150036

S0-BMD-382

God, Creation, and Providence
in the Thought of Jacob Arminius

God, Creation, and Providence in the Thought of Jacob Arminius

Sources and Directions of Scholastic Protestantism in the Era of Early Orthodoxy

Richard A. Muller

BAKER BOOK HOUSE
Grand Rapids, Michigan 49516

Copyright 1991 by
Baker Book House Company

Printed in the United States of America

Library of Congress Cataloging-in-Publication Data

Muller, Richard A. (Richard Alfred), 1948–
    God, creation, and providence in the thought of Jacob Arminius : sources and
directions of scholastic Protestantism in the area of early orthodoxy / Richard A. Muller.
        p.   cm.
    Includes bibliographical references.
    ISBN 0-8010-6279-9
    1. Arminius, Jacobus, 1560–1609. 2. Theology, Doctrinal—History—16th century. 3.
Theology, Doctrinal—History—17th century. I. Title.
BX6196.M84   1991
230'.49'092—dc20   91-6417
                                                                        CIP

30.49092
19169

LIFE Pacific College
Alumni Library
1100 West Covina Blvd.
San Dimas, CA 91773

In memoriam

Heinrich Angelus Müller (1885–1968)
Elizabeth Eichner Hinsch Müller (1888–1962)
George Robert Emil Spiess (1890–1977)
Katherine Marie Bergmann Spiess (1892–1990)

L.I.F.E. BIBLE COLLEGE EAST
LIBRARY
CHRISTIANSBURG, VA   051222

Contents

Preface

This study of the thought of Jacob Arminius arose out of the gradually formed recognition that Arminius, despite his importance to the history of Protestant doctrine and despite the large literature contrasting the Arminian and the Calvinist views on sin, free choice, grace, and predestination, is one of the most neglected of the major Protestant theologians. Apart from discussions of these topics, framed with reference to later debate, virtually none of the topics treated in Arminius' thought have been discussed at length and Arminius has never, to my knowledge, been accorded his rightful place in the development of scholastic Protestantism. It is my hope that this essay will contribute both to the reappraisal of Arminius' theology and to a renewal of interest in his work.

Thanks are due to several of my students whose enthusiasm for the study of Arminius' thought convinced me to attempt a monograph on the subject: Stephen Cary, Kathy Greene Van Huizen, and Michael Milway. Their energetic interest in the subject and their frequently insightful participation in seminars on Arminius and on early orthodox Reformed thought is deeply appreciated. I also owe much to John Patrick Donnelly, who read the manuscript with great care and insight, to his colleague at Marquette, Jack Treolar, whose expertise on Suárez was helpful at several points, and to Brian Armstrong, whose painstaking examination of the manuscript has led to numerous refinements and whose ongoing dialogue concerning the nature and character of Protestant scholasticism has provided a continuing impetus to the refinement of arguments and definitions. I owe a similar debt to Charles Partee, whose thoughtful reading of the manuscript contributed several refinements of argument and focus. And if one of his suggestions has seemed to have gone unheeded, that is only because it has stimulated yet another project.

Perhaps the greatest incentive toward the completion of this project came from a theologian who claimed that the various distinctions found in the thought of Arminius—*potentia absoluta/potentia ordinata, voluntas antecedens/voluntas consequens* and so forth—were hardly evidence of scholasticism and might just as easily have been cited from the fathers. He also indicated that he thought any scholastic influence on Arminius had to be interpreted either as a result of the Renaissance revival of scholasticism or as a result of Arminius' reading of the medieval scholastics—probably, he claimed, as a result of the former, but surely not of both. I note these comments because they are indicative of the contemporary ignorance of the movement of theology through the late sixteenth and early seventeenth centuries—even among those who ought to know better. The likelihood of contemporary Protestantism understanding itself when it is ignorant of its past is very slim. To this particular interlocutor and others like him, I offer thanks, if only for the incentive to write.

A profound word of thanks must also be offered to the persons who made this work technically possible. David Sielaff and his staff at the Fuller word processing office have worked painstakingly with the manuscript and have produced superb final copy. Thanks are also due to Maria denBoer of Baker Book House for her careful scrutiny of the text and its format.

Finally, some comment is necessary concerning the text and translations of Arminius' writings. Throughout this essay, I have followed the text of the 1629 edition of Arminius' *Opera theologica* in consultation with the London edition of Arminius' *Works*, as translated by James and William Nichols. Citations from the *Disputationes* (both private and public) give the number of the disputation and the number of the subsection and are therefore sufficient for checking references in the Latin or in either English edition of the *Works*. Citations from the less closely outlined works like the *Orationes* give page references to the Latin text followed by page references in brackets to the London edition, following the repagination of volume 1 in the latest reprint (Grand Rapids: Baker Book House, 1986). The London edition of the *Works* has been used because it includes materials not present in the American edition edited by William Bagnall and because Bagnall's reworking of the Nichols translation (i.e., of volumes 1 and 2) lacks merit. Indeed, because of James Nichols' massive gathering of Arminiana in the notes to volume I (omitted by Bagnall from the American edition), the London edition remains the best English-language resource on Arminius' theology.

Some comment must also be made about the merits and demerits of the Nichols translation. On the whole it is a solid and serviceable translation that faithfully renders Arminius' thought. It deserves to be modernized and emended and ought rightfully to be the basis of any subsequent English-language edition of Arminius' writings. Nonetheless, it does embody pitfalls and problems, not the least of which is the often unnecessarily burdensome syntax it employs. In addition to this problem of style, however, there is an occasional problem of misunderstanding: James Nichols was an adept amateur theologian and historian but not a scholastic trained in the technical philosophical niceties of the late sixteenth century. Thus, his rendering of *momentum* as "cause of motion" in the disputations on the nature of God represents a serious blunder. Other, similar, problems could be noted. Readers will note my grateful reliance on Nichols but also my frequent alteration, emendation, and re-working of the text.

PART 1

Arminius' Theology in Context

1

Arminius and the Historians

James or, as he is more rightly called, Jacob Arminius (1559–1609) is one of the dozen or so theologians in the history of the Christian church who has given lasting direction to the theological tradition and who, as a result, has stamped his name upon a particular doctrinal or confessional viewpoint. It is all the more surprising, therefore, that Arminius has received little positive attention from scholars and still awaits the definitive discussion of his system of thought. There are, of course, numerous biographies of Arminius and equally numerous discussions of the debate between Arminius and his Reformed colleagues at the University of Leiden that precipitated the larger controversy leading to the Synod of Dort (1618–19) and to the establishment of an Arminian or Remonstrant Church in the Netherlands alongside of the Reformed Church. Nevertheless, there is no substantive treatment of the whole of Arminius' theology— most of the topics of which were not debated either during his lifetime or in the later controversy. Equally so, there is no scholarly monograph on the relation of Arminius' thought to its intellectual environment—the early orthodox or early scholastic thought of confessional Protestantism. Nor is there a critical edition of Arminius' works or even an up-to-date critically annotated translation. I hope, in the following pages, to provide a discussion of Arminius' views on God and the world that sheds new light on his theology as a whole and on the place occupied by his thought in the intellectual history of the seventeenth century.

After the Reformation, in the period extending roughly from 1565 to 1700, Protestantism faced the crisis of being forced to defend its nascent theology against attack from the highly sophisticated and carefully articulated vantage point of Roman Catholic scholastic theology. It faced the problem of institutionalization—of passing from its beginnings as a protest movement within the Catholic Church to its destiny as a self-sufficient ecclesiastical establishment with its own

3

distinct academic, confessional, and dogmatic needs. It also faced, together with the Roman Catholic Church, the twin challenges of modern philosophical rationalism and the dawn of modern science. As scholars in the Roman Catholic tradition have long recognized and as students of the late development of Protestantism have acknowledged, albeit frequently with some reluctance, scholasticism did not pass away with the Renaissance and Reformation. Scholasticism, rightly understood as a method or approach to theological and philosophical discourse rather than as a particular doctrine or set of doctrines, provided a vehicle for Roman Catholic and Protestant thought long past the era of the Reformation. Far from breaking down at the close of the Middle Ages, scholasticism underwent a series of modifications that enabled it to adapt to the renewed Aristotelianism of the Renaissance, to the decline of Aristotelianism in the seventeenth century, and to the rise of Wolffian rationalism in the eighteenth century.[1] Arminius, as much as any of his opponents and detractors, belongs to this history. His theology must be understood against this background of theological and philosophical development and debate.

Arminius' place in the history of doctrine is assured by the direct relationship between his teaching on the doctrine of predestination and the *ordo salutis* and the great theological debate leading to the Synod of Dort. All major histories of doctrine discuss the debate, and virtually every history of Protestant thought traces in some detail the education of Arminius in Reformed theology at Leiden and Geneva, the gradual formulation by Arminius of an alternative view of predestination, and the great controversy in the Dutch church that revolved around the soteriology taught by Arminius during his tenure as professor of theology at Leiden. "Arminius," "Arminianism," "Dort," and "TULIP" are part of the common language of modern Protestantism. Nonetheless, the fame of Arminius' views on this one issue has only served to obscure the larger, general outlines of his theology and to conceal utterly the positive relationships that existed between Arminius' thought and method and the intellectual life of post-Reformation Protestantism.

---

[1] See G. Fritz and A. Michel, "Scolastique," DTC 14/2, cols. 1691–1728; J. A. Weisheipl, "Scholastic Method," in NCE, 12, pp. 1145–46; I. C. Brady, J. E. Gurr, and J. A. Weisheipl, "Scholasticism," in *NCE*, 12, pp. 1153–70; and note M.-D. Chenu, *Toward Understanding St. Thomas*, trans. A. M. Landry and D. Hughes (Chicago: Henry Regnery, 1964), pp. 58–69. On Protestant scholasticism, see the discussion in Robert Preus, *The Inspiration of Scripture: A Study of the Seventeenth Century Lutheran Dogmaticians* (London: Oliver and Boyd, 1955), pp. xv–xvi; Henry E. Jacobs, "Scholasticism in the Lutheran Church," in *The Lutheran Cyclopedia*, pp. 434–35; and Richard A. Muller, *Post-Reformation Reformed Dogmatics* (Grand Rapids: Baker, 1987), I, pp. 13–40.

From the very first, the biographers of Arminius have contributed to this problem. Arminius' first biographer, his friend and colleague Petrus Bertius, focused apologetically on Arminius' career with the intention of vindicating the recently deceased theologian from the vicious rumors that had been spread about Arminius' life and from the frequently unfair and distorted accusations of heresy leveled against his theology.[2] Arminius emerges from Bertius' essay as a studious, sincere, temperate, and, above all, orthodox Protestant who had been acclaimed by all his teachers, including the predestinarian Beza, as a brilliant and most promising young theologian. Bertius reflects on Arminius' theology only in relation to the debate over predestination and gives the impression that the young Arminius stood in basic agreement with the doctrine of his Reformed teachers. When Arminius prepared to do battle on behalf of the Dutch church against the doctrines of Dirck Coornhert, his doctrine of predestination most probably followed the line of Theodore Beza. Further studies, undertaken for the refutation of Coornhert, turned Arminius away from Beza's doctrine toward a view similar to that of the Lutheran dogmatician, Nicholas Hemmingius or Hemmingsen (1513–1600) of the University of Copenhagen. Bertius goes on to note that the church in the Netherlands had traditionally allowed considerable breadth of opinion on this doctrine inasmuch as the point had never been resolved by any of the ancient synods or councils of the church. The noted professor of theology at Leiden, Johannes Holmanus Secundus (d. 1586), had held views identical to those of Hemmingsen and Arminius.[3] Bertius makes no attempt to discuss Arminius' views on any other subject—and no attempt to survey Arminius' written works.

A very similar approach is taken by Gerard Brandt in his massive *History of the Reformation ... in ... the Low Countries.*[4] Here, however, the history of Arminius' debate in the university and of the subsequent debate between Remonstrants and Contra-Remonstrants leading to the Synod of Dort is rehearsed in great detail. Brandt's discussion of Arminius begins with the debate over Arminius' appointment as Junius' successor at the University of Leiden. Brandt provides considerable detail concerning the debate, including exchanges

---

[2] Petrus Bertius, *De vita et obitu reverendi & clarissimi viri D. Iacobi Arminii oratio*, in *Opera* (1629), translated as *The Life of James Arminius*, in *Works*, I, pp. 13–47.

[3] Bertius, *De vita et obitu*, p. **iv recto (*Works*, I, pp. 30–31).

[4] Gerard Brandt, *Historie der Reformatie en andre Kerkelyke Geschiedenissen, in en ontrent de Nederlanden*, 4 vols. (Amsterdam, 1671–1704), translated as *The History of the Reformation and Other Ecclesiastical Transactions in and about the Low Countries, down to the Famous Synod of Dort*, 4 vols. (London, 1720–23; repr. New York: AMS, 1979). References are to the translation.

between Helmichius (a minister in Amsterdam), Gomarus, and Arminius' friend and ally Uitenbogaert over the doctrine of predestination.[5] Indeed, Brandt's *History* remains the most detailed gathering of materials related to the debate over predestination that developed during the time of Arminius' professorship at Leiden.

Even more important is the way in which Brandt fills out the history behind the point made by Bertius concerning diversity of opinion in the Netherlands over the doctrine of predestination. Brandt first argues the consent of the early church to a doctrine of human free will and responsibility and to the belief that "all those which God foresaw would lead good and godly lives were ordained to eternal life."[6] It was Augustine, argues Brandt, who created the strict doctrine of predestination in polemic against Pelagius. Brandt notes the impact of Augustine on medieval doctrine and the efforts of Franciscan, Dominican, and, later on, Jesuit theologians to overcome the problems of the Augustinian teaching. These problems were brought over into Protestantism in the thought of Luther, whose teaching was carried forward by Calvin, Beza, Ursinus, Zanchi, and Piscator. Among the Lutherans, however, Brandt argues, the humanist Melanchthon was convinced by Erasmus' treatise against Luther, and so convincingly moderated his teaching on election that virtually all Lutherans, perhaps even Luther himself, gave up a strict Augustinian view of predestination.[7] These opposing Protestant views were both present in the Netherlands before the debate over Arminius' theology.

Brandt argues that, early on, the Dutch church made no controversy over the issues, but that the gradual influx of teachers and ministers educated in Geneva and Heidelberg led to a concern among the indigenous Protestant thinkers that those who held a non-Calvinistic doctrine would be excluded from the ministry. Next came complaints against the Melanchthonian teaching of established teachers and ministers like Anastasius Veluanus, Gellius Snecanus, Hubert Dovehouse, Johannes Holmanus Secundus, Clement Martenson, and Herman Herberts, none of whom could have been called anything less than orthodox Protestants.[8] The disputes in which these theologians were involved are recounted at length.[9] Arminius appears, therefore, in Brandt's well-documented account, as yet another teacher of the moderate Protestant line, setting forth the old Melanchthonian doctrine against the harsh Augustinianism of the Reformed

---

[5] Brandt, *History*, II, pp. 27–28.
[6] Ibid., p. 31.
[7] Ibid., p. 32.
[8] Ibid.
[9] See Brandt, *History*, I, pp. 308–9, 312–13, 336–37, 369–70, 441–42, 450–51.

or Calvinist teachers.[10] This view is essentially the same as that of Carl Bangs, Arminius' foremost modern biographer.[11] Brandt does not, however, examine Arminius' doctrine closely enough to see whether it is Melanchthonian or Lutheran—nor does he examine any of Arminius' other teachings with a view to identifying their actual sources and antecedents.

In particular, medieval antecedents of Arminius' theology and parallel developments in Roman Catholic doctrine are left unmentioned. Nor should we expect a late seventeenth-century historian of the Dutch Reformation to note Roman Catholic or medieval parallels to Arminius' teaching: on the one hand, Arminius himself deemphasized such sources and, indeed, strenuously denied having any affection for scholastic theology,[12] and, on the other hand, polemic was still intense in Brandt's time and it would hardly have coincided with his purpose in describing the events of the Dutch Reformation to have searched out positive relationships between Protestant and Roman Catholic thought. Nonetheless, it is not without significance to the development of Protestant theology in the late sixteenth and early seventeenth centuries that the predestinarian controversies in England and the Netherlands were paralleled by a major predestinarian controversy in Roman Catholicism, generated by the strict Augustinianism of Michael Baius and the attempt of the Jesuit theologian Luis de Molina to reconcile the concept of an eternal decree with human freedom and responsibility.[13]

Arminius' second biographer was Caspar Brandt, son of the historian Gerard Brandt and, like him, a Remonstrant minister of Amsterdam.[14] Brandt took up the apologetic task begun by Bertius but

[10] Ibid., II, pp. 32–35, etc.

[11] Carl Bangs, *Arminius: A Study in the Dutch Reformation* (Nashville: Abingdon, 1971), pp. 103–4; and see further, below, this chap.

[12] See further, below, this chap.

[13] Cf. Vansteenberghe, "Molinisme," *DTC* 10/2, cols. 2099–2101 with Mandonnet, "Bañez, Dominique," *DTC* 2/1, cols. 140–45; Le Bachelet, "Baius, Michel," *DTC* 2/1, cols. 38–111; Henri de Lubac, *Augustinianism and Modern Theology*, trans. Lancelot Sheppard (London: Geoffrey Chapman, 1969), pp. 1–33, 118–22, 145–85; Dewey D. Wallace, *Puritans and Predestination: Grace in English Protestant Theology, 1525–1695* (Chapel Hill: University of North Carolina Press, 1982), pp. 65–70; John Hunt, *Religious Thought in England from the Reformation to the End of Last Century*, 3 vols. (London, 1870–73), I, pp. 91–93. A detailed discussion of the Roman Catholic controversy that surveys the views of Bañez, Molina, Suárez, and Bellarmine is found in Raoul de Scorraille, *François Suárez de la Compagnie de Jésus, d'après ses lettres, ses autres écrits inédits et un grand nombre de documents nouveaux*, 2 vols. (Paris: Lethielleux, 1912), I, pp. 401–78.

[14] Caspar Brandt, *Historia vita Jacobi Arminii* (Brunswick, 1725); translated by John Guthrie as *The Life of James Arminius, D.D.* (London, 1854; also issued with an introduction by Thomas O. Summers, Nashville, 1857).

developed it on a far greater scale, incorporating into Bertius' basic narrative a wealth of material drawn from the published letters of Uitenbogaert and other eminent Remonstrants together with previously unpublished remains (mostly letters) of Arminius. Brandt does not, however, avail himself of the historical research of his father into the theological antecedents of Arminianism—inasmuch as he accepts completely the story of Bertius that Arminius altered his views on predestination in 1589 when confronted by the debate over the teachings of Coornhert.[15] The remainder of Brandt's work surveys the controversies that swirled around Arminius' teaching and that led, ultimately, to the Remonstrance and the Synod of Dort. In other words, even though the actual terminus of Brandt's work is the death of Arminius, his treatment of Arminius' thought is defined by the course of the controversy. Doctrines held and taught by Arminius but not touched on in debate fall outside of the scope of Brandt's study.

This basic pattern of argument is maintained in two studies by A. W. Harrison. His *Beginnings of Arminianism to the Synod of Dort* and *Arminianism* both trace the development of Arminian theology from the debates at the University of Leiden during Arminius' lifetime to subsequent argumentation on grace, predestination, sin, and human responsibility that crystallized around the *Remonstrance*, the *Contra-Remonstrance*, and the *Canons* of the Synod of Dort.[16] There can, of course, be no complaint with a monographic study tracing the course of this major controversy—but Harrison is so concerned with the polemics between the Arminians and the Reformed that he makes no attempt to place either the thought of Arminius or the theology of his successors into the context of the positive, nonpolemical development of orthodoxy and scholastic Protestantism. In Harrison's treatment, because of the narrow attention to the course of the controversy, Arminius' theology is discussed only in fragmentary form, indeed, in a form supplied largely by theological polemics and, therefore, not in a form that is designed to manifest either the positive development of Arminius' doctrine or the way in which the debated doctrines fit into the structure of Arminius' theology as a whole.

---

[15] Brandt, *Life of James Arminius*, pp. 63–64.

[16] A. W. Harrison, *The Beginnings of Arminianism to the Synod of Dort* (London: University of London Press, 1926); *Arminianism* (London: Duckworth, 1937). Cf. also D. Tjalsma, *Leven en Strijd van Jacobus Arminius* (Lochem: Uitgave de Rijstroom, 1960), which surveys Arminius' life and offers a few pages on "aspects" of Arminius' theology: he notes Arminius' association with Ramism, compares Arminius' thought on predestination to Castellio, and then briefly reviews the teaching of Arminius' letter to Hippolytus à Collibus and the *Declaration of Sentiments*.

The same problem of a narrowed focus is evident in Hans Emil Weber's *Reformation, Orthodoxie, und Rationalismus*, although here the problem is compounded by Weber's adherence to a theory of the development of Protestant theology around "central dogmas." Weber's assumption that Lutheranism is "the system of the doctrine of justification" and that Calvinism is "the system of predestinarianism," each system being rationally and deductively constructed around a central systematic concept, leads him to view Arminius' theology and Arminianism in general as a humanistic and biblicistic protest against rationalizing predestinarianism. Inasmuch as the decree functioned "as a systematic foundation (*Prinzip*) for dogmatics" in Reformed theology, the Arminian opposition to strict predestinarianism was viewed by the Reformed as an utterly "offensive" and "contemptible" assault on orthodoxy.[17] The Arminian protest, like the Jesuit concept of a divine *scientia media*, undermined the Reformed presupposition of the utter dependence of all things on God.[18] Weber does not, however, attempt to view Arminianism as more than a protest; he does not propose a central dogma for Arminianism, does not develop the parallel between Arminian doctrine and the Jesuit *scientia media*, and does not accord Arminianism the status of system.

Thanks to the efforts of Carl Bangs, we do have a superb critical biography of Arminius based on archival sources and a wide variety of late sixteenth- and early seventeenth-century sources.[19] Not the least of Bangs' contributions to the study of Arminius' life and thought is his careful reappraisal of the development of Arminius' thought on predestination. Rather than follow Bertius and Brandt in arguing a change of mind on Arminius' part after his university studies and during his pastorate in Amsterdam, Bangs points out that little or no evidence exists for an early, Bezan, supralapsarian Arminius and that the story of Arminius' attempt to refute Coornhert's doctrine of predestination is probably apocryphal.[20] Bangs presents us with a picture of Arminius as a moderate predestinarian, standing in the pre-Calvinist tradition of Dutch Protestantism and reflecting the views of grace and salvation found in early Reformation catechisms like that written by Laurens Jacobszoon Reael. According to Bangs, therefore, Arminius' theology stands firmly in the Reformed tradition.[21]

---

[17] H. E. Weber, *Reformation, Orthodoxie und Rationalismus*, 2 vols. (Gütersloh, 1937–51; repr. Darmstadt, 1966), II, pp. 120–21.

[18] Ibid., p. 121.

[19] Carl Bangs, *Arminius: A Study in the Dutch Reformation* (Nashville: Abingdon, 1971).

[20] Ibid., pp. 139–41.

[21] Ibid., pp. 103–4; cf. pp. 333, 336–37, 340, 349, 354, where Bangs argues that Arminius was a Reformed theologian; also see Carl Bangs, "Arminius as a

Apart from the question of whether Arminius can be considered a Reformed theologian, Bangs' argument is quite convincing. All of Arminius' writings on predestination and related topics manifest dissent from the teaching of his Reformed contemporaries, whether infra- or supralapsarian. Unfortunately, we do not possess any writings from the pen of Arminius that predate the famous dispute of 1589 over the doctrines of Dirck Coornhert and the modified Calvinism of two ministers from Delft, Arent Corneliszoon and Reynier Donteklok. It was during this dispute that Bertius and Brandt assume Arminius changed his mind.[22] Arminius began his investigation into problems of predestination and the *ordo salutis* in 1591 in a series of sermons. These sermons became the basis for his *Dissertation on ... Romans 7*.[23] Arminius' *Analysis of Romans 9* followed in 1596 and, in the same year, the *Conference* with Junius on predestination.[24] In all of these writings Arminius appears to be conducting an inquiry into the doctrines rather than to be stating a settled opinion—a fact which would tend to confirm Bangs' theory.

What Bangs fails to do, however, is to provide a full account of reasons for Arminius' theological development. Granting that Arminius' thoughts on predestination may reflect a pre-Calvinist theology resident in the Netherlands, it must still be explained why Arminius' doctrine developed along certain technical lines and with attention to such questions as the internal logic of the divine will, the character of human beings in their original created state, the relationship of divine will, in its providential concurrence, to the acts of human beings, and the nature of the divine foreknowledge of future contingents. These are all highly technical, indeed, scholastic issues—and the antecedents of these particular elements of Arminius' teaching must be noted before the character of his teaching can be fully understood. The one point that Bangs retains from Bertius is the assumption that Arminius reacted against or opposed himself to a specifically Bezan supralapsarianism.[25]

Unfortunately the theology of Arminius has not received the close attention that has been accorded his life. Bangs does present a brief examination of Arminius' conception of the idea and method of

---

Reformed Theologian," in *The Heritage of John Calvin*, ed. John H. Bratt (Grand Rapids: Eerdmans, 1973), pp. 209–22.

[22] Ibid., pp. 138–40; cf. Bertius, *De vita et obitu*, p. **iii verso–**iv recto (*Works, I*, pp. 29–30) and Brandt, *Life of James Arminius*, pp. 60–63.

[23] See Bangs, *Arminius*, p. 186; Brandt notes the completion date of the treatise as early 1600: see *Life of James Arminius*, p. 71.

[24] Ibid., pp. 194, 199.

[25] Bangs, *Arminius*, pp. 66 71, 77, 138–41, 148–49.

theology,[26] and he has surveyed the various writings of Arminius on grace and predestination that led up to the final struggle between Arminius and his Reformed contemporaries in the Netherlands— the *Dissertation on Romans 7*,[27] the *Short Analysis of Romans 9* and the *Conference with Franciscus Junius*,[28] and the *Examination of Perkins' Pamphlet*.[29] Bangs also surveys the contents of Arminius' *Declaration of Sentiments*[30] and provides an overview of Arminius' thought on the topics of church, sin, free will and grace, synergism, justification, sanctification, assurance, perseverance, and predestination.[31] Without taking anything away from the value of Bangs' study, there are two basic problems with these surveys. On the one hand, with the exception of the discussion of the concept of theology, they address only the ideas of Arminius that point toward the debate at Dort and make no attempt to present Arminius' theology as a whole; on the other hand, Bangs merely summarizes Arminius' thought without attempting to analyze it in terms of either the development of late sixteenth- and early seventeenth-century Reformed theology or of its possible antecedents in the Middle Ages and the Reformation. The one exception to this generalization is Bangs' recognition of a Melanchthonian influence on Dutch predecessors of Arminius like Johannes Holmanus Secundus and Gellius Snecanus.[32]

Similar and somewhat more severe criticisms must be leveled against Harold Slaatte's presentation of Arminius' theology in his comparative study of the thought of Joseph Fletcher and Arminius, *The Arminian Arm of Theology*.[33] Slaatte not only assumes that it is theologically and historically legitimate to leap from Fletcher into Arminius without consideration either of the development of continental Arminianism after Arminius in the thought of Simon Episcopius, Stephanus Curcellaeus, and Philipp Limborch or of the indigenous English antecedents of Wesleyan Arminianism, but he also assumes that a discussion of the topics of predestination and the *ordo salutis*—again, the *loci* debated at Dort—is sufficient to the comprehension of Arminius' theology. In addition, Slaatte's study is based entirely on English-language sources and, therefore, has no contact with the actual theological vocabulary of Arminius.

---

[26] Ibid., pp. 256–61.

[27] Ibid., pp. 186–92.

[28] Ibid., pp. 193–205.

[29] Ibid., pp. 206–21.

[30] Ibid., pp. 307–13.

[31] Ibid., pp. 332–55.

[32] Ibid., pp. 139, 193–94.

[33] Harold Slaatte, *The Arminian Arm of Theology: The Theologies of John Fletcher, First Methodist Theologian, and His Precursor, James Arminius* (Washington, D.C.: University Press of America, 1978).

A very important contribution to the study of Arminius' thought
and of early orthodox Dutch Reformed theology in general has
been made in John Platt's *Reformed Thought and Scholasticism*.[34]
Although Platt restricts his study to a close examination of the proofs
of the existence of God as they developed in Dutch theology between
1575 and 1650, his essay has broad implications for the study of Protestant scholasticism. Platt clearly demonstrates a massive, positive
interest on the part of Dutch Protestant theologians in scholastic categories. He also convincingly sets Arminius into the context of this
developing Protestant scholasticism and shows that there were elements of a positive theological and philosophical dialogue between
Arminius and his colleagues on the faculty at Leiden. Even though
the section on Arminius is quite brief, it serves to demonstrate the
importance of understanding Arminius' thought in the context of
Reformed orthodoxy and scholasticism at Leiden following the semi-
nal work of Franciscus Junius.[35]

With the exception of Platt's study—and here the thought of
Arminius is discussed briefly in a few pages—there has been no
attempt to set Arminius' theology into its intellectual context.
Nowhere, moreover, has Arminius' thought been described in terms
of the scholarly discussion of post-Reformation Protestantism: the
standard monographic studies and the various biographies of
Arminius do not refer to the problem of the development of confessional orthodoxy and Protestant scholasticism. Thus, the older histories of Protestant thought, like those of Dorner and Ritschl, have not
been consulted;[36] and the more detailed examinations of the impact
of philosophy and scholastic method on Protestant thought by H. E.
Weber, Eschweiler, Wundt, Lewalter, and Dibon have also been
ignored.[37] (There is a small irony in the fact that Weber did not apply

---

[34] John Platt, *Reformed Thought and Scholasticism: The Arguments for the Existence of God in Dutch Theology, 1575–1650* (Leiden: Brill, 1982).

[35] Ibid., pp. 148–59.

[36] I. A. Dorner, *History of Protestant Theology*, trans. George Robson and Sophia Taylor, 2 vols. (Edinburgh: T. and T. Clark, 1871); Otto Ritschl, *Dogmengeschichte des Protestantismus*, 4 vols. (Leipzig and Göttingen: J. C. Hinrichs/Vandenhoeck and Ruprecht, 1908–27).

[37] Hans Emil Weber, *Die philosophische Scholastik des deutschen Protestantismus in Zeitalter der Orthodoxie* (Leipzig: Quelle und Meyer, 1907); idem, *Der Einfluss der protes-tantischen Schulphilosophie auf die orthodox-lutherische Dogmatik* (Leipzig: Deichert, 1908); Karl Eschweiler, "Die Philosophie der spanischen Spätscholastik auf den deutschen Universitäten des siebzehnten Jahrhunderts," in *Gesammelte Aufsätze zur Kulturgeschichte Spaniens*, ed. H. Finke (Münster: Aschendorff, 1938); Max Wundt, *Die Deutsche Schulmetaphysik des 17. Jahrhunderts* (Tübingen: J. C. B. Mohr, 1939); Ernst Lewalter, *Spanisch-jesuitisch und deutsch-lutherische Metaphysik des 17. Jahrhunderts* (Hamburg, 1935; repr. Darmstadt: Wissenschaftliche Buchgesellschaft, 1968); Paul Dibon, *L'Enseignement philosophique dans les Universités néerlandaises à l'époque précartesienne* (Paris: Elsevier, 1954). Note that Dibon's *L'Enseignement*

the results of his early investigations of the impact of scholastic philosophy and method on the thought of Bartholomaus Keckermann and on the theology of early Lutheran orthodoxy to the discussion of Arminius and Arminianism in his later analysis of the phenomenon of Protestant orthodoxy. There, we recall, Arminius appears only as the biblicistic and "humanistic" opponent of the Reformed "predestinarian system."[38] The shorter essays of Bakhuizen van den Brink, Van Holk, and Hoenderdaal fall under the same critique.[39]

The historians leave us with what might be called, somewhat tongue-in-cheekishly, the problem of the historical Arminius. The Arminius "of faith" who rises up against the scholastic predestinarianism of the Reformed with an antischolastic and therefore antipredestinarian biblicism is at once considerably more and considerably less than the Arminius "of history"—considerably more because the view of grace and election expressed by Arminius was not some new invention brought about by a close analysis of problems in the Reformed doctrine, but a doctrinal perspective similar both to late medieval doctrines of grace and election and to the views of several British writers who protested against the Reformed doctrine of predestination at Cambridge only a decade before Arminius and profoundly akin to the views expressed by Roman Catholic opponents of Michael Baius during the same period. Considerably less because Arminius' works manifest not only an alternative view of predestination but a large-scale theological system differing at many points from the Reformed theology of the day. Indeed, a close examination of Arminius' theology demonstrates that he did not take predestination as a central dogma, offer a different formulation, and then build a system around it. Rather, Arminius' doctrine of predestination appears as but one aspect of a larger developing system and, perhaps, as a result of other, prior doctrinal considerations, such as Arminius'

---

philosophique was published both as his dissertation at the University of Leiden and (without alteration) as volume 1 of his projected *La Philosophie néerlandaise au siécle d'or.*

[38] See Weber, *Reformation, Orthodoxie und Rationalismus*, II, pp. 99–100, 111–14.

[39] J. N. Bakhuizen van den Brink, "Arminius te Leiden," *Nederlands Theologisch Tijdschrift*, 15 (1960–61), pp. 81–89; G. J. Hoenderdaal, "De theologische Betekenis van Arminius," *Nederlands Theologisch Tijdschrift* 15 (1960–61):90–98; idem, "The Life and Struggle of Arminius in the Dutch Republic," in *Man's Faith and Freedom: The Theological Influence of Jacobus Arminius*, ed. Gerald O. McCulloh (Nashville: Abingdon, 1963), pp. 11–26; idem, "The Debate about Arminius Outside the Netherlands," in *Leiden University in the Seventeenth Century: An Exchange of Learning*, eds. Th. H. Lunsingh Scheurleer and G. H. M. Posthumus Meyjes (Leiden: Brill, 1975), pp. 137–59; and Lambertus van Holk, "From Arminius to Arminianism in Dutch Theology," in *Man's Faith and Freedom*, pp. 27–45.

views on Christology,[40] the doctrine of God, and the doctrines of creation and providence.

---

[40] See Richard A. Muller, "The Christological Problem in the Thought of Jacobus Arminius," *Nederlando Archief voor Kerkgeschiedenis* 68 (1988): 145–63.

2

Arminius' Theological Development in Its Historical Context

In 1575, Arminius journeyed from Utrecht to Marburg to begin studies in the university under the patronage of Rudolph Snellius, professor of philosophy at Marburg and a celebrated logician, mathematician, and linguist. In the same year, the University of Leiden was founded. Arminius studied at Marburg under Snellius for about one year and then returned to the Netherlands and registered for the liberal arts course in the new university on October 23, 1576. Bangs indicates that Arminius was the twelfth student to be registered.[1] From Bertius' funeral oration we learn that Arminius studied theology, mathematics, and "other branches of philosophy," and that Lambert Daneau, brought to Leiden as professor of theology in 1581, praised Arminius for his intelligence and proficiency and also urged the other "Divinity students to imitate the example of Arminius, by the same cheerful and diligent attention to the study of sacred theology."[2] In addition to Daneau, Arminius studied with Guilhelmus Feuguereus and perhaps again, briefly, with Snellius, who was appointed professor of mathematics at Leiden in 1581, just before Arminius completed his studies and left for Geneva.[3]

The impact of these three professors on Arminius is difficult to assess, granting the relatively brief association of Arminius with Daneau and Snellius. From Snellius, Arminius may well have acquired the taste for Ramist logic that would later bring him to disagree with his Genevan mentors, including Beza, and that would also help him to shape his theological arguments during his years as a

---

[1] Bangs, *Arminius*, p. 47.
[2] Bertius, *De vita et obitu*, p. **ii verso (*Works*, I, pp. 21–22).
[3] See Bangs, *Arminius*, pp. 50, 55, 64.

15

professor at Leiden. Snellius had been trained in the philosophy of Aristotle—both the older Aristotelianism of the scholastic tradition as mediated and modified by late medieval logicians like Rudolf Agricola, and the newer Aristotelianism of the Renaissance with its recourse to the original works of Aristotle. As a professor at Cologne, Snellius had taught Aristotelian philosophy and logic, but shortly after his arrival at Marburg, he encountered the new logic of Ramus and was so impressed by it that he devoted himself to teaching it at the university.[4] As Bangs well recognizes, Ramism had more influence on Arminius' logic than on his theology. Ramist logic was the exclusive property of no single theological party: one of the most thoroughgoing Ramists of the day was the supralapsarian Perkins.[5] Nonetheless, it was characteristic of Ramus' own theology that he viewed the system of Christian doctrine as practical rather than theoretical—a point that, despite their fundamental disagreement over the decrees, carried over into the theology of both Perkins and Arminius.[6]

It would be a mistake to view Ramus as either an adversary of all things Aristotelian or as a humanistic liberator of theology from "scholastic subtleties."[7] Ramus' thought is better understood as a modified Aristotelianism in the tradition of the late medieval logician Rudolf Agricola and in the wake of the development of Galenic logic and method in the sixteenth century. Moreover, as pointed out in Ramus' own day, some of his best arguments were drawn directly from Aristotle.[8] It is also a matter of history that Ramus' neat bifurcations, far from standing in the way of the development of Protestant scholasticism, became the logical vehicle for the creation of comprehensive and cohesive scholastic systems by writers like Perkins, Polanus, Piscator, Ames, and Maccovius.[9] This architectonic, systematizing capacity of the Ramist logic was not lost on Arminius.

---

[4] See appendix C in *Works*, I, p. 55.

[5] Bangs, *Arminius*, p. 63. For an assessment of the considerable influence of Ramus on Perkins, see Donald K. McKim, *Ramism in William Perkins' Theology* (New York and Bern: Peter Lang, 1987); also see Keith L. Sprunger, "Ames, Ramus, and the Method of Puritan Theology," *Harvard Theological Review* 59 (1966): 133–51.

[6] Cf. Ramus, *Commentariorum de religione christiana* (Frankfurt, 1576), I.i with Perkins, *Golden Chaine*, in *Works*, I, p. 11, col. 1, and Arminius, *Disp. priv.* I.iii, v; and see the discussion in *PRRD*, I, pp. 108–9, 219–23.

[7] Contra Graves, *Peter Ramus*, pp. 141–43 and Bangs, *Arminius*, p. 58.

[8] Ong, *Ramus*, pp. 214–20, 254–62; Bangs, *Arminius*, pp. 59–60.

[9] Cf. McKim, *Ramism in William Perkins' Theology*; Sprunger, "Ames, Ramus, and the Method of Puritan Theology," pp. 133–51; Walter Ong, "Johannes Piscator: One Man or a Ramist Dichotomy," *Harvard Library Bulletin* 8 (1954): 151–62; idem, *Ramus*, pp. 298–300; Perry Miller, *The New England Mind: The Seventeenth Century* (1939; repr. Boston: Beacon, 1961), chaps. 5 and 6, passim.

Very little, if anything, can be said about the kind of theology that Arminius may have learned from Feuguereus, who was professor of theology at Leiden from 1575 to 1579. Feuguereus had edited Augustin Marlorat's *Scripture thesaurus*, a topical concordance to both Testaments, and had edited with commentary the eucharistic treatise of Ratramnus of Corbie.[10] His only major independent essay was a treatise on the church.[11] The *Scripture thesaurus* was published in London in 1574, before Feuguereus came to Leiden; the other two works appeared in Leiden in 1579, during his last year as a professor in the university.

Lambert Daneau, who was professor of theology during Arminius' final year at Leiden (1581), knew Arminius long enough to develop a rather high estimation of his abilities. We cannot say precisely what Daneau imparted to or perceived in Arminius' work—but we can identify from Daneau's own works some of the characteristics that he valued in theology. Daneau had studied with Calvin in 1560 and had formed a close friendship with Beza when he was a pastor in Geneva from 1574 to 1581. With Beza, Ursinus, and Zanchi, he was one of the formulators of the early scholastic form of Protestantism. For one thing, Daneau did not follow Beza toward a supralapsarian view of predestination but, like Zanchi, adopted an infralapsarian formulation.[12] Daneau did not, therefore, teach Arminius the supralapsarian doctrine against which he later argued so strenuously. More importantly, Daneau turned toward medieval scholasticism for theological models. Daneau was so intrigued with the systematizing efforts of Peter Lombard that he composed a Protestant commentary on the first book of the *Sentences*.[13] He also read deeply in the writings of Thomas Aquinas and incorporated many of Aquinas' arguments, including the proofs of the existence of God, into his theological system, the *Christianae isagoges*. Daneau even points out that the Occamist *Centiloquium theologicum* denies the possibility of proving the existence of God: this, he adds, is false whereas the five ways of Aquinas are correct and useful arguments. Daneau's references show an acquaintance with both Aquinas' *Summa* and with Aquinas' commentary on the *Sentences*. As Fatio has shown, moreover, Daneau's

[10] Guilhelmus Feuguereus, *Bertramni presbyteri, De corpore et sanguine Domini liber ad Carolum Magnum imperatorem G. Feugueraei opera emendatus et commentario illustratus* (Leiden, 1579).

[11] Guilhelmus Feuguereus, *Responsa ad quaestiones cuiusdam obscuri inquisitoris in Zelandia delitescentis, de ecclesiae perpetuitate et notis, deque alius quinque eodem pertinentibus capitibus* (Leiden, 1579).

[12] Lambert Daneau, *Christianae isagoges ad christianorum theologorum locos communes, libri II* (Geneva, 1583).

[13] Lambert Daneau, *In Petri Lombardi Episcopi Parisiensis ... librum primum Sententiarum ... Lamberti Danaei commentarius triplex* (Geneva, 1580).

scholasticism, while resting on a broad reading of the medieval
doctors, favored a critical reading of Peter Lombard, Thomas Aquinas,
and Durandus of Sancto Porciano. Arminius, as we will see further
on, had a fairly extensive knowledge of Lombard, surely used
Aquinas' works but, most probably, did not take much from Durandus.[14] The pairing of Thomas and Durandus in Daneau's work,
however, does provide a significant indication of the direction of
Reformed scholastic theology. Just as the Thomism of Vermigli and
Zanchi was consistently modified in the direction of Augustinian and
Calvinistic views on human nature, sin, and grace, so also does
Daneau's juxtaposition of the rather independent Dominican thinker,
Durandus, with Thomas Aquinas point toward an interest in episte-
mologically critical and, frequently, Augustinian modifications of the
Thomist position. Contrary to older views of Durandus, his theories
cannot be claimed as clear predecessors of Ockham.[15] Daneau's
approach to the proofs, moreover, makes clear that he rejected the
nominalist denial of a rational, analogical approach to the divine in
favor of the Thomistic approach.[16] It is worth raising the question of
whether Daneau's enthusiasm for Arminius' theological work was

[14] Daneau, *Christianae isagoges*, I.iii; see Olivier Fatio, *Méthode et théologie: Lambert
Daneau et les débuts de la scolastique reformée* (Geneva: Droz, 1976), pp. 118–30.

[15] See Copleston, *History of Philosophy*, III, pp. 26–28.

[16] Recent studies have demonstrated that the term "nominalism" must be used
cautiously. Indeed, one scholar has argued against its use as a characterization of
late medieval theology: see William J. Courtnay, "Nominalism in Late Medieval
Religion," in Trinkhaus and Oberman, eds., *The Pursuit of Holiness in Late Medieval
and Renaissance Religion* (Leiden, 1974), pp. 26–59; and note the very detailed work of
Katherine Tachau, *Vision and Certitude in the Age of Ockham: Optics, Epistemology and
the Foundations of Semantics, 1250–1345* (Leiden: Brill, 1988), which indicates broad
areas of investigation in the later Middle Ages—including problems of cognition
noted in commentaries on the *Sentences*—that, contrary to received opinion, were
utterly untouched by Ockham's critical approach to the problem of knowledge.
Thus "nominalism" certainly cannot be used any longer as a broad and
indiscriminate category for labeling the dominant theology of the later Middle Ages
without attention to the details of the views of individual thinkers. Its application
in the field of logic and metaphysics, however, to a critical temper that emphasized
knowledge as a knowledge of particulars and refused to grant either the real, extra-
mental existence of universals or the "real existence of the universal in
individuals," remains, I think, unchallenged. Cf. Philotheus Boehner, "The
Realistic Conceptualism of William of Ockham," in *Collected Articles on Ockham*, ed.
Eligius M. Buytaert (St. Bonaventure, N.Y.: Franciscan Institute, 1958), p. 159, with
the somewhat pointed comments of Kristeller, "The Validity of the Term:
'Nominalism'," in Trinkhaus and Oberman, eds., *Pursuit of Holiness*, pp. 65–66. In
the present essay, the term "nominalism" is used in this restricted sense. Similarly,
"Scotism" is used to refer directly to particular motifs belonging to the thought of
Duns Scotus, such as the distinction between *theologia in se* and *theologia nostra*
underlying later language of archetypal and ectypal theology

an indication of Arminius' interest in the methods and patterns of scholastic theology or the recognition of a nascent admiration of Thomism in the theology of young Arminius.

In the autumn of 1581, the twenty-two-year-old Arminius left Leiden for study in Geneva. The six years of study, based in Geneva but including extended trips to Basel and Padua, are crucial for an understanding of Arminius' theology. It was the opinion of Bertius and Brandt that Arminius had advocated a strict Calvinism, akin to that of Theodore Beza, until he was faced, as a minister in Amsterdam, with the alternative forms of the doctrine of predestination proposed by Coornhert in the Netherlands and Hemmingius in Denmark.[17] Bangs is able to show that Arminius' own theology underwent a development rather than experiencing a sudden change in encounter with Coornhert. In addition, Bangs quite convincingly argues that Arminius probably never held a supralapsarian doctrine like that of Beza.[18] Nonetheless, Bangs also assumes that Beza's supralapsarianism was the dominant theology of the day and, also, the backdrop against which Arminius' alternative must be understood.[19]

Bangs does recognize that Beza was "not a despot" in the Genevan Academy and that other views than his own were tolerated.[20] What Bangs does not note, however, is that Geneva was not at all dominated by supralapsarianism and that Beza himself probably did not claim confessional status for his doctrine but recognized the generally infralapsarian view of Bullinger and others as the confessional norm for the Reformed churches: it was Bullinger's *Confessio Helvetica posterior* that became the basis for the *Harmony of the Reformed Confessions* developed in Geneva in 1580 under the supervision of Beza.[21] In addition, Arminius' theology is not to be viewed as an essentially Reformed rejection of supralapsarianism: Arminius also rejected the infralapsarianism of the Reformed confessions.[22] Other students of Beza, like Johann Polyander—later one of the authors of the great Leiden University *Synopsis purioris theologiae*—came away from Geneva confirmed in a confessional, infralapsarian view of predestination.[23]

---

[17] Bertius, *De vita et obitu*, pp. **ii verso–**iii recto (*Works*, I, pp. 29–31); Brandt, *Life of James Arminius*, pp. 60–64.

[18] Bangs, *Arminius*, pp. 138–41.

[19] Ibid., pp. 66–71, 77, 148–49, 253.

[20] Ibid., p. 75.

[21] See Philip Schaff, *The Creeds of Christendom*, 3 vols. (New York, 1931; repr. Grand Rapids: Baker, 1983), I, p. 354.

[22] Cf. *Dec. sent.*, pp. 116–17 (*Works*, I, pp. 645–47).

[23] Cf. *Propositions and principles of divinitie propounded ... in the University of Geneva ... under M. Theod. Beza and M. Anthonie Faius* (Edinburgh, 1595), p. 26, where Poliander's infralapsarian thesis is recorded as successfully defended, with the *Synopsis purioris theologiae* (Leiden, 1625; 6th ed., 1881), XXIV.xiv, where Polyander's colleague,

What, then, did Arminius gain from his experience in Geneva? He gained, perhaps for the first time, a sense of the magnitude of the philosophical debate between Ramists and traditional Aristotelians. In Geneva, Ramus' philosophy came under fire from Theodore Beza and from the philosopher, Petrus Galesius, a Spanish Aristotelian. Indeed, in 1570, Beza blocked the efforts of Ramus to join the faculty at Geneva—in part because of finances and in part out of a "determination to follow the position of Aristotle, without deviating a line, be it in logic or in the rest of our studies."[24] Bertius records that Arminius retained an "invincible attachment" to the philosophy of Ramus "which he publicly defended in the warmest manner, and which he taught in private to such auditors as were admirers of that logical system."[25] Among these auditors was Arminius' friend and ally of later years, Uitenbogaert. Galesius was irate and Arminius was forbidden to teach Ramism. Arminius left for Basel, where he remained from September 1583 until August 1584. At that time, Arminius returned to Geneva and again took up studies with Beza, Faius, and Perrot—with whom he had maintained a cordial relationship.[26]

After his studies in Geneva and before his departure for pastoral work in Amsterdam, Arminius made a journey to Italy. His stay may have been as long as a year—from the summer of 1586 to the summer of 1587—but certainly no longer. We know that he studied in Padua under Jacob Zabarella. The significance of this journey in Arminius' theological development has been hotly debated since the early seventeenth century. Even before his death, some of Arminius' opponents and detractors circulated the rumor that Arminius had converted to Roman Catholicism, had an audience with the pope, had kissed the pope's slipper, had "frequented the company and the assemblies of the Jesuits," and had become fast friends with the great anti-Protestant polemicist, Robert Bellarmine.[27] There is, surely, no truth in any of these allegations. After the year in Italy, Arminius

---

Walaeus, supplies a similar infralapsarian definition. On the theology of the *Synopsis* and its significance, see G. P. van Itterzon, "De 'Synopsis purioris theologiae': gereformeerd Leerboek der 17de Eeuw," *Nederlands Archief voor Kerkgeschiedenis* 23 (1930): 161–213, 225–59; C. A. Tukker, "Vier liedse Hoogleraren in de gouden Eeuw: De Synopsis purioris theologiae als theologisch Document (1)" in *Theologia Reformata* 17 (1974): 236–50; and idem, "Theologie en Scholastiek: De Synopsis purioris theologiae als theologisch Document (2)," *Theologia Reformata* 18 (1975): 34–49.

[24] Beza, as cited in Waddington, *Ramus*, pp. 229–30; cf. Bangs, *Arminius*, pp. 60–61.

[25] Bertius, *De vita et obitu*, **ii verso (*Works*, I, p. 23).

[26] See Bangs, *Arminius*, pp. 71–73.

[27] Bertius, *De vita et obitu*, **iii recto (*Works*, I, pp. 26–27); cf. Bangs, *Arminius*, pp. 78–80.

returned to Geneva—again without experiencing any deterioration of his cordial relationship with Beza.

Do these events suggest anything to us about Arminius' theological development? Bertius, on whose life of Arminius we depend for the outlines of this narrative, assumes that Arminius broke with Beza theologically only after his departure from Geneva but is disposed to view Arminius' Ramism as a basic point of difference between professor and student. Both Brandt and Bangs assume that Arminius maintained his opposition to Aristotle and remained thoroughly Ramist throughout his years as a professor at Leiden.[28] The events seem, however, to point in a somewhat different direction, particularly in view of the eclectic character of Arminius' later philosophical usage. Arminius did retain the Ramist definitions of theology, but his patterns of theological exposition in the *Orations* and *Disputations* manifest little impact of Ramist logic—quite in contrast to the consistent use of bifurcation by writers like Perkins, Polanus, and Ames. Arminius' journey to hear Zabarella, who was one of the foremost exponents of the newly revived Aristotelianism of the late Renaissance, suggests that he was not nearly as enamored of Ramus' anti-Aristotelian polemic as is frequently assumed. In addition, Arminius' later interest in the metaphysics of Spanish Aristotelians like Suárez and Molina,[29] when added to his interest in Zabarella, suggests that Galesius' influence may not have been entirely negative!

Although it is not at all clear precisely what philosophical perspectives Arminius gained during the Genevan phase of his education, it is fairly certain that the scholastic tendencies of his thought, as instilled by Daneau and to a certain extent by Snellius, were confirmed by the teaching of Beza and Faius. The scholastic method and Aristotelian philosophy inculcated by Daneau's Thomism were reinforced by the method of academic disputation employed in the academy. By teaching theology and conferring degrees on the basis of successful defense of academic theses, Geneva both drew on the pedagogical methods of medieval scholasticism and provided students with a scholastic pedagogy for use in their own subsequent teaching careers. Junius, educated in Geneva toward the end of Calvin's career, adopted this method in Heidelberg and refined it in Leiden. Arminius and other Leiden theologians learned it in Geneva under Beza and retained it in their classrooms in Leiden. As for the famous letter of commendation written by Beza for Arminius, it ought not to be viewed either as a glowing but empty letter of a professor who did not know his student well enough to understand where they differed on

[28] Cf. Brandt, *Life of James Arminius*, pp. 41–42 with Bangs, *Arminius*, pp. 62–63, 257.

[29] See below, chaps. 6, 10, 11, 12, et passim.

key points of doctrine or as a sign that Arminius once held a view of
predestination that was substantially the same as Beza's and subsequently changed his mind. The Arminius that Beza knew in Geneva
may not yet have clearly articulated his views on predestination—
that was the result of the unpublished correspondence with Junius
and the (also unpublished) refutation of Perkins, both written after
Arminius' departure from Geneva. Beza, like Daneau, may simply
have been commenting on the aptitude of the young Arminius for
the scholastic theology then coming into vogue in Protestantism. As
Bangs correctly observes, predestination is not noted in the letter.[30]

Arminius' theological development between the time of his departure from Geneva in 1587 and the beginning of his professorial duties
in 1603 is chronicled in the pages of the disputations written during
those years but only published posthumously, particularly in the epis-
tolary debate with Franciscus Junius[31] and in the lengthy refutation of
William Perkins' treatise on predestination.[32] In both cases, the
reader is struck by Arminius' facility in scholastic debate and by his
ability to use the same scholastic distinctions as his opponents, but for
the sake of arguing an opposite position. The conference with Junius,
although it was conducted by letter, takes the form of a scholastic academic disputation: Arminius states a thesis or proposition to which
Junius offers objections and then, by way of conclusion, Arminius
replies to the objections in defense of his thesis. This pattern is followed through twenty-seven propositions. Much of the argument is
developed syllogistically and refutation frequently proceeds through
demonstration of logical errors.[33]

Not only the method but also the content of the *Conference* is
scholastic. Arminius worries through such issues as the distinction
among absolute necessity, necessity of the consequent, and the
necessity of the consequences and the distinction between the certainty of knowledge and the necessity resulting from acts of will.[34] He
raises questions about the correctness of identifying human beings in
their original state as existing in *puris naturalibus* and argues the
Thomist case for the *donum superadditum* or superadded gift of grace as
belonging to the human being in the initial act of creation.[35]

---

[30] See Bangs, *Arminius*, pp. 73–75 and cf. the extended excerpt of the letter in
Works, I, pp. 24–25 and in Brandt, *Life of James Arminius*, pp. 48–49.

[31] *Amica cum Francisco Iunio de praedestinatione per litteras habita collatio*, in *Opera*,
pp. 445–619 (*Works*, III, pp. 1–248).

[32] *Examen modestum libelli Perkinsianae*, in *Opera*, pp. 621–777 (*Works*, III, pp. 249–
484).

[33] See *Amica collatio*, pp. 523, 554–66 (*Works*, III, pp. 110, 153–71).

[34] Ibid., p. 572 (*Works*, III, p. 180).

[35] Ibid., pp. 521–25 (*Works*, III, pp. 108–14).

He also raises a series of scholastic distinctions concerning the relation of the divine knowledge to its objects.[36]

Similarly, the *Modest Examination* follows the disputative scholastic method by dividing Perkins' treatise into separate arguments and then disproving the syllogistic structure of those arguments by manifesting errors in either the major or minor propositions of the syllogism.[37] Arminius also argues against Perkins on the grounds of a scholastic view of the divine attributes—noting, for example, that Perkins' teaching fails to take cognizance of the logic of justice, will, and freedom in God: Perkins wrongly argues divine freedom by placing will prior to justice, when the proper view would argue that justice is the rule of will and will is free because it is not constrained by externals.[38] As in the *Conference* with Junius, Arminius here also has recourse to the distinction between necessity of the consequent and the necessity of the consequences.[39]

On 23 October 1602, Franciscus Junius, professor ordinarius of theology at the University of Leiden died of plague. Scarcely two months earlier, Junius' colleague, Lucas Trelcatius the Elder, had been taken by the same disease. Franciscus Gomarus, Trelcatius' successor, was left alone to bear the burden of teaching in the university. A successor to Junius was desperately needed, but the candidate whose name was brought forward by the curators of the university immediately became a focus of debate and dissension. The curators favored Arminius, then a Reformed minister in Amsterdam. The faculty, particularly Gomarus, believed that there was reason to doubt Arminius' orthodoxy and proposed several more trustworthy candidates. Arminius had as yet published nothing and the complaints against him were based largely on rumor. Despite the intensity of the objections, the curators settled on Arminius.[40] As a final preparation for his post as professor, Arminius was examined for the doctorate at Leiden: he was first interviewed in private and then in a public disputation on the nature of God. On the following day, 11 July 1603, Arminius presented an oration "On the Priesthood of Christ" before the convocation of the university.

When Arminius began his teaching duties in September 1603, he chose as the topic of his inaugural lectures a series of issues central to the development and construction of theological prolegomena: the

---

[36] Ibid., p. 492 (*Works*, III, pp. 65–66).

[37] *Examen modestum*, pp. 673–79 (*Works*, III, pp. 328–36).

[38] Ibid., pp. 680–81 (*Works*, III, pp. 342–43).

[39] Ibid., pp. 712–13 (*Works*, III, pp. 387–88).

[40] Cf. Brandt, *Life of James Arminius*, pp. 133–81 with Bangs, *Arminius*, pp. 232–39.

object, author, goal, and certainty of theology.[41] The significance of this choice, given the academic setting of Arminius' first term at Leiden, has escaped the notice of Arminius' biographers and of the few scholars who have examined his theology in any depth. Harrison, for example, notes the "practical and evangelical temper" of Arminius' teaching and states that the orations "show [Arminius'] sense of responsibility as a teacher of the Christian ministry."[42] Bangs provides an accurate summary of the contents of the orations but makes no effort to place them into the context of intellectual or doctrinal history—with the exception of a brief comment that, quite rightly, establishes a relationship between Arminius' definition of theology as practical and his appreciation of Ramist thought and logic.[43]

It was not the case that Arminius simply chose to begin his lectures at the beginning by selecting the foundational topics of the definition of theology as his initial subject. Most of the Protestant theological systems written before 1590 had not discussed these topics. Even Arminius' scholastically inclined teacher at Leiden, Lambert Daneau, had not introduced his *Christianae isagoges* with a formal prolegomenon, but simply began with the doctrine of God.[44] Protestantism survived more than a half-century of debate, confessional formulation, and systematic development before it turned to the work of constructing methodological prolegomena to its dogmatic systems. One of the first theologians, if not the first, to write a full-scale prolegomenon was Franciscus Junius. As demonstrated by the theological systems of Polanus, Scharpius, Alsted, Walaeus, and even the Lutheran, Johannes Gerhard, Junius' treatise, *De vera theologia* (1594), was enormously influential.[45]

In lecturing on theological prolegomena, therefore, Arminius chose to place himself firmly on the path indicated for Protestant theology by his predecessor at Leiden. He also took up—before the publication of the major theological systems of Polanus, Scharpius, Alsted, Walaeus, and Gerhard—a topic that was not only new to

---

[41] *Orationes tres: I. De obiecto theologiae. II. De auctore & fine theologiae. III. De certitudine ss. theologiae*, in *Opera*, pp. 26–41, 41–55, 68–71.

[42] Harrison, *Arminianism*, p. 27.

[43] Bangs, *Arminius*, pp. 63, 256–61.

[44] Daneau, *Christianae isagoges*, I. i–xxv.

[45] On Junius, see Althaus, *Die Prinzipien*, pp. 230–31; and note Amandus Polanus von Polansdorf, *Syntagna theologiae christianae* (Geneva, 1617), I.i–ii; Johann Heinrich Alsted, *Praecognita theologiae*, I.iv–viii; Johannes Scharpius, *Cursus theologicus* (Geneva, 1620), I, col. 1; Antonius Walaeus, *Loci communes s. theologiae*, in *Opera omnia* (Leiden, 1643), p. 114; and Johann Gerhard, *Loci communes* (1610–21), ed. Preuss (Berlin: Schlawitz, 1863–75), I.1–12, all of which appear to borrow substantively from Junius.

Protestants but was, more importantly, indicative of the Protestant acceptance of the method and interests of medieval scholastic theology. Arminius, in other words, cast his theological lot with the new scholasticism. What he developed at considerable length in his three inaugural orations on theology he also set forth, in briefer form, as the first set of theses in his *Private Disputations*.

Much of Arminius' theological writing came from the years prior to the debate over his doctrines and dealt with topics that were never drawn into the debate. Indeed, the two sets of "disputations" or, more precisely, theses presented as the basis of academic discussion in the basic classes in theology, date from the years after 1603: as late as 10 August 1605, Arminius could join with his two future opponents on the theological faculty at Leiden, Franciscus Gomarus and Lucas Trelcatius the Younger, in a profession of mutual agreement on fundamental matters of doctrine. What is more, the set of *Disputationes privatae* begun by Arminius in 1603 were intended by him as the basis for an entire system of theology, dealing with such topics as the etymology, meaning, method, and proper object of theological discourse; the nature of religion; the authority, certainty, perfection, and perspicuity of Scripture; the essence, life, understanding, and will of God; and the sacraments of the church—topics not taken up in the later debate over predestination, Christology, and the order of salvation.

It is one of the ironies of later discussions of Arminius and his theology, including contemporary scholarly discussion, that Arminius' thoughts on these topics have been studiously ignored, even though the noncontroversial and nonapologetic character of Arminius' work on these fundamental topics renders them a significant index to the tenor and intention of his thought as a whole. Whereas it is frequently rather difficult to ascertain all of the implications of the statements made by Arminius in polemical and apologetic essays like the *Declaration of Sentiments* or the *Apology Against Thirty-one Defamatory Articles*, the virtually unperturbed flow of his thought in the *Orations* and in the two sets of disputations lends itself to a clearer analysis of his arguments, particularly their direction and their implication. In addition, the *Orations* and two sets of disputations include Arminius' discussions of the presuppositions and foundational topics of theological system, the prolegomena and *principia* of theology as typically stated in the early Protestant scholastic systems. It is arguable that whatever view of predestination and the *ordo salutis* Arminius espoused, its roots may be found in the presuppositional structure and foundational principles of his system, which is to say, in the definition of theology and in the doctrine of God, the so-called *principium essendi* of theological system.

Examination of Arminius' academic disputations on theology, God, creation, and providence also sheds light on his choice of Franciscus Junius as his correspondent or academic referee during his early studies in and worries about the Reformed doctrine of predestination. Junius was a known moderate—an infralapsarian—in his view of predestination and not merely an irenic thinker who sought the peace and unity of the church. Junius was also a major formulator of early Reformed orthodoxy, a creator of new theological models for the exposition of doctrine. Arminius early on sought his advice on predestination and, some years later, after Junius' death, when Arminius was appointed to succeed Junius at Leiden, he looked to Junius' *Theses theologicae* for help in his own preparation of theological system. Arminius' own intellectual struggles with the doctrines of God, creation, and providence not only manifest striking parallels with and developments of Junius' formulations, they also— as we will see more clearly in subsequent discussion—follow the pattern established by Junius, together with other eminent Reformed writers like Zanchi and Daneau, to search the works of medieval scholastics for basic definitions and dogmatic paradigms. Not only do these resemblances indicate an interest in the theological patterns established in Reformed theology by his predecessors and teachers, they also indicate Arminius' close reading of works like Junius' *De vera theologia*, Zanchi's *De natura Dei*, and Daneau's *Christianae isagoges* —the titles of which all appear in the catalogue of Arminius' library.[46]

Arminius' teaching at Leiden, then, should not be viewed as somehow antischolastic and in methodological as well as doctrinal dissent from the Reformed position. The frequent characterization of his thought as a biblical and exegetical reaction to the onset of a speculative and scholastic style in Reformed theology falls wide of the mark.[47] Examination of his style of argument and of the rather speculative teaching of his theses on the essence and attributes of God evidences clear parallels with the thought of his orthodox Reformed colleagues and opponents and, together with their efforts, an equally clear rootage in medieval theology. It is quite true that Arminius— and the early orthodox Reformed writers as well—could echo Luther's and Calvin's harsh words about the excesses and abuses of medieval scholastic thought. Arminius is remembered as having objected to the use of certain scholastic distinctions at a public disputation of 1609 with the comment "that the Schoolmen were not to

---

[46] *The Auction Catalogue of the Library of J. Arminius*, a facsimile edition with an introduction by C. O. Bangs (Utrecht: HES, 1985), pp. 7, 11, 12.

[47] See the summary of discussion in Richard A. Muller, "Arminius and the Scholastic Tradition," *Calvin Theological Journal* 24/2 (1989): 263–77.

him the rule either of speech or of faith, because they first came into notice at the time when Antichrist was revealed; and because Scholastic Divinity had never become prevalent, except when that which was true and apostolical had been banished."[48]

Such objection to scholasticism was quite typical of Arminius' time, as Protestant theologians felt the attraction and sensed the dangers, both theological and ecclesiastical, of late medieval thought. Protestant theology in the late sixteenth and early seventeenth centuries was ineluctably drawn toward the methodological and the metaphysical insights of scholastic theology and, at the same time, hesitant to avow openly any intellectual alliance with this supposed enemy. As Lewalter has argued, the topics of a fully developed theological system raised issues and questions that demanded the use of metaphysical concepts for their resolution.[49] The reconstructed Christian Aristotelianism of Zabarella, Fonseca, Suárez, Piccolomini, and J. C. Scaliger was enormously influential in Protestant as well as in Catholic circles.[50] Even so, the movement toward scholastic method was noted by writers like Antoine de Chandieu (1534–91) and Johann Heinrich Alsted (1588–1638) who strongly criticized medieval scholasticism and, at the same time, took over the method and even the term "scholastic" for their own use.[51]

In his history of Dutch theology in the sixteenth and seventeenth centuries, Sepp records the comments of one Caspar Sibelius, a student at the University of Leiden during the years 1608 and 1609:

> I observed, among a number of fellow students enrolled in the private theological class of doctor Arminius, many things that, had I been ignorant, might easily have led me into dark and abominable errors. For in that class we were utterly drawn away from reading the works and treatises of Calvin, Beza, Zanchi, Martyr, Ursinus, Piscator, Perkins, and other learned and valuable theologians of the church of Christ, we were commanded to examine only holy scripture, but equally so the writings of Socinus, Acontius, Castellio, Thomas

[48] Cited in *Works*, I, p. 301 (appendix W).

[49] Lewalter, *Metaphysik*, pp. 8–19.

[50] Cf. Lewalter, *Metaphysik*, pp. 63–64 with Weber, *Die philosophische Scholastik*, pp. 15–20, 48–54.

[51] Cf. Antoine de Chandieu (Sadeel), *De verbo Dei scripto ... praefatio de vera methodo theologice simul et scholastice disputandi*, in *Opera theologica* (Geneva, 1593), pp. 7–9; Johann Heinrich Alsted, *Praecognita theologiae* (Hanoviae, 1614), I.xviii; with the system of Arminius' colleague, Lucas Trelcatius the Younger, *Scholastica et methodica locorum communium institutio* (London, 1604); also see the extended analyses of the problem of scholasticism in Burmann, *Synopsis theol.*, I.ii. 46–47 and Voetius, *De theologia scholastica*, in *Selectarum disputationum theologicarum* (Utrecht, 1648–69), I, pp. 12–29; and note the discussion of Protestant orthodox use of the terms "scholastic theology" and "scholasticism" in *PRRD*, I, pp. 76, 259–63 and in Muller, "Arminius and the Scholastic Tradition," pp. 264, 276–77.

Aquinas, Molina, Suárez and other enemies of grace were commended to us.[52]

Sepp draws attention to the point that Arminius was known as a biblical teacher and argues that a contrast must be made between the "churchly dogmatics" of Gomarus—who drew on Calvin, Beza, Zanchi, and the others—and the "biblical theology" of Arminius.[53] This view of Arminius is typical of those who contrast his thought with scholastic orthodoxy.

A similar accusation is recorded in the preface to the Acts of the Synod of Dort and taken up by Brandt in his life of Arminius together with the claim that Arminius and Uitenbogaert had received a letter from the pope promising financial rewards in return for advocacy of Roman theological views.[54] Brandt refutes the charges with an excerpt from a letter of Arminius to Sebastian Egbertszoon, the burgomaster of Amsterdam, where Arminius denies that he ever recommended "the works of the Jesuits and of Coornhert" and states that he continually encouraged students to read commentaries and the *Institutes* of Calvin. Arminius expresses a high appreciation of Calvin's commentaries and adds that the *Institutes* must be read "with discrimination, as the writings of all men ought to be read."[55]

Arminius' protestations notwithstanding, the accusations continued to be made. In December 1608, Gomarus spoke before the States of Holland and West Friesland of the "various heresies and gross errors" of Arminius, noting that Arminius' theology "agreed with the Pelagians and the Jesuits." Gomarus claimed that Arminius had worked to "invalidate" the "orthodox doctrine" of the Reformed churches in his private classes and that he had supported the theology of "Jesuits and other adversaries" specifically in areas of conflict with Reformed theology.[56] At very least, Gomarus had noted the parallels between Arminius' views on predestination and the teachings of Lessius, Molina, and other Jesuit adversaries of Baius. In addition, as Dibon has shown, the conflict between Arminius and Gomarus must be understood in the context of philosophical developments at the University of Leiden—specifically, in the context of the development of a Protestant Aristotelianism under the impact of Suárezian metaphysics. Gilbert Jacchaeus, who taught philosophy at Leiden during the time of the debates between Arminius and Gomarus, was deeply influenced by Suárez on such topics as causality, divine

---

[52] Christiaan Sepp, *Het Godgeleerd Onderwijs in Nederland, gedurende de 16e en 17e Eeuw* (Leiden: De Breuk and Smits, 1873–74), I, p. 118.

[53] Ibid., pp. 118–19.

[54] Brandt, *Life of James Arminius*, p. 298.

[55] Ibid., pp. 299–300; also cited in the elder Brandt's *History*, II, pp. 49–50.

[56] Brandt, *Life of James Arminius*, pp. 343–44.

concursus, and creaturely contingency—precisely the topics of dispute between Gomarus and Arminius. Indeed, Gomarus had also spoken of the deficiencies of Arminius' theology on such topics as contingency, necessity, divine *concursus,* and velleity. Dibon leaves open the extent of the influence of Suárez on the two theologians.[57]

Suárez, it must be remembered, was the metaphysician par excellence of the seventeenth century. It was Suárez who, dissatisfied both with the poor organization of Aristotle's *Metaphysics* and, therefore, with the scholastic metaphysics that had been based upon it, developed a topically arranged and perspicuously organized study of the entire field of metaphysics.[58] In producing his *Disputationes metaphysicae,* moreover, Suárez mastered, more thoroughly than any of his contemporaries, the history of the development of scholastic philosophy. His mastery of scholastic sources and broad range of precise citation and analysis are virtually unparalleled.[59] The excellence of Suárez' work led to the rapid adoption of the *Disputationes* as a standard text and of Suárezian metaphysics as the basic perspective in European universities, particularly in the Netherlands and Germany, whether Catholic or Protestant.[60]

Arminius was certainly not a crypto-Catholic or a Jesuit sympathizer. Like virtually every other Protestant theologian of his day, however, Arminius did dip heavily into medieval scholastic sources. And it is also the case that even when some account is taken of the polemical nature of the accusations made against him, the views of the theologians noted in the accusations—Thomas Aquinas and two of the three Jesuits mentioned, Molina and Suárez—do appear to have influenced his thought at certain crucial points.[61] Similarly, the views of Castellio are reflected in Arminius' teaching on toleration, and perhaps those of Acontius as well.[62] The reference to Socinus may reflect a suspicion that Arminius' doctrines of Christ and the Trinity were not quite in accord with the views of his Reformed

---

[57] Dibon, *L'Enseignement philosophique,* pp. 66–68. On "velleity" or *velleitas,* see below, chap. 10; on contingency, necessity, and *concursus,* see chap. 12.

[58] Cyril Vollert, "Introduction," in François Suárez, *On the Various Kinds of Distinctions* (Milwaukee: Marquette University Press, 1947), pp. 7–8.

[59] See Norman J. Wells, "Suárez, Historian and Critic of the Modal Distinction Between Essential Being and Existential Being," *New Scholasticism* 36 (1962): 419–44; and idem, "Introduction," in François Suárez, *On the Essence of Finite Being as Such ...* (Milwaukee: Marquette University Press, 1983), pp. 6–13; cf. Vollert, "Introduction," pp. 10–11.

[60] See Karl Eschweiler, "Die Philosophie der spanischen Spätscholastik," p. 283.

[61] See below, pp. 88, 110–21, 163, 192–93, 197–98.

[62] Cf. Arminius, *Oratio de componendo religionis inter Christianos dissidio,* in *Opera,* pp. 71–91 (*Works,* I, pp. 434–540) with Sebastian Castellio, *Concerning Heretics Whether they are to be Persecuted ...,* trans. Roland Bainton (New York: Columbia University Press, 1935).

colleagues—although this one element of the accusation has no real basis in Arminius' teaching. His doctrines of Christ and the Trinity did differ with Reformed theology, but they were not at all in sympathy with Socinian doctrine.[63]

The opponents of Arminius could not deny his biblicism—but neither did they have to invent his ties to scholastic theology. Sepp's generalization is, therefore, only partly correct. Indeed, Arminius' opponents were as intent on developing a biblical theology as he was, and their scholasticism was certainly the equal of Arminius' own. What Sepp's characterization of Gomarus' theology as a "churchly" or Reformed confessional dogmatics rightly emphasizes is the orthodox and confessional interest of Gomarus both in his biblicism and in his scholasticism—and this, as Sepp did not fully recognize, stands in contrast to the nonconfessional tendencies of Arminius, both in his biblicism and in his scholasticism. The theological or interpretive grid placed by Arminius over his reading of the body of Christian doctrine was different from the grid employed by Gomarus: the latter stood more firmly in the confessional tradition of the Reformed churches and drew on the scholastic tradition in an attempt to create an orthodox Reformed system; the former, whatever one decides about his relation to the confessional tradition of the Reformed churches, drew on the scholastic tradition, including the contemporary efforts of Suárez and Molina, in order to move away from what he considered to be some of the more problematic formulations of his orthodox Reformed colleagues and contemporaries.

[63] See Muller, "Christological Problem," pp. 153–54.

3

Arminius
and the Scholastic Tradition

A perusal of the disputations on "theology," "the manner in which theology must be taught," and "blessedness, the end or goal of theology" manifests Arminius' interest in the themes enunciated by Junius only a few years before at the University of Leiden and, via the connection established in the language and argument of Junius' work, an interest in the theological prolegomena of the scholastic doctors of the later Middle Ages. The scholasticism of Arminius, like that of Junius and other writers, both Reformed and Lutheran, of the early orthodox era, represents primarily a methodological and pedagogical direction in Protestant theology connected with the development of theological system in a university context. Protestant scholasticism, including the work of Arminius, is a school theology, identified by its careful division of topics and definition of component parts and by its interest in pressing the logical and metaphysical questions raised by theology toward rational answers.[1]

A few paragraphs must suffice on the nature and character of Protestant scholasticism and its relation to the teaching of the Reformers. It is very clear that Protestant theology at the beginning of the sixteenth century was different from Protestant theology at the beginning of the seventeenth century, and that the difference can be identified in part by the adoption of scholastic method by the Protestant theologians of the late sixteenth and early seventeenth centuries.[2] The method itself, however, does not account for all of the differences—inasmuch as they relate to the thematic development of ideas as well as to patterns of exposition. Specifically, Protestant

[1] Cf. Muller, *Christ and the Decree*, pp. 11–13 with *PRRD*, I, pp. 17–19, 28–40.
[2] Cf. the definitions of Protestant scholasticism given by Armstrong, *Calvinism and the Amyraut Heresy*, pp. 32, 131–39 and Preus, *Inspiration of Scripture*, pp. xv–xvi.

theology at the end of the sixteenth century had become a confessional orthodoxy more strictly defined in its doctrinal boundaries than the theology of the early Reformers but, at the same time, broader and more diverse in its use of the materials of the Christian tradition, particularly the materials provided by the medieval doctors.[3]

The adoption of scholastic method by Protestants can be understood as one of the first and, perhaps, the most obvious of the indications of this broader use of the tradition. The Reformers themselves, particularly the trained theologians among them—Luther, Bucer, Bullinger, Musculus, Vermigli—were all versed in scholastic method and, although they set themselves polemically against scholasticism, they were never at a loss to understand their own theological task, at least in part because they were technically trained in the mechanics of theology. The problem for later generations of Protestants, particularly for the third and fourth generations of Protestant teachers, was that the revolution had succeeded and they represented no longer a protest movement but an established confessional church. In order to teach theology in their universities they needed, once again, to address issues of definition and method. Their sources for definition and method, selectively and critically chosen, were late medieval scholastic theologies. The Reformers themselves had virtually never discussed these basic academic issues and had not written full-scale theological systems; their successors returned to the older theology, the scholastic theology in which their own teachers had been trained, for answers to the questions of definition and method.[4]

The development of this Protestant scholasticism, like the related development of Protestant theological system, took several generations. Second- and third-generation Protestant codifiers produced works that were more systematic than the works of the first Reformers both in their organization and in their coverage of theological topics. Several of these third-generation writers, notably Ursinus, Daneau, and Zanchi, adopted fully scholastic methods of *quaestio* and *disputatio* and, in the cases of Daneau and Zanchi, drew explicitly on the more remote scholastics of the Middle Ages, like Aquinas, in the

---

[3] Muller, "Scholasticism Protestant and Catholic: Francis Turretin on the Object and Principles of Theology," *Church History* 55 (1986): 204–5 and cf. idem, "*Vera Philosophia cum sacra Theologia nusquam pugnat*: Keckermann on Philosophy, Theology, and the Problem of Double Truth," *Sixteenth Century Journal* 15/3 (1984): 341–65.

[4] Cf. Weber, *Die philosophische Scholastik*, pp. 38–40; idem, *Der Einfluss der protestantischen Schulphilosphie*, pp. 17–94, passim; Althaus, *Die Prinzipien*, pp. 230–34; Lewalter, *Metaphysik*, pp. 22–26; and note my longer discussions of this issue in *PRRD*, I, pp. 63–82 and "Scholasticism Protestant and Catholic," pp. 193–205.

attempt to claim that part of the tradition for Protestantism. By the time of Arminius, the theological style is that of a fourth or fifth generation and the scholastic method together with aspects of the thought of the medieval teachers had become an integral part of the theology of the Protestant universities. The contrast between the style and method of these thinkers and the style and method of the Reformers is obvious, indeed, striking.

Despite these differences, however, Protestant theology maintained a profound doctrinal continuity with the theology of the Reformers on such issues as the sole normative authority of Scripture, justification by grace through faith alone, the direct accessibility of Christ and his benefits to faith, and the limitation of the sacraments to baptism and the Lord's Supper. Among the Reformed, continuity in development can also be argued on such topics as the details of Christology, the doctrines of predestination and covenant, and the approach to natural revelation.[5] There is an increasing recognition among scholars, moreover, that the view of orthodoxy and scholasticism as distortions of the Reformation is inadequate and that neither term, orthodoxy or scholasticism, ought to be used pejoratively.[6] It is, after all, a theological and not a historical judgment to claim that the method and the teachings of Calvin's 1559 *Institutes* are somehow better than or preferable to the method and teachings of Polanus' 1609 *Syntagma theologiae*. In addition, inasmuch as the theologians of the Reformation neither produced a monolithic Protestant system nor set up their own theological systems as norms apart from the exegesis of Scripture, it is quite impossible to speak of distortions. For example, when Polanus speaks of a divine permission or permissive willing in agreement with Calvin's contemporary Peter Martyr Vermigli but in disagreement with Calvin, is this a distortion of Calvin's teaching, or

---

[5] See Donald W. Sinnema, "The Issue of Reprobation at the Synod of Dort (1618–1619) in the Light of the History of This Doctrine," Ph.D. diss., University of St. Michael's College, 1985; Gottlob Schrenk, *Gottesreich und Bund im älteren Protestantismus vornehmlich bei Johannes Coccejus: Zugleich ein Beitrag zur Geschichte des Pietismus und der heilsgeschichtlichen Theologie* (Gütersloh: Bertelsmann, 1923); Muller, *Christ and the Decree*, pp. 171–82; and idem, *PRRD*, I, pp. 167–93, 302–11.

[6] E.g., Jill Raitt, *The Eucharistic Theology of Theodore Beza: Development of the Reformed Doctrine* (Chambersburg, Pa., 1972); John Patrick Donnelly, *Calvinism and Scholasticism in Vermigli's Doctrine of Man and Grace* (Leiden, 1972); idem, "Calvinist Thomism," *Viator* 7 (1976): 441–45; Tadataka Maruyama, *The Ecclesiology of Theodore Beza: The Reform of the True Church* (Geneva, 1978); Lyle D. Bierma, "The Covenant Theology of Caspar Olevian," Ph.D. diss., Duke University, 1980; Olivier Fatio, *Méthode et théologie: Lambert Daneau et les débuts de la scolastique réformée* (Geneva: Droz, 1976); Donald W. Sinnema, "The Issue of Reprobation"; Martin Klauber, "The Context and Development of the Views of Jean-Alphonse Turrettini (1671–1737) on Religious Authority," Ph.D. diss., University of Wisconsin-Madison, 1987.

is it simply the expression of an intellectual preference for one rather than another of the two sources for later Reformed opinion?

The place of Arminius' thought in this development must be viewed, moreover, somewhat differently than the place of Zanchi's or Junius' or Polanus' thought. Whereas the Reformed scholastics endeavored, despite the obvious changes in method and, at least in terms of the breadth of sources used and issues addressed, in content as well, to stand in doctrinal continuity with the basic teachings of the Reformers, Arminius endeavored, in his teachings on grace, free will, and predestination, to alter substantively the doctrines of Reformed Protestantism. Arminius most certainly disagreed with Calvin, Vermigli, Musculus, Bullinger, and other early codifiers of Reformed doctrine.[7] It should be obvious, however, that a characterization of his thought as a distortion of earlier Reformed theology utterly misses the point of his work. Equally obviously, his disagreement with the Reformed on grace, free will, and predestination cannot be attributed to his adoption of scholastic method, inasmuch as his method was no more and no less scholastic than the method used by his Reformed opponents.

Finally, we must address the question of the intellectual tendency of Protestant scholasticism, particularly the tendency of Arminius' theology. Why did Protestant scholasticism take on a decidedly Thomistic character—why, specifically, did Arminius' theology lean toward Thomism rather than toward Scotism or nominalism, despite the clear impact of a more Scotistic or nominalistic perspective on Reformed epistemology and on the definitions of theology found in the Reformed theological prolegomena?[8] In the first place, the relationship of the earlier codifiers of Reformed theology was quite different and considerably more pronounced than the relationship of members of the same generations of Reformers to either Scotism or nominalism. Of the early codifiers of Reformed theology, only Musculus was trained in Scotist and nominalist theology.[9] As Ganoczy

---

[7] On the development of the Reformed doctrine of predestination, see Alexander Schweizer, *Die protestantischen Centraldogmen in ihrer Entwicklung innerhalb der reformierten Kirche*, 2 vols. (Zürich, 1854–56), which remains the most exhaustive study. Schweizer assumed, throughout his work, a continuity of teaching between the Reformation and orthodoxy. Later writers, like Basil Hall, "Calvin Against the Calvinists," in *John Calvin: A Collection of Distinguished Essays*, ed. Gervase Duffield (Grand Rapids: Eerdmans, 1966), pp. 27–29, have tended to argue a discontinuity. Muller, *Christ and the Decree*, pp. 69–71, 121–25, 149–82; and Sinnema, "Issue of Reprobation," pp. 52–197 once more argue continuity, although without Schweizer's "central dogma" thesis.

[8] See Muller, *PRRD*, I, pp. 123–32.

[9] Wilhelm Hadorn, "Musculus, Wolfgang," in *RE*, vol. 13, p. 581, notes Musculus' studies in the Benedictine monastery at Lixheim. On Musculus' use of Scotus, Occam, and Biel, see Muller, *Christ and the Decree*, pp. 47, 49.

has shown, the Scotist tendencies in Calvin's thought relate not to early training in Paris but to later reading and they hardly indicate an immersion in Scotist theology.[10] By way of contrast, Bucer, Vermigli, and Zanchi were all trained as Thomists and, in the case of the latter two thinkers, elements of Thomism were integrated into full-scale theological systems.[11] The Thomistic model, particularly as developed by Zanchi, was highly influential in Reformed circles—as is witnessed by the parallel interest in Aquinas by other writers of Zanchi's generation like Lambert Daneau. In addition, contemporaries of Arminius instrumental in the development of early Protestant orthodoxy—thinkers like Arminius' predecessor at Leiden, the Basel theologian Amandus Polanus von Polansdorf, and the great Lutheran dogmatician Johannes Gerhard—all drew heavily on the scholastic tradition, in particular on the work of Thomas Aquinas.[12]

In the second place, the revival of Aristotelianism and of scholasticism in Roman Catholic circles in the sixteenth century had, as its intellectual centerpiece, a revival of Thomism. Not only was there a flowering of interest in Aquinas' thought as witnessed by the many fine editions and commentaries on Thomas' works printed in the sixteenth century, there was also a notable shift of emphasis in the study of Aquinas. Whereas medieval Thomism, due to the reliance of medieval theological study on the *Sentences* of Peter Lombard, had focused on Aquinas' commentary on the *Sentences*, the sixteenth century, because of the work of Thomas de Vio, Cardinal Cajetan, and others found the greater Aquinas, the mature Aquinas of the *Summa theologiae*.[13] Although many other scholastics received attention in the sixteenth century—many scholastic systems and treatises appeared in print—none were given the close analytical attention that Thomas received. Not only were the *Summa theologiae* and the *Summa contra gentiles* printed in five editions, they were also the subject of numerous commentaries. Here again, the work of Cajetan must be noted.[14] In addition, this interest went beyond the bounds of

[10] Alexandre Ganoczy, *The Young Calvin*, trans. David Foxgrover and Wade Provo (Philadelphia: Westminster, 1987), pp. 174–78.

[11] See Johannes Müller, *Martin Bucers Hermenutik* (Gütersloh: Gerd Mohn, 1965), pp. 20 (25), 93–94; John Patrick Donnelly, *Calvinism and Scholasticism*, pp. 24–29, 47–48, 69–70, 80, 85, 100, etc.; and "Calvinst Thomism," pp. 442–44; also see Philip McNair, *Peter Martyr in Italy: An Anatomy of Apostasy* (Oxford: Clarendon, 1967), pp. 105–6.

[12] See Heiner Faulenbach, *Die Struktur der Theologie des Amandus Polanus von Polansdorf* (Zurich, 1967), pp. 48–49, 53, 55; and Robert Scharlemann, *Aquinas and Gerhard: Theological Controversy and Construction in Medieval and Protestant Scholasticism* (New Haven: Yale University Press, 1964).

[13] Copleston, *History of Philosophy*, III, p. 344.

[14] See Paul Oskar Kristeller, *Medieval Aspects of Renaissance Learning: Three Essays*, ed. and trans. Edward P. Mahoney (Durham, N.C.: Duke University Press, 1974), pp.

the Dominican order: the Jesuit order, at the insistence of its founder, Ignatius of Loyola, looked to Thomas Aquinas as its primary theological guide.[15] This revival of Thomism represented a marked shift from the theological and philosophical tendencies of the fifteenth century. As Oberman has argued, the Thomism of the later Middle Ages was hardly the force that it eventually came to be. Not only was it the "young Thomas" of the sentence commentary who "determined the profile of the total Thomas," it was also a highly "metaphysical Thomas" who was taught by the late medieval Dominicans rather than the careful interpreter of Scripture and the fathers. In this context, Franciscan theology, particularly the theology of Scotus, appeared as a powerful and attractive alternative,[16] which worked its way into some of the theology of the early Reformation. The rising tide of Thomism in the sixteenth century, presenting as it did the Thomas of the *Summa*, offered the world a more strictly Augustinian doctrine of grace than that found in the commentary on the *Sentences* and, in addition, a Thomas more adept at scriptural and patristic argumentation.[17]

The philosophy, particularly the metaphysics, propounded by sixteenth-century Dominicans and Jesuits was adopted with surprising rapidity by philosophers and theologians in the German and Dutch universities. The revived Thomism of the Dominican order spread northward from the universities of Padua and Bologna while the Thomistic teachings of the Jesuits were mediated by Spanish thinkers like Suárez and Vitoria to Lyon, Louvain, Antwerp, and thence to the Protestant universities.[18] The Protestant scholasticism that arose out of the contact of the teachings of the Reformers, the scholastic background of the Reformation itself, and this renewed, fundamentally Thomistic, scholasticism of the Dominicans and Jesuits, of the Italian and Spanish universities, was no mere reproduction of medieval scholasticism but a critical and at times somewhat eclectic modification of the medieval models that adapted them to the new intellectual context of the post-Reformation period.[19] Thus, Thomism must be regarded as a center of reference which—just as Aquinas had appropriated and modified Aristotle—was modi-

---

40–42, for a discussion of the revival of the summas and pp. 49–50, 54, for an assessment of Cajetan's work.

[15] Copleston, *History*, III, p. 344; cf. Charles Jourdain, *La philosophie de Saint Thomas d'Aquin*, 2 vols. (Paris: Hachette, 1858), II, pp. 254–55.

[16] Heiko A. Oberman, *The Dawn of the Reformation: Essays in Late Medieval and Early Reformation Thought* (Edinburgh: T. and T. Clark, 1986), pp. 4–6.

[17] Ibid., p. 5.

[18] Cf. Escheweiler, *Die Philosophie*, pp. 262–66 with Weber, *Die philosophische Scholastik*, pp. 38–46.

[19] Weber, *Die philosophische Scholastik*, pp. 45–46.

fied by the writers of the period in terms of late medieval critiques of Thomism such as had already modified the thought of Dominicans like Capreolus, in terms of the strict Augustinianism and the epistemological concerns of the Reformers, and in terms of the new developments in logic and metaphysics represented by thinkers like Rudolf Agricola, Ramus, Zabarella, and Suárez.

As for Arminius' own interest in Aquinas, it certainly can be explained in general on the basis of the two already noted points and more specifically, on the influence of Arminius' teacher, Lambert Daneau, and on Arminius' participation in the early Protestant orthodox quest for systematic models which, early on, became aware of the Thomistic renaissance of the sixteenth century. Perhaps more importantly, Arminius' own theological concern for the problem of grace and human ability raised anew the epistemological problem of the relationship of the fall to the human faculties and—against Calvin—Arminius argued the ability of the intellect to know the good and to direct the will despite the problem of sin.[20] In the intellectualism of Thomas Aquinas, Arminius could find a philosophical and theological position suitable to his own concerns. As we will see in the following study, philosophical intellectualism had an enormous impact on Arminius' theology. As Donnelly has observed, "Lutheran and Calvinist scholasticism did not build on medieval nominalism ... insofar as the roots of Protestant scholasticism go back to the Middle Ages, they tend to go back to the *via antiqua* and Thomism."[21]

That there are late medieval scholastic sources underlying many of Arminius' formulations will be evident from the very outset of our discussion of Arminius' theological prolegomena and doctrines of God, creation, and providence. The identity of particular thinkers and specific works used by Arminius, however, presents a major problem for historical investigation. Arminius virtually never cites his sources. This absence of clear or direct citation of medieval sources is, it ought to be noted, quite typical of Protestant theology and philosophy in Arminius' day. The polemic between Protestant and Roman Catholic theologians was so heated in the late sixteenth and early seventeenth centuries that any positive citation of a potential adversary could easily bring down charges of heresy on one's head. Protestants were naturally averse to citing Roman Catholic authors, particularly their contemporaries. Thus, the more daring of the early Reformed orthodox—like Daneau, Zanchi, and Polanus—cite positively and relatively frequently only the long dead scholastics. More recent Catholic thinkers, such as Cajetan, Cano, Suárez, or Molina, are cited seldom, if ever, and then not favorably, even

[20] *Disp. pub.,* XI. i, v, vii, ix, x.
[21] Donnelly, "Calvinist Thomism," p. 454.

though their works were probably being read with care and despite the frequent theological and philosophical agreement between their views and the nascent Protestant scholasticism.

Arminius' emphasis on the problem of intellect or understanding and will, and his adoption of a Thomistic approach to that problem, together with the Thomistic rootage of several of the important Reformed teachers of the sixteenth century, makes the thought of Thomas Aquinas, the foremost exponent of the medieval intellectualist tradition, a crucial element in any discussion of the place of Arminius in the development of Protestant scholasticism.[22] Inasmuch, moreover, as many aspects of the teaching of Reformed orthodoxy can be described as resting on Thomism while at the same time modified in the direction of an Augustinian and a Scotist critique of Aquinas' trust in the instrumentality of reason,[23] the way in which Arminius receives and modifies the Thomistic heritage or disagrees with it will also be important to an understanding of his relation to the Reformed development. Even so, Arminius' relationship to and possible use of the revived Aristotelianism of the late sixteenth century and its modifications of Thomism is also crucial to the evaluation of his theology.

As Kristeller observes, "It is important to distinguish clearly those authors who rely principally on [Aquinas'] authority and who tend to support most of his major and characteristic doctrines from those who combine his ideas with other ideas that are original or from another source, or who are content simply to borrow certain of his ideas or assertions without giving them a central position in their own writings or thought."[24] Arminius clearly does not fall into Kristeller's first category nor does he borrow so little that he can be relegated to the third. Rather Arminius appears to have combined fundamental teachings of Aquinas with ideas gathered from a variety of divergent sources. These other sources will be particularly evident in Arminius' definitions of theology and in his views on divine knowledge and providence. Nonetheless, in the main outlines of the

---

[22]On Aquinas, see Pierre Rousselot, *The Intellectualism of Saint Thomas*, trans., with a foreword by James E. O'Mahony (New York: Sheed and Ward, 1935).

[23] Cf. Richard A. Muller, *"Vera Philosophia cum sacra Theologia nusquam pugnat:* Keckermann on Philosophy, Theology and the Problem of Double Truth," *Sixteenth Century Journal* 15/3 (1984): 362–65 with John Patrick Donnelly, "Calvinist Thomism," *Viator* 7 (1976): 441–45; and idem, *Calvinism and Scholasticism in Vermigli's Doctrine of Man and Grace* (Leiden, 1975). Donnelly shows, in both essays, that the Thomistic models are adapted both in the case of Vermigli and of Zanchi, to the demands of Reformed theology: both writers may sometimes disagree with Calvin for the sake of following Aquinas but, equally frequently interpret Thomas "in a Calvinistic sense" and, therefore, in a powerfully Augustinian manner in the doctrines of sin, fall, and law (see "Calvinist Thomism," pp. 451–52).

[24] Kristeller, *Medioval Aspects,* p. 37.

doctrine of God, Aquinas' influence will be evident and, even in the modifications of the doctrine of the *scientia Dei*, Aquinas remains a crucial point of reference. Some of the Thomistic features of Arminius' theology could easily have come from Daneau and Zanchi, but the larger part, as will be argued below, most probably come from Aquinas himself. The other elements of Arminius' thought, taken from various late medieval, Reformation, and late sixteenth-century sources, were blended by Arminius into a whole that can no longer be called Thomism in the strictest sense but which certainly retains strongly Thomistic tendencies. Perhaps more important even than the direct borrowings from Aquinas is the consistency with which Arminius uses Aquinas and other scholastic sources to plot out a theological path with strong affinities to the *via antiqua* rather than to the *via moderna*. Even when we cannot be certain of the precise point of reference underlying a given statement in Arminius' theology, there are powerful emphases on the analogical relation between God and world, the existence of all things by participation in the divine being and goodness, and the assumption that the divine intellect is prior to the divine will, all of which point away from a nominalist *via moderna* to the *via antiqua*: and, more or less directly, to Aquinas, despite the frequently eclectic detail of the system.

There remains, therefore, a bit of a nomenclature problem. This study evinces no desire to set aside previous analyses of developing Reformed orthodoxy that have noted a shift away from the *via moderna* toward the *via antiqua*; have shown an important impact of Aquinas on writers like Vermigli, Zanchi, Polanus, and, among the Lutherans, Gerhard; and have been able to speak, within parameters like those set by Kristeller's second category of Thomistic influence, of a "Calvinist Thomism." Another term, however, is required for the discussion of Arminius' thought, if only because it serves no purpose to call him a "Calvinist" and, inasmuch as he veers away from Calvinism, his use of the medieval tradition will also manifest differences between his thought and that of his teachers. Rather than use the term "Calvinist Thomism," this essay will speak of an eclectic theology with a Thomistic center or of a modified Thomism. The issue, as I hope will become clear, is not merely that Arminius draws on certain central concerns of Aquinas but rather how he takes up those concerns and uses them as primary foci in his own theology after modifying sometimes their context and, other times, their direction.

A final question that must be answered concerns the character and import of the Arminian system itself. Granting the varied sources of Arminius' theology and its frequent use of arguments that would, under other circumstances, not only seldom be linked with one another, but would also be viewed as potentially contrary, is there a unity and, indeed, a specific, unifying program in Arminius' thought? For example, Arminius accepts a distinction between an archetypal divine self-knowledge and a limited, ectypal human theology and a definition of theology as a practical discipline, both associated with Scotism, and binds these concepts to a profoundly intellectualistic doctrine of God that bears marked similarities to the teaching of Thomas Aquinas. Having once accepted this intellectualist premise and its corollary, a profound analogy of being between God and world, Arminius moves by way of a concept of middle knowledge or *scientia media* to lessen the impact of the intellectualist perspective on his doctrine of divine causality. With all of these modifications, does Arminius' theology coalesce and find its own unity and systematic identity?

Another indication of the direction of Arminius' scholasticism can be found in the comment of Brandt:

> as ... the illustrious Junius himself, treading in the footsteps of the Thomists, seemed not so much to abandon as merely to shade off that harsher sentiment of Calvin and Beza (for he held the subject of pre-destination to be, not man as whom God had not yet decreed to create, nor man viewed as created with the foreknowledge of his fall, but man viewed as created ...,) Arminius attempted to prove ... that both opinions [i.e., Calvin's and Junius'] in addition to other disadvantages, involved the necessity of sin, and, consequently, that recourse must be had to a third, which presupposed the creation and the fall.[25]

Brandt's point is significant inasmuch as it points both toward the spectrum of Protestant opinion on predestination and to the directions taken by Protestant thought in its encounter with and appropriation of scholastic tools. The infralapsarianism of Junius, like that of Vermigli and Zanchi before him, rested on a use of Thomist categories.[26] These founders of Protestant scholasticism need to be credited with a modification of the doctrine of predestination away from the strict causal and virtually deterministic patterns of Calvin and Beza toward a less deterministic model—indeed, they demonstrate just how little truth there is in the frequent association of scholastic method with a deterministic or predestinarian tendency in Protestant thought. If, moreover, a scholastic influence or, more precisely, a modified Thomism, may be credited in part with the shift away from a supralapsarian view of predestination toward an infralapsarian perspective in thinkers like Vermigli, Zanchi, and Junius,[27] there is all

[25] Brandt, *Life of James Arminius*, pp. 106–7.

[26] See Donnelly, "Calvinist Thomism," pp. 441–45 and idem, "Italian Influences on the Development of Calvinist Scholasticism, *Sixteenth Century Journal* 7/1 (1976): 81–101.

[27] On this point, see in particular Sinnema, "Issue of Reprobation," pp. 73–78, 137–40, 449–50, where Zanchi's and Junius' scholastic formulae are convincingly

the more reason for looking to scholastic thought and, specifically, to other sixteenth-century uses and modifications of Thomism for the roots of Arminius' own movement beyond the views of Junius and still further away from the teaching of Calvin and Beza.

As a fairly large body of recent scholarship has demonstrated, it is a mistake to define Protestant scholasticism primarily in terms of the rise of a Reformed predestinarianism. On the one hand, the Reformed developed other doctrines in a scholastic fashion and they did not actually use the doctrine of predestination as their "central dogma."[28] On the other hand, the Lutheran writers—who strongly rejected the Reformed view of predestination—manifest the increasing impact of scholastic method as much as the Reformed.[29] Even so, the opposition of Arminius to the Reformed doctrine of predestination ought not to be viewed as a sign of opposition to the increasingly scholastic character of Reformed (or Lutheran) theology. Indeed, for all his debate with his Reformed adversaries at Leiden, Arminius was one with them in his fundamental acceptance of scholastic method and of the intricacies of scholastic argumentation. In this essay, I propose to examine this rather different Arminius—the scholastic Arminius—in terms of the themes of the early orthodox or Protestant scholastic theological prolegomena and doctrine of God, creation, and providence. In these doctrinal *loci*, moreover, we can expect to find the beginnings of an Arminian system in which a revised view of predestination and of the *ordo salutis* will stand not as lonely points of protest against Reformed orthodoxy but as arguments set forth in harmony with (and as results of) a larger theological and philosophical concern.

If Arminius was in fact attempting to produce a full systematic alternative to the teaching of his orthodox Reformed contemporaries, the character of his plea for confessional revision in the Reformed churches must also be placed in a new light. In his *Declaration of Sentiments* Arminius had, on the one hand, argued for a revision of the *Heidelberg Catechism* and *Belgic Confession* and for a revised understanding of which confessional articles were necessary for faith,[30]

---

shown to belong to a moderating tendency in Reformed doctrine and part of the reason why the Canons of Dort are not only more precise but also "less stringent" than Calvin's formulae. Cf. Muller, *Christ and the Decree*, pp. 62–67, 70–71, 116–17.

[28] Cf. Muller, *Christ and the Decree*, pp. 1–13, 79–96, 121–25, 154–59, 164–82; PRRD, I, pp. 82–87, 197, 308 with the conclusions of Tadataka Maruyama, *The Ecclesiology of Theodore Beza: The Reform of the True Church* (Geneva: Droz, 1978), pp. 22, 139–48, 198–99.

[29] See, in particular, H. E. Weber, *Der Einfluss der protestantischen Schulphilosophie auf die orthodox-lutherische Dogmatik.*

[30] *Dec. sent.*, pp. 130–32 (*Works*, I, pp. 713–30).

while, on the other, he had claimed agreement with both documents on specifically those points of doctrine at issue between him and his Reformed brethren.[31] The confessional documents themselves, particularly the catechism, state doctrine broadly and are, therefore, more inclusive than the doctrinal statements of either Arminius or his opponents. Arminius could, perhaps, argue that his theology was Reformed enough to fit within the bounds of the catechism—but if that were so, why the call for revision? If Arminius' arguments for confessional agreement are scrutinized in terms of the meaning intended by the authors of the confessional documents, however, a rather different impression emerges. This is particularly the case with the *Heidelberg Catechism*, where Arminius had at his disposal not only the confessional document itself, but also the catechetical lectures of one of its authors, Zacharias Ursinus.[32] Had Arminius compared Ursinus' doctrines of the causes of faith and of predestination, elaborated at some length in the catechetical lectures, he would have found Ursinus' teaching in agreement with one of the views he rejected. In addition, Arminius would have found Ursinus to be in disagreement with his own catechism—at least as interpreted by Arminius![33] In other words, if confessional revision did not proceed quickly, Arminius' protestations of agreement with the confessions would be (and were) called into question in very short order. Granting, moreover, Arminius' rather ambivalent relationship to the Reformed confessions, Ursinus' confessional theology stands as a significant index to the tendency of Arminius' own system of doctrine.

Although Arminius cannot be identified as a Reformed theologian he must nevertheless be understood in relation to the Reformed tradition and, specifically, in relation to the developing Reformed orthodoxy of the University of Leiden between the time of Franciscus Junius and the era of the great *Synopsis purioris theologiae* (1626). For all his disagreement with crucial elements of Reformed theology, Arminius stands in positive relationship with the movement of theological method and with the drive toward technical definition characteristic of Protestant thought in the final quarter of the sixteenth and the first quarter of the seventeenth century. His own theological theses frequently draw upon the work of his predecessor, Junius, and

---

[31] Ibid., pp. 105, 119–20 (*Works*, I, pp. 622–23, 654).

[32] *Doctrinae christianae compendium sive commentarii catechetici* (Neustadt, Leiden, and Geneva, 1584; Cambridge, 1585); published as *Explicationes catecheseos* in Ursinus' posthumous *Opera theologica*, 3 vols., ed. Quirinius Reuter (Heidelberg, 1612); also note *The Commentary of Dr. Zacharias Ursinus on the Heidelberg Catechism*, trans. G. W. Williard (Columbus, Ohio, 1852; repr. Phillipsburg, N.J.: Presbyterian and Reformed, 1985).

[33] Cf. *Expl. cat.*, cols. 107–9, 212–18 (*Commentary*, pp. 112–16, 293–303) with *Dec. sent.*, pp. 116–21 (*Works*, pp. 616–57).

equally frequently point positively toward the theses of successors like Poliander and Walaeus, authors of the *Synopsis*. Even more clearly, they point toward the Remonstrant theology of Episcopius and Limborch. For all his ultimate disagreement with their confessionalism, Arminius joined with them, historically, in the development of scholastic orthodoxy at Leiden.

The continuity and discontinuity of Arminius' theology with the thought of colleagues and successors at Leiden, therefore, is an important index to the meaning and import of his doctrinal formulations. Their scholasticism and its sources can and must be measured against his. It is precisely this task, however, that manifests the underlying difficulty of analyzing Arminius' thought and the probable reason for the neglect, in previous scholarship, of any consideration of the scholastic roots of Arminius' teaching. Of the great medieval scholastics, Arminius cites only one, Thomas Aquinas, as a positive source of his own opinion. In addition to Arminius' one direct citation of Aquinas in the *Public Disputations*, there are quite a few places in the two sets of disputations where the language evinces a reading of both *Summas*.[34] There are also passing references to "the Master of the Sentences," Peter Lombard,[35] and there are several general references to the opinions of the "scholastics" or "schoolmen" plus fairly consistent reference in disputation to Thomas Aquinas, Pierre d'Ailly, Francis of Mayronnes, Francis de Sylvestris (Ferrariensis), and Dominic Bañez.[36] The reference to Bañez illustrates the problem, noted above, of the early Protestant scholastic citation of Roman Catholic sources. Bañez, a Dominican, had argued, in good Thomistic fashion, that God's gracious activity is the first cause of salvation and must, therefore, stand prior to the human will in the order of salvation—a point of doctrine also in accord with Reformed theology and in its causal language in profound agreement with the theology of Reformed Thomists like Vermigli and Zanchi. Arminius was quite willing to cite Bañez somewhat unfavorably in order to press home the point that he, Arminius, hoped to make against his Reformed opponent, William Perkins. But Arminius did not draw explicitly on the thought of Bañez' Jesuit adversary, Louis Molina—even though the influence of Molina is quite apparent in several places in Arminius' system and even though the debate between Bañez and Molina, which had taken place only a few years before, was probably well known to Arminius.[37] The actual sources of Arminius' scholastic

---

[34] *Disp. pub.*, IV.iv.

[35] *Examen modestum*, pp. 654, 691 (*Works*, pp. 299, 354).

[36] *Examen modestum*, pp. 638, 643, 692–93 (*Works*, III, pp. 273, 281, 354, 358); *Disp. pub.*, IV.xliii; *Disp. priv.*, XVII.x.

[37] On the debate between Bañez and Molina, see Vansteenberghe, "Molinisme," *DTC* 10/2, cols. 2142–45; Mandonnet, "Bañez, Dominique," *DTC* 2/1, cols. 143–44;

teachings can be inferred by the comparison of his views with the teaching of various scholastic thinkers and schools of thought.

A crucial tool in this work of the comparative reconstruction of the intellectual background and immediate theological sources of Arminius' thought is the catalogue of his library printed for its auction in 1610.[38] Arminius owned a superb theological library containing a wealth of materials, including Erasmus' *Annotationes* on the New Testament, virtually all of Calvin's commentaries, commentaries by Luther, Oecolampadius, Bucer, Melanchthon, Zanchi, Junius, Aretius, and numerous other writers of the sixteenth century, a Vulgate, a Stephanus Bible, a broad selection of patristic texts, major works by theologians and philosophers of the Middle Ages and Renaissance, and a considerable gathering of works by early orthodox Lutheran and Reformed thinkers, including virtually all of the major theological systems written by Protestants in the second half of the sixteenth century. If we restrict ourselves to works belonging specifically to the category of systematic theology, we can discern an interest in developing Lutheran dogmatics evidenced by the Melanchthonian *Corpus doctrinae*,[39] Urbanus Rhegius' *Loci communes*,[40] Hemmingsen's *Enchiridion*,[41] and Chemnitz' *Examen concilii Tridentini* and *Loci communes*.[42] On the Reformed side, Arminius most probably possessed Ursinus' lectures on the Heidelberg Catechism.[43] He also owned virtually all of the major dogmatic treatises of Zanchi,[44] Beza,[45] Daneau,[46] Junius,[47] Sadeel,[48] and Aretius,[49] together with the loci or disputations of Szegedin, Grynaeus, the Leiden faculty (1597), Snecanus, Ramus,

---

Pegis, "Molina and Human Liberty," pp. 91–121; a lengthy discussion of the history and implications of the concept at the heart of the debate, the divine *scientia media*, is found in Paul Dumont, *Liberté humaine et concours divin d'après Suárez* (Paris: Beauchesne, 1936), pp. 77–170.

[38] *Catalogus librorum clarissimi viri D.D. Iacobi Arminii, quondam in academia lugdunensi theolog. professoris, quorum auctio habebitur ...* (Leiden, 1610). This extremely rare item, the only known copy of which is in the British Museum, has recently been made available through the good offices of Carl Bangs.

[39] *Auction Catalogue*, p. 13.

[40] Ibid., p. 17. This is probably a reference to Rhegius' *Formulae ... loquendi de praecipuis christianae doctrinae locis* (1535).

[41] Ibid., pp. 14 and 17 (two copies?).

[42] Ibid., pp. 4, 8.

[43] Ibid., p. 4: "Tomus primus operum Theolog. Urzini" and p. 18: "Catechesis Ursini."

[44] Ibid., pp. 4, 7.

[45] Ibid., pp. 9, 15, 16.

[46] Ibid., pp. 5, 12, 15, 18, 21.

[47] Ibid., pp. 7, 8, 9, 11.

[48] Ibid., pp. 9, 12.

[49] Ibid., pp. 13, 19, 22.

Keckermann, Sohn, Martinius, and Polanus.[50] The catalogue also cites works by Landesberg, Bastingius, Mornaeus, and Gomarus.[51]

The Lutheran materials, which represent the Philippist or Melanchthonian side of early Lutheran orthodoxy, provided Arminius with a less predestinarian and even synergistic model for Protestant theology. This is certainly the case with Hemmingsen's *Enchiridion*, which Arminius cited in later dispute as an instance of orthodox Protestant system favorable to his own views on predestination.[52] Chemnitz' works, both the *Loci communes* and the *Examen*, although not examples of Philippist synergism, also surely served as models for a system in which a thoroughly Protestant view of justification by grace through faith could be posed against the teachings of Trent without recourse to a strict and rigid doctrine of predestination.[53] In neither case, however, do these Lutheran theologies provide the philosophical and theological foundation for the scholastic distinctions on which Arminius' theology would ultimately rest. (It is equally clear that neither Arminius' patristic collection nor his library of early Reformation treatises provided him with his language of the priority of intellect in its direction of the divine will toward a known good, of the character of theology as a practical *scientia*, of the distinctions between antecedent and consequent will, absolute and ordained power in God, or of the divine *concursus* with the acts of finite causes in the temporal ordering of providence.)

The Reformed materials make clear, on the one hand, that Arminius had a strong interest in the exegetical theology of the Reformation and that, for all of their doctrinal disagreement over the doctrine of predestination, he retained a profound sense of the importance of Calvin's work, particularly as found in the commentaries. On the other hand, they evidence Arminius' immersion in the thought of his teachers and immediate predecessors in the Reformed tradition. By far the greatest portion of the Protestant materials in his library were those from the era of early Protestant orthodoxy. From Zanchi he surely learned that Thomistic foundations were no hindrance to Reformed system. From Junius' treatise on "true theology" Arminius gained the most advanced discussion yet available of theological prolegomena; and from Sadeel's *Opera* and *De verbo Dei*, he

---

[50] Ibid., pp. 4, 9, 11, 13, 21, 22 (respectively as above).

[51] Ibid., pp. 8, 11, 13 (respectively as above).

[52] *Dec. sent.*, p. 115; cf. Niels Hemmingsen, *Enchiridion theologicum* (London, 1580), III.i. (pp. 237–38).

[53] Martin Chemnitz, *Loci theologici*, pars II, De iustificatione, iv, esp. pp. 273–76; cf. idem, *Examination of the Council of Trent*, trans. Fred Kramer (St. Louis: Concordia, 1971–86), I, pp. 605–6.

received, if nothing else, a basic discussion of a program for scholastic Protestantism.[54]

Arminius' library also contained a substantial number of medieval scholastic and sixteenth-century Roman Catholic works, including a significant number of the writings that his adversaries accused him of recommending to students. The catalogue notes Bonaventure on the third and fourth books of the *Sentences*, Albert the Great on the first and second books of the *Sentences* and on the eucharist, Scotus' *Opera* in the Venice edition of 1503,[55] Aquinas' *Summa contra gentiles* and *Summa theologiae*,[56] Biel's essay on the canon of the mass, Lombard's *Sentences*, and the *Opuscula* of St. Anselm.[57] The presence of the two summae of Aquinas is significant inasmuch as several main themes in Arminius' theology, as examined below, appear to draw on both. Even more significant is the emphasis on Jesuit theology: in addition to copies of the *Catechismus concilii tridentini* or *Catechismus Romanus*,[58] Arminius owned the *Opuscula* of Suárez, Bellarmine's *Disputationes*, Molina's *Concordia*, and two volumes entitled *Capitum doctrinae Jesuiticae*.[59] In addition, Arminius' library also contained three works by John Driedo of Louvain, including his *De concordia liberi arbitrii et praedestinationis divinae* (1537), an important precursor of Molina's *Concordia*.[60] The impact of these works, particularly those of Suárez and Molina, upon Arminius appears to have been considerable. Finally, the catalogue lists, without referencing either the author or the place and date of publication, a *Vocabularum theologicum*. The most likely identification of this work would seem to be Altenstaig's eminent theological dictionary, first published in 1517 and available to Arminius in several editions—Antwerp (1576), Venice (1579, 1582, 1583), Lyon (1580), Leiden (1580), plus two printings of an abridgment (Paris, 1567, 1580).[61]

Arminius' library also contained several major patristic works—and it is clear that here, too, we can discern the source of an important influence upon his thought, specifically his trinitarian and chris-

---

[54] See Franciscus Junius, *De vera theologia* (1594) in *Opuscula*, ed. Abraham Kuyper (Amsterdam, 1882); and Antoine Chandieu (Sadeel), *De verbo Dei scripto* .... *Praefatio de vera methodo theologice simul et scholastice disputandi*, in *Opera theologica* (Geneva, 1593), pp. 7–9; cf. the discussions in *PRRD*, I, pp. 76–77, 123–26, 297–98.

[55] *Auction Catalogue*, p. 3.

[56] Ibid., pp. 3, 4. *N.B.*: the Antwerp (1585) edition of the *Summa theologiae* owned by Arminius was complete in five folio volumes, with a sixth volume of indices.

[57] Ibid., pp. 5, 7.

[58] Ibid., pp. 18, 22.

[59] Ibid., pp. 8, 11, 14.

[60] Ibid., p. 7.

[61] Ibid., p. 6 and cf. de Lubac, *Augustinianism and Modern Theology*, p. 152 on the importance of Altenstaig.

tological formulations.[62] Nonetheless, like the writings of the Reformers, these patristic sources cannot be counted as providing Arminius with his style and method or, indeed, with foundational themes of his teaching on theology, God, creation, and providence. As this essay hopes to demonstrate, Arminius' style, method, and the foundational themes of his teaching derive from the scholasticism of the age, both Protestant and Catholic, and manifest his participation in the movement toward the intellectual institutionalization of Protestantism. Continuity with the Reformation, particularly on such issues as church and sacraments and, indeed, on the doctrine of justification, cannot be denied nor should Arminius' interest in the patristic period, quite characteristic of the spirit of early Protestant orthodoxy, be overlooked, but continuity with the scholastic tradition is present also as a dominant tendency in Arminius' thought. These several lines of continuity (together with the discontinuities caused by, for example, the application of scholastic method to Reformation doctrines) are typical of the Protestant theology of Arminius' era—indeed, are part and parcel of the Protestant scholastic enterprise of constructing an orthodox and catholic body of doctrine for the Protestant churches.[63]

The contents of a professor's library are not, of course, identical with the contents of his mind. Some books are purchased and not read; others are read without having been purchased. Many are read and are mentally set aside as less than important while a few are read over and over for the sake of mastery. We cannot, therefore, make hasty conclusions based on the catalogue of Arminius' library. The presence of a title in the library, however, together with a clear resemblance between Arminius' thought and the thought of the author of the volume does, however, point toward a source of Arminius' theology almost as clearly as an actual reference in Arminius' text. And, granting the absence of references, the catalogue provides considerable assistance.

The purpose of this study, then, is to provide an explanation of several of the foundational motifs of Arminius' theology in the context of late sixteenth- and seventeenth-century scholasticism, by noting the probable and possible antecedents of Arminius' teachings and by indicating the implications of Arminius' theological formulations in their relationship to and distinction from the doctrinal formulae of orthodox Protestantism and of the scholastic tradition—both medieval and sixteenth-century Roman Catholic. It is clear from

[62] See Muller, "Christological Problem," pp. 150, 153–54, 161. Arminius' use of patristic sources and the extent of their influence on his theology is a topic warranting further study.

[63] See Muller, "Vera Philosophia," pp. 356–65 and idem, "Scholasticism Protestant and Catholic," pp. 193–96, 200–201, 204–5.

an examination of Arminius' writings that he used a scholastic method and adopted scholastic models similar to those used by his Protestant contemporaries. Thus, the phenomenon of Reformed or "Calvinist Thomism,"[64] as inaugurated in the writings of Vermigli and Zanchi and carried forward with modifications in the works of such authors as Daneau, Ursinus, Junius, Polanus, and Alsted had its impact also on Arminius. What is most significant in Arminius' thought is the direction of his modifications of this Protestant Thomist trajectory—insofar as they are different from the modifications made by his Reformed contemporaries and indicate probable and possible antecedents different from the sources of the Reformed arguments.

This eclectic aspect of Arminius' thought was hardly uncharacteristic of the age. The theology and philosophy of Keckermann can easily be described in the same way—and the eclecticism of the Herborn school and its most eminent exponent, Johann Heinrich Alsted, stands as the most influential Reformed approach to the method and substance of the university curriculum in the early seventeenth century.[65] On the Roman Catholic side, the eclectic approach to philosophy was characteristic of Francis Suárez, whose metaphysics was the most important contribution of the century to Protestant and Catholic philosophy, surpassing easily the influence of Descartes for the greater portion of the seventeenth century.[66] This eclecticism of the age was not, moreover, haphazard. As Loemker and Mahieu have shown, it represented an attempt to appropriate critically the diverse materials of a rich tradition and to draw them together toward a new synthesis—a synthesis capable of sustaining the philosophical and theological mind of the West through the crisis brought on by the vast philosophical, scientific, and political changes that troubled the seventeenth century.

The importance of Arminius' contribution to this "struggle for synthesis" must not, of course, be assessed merely negatively in comparison with the Reformed model or merely internally or intrinsically in view of the alterations in perspective brought about by Arminius'

---

[64] Cf. John Patrick Donnelly, "Calvinist Thomism," pp. 441–55; idem, *Calvinism and Scholasticism in Vermigli's Doctrine of Man and Grace* (Leiden: Brill, 1975); and idem, "Italian Influences on the Development of Calvinist Scholasticism," pp. 81–101.

[65] On Keckermann, see W. H. Zuylen, *Bartholomaus Keckermann: Sein Leben und Wirken* (Leipzig: Noske, 1934), pp. 44–47 and Muller, *"Vera Philosophia,"* pp. 341–65; on eclecticism in relation to Alsted and Herborn, see Leroy E. Loemker, *Struggle for Synthesis: The Seventeenth Century Background of Leibniz's Synthesis of Order and Freedom* (Cambridge, Mass.: Harvard University Press, 1972), pp. 45–48, 141–44.

[66] Cf. Loemker, *Struggle for Synthesis*, pp. 48, 139 with Léon Mahieu, "L'eclectisme Suarézien," *Revue Thomiste* 8 (1925): 250–85.

borrowings from medieval and sixteenth-century sources.[67] The assessment must also be made with an eye to the subsequent trajectory of Arminius' ideas, particularly of those theological and philosophical constructions representing major modifications either of the tradition in general or, specifically, of the developing Reformed scholastic perspective. The work of Arminius' successors in the Remonstrant tradition, Episcopius and Limborch, is, therefore, crucial to the assessment of the significance of Arminius' own thought. Episcopius in particular, as a student of Arminius who most certainly participated in the discussions generated by Arminius' theological *Disputations*, is an index to the implications and the importance of Arminius' distinctive contributions to seventeenth-century Protestant thought.

Our basic source for Arminius' views on theology, God, and creation, apart from the three inaugural orations on the subject of theology,[68] are two sets of theses for classroom disputation or discussion, the *Disputationes publicae* and the *Disputationes privatae*.[69] This pattern for the presentation, at some length and with no loss of intellectual complexity, of the outlines of a theological system was typical of the age. Arminius' predecessor at Leiden, Franciscus Junius, left behind two major sets of theological theses—one from his earlier post at the University of Heidelberg and one reflecting his years of maturity at Leiden.[70] Franciscus Gomarus, Arminius' bitter opponent at Leiden, also developed his system in the form of theses for disputation.[71] Indeed, some of Gomarus' theses were written for the same general, jointly taught course in theology as Arminius' public disputations.[72] We also have a basic set of theses from Amandus Polanus of Basel, written out in Agricolan or Ramist fashion as a logically interrelated series of divisions of the topic of theology.[73] Polanus' theses, the *Partitiones theologicae*, also serve to show the ultimate goal of such collections: they became the basis of a fully developed system, the *Syntagma theologiae christianae*.[74] Had circumstances permitted,

---

[67] N.B.: "struggle for synthesis" is Loemker's apt characterization of the philosophical movement of the early seventeenth century.

[68] *Orationes tres: I. De obiecto theologiae. II. De auctore & fine theologiae. III. De certitudine ss. theologiae*, in *Opera*, pp. 26–71 (*Works*, I, pp. 321–401).

[69] *Disputationes publicae*, in *Opera*, pp. 197–333 (*Works*, II, pp. 77–317); *Disputationes privatae*, in *Opera*, pp. 339–444 (*Works*, II, pp. 318–469).

[70] In Franciscus Junius, *Opuscula theologica selecta*, ed. Abraham Kuyper (Amsterdam, 1882), pp. 103–289 (Leiden); 289–327 (Heidelberg).

[71] Franciscus Gomarus, *Disputationes theologicae*, in *Opera theologica omnia* (Amsterdam, 1644), pars III.

[72] See Bangs, "Introduction," in *Works*, I, pp. xvii–xviii.

[73] Amandus Polanus von Polansdorf, *Partitiones theologicae* (Basel, 1590).

[74] Amandus Polanus von Polansdorf, *Syntagma theologiae christianae* (Geneva, 1617); cf. Muller, *Christ and the Decree*, p. 130 and p. 217, n. 2.

Junius, Arminius, and Gomarus would probably have developed lengthy systems on the basis of their disputations.

The relationship of Arminius' public and private disputations is also of importance to an understanding of his theology. As Bangs indicates, James Nichols' hypothesis of the early origin of the private disputations (1599ff), during Arminius' pastorate in Amsterdam, is surely incorrect. Bangs argues from the form and content of the disputations that they were written for university students and notes that they were most probably left incomplete because of Arminius' death.[75] The last of the set, on the sixth commandment, was delivered on 31 July 1609, just before Arminius' last conference at the Hague. On his return from the Hague, his illness worsened and he was confined to bed; he died on 19 October 1609. The entire set was most probably written out, parallel to the public disputations and for the use of a closer circle of students, between 1603 and 1609.

There is also evidence that the *Private Disputations* arose somewhat later than the *Public Disputations*, probably as a revision and correction of the earlier set. At one point in his discussion of the nature of God in the *Private Disputations*, Arminius simply notes the essential attributes, simplicity, infinity, eternity, immensity, immutability, and so forth, without elaboration, commenting that these issues had been discussed in his "public theses on this subject."[76] The *Private Disputations*, at least those on the doctrine of God, were, therefore, written second. In addition, the *Private Disputations* are, almost invariably, both verbally similar to the *Public Disputations* but far more smoothly written and, typically, better argued. The points presented only in the longer form of the *Public Disputations* are, on occasion, quite poorly stated and difficult to understand, not having benefited from the subsequent debate and discussion.[77] Arminius also tends, in the *Private Disputations*, to present his arguments cohesively, without the intrusion of the masses of *dicta probantia*, scriptural proof-texts, that clog the *Public Disputations*. This may indicate a freer, less troubled climate in the closer circle of students, with less need to provide direct biblical justification of theological arguments.

The list of theses entitled in the *Opera*, *Articuli nonnulli diligenti examine perpendendi* (certain articles to be diligently examined and weighed), have a limited usefulness in deciphering Arminius' thought. They are prefaced with the statement that some of the articles are denied or affirmed decisively and others denied or affirmed

---

[75] Bangs, "Introduction," in *Works*, I, p. xviii.

[76] *Disp. priv.*, XV.vii.

[77] E.g., *Disp. pub.*, IV, l–li on the relation of goodness, understanding, and will in the divine willing of finite things.

with doubt and that these various understandings are indicated by signs added to the articles. There are, however, no such signs in any of the printed editions of the *Articles*. Bangs quite rightly states that some of the articles clearly express Arminius' own thoughts while others appear to be "raising leading questions."[78] Indeed, the statements on the decree of salvation in the *Articles* are identical with those found in the *Declaration of Sentiments*.[79] Nonetheless, where corroboration cannot be found in other writings of Arminius, the points made in the *Articles* cannot—given the prefatory remarks and the absence of the signs—be taken as definitive of Arminius' position.

[78] Bangs, "Introduction," in Arminius, *Works*, I, p. xix.
[79] *Articuli nonnulli*, XV.1–4; cf. *Dec. sent.*, p. 119 (*Works*, I, p. 653–54).

PART 2

The Idea and Method of Theology

4

Theology as a "Practical" Discipline

Arminius wrote at considerable length on the idea and method of theology. Indeed, there is no topic in the whole of theological system —apart from the doctrine of predestination—on which Arminius discoursed at such length and in such detail. As Bangs notes, Arminius' three "orations" on theology "were polished productions, non-controversial, and widely applauded."[1] They represent a moment in Arminius' career that was free of debate and open to the presentation and elaboration of ideas. Together with the much briefer *Private Disputation*, "De theologia," they provide a virtually complete prolegomenon to theological system as it was being developed in the early years of the seventeenth century. As noted in the preceding chapter, Arminius' interest in the construction of theological prolegomena placed him directly in the main line of the development of Protestant scholasticism and, perhaps even more importantly, identified him as a true successor of the revered Junius who had written the highly influential *De vera theologia*. More than this, Arminius' choice of prolegomena as his subject placed him, with other Protestant scholastics of his day, in reliance upon the medieval tradition of prolegomena: the Reformers had never defined the discipline of theology in and for the university context, leaving their successors the problem of deciding which elements of earlier discussion were suitable to the Protestant theological enterprise.[2] In the following analysis, I have drawn on both the orations and the disputation. Taken together, these essays on theological prolegomena not only provide a view of basic definitions held by Arminius, they also adumbrate, with remarkable consistency, the basic themes of his doctrines of God,

---

[1] Bangs, *Arminius*, p. 261.
[2] Cf. the discussion in *PRRD*, I, pp. 63–80.

creation, and providence—themes that are, in turn, constitutive of his theology and formative in his development of an alternative to the Reformed dogmatics of his day.

After a somewhat flowery introductory paragraph addressed to his colleagues and prospective students in the university, Arminius moves to a series of general remarks on the nature of *sacra theologia*. He avers that he means no insult to other disciplines or to his esteemed colleagues in those fields when he identifies theology as first among the sciences. In order to demonstrate the excellence of theological science, Arminius points out that all forms of human knowledge (*disciplina humana*) are "estimated according to the excellence of their object, their author, and their end."[3] He proposes to discuss these points in order and then to conclude with a discussion of the certainty of theology: the three orations, therefore, are to be considered as a unified argument.

Arminius' thought in these three orations and in the corresponding section of the *Private Disputations*, like the thought of his Protestant contemporaries and predecessors on these points, is at its most eclectic. The Protestant search for models for theological prolegomena brought the early orthodox writers into contact with a rather diverse and, in addition, gradually developing medieval tradition. The distinction between *theologia* and the interpretation of *sacra pagina* was not made before the rise of the schools in the eleventh century and the first denomination of theology as a *scientia*, probably by Alain of Lille, did not occur until the second half of that century. The doctors of the thirteenth century debated whether theology was a *scientia* or, more properly, a *sapientia* and—if indeed a science—what kind of science, speculative or practical.[4] Protestant theologians, beginning with Junius, began the appropriation of these materials, in some cases, notably that of the Lutheran dogmatician, Johann Gerhard, by setting forth an entire paradigm of the medieval discussion and choosing those elements and definitions most suitable to Protestant theology.[5]

The term "theology" means, literally, "a word or rational discourse about God" (*sermo sive rationem de Deo*).[6] Like most of his contemporaries, Arminius appears somewhat sensitive to the fact that it is not a biblical term—and perhaps to the fact that it was seldom used by the Reformers as a description of the content of their writings. *Religio*

---

[3] *De obiecto*, p. 28 (*Works*, I, p. 324).

[4] See Congar, *History of Theology*, pp. 79–165.

[5] Johann Gerhard, *Loci theologici*, I, prooemium, 11–12; cf. Paul Althaus, *Die Prinzipien der deutschen reformierten Dogmatik in Zeitalter er aristotelischen Scholastik* (Leipzig: Deichert 1914), pp. 230–31.

[6] Ibid.

had been the term preferred by the Reformers.[7] The idea of theology is biblical, however, and Arminius notes that *theologia* is precisely the "science" identified by Paul as "the truth which is after godliness" (Titus 1:1). The term for godliness, *eusebeia*, is more precisely given by Paul in 1 Timothy 2:10 as *theosebeia*. *Theologia*, then, is rightly and properly identified as "a rational discourse about God" and the definition itself points to God as the "object of theology" (*obiectum theologiae*).[8] These basic definitions follow the paradigm established by Junius and echo the direction being taken by contemporaries of Arminius like the Reformed thinkers Polanus, Alsted, and Scharpius, and the great inaugurator of Lutheran scholasticism, Johann Gerhard.[9] As noted in the previous chapter, much of this development must be credited directly to the influence of Junius' *De vera theologia*.

All sciences can thus be defined in terms of their proper object and, when this definition is accomplished, the excellence of theology quite clearly appears. The object of general metaphysics, notes Arminius, adopting the standard scholastic definition, is "being with reference to its being" (*ens qua ens*); particular metaphysics takes as its object minds or intelligences abstractly considered, while the objects of physics are "bodies as having the principle of motion in themselves."[10] Definitions follow for mathematics, medicine, jurisprudence, ethics, oeconomics, and politics.[11] "All these sciences," concludes Arminius,

> are ordered in subordination to God, for indeed they all have their origin in him, are dependent on him alone, and return to him in their ultimate direction and tendency. This science [i.e., theology] is the only one that occupies itself with the Being of beings and the Cause of causes, the foundation or ground (*principium*) of nature and of the grace existing in nature, by which nature is assisted and surrounded. This object therefore is the most worthy and dignified of all.[12]

The language here is of some interest because of its clear scholastic rootage. The preeminent example of the theory of the unity of all

---

[7] Cf. *PRRD*, I, pp. 112–15.

[8] *De obiecto*, p. 28 (*Works*, I, p. 324); cf. *Disp. priv.*, I.ii, iv: "Theologiae voce non conceptum seu sermonem ipsius Dei, quod etymon permittit, sed de Deo rebusque divinis intelligimus, secundum vulgarem usum eius. ... Qui Deus propterea in Theologia ut objectum illius officii considerandus est."

[9] Polanus, *Syntagma theol.*, I.i–ii; Alsted, *Praecognita theol.*, I.i; Scharpius, *Cursus theol.*, I, col. 1; Gerhard, *Loci theol.*, I.1–12.

[10] *De obiecto*, p. 28 (*Works*, I, pp. 324–25).

[11] Ibid.; note that *oeconomia* or oeconomics referred, in the sixteenth and seventeenth centuries, not to banking and finance but, as in classical usage, to "household management."

[12] Ibid., p. 28 (*Works*, I, p. 325).

knowledge in the light of divine truth is surely Bonaventure's *De reductione artium ad theologia (On the retracing of the arts to theology).*[13] Although it is impossible to prove whether Arminius knew this particular treatise, it is clear that the concept does not come from the Reformers and that Arminius did have some acquaintance with the theology of Bonaventure.[14]

The point might also be derived from Ramus and be another of the occasional signs of Arminius' admiration of Ramist dialectics. Like Bonaventure, Ramus argued the ascent of the mind from the sensible to the intelligible order and from thence, by means of the divine light that shines through intelligible things, toward the divine mind itself. This ascent is accomplished by the art of dialectic which, as the one, unitary method for grasping the whole of reality and as the art of arts, serves, in effect, to draw or retrace all of the arts toward theology.[15] The unity of all knowledge is to be found, by means of dialectic, in the ultimate source of all knowledge, God.[16]

Clearly, the most excellent object of any possible inquiry will be the object "which is in itself the best and the greatest, and immutable," which is also "most lucid and clear," and which is capable "by its action on the mind completely to fill it and to satisfy its infinite desires."[17] These three conditions are satisfied only by God, the proper object of theological study. Thus, it can hardly be debated that God is the best—that is, the superlatively good—being, inasmuch as God is the *summum bonum* and goodness itself. God alone is capable of communicating this goodness—limited only "by the capacity of the recipient, which he has appointed as a limit and measure of the goodness of his nature and of his self-communication."[18] This point —which seems not to have caused debate either in 1603 or at any later point in Arminius' career—is foundational to his theological perspective and, ultimately, to his disagreement with his Reformed colleagues, as will become apparent in the discussion of his doctrines of God and providence.

Equally so, God is great and immutable—great because "he is able to subject to his power even nothing itself, that it may be capable of divine good by the communication of himself"; immutable because

---

[13] In *Opera*, V, pp. 319–25.

[14] See *Auction Catalogue*, p. 3.

[15] Cf. Peter Ramus, *Dialecticae institutiones Aristotelicae animadversiones* (Paris, 1543; repr. Stuttgart, 1964), pp. 34v–36v with the discussion in Kent Emery, Jr., *Renaissance Dialectic and Renaissance Piety: Benet of Canfield's Rule of Perfection, Medieval and Renaissance Texts and Studies*, vol. 50 (Binghamton, N.Y.: State University of New York, 1987), p. 39.

[16] McKim, *Ramism in William Perkins' Theology*, pp. 130–31.

[17] *De obiecto*, p. 28 (*Works*, I, p. 325).

[18] *De obiecto*, p. 29 (*Works*, I, p. 326).

"nothing can be added to him and nothing can be taken away from him."[19] It is "delightful" to contemplate the goodness of God, "glorious" to consider his greatness, and "certain" to ground discussion in his immutability. Theology alone, therefore, meets the first criterion of excellence. Even so, in reference to the second criterion of lucidity and clarity, God must be recognized as "most resplendent and bright," as "light itself" and "that which [is] most disposed [to be known] by mind." This clarity of the divine truth is such that no object can be rightly understood unless all that is known in and through that object has been first "seen and known" in God. God is, thus, offered to the understanding as "Being itself" (*Entitas ipsa*) from which all finite beings, whether visible or invisible, have their essence and upon which their existence is grounded. All creatures bear signs of this divine origin and signs indicating their place in the "number and order" of beings.[20] It is significant for the reappraisal of Arminius' thought that this language of Being and of the order of finite beings is neither directly biblical and exegetical nor rooted in the theological pronouncements of the Reformers. The language itself demonstrates the presence of a scholastic turn of mind and the participation of Arminius in the return of Protestant theology to the metaphysical concerns of earlier centuries. That Arminius raises these issues at the point of declaring the presuppositional structure of his theology manifests their importance for his system as a whole. In view, moreover, of the Scotist tendencies already resident in Junius' prolegomena and of Scotus' declaration that the proper object of theology is God considered as God while the proper object of metaphysics is God considered as Being (*Ens*), Arminius appears far more willing than Protestants of previous generations to draw rational metaphysics into the service of theology. At very least, Arminius appears here to set aside the cautions of Scotism concerning the separation of theology from metaphysics and to advocate the use of the concept and language of Being in theology at the fundamental level of the identification of the object of the discipline.[21]

The claim, moreover, that God, considered as *Ens* or *Entitas* in an ultimate sense, provides the proper ground for an understanding of all finite or contingent beings provides Arminius with much more than a basis for arguing that theology is the highest of the sciences. It also provides him with a theme of the interconnectedness and dependence of being which is of profound importance to the whole of his theology. If the understanding of all finite beings depends upon

---

[19] Ibid.

[20] Ibid., p. 29 (*Works*, I, pp. 326–27).

[21] Scotus, *Op. oxon.*, I, prol.3, q.2; cf. *PRRD*, I, pp. 124, 158, 200.

the vision of God as Being itself, that can only be true because the Being of God is the source and ground of all being and, indeed, because the divine self-understanding—ultimate Being knowing itself in its own fullness—is the source and the ground of the intelligibility of all finite beings. By pointing toward this theme of the intelligibility of being on the basis of an analogy between the Being of God and the being of the finite order (the *analogia entis*) Arminius has, from the very beginning of his system, pointed toward a more Thomistic orientation than indicated in Junius' prolegomena and has drawn out a point of connection between his presuppositions about the character of theology and his approach to the problem of the relationship of God to the created order.

God alone, Arminius continues, is capable of filling the mind, of totally occupying the mind in its desire to know. This fact arises from the infinitude of the divine essence in its wisdom, goodness, and power and from the identity of God as truth itself, truth in itself, in the abstract. The human mind is finite and "incapable of comprehending" God in his fullness even as it apprehends the divine.[22] (Albert the Great is usually credited with making the distinction between the possibility *Deum intellectu attingere* and the impossibility *Deum intellectu comprehendere!*[23]) The divine fullness is more than the mind will ever need—and thus, "he who knows this one thing, and who is ignorant of all else, attains complete repose."[24] The point coincides precisely with the practical or goal-oriented character of theology as defined in Arminius' *Private Disputations* and, in addition, with the intellectualist and Thomist conception of the beatific vision that guides the whole of Arminius' definition.[25]

The last point concerning the ultimacy of God as an object of knowing—an object to be apprehended but not comprehended or grasped—leads Arminius to a closer consideration of the character of "our theology" (*nostra theologia*) and its object. The issue is to understand the "mode" or "manner" by which "we have a knowledge of God in this life." Very much after the pattern established at Leiden by Junius, Arminius makes a distinction between the infinite nature of God and the limited character of human knowing: the *obiectum theologiae*, God himself, must be presented to the mind "in a manner that is accommodated to our capacity."[26] As Junius argued, there is an infinite, archetypal divine self-knowledge (*theologia archetypa*), that

---

22 *De obiecto*, p. 29 (*Works*, I, p. 327).
23 Cf. *Summa theologica*, I, tract.iv, q.18, memb.3.
24 *De obiecto*, p. 30 (*Works*, I, p. 327).
25 Cf. Aquinas, *SCG*, III.25 with the discussion below, this chap.
26 *De obiecto*, p. 30 (*Works*, I, p. 328).

cannot be known by finite rational creatures (*theologia ectypa* suited to the mind of the creature).[27]

It is not sufficient, however, simply to state that theology must be an accommodated way of knowing. Rational creatures have a capacity for knowledge that varies according to their condition: we now know of God by grace through revelation but, in heavenly blessedness, illuminated by "the light of glory" we shall know by sight. Here, Arminius echoes Junius' distinction between the theology of revelation in this life (*theologia revelationis in hac vita*), also called the theology of pilgrims (*theologia viatorum*), and the theology of vision in heaven (*theologia visionis in caelis*), also called the theology of the blessed (*theologia beatorum*).[28] To these distinctions, Arminius adds that fact that "this object is not presented to our theology merely to be known but, when known, to be worshipped."[29] This view of theology stands clearly in continuity with the medieval prolegomena—not only in its emphasis on *nostra theologia* as a theology of the *viator* but also in its distinction between the two modes of knowing, revelation and vision, as characteristic of our theology in this life (*in via*) and of our theology in its heavenly fulfillment (*in patria*).[30]

The ectypal character of theological knowing together with the purpose of revelation—the worship as well as the knowledge of God—leads Arminius to conclude that

> the theology which belongs to this world is practical, through faith: theoretical theology belongs to the other world, and consists of pure and unclouded vision.... For this reason we must clothe the object of our theology in such a way that it inclines and persuades us to worship God.[31]

This is a conclusion somewhat different from that of Junius. Junius' distinctions between the infinite and archetypal divine "theology" and the finite, ectypal, and accommodated human theology, for all its resemblance to the Scotist definition of "our theology," *theologia nostra*, had not led to the typically Scotist conclusion that our theology, granting its finitude and penultimate purpose, is essentially practical and not theoretical or speculative.[32] Junius and, eventually, most of the Reformed orthodox, assumed that theology was a

---

[27] Junius, *De vera theologia*, III; idem, *Theses theologicae* (Leiden), I.4; and *PRRD*, I, pp. 123–36.

[28] Cf. *De obiecto*, p. 30 (*Works*, I, p. 328) with Junius, *De vera theologia*, VII and VIII and *DLGT*, s.v. "*theologia*."

[29] *De obiecto*, p. 30 (*Works*, I, p. 328).

[30] Cf. Aquinas, *I sent.*, prol. with the discussion in *PRRD*, I, pp. 132–33, 153–55.

[31] *De obiecto*, p. 30 (*Works*, I, p. 328).

[32] Cf. *PRRD*, I, pp. 124, 132 with Scotus, *Op. oxon.*, prol. q.4 and Minges, I, pp. 517–18.

"mixed discipline," both speculative and practical in its approach to knowledge of God.[33] The burden that this definition places on Arminius' system is to find a way to merge what began as a Scotist view of the character of theology (i.e., theology as practical), rooted in a voluntarist theory of the operations of mind, with a Thomist approach to the relationship of infinite to finite being, rooted in an intellectualist theory of the operations of mind.

The key to Arminius' resolution of this problem lies in his claim that theology *in patria* is theoretical or speculative. By definition, knowledge that is theoretical or speculative grasps its object as an end in itself while knowledge that is practical looks beyond its immediate objects toward a higher goal. Arminius can, therefore, construct a theology that is directed toward God as its goal and that argues the attainment of that goal by means of an intellectualist rather than a voluntarist dynamic. Given both the incompleteness of the Protestant scholastic system in Arminius' day and the rather eclectic reception of medieval scholastic elements into Protestant teaching, such options ought not to be surprising nor should the relative continuity between Arminius' wrestlings and those of his Reformed colleagues.

Like his Reformed contemporary, Keckermann, Arminius concluded both that theology is an essentially practical knowing and that its method of exposition would be suitable to a *praxis*. Theology does not deal, after all with knowledge of God as he is in himself (*in se*). Rather, theology is a knowledge of God and the "things" or works of God that are directed toward the salvation of human beings in the context of their life in the world. Theology may therefore be defined as the doctrine or science of the truth, which is according to godliness (*secundum pietatem*), revealed to man by God, that he might know God and divine things, believe in him, and may through faith perform acts of love, fear, honor, worship, and obedience, and in return expect and obtain blessedness from him, through union with him, to the glory of God.[34]

Granting this definition, "the proximate and immediate object of this doctrine or science is, not God himself, but the duty and act of man which he is bound to perform to God."[35]

Some clarification of terms is probably warranted here. The scholastic concepts of the practical and the speculative are quite different from the modern usage of those terms. Practical knowledge (*scientia practica*) is knowledge that is not an end in itself but that leads toward a goal beyond itself; speculative, theoretical or, as it is sometimes

---

[33] On the medieval paradigm at the root of these definitions, see Muller, "Scholasticism Protestant and Catholic," pp. 198–99.

[34] *Disp. priv.*, I.iii.

[35] Ibid., I.iv.

called, contemplative knowledge (*scientia speculativa/contemplativa*) is knowledge that is known in and for itself as a proper end or goal. The terms correspond to the two Augustinian terms for love: use (*uti, utilitas*) and enjoyment (*frui, fruitio*). Since God alone is the ultimate good, the *summum bonum*, and the goal of all things, all other objects of knowledge belong to the category of use and are to be loved in a penultimate sense. The question, then, for theological knowledge is whether it should be viewed as somehow attaining the goal of God and therefore as speculative; or whether it should be viewed as an avenue to final vision of God and therefore as practical; or whether it is both a goal and an avenue and therefore both speculative and practical. In Arminius' day, it was fairly common knowledge among Protestant theologians that the Augustinians, following Thomas of Strasburg, had identified theology as a mixed, speculative, and practical discipline, that emphasized the practical; that Aquinas had stated the opposite as characteristic of his own approach to theology (theology was a mixed, speculative, and practical discipline, with emphasis on the speculative); and that Scotus had argued a totally practical while theologians like Marsilius of Inghien and Durandus had posed a totally speculative view of theology.[36]

From these comments it ought to be clear that the identification of theology as *scientia practica* does not reduce theology to a study of ministerial praxis—worship, liturgy, homiletics, and the like—any more than definition of theology as *scientia speculativa* restricts theology to the abstractions of a priori metaphysics. Such connotations did not belong to the terms in the medieval and early modern periods. The movement or action that is generated and the direction that is given by a practical knowledge can and, in fact, must lead to a considerable emphasis on metaphysical categories, inasmuch as the goal of the praxis is the transcendent being of God. Arminius' claim that theology is practical, therefore, indicates that his thought will have a profound metaphysical interest, indeed, a metaphysical interest in the meaning and implication of the relationship between the world and God, the goal of all things.

Significantly, Arminius' basic definition of theology as "the doctrine or science of the truth which is according to godliness" that directs man toward the final goal of "blessedness" and "union" with God stands in continuity with the Ramist and with the Scotist or nominalist tendencies of the early orthodox Protestantism of his day. Petrus Ramus, whose definitions and logic provided much of the framework of early orthodox Reformed thought in such writers as

---

[36] Cf. Gerhard, *Loci theologici*, I, prooemium, 11–12, with Altenstaig, *Lexicon*, s.v. "theologia"; also Walaeus, *Loci communes*, p. 114, cols. 1–2, where the various scholastic options are discussed without citation and the Thomistic model is affirmed.

Perkins, Polanus, Scharpius, and Ames, had defined theology as *doctrina bene vivendi*, "the doctrine of living well,"[37] a definition followed explicitly by Perkins and Ames and carried forward in the Dutch theological tradition, not only by Arminius, but also by such staunch proponents of Reformed orthodoxy as Maccovius and Mastricht.[38] From a very similar point of view, the Scotist or even nominalist tendency of the early orthodox Reformed view of theology as an ectypal reflection of the divine archetype, a form of knowing given definition by the finite capacities of the human subject rather than by the infinite being of its divine object, led a writer like Keckermann to conclude that theological knowing is of penultimate, not ultimate, significance—that it exists primarily for a purpose or a use and not primarily as a goal or object of intellectual enjoyment. The Christian must not contemplate theology as an end in itself; such contemplation belongs to the final *visio Dei* alone.[39]

This goal-directed character of theology pointed Arminius to the conclusion reached also by Perkins, Ames, and Keckermann, that theology is not a contemplative or speculative discipline, but rather a practical discipline or, more simply, a *praxis* to be used as a means to the end of blessedness and union with God. If, moreover, theology is practical, Arminius reasoned, it must adopt a method that is suited to this practical character:

> It is established among the philosophers who are masters of method and order, that the theoretical sciences ought to be taught in a compositive order, the practical in a resolutive order, granting the nature and goal of these sciences: for which reason, since theology is a practical science, it follows that it must be treated according to the resolutive method.[40]

This statement of the problem of method with its language of *methodus* and *ordo* and its presentation of the compositive (*compositiva*) and resolutive (*resolutiva*) patterns of argument is itself indicative of the sources of Arminius' scholasticism: it derives directly from the tradition of Renaissance Aristotelianism—specifically from the philosophy of Zabarella, the great logician of Padua in the latter half

---

[37] Petrus Ramus, *Commentariorum de religione christiana* (Frankfurt, 1576), I.i.

[38] Cf. Perkins, *Golden Chaine*, p. 11, col. 1; Ames, *Medulla*, I.i; Maccovius, *Loci communes*, I; Mastricht, *Theoretico-practica theologia*, I.i.16; and the discussion in PRRD, I, pp. 108–9.

[39] Cf. Keckermann, *Systema*, cols. 1–2; and the arguments of Scotus, *Op. oxon.*, I, q.1 in Minges, I, pp. 517–20.

[40] *Disp. priv.*, II.i: "Constitutum est a Philosophis Methodi & Ordinis Magistris ut scientiae Theoreticae ordine compositivo, practicae vero resolutivo traderentur, idque secundum ipsarum scientiarum naturam & finem, qua de causa quum Theologia sit scientia practica, sequitur illam Methodo resolutiva esse tractandam."

of the sixteenth century.[41] We know that Arminius held Zabarella in such high esteem that he journeyed to Padua in 1583 to hear Zabarella's lectures.[42] This perspective on method and order, moreover, marks the point at which the influence of Ramism, with its stress on movement from the general to the specific and its distaste for a more analytical perspective,[43] was met and overmatched in Arminius' thought by the revived Aristotelianism of the late sixteenth century. Where Perkins, Ames, Piscator, and Polanus saw the chief value of Ramism—in the architectonic disposition of the whole of theological system—Arminius perceived instead the importance of Zabarella's teaching. Ramus' influence on Arminius must be restricted to the basic definition of theology and to the occasional use of logical bifurcation to illustrate individual points under discussion.[44]

As Keckermann also saw, at roughly the same time as Arminius, the resolutive or analytical method would provide a key to the organization of the entire theological system. In Arminius' words:

> the beginning, therefore, of the presentation of this doctrine must be its goal, first with a brief presentation considering that this goal exists and what it is; then by teaching through the course of the whole discourse, the means for attaining this end; to which the obtaining of this end must be subjoined, and, at this, the whole discussion will conclude.[45]

Keckermann makes virtually the identical point: his system is practical or analytical in method because it is directed toward the goal of

[41] See Jacob Zabarella, *Opera logica*, intro. by W. Risse (Hildescheim: Olms, 1966). On Zabarella, see Neal W. Gilbert, *Renaissance Concepts of Method* (New York: Columbia, 1960), pp. 171–72; an important summary of Zabarella's place in the sixteenth-century revival of Aristotelianism and scholasticism is found in Paul Oskar Kristeller, *Renaissance Thought: The Classic, Scholastic, and Humanist Strains* (New York: Harper and Row, 1961), pp. 37–38, and in John Herman Randall, "The Development of Scientific Method in the School of Padua," *Journal of the History of Ideas* 1 (1940): 177–206. Also see William A. Wallace, *Causality and Scientific Explanation*, 2 vols. (Ann Arbor: University of Michigan Press, 1972–74), I, pp. 144–49.

[42] I owe to John Patrick Donnelly the significant note that Zabarella, unlike most of the Paduan Aristotelians, was esteemed by Jesuits like Antonio Possevino and, in return, was an academic "friend" of the Jesuits at Padua. Perhaps some of Arminius' positive interest in and use of Molina and Suárez is also traceable to his time of study in Padua.

[43] Cf. McKim, *Ramism in William Perkins' Theology*, pp. 27–28, 37–39.

[44] Note, for example, the division of divine nature into categories of essence and life and the divine life into categories of intellect and will (which may not be self-consciously Ramist) in *Disp. priv.*, XV.iii; XVI.ii, vi and the charts in *Opera*, pp. 831–32.

[45] *Disp. priv.*, II.ii: "Initium igitur in hujus doctrinae tractatione faciendum a fine eius de quo tum quod sit, tum quid sit breviter praelibandum: inde medium ad finem adsequendum tota tractatione docendum: cui finis adeptio est subjungenda, inque ea tractatio tota finienda."

man's salvation in the ultimate *fruitio Dei*.[46] The system, therefore, states this goal, follows the statement with the doctrine of God, and then develops the doctrines concerning the means of salvation as they are directed toward their end.[47]

In other words, an essentially proleptic discussion of eternal blessedness as the goal of theological teaching becomes an integral part of the preliminary definition and discussion of theology and acts as a focal point for the ordering and exposition of doctrines within the system of doctrine. The arrangement of doctrine in the system from the doctrine of God, through creation and redemption, to the doctrine of the *consummatio mundi*—the last things and the final union with God—is not a synthetic or deductive but a "resolutive," an analytical and teleological arrangement:

> according to this order, not only the whole of doctrine, but also all its parts, will be discussed with its principal goal in view; and each article will be set in the place that belongs to it according to its fundamental relationship both to the whole [of doctrine] and to the goal or end [of theology].[48]

This basic definition of the nature of theology and its method serves to underline the importance of the doctrine of God to Arminius' theology. Beyond the fact that God is to be understood, in the words of Arminius' colleagues and contemporaries, as the essential foundation of theology (*principium essendi theologiae*) and, therefore, as the being without whom there (obviously!) could not be a theological enterprise, God functions in Arminius' theology as the goal of both theological discussion and the salvific *praxis* identified and defined by theological system. God, known to theology as the *summum bonum*, is discussed first and foremost in theological system, but is not, in a sense, left behind as the discussion progresses. Because God is not merely first, but also final cause, the doctrine of God remains constantly before the reader of Arminius' goal-oriented theology as the point from which the whole has emanated forth, "echoing the ontological procession of creatures from God,"[49] and toward which the whole moves in reconciliation.

These reflections on the relation of Arminius' prolegomena to the structure and implication of his system as a whole point toward the considerable irony in standard characterization of Reformed theology

---

[46] Keckermann, *Systema*, I.ii.

[47] Ibid.

[48] *Disp. priv.*, II.iii: "Secundum hunc enim ordinem tum ipsa tota doctrina, tum omnes eius partes ex fine praecipuo suo tractabuntur, & singula capita illum locum obtinebunt, qui ipsis competit secundum principalem respectum, quem habent ad totum suum, & ad finem totius."

[49] The term is from Aquinas, *Summa*, Ia, p. 44.

as a system with predestination as its central dogma and Arminianism as a rebellion against that central dogma. If asked the question of central dogmas or, in terms more suitable to the post-Reformation era, of essential foundations, both Arminius and his Reformed contemporaries would have pointed, not to the decrees, but to God as *principium essendi theologiae*. It ought to be fairly clear that the way in which a theology understands God as its primary object is more fundamental than and, indeed, determinative of the way in which that theology defines the eternal decree as willed by God. To make the same point in another way, the language of God—both, as Burrell informs us,[50] in the proofs of God's existence, and in the parallel language of the divine *potentia* for the being of the world, as the proofs and the language of emanation of being draw on the fundamental conception of the divine essence, intellect, and will—is hardly an abstract discussion unrelated to the subsequent discussions of creaturely existence, human nature, freedom, moral responsibility, and salvation. Rather, this God-language is constitutive of all subsequent discussion. This is intentionally the case in an analytically ordered system like Arminius' disputations.

This analytical or resolutive method does not indicate, of itself, a disagreement with the doctrinal content of Reformed theology. Keckermann was, after all, a thoroughly orthodox Reformed theologian. It does, however, indicate a major attitudinal difference between its practitioners and the majority of orthodox Reformed writers, who had followed the synthetic or compositive model of theological system. In addition, there is some correlation between the use of the synthetic, compositive model and the Reformed doctrine of providence and predestination—even if it is only an indication of a rather Thomistic orientation of the system toward the divine *principium essendi* understood as the first efficient cause. Equally so, the analytic or resolutive order conforms better to the demands of a less predestinarian structure, such as was typical of the Lutheran orthodox system or, indeed, of Keckermann's and Arminius' emphasis on the final causality of system. (Emphasis on final causality that deemphasizes the first efficient causality indicates, surely, a different approach to the basic Thomistic model than that adopted by the Reformed.)

By extension, the analytical method, with its assumption that the doctrine of God, first stated in the order of system, is to be understood as a declaration of the final goal both of theological discussion and of all existence, asks as a primary question underlying the entire system the question of the relation of God and world. The point is *not* that

---

[50] David B. Burrell, *Knowing the Unknowable God: Ibn-Sina, Maimonides, Aquinas* (Notre Dame: University of Notre Dame Press, 1986), pp. 5–6.

the analytical model generates a more or less synergistic approach to problems of free will and salvation while the synthetic model generates a more monergistic approach. Reformed and Lutheran use of the analytical model noted in the preceding paragraph is sufficient to refute that notion. The point, rather, is that the analytical model can lend itself, as in the case of Arminius' theology, to a deemphasis on efficient and an emphasis on final causality and can become a vehicle suitable to the declaration of a mutuality of relation between God and world. Since the doctrine of God, despite its prior placement, is understood primarily as final goal, the world, as defined in the doctrines of creation and providence, appears less as determined in a prior sense by the first cause than as drawn in an ultimate sense by the final cause. The way is left open for a greater emphasis on freedom and contingency than in the synthetic model. Indeed, Arminius will labor in his doctrines of creation and providence to open the relationship and to loosen the causal link between God and creatures.

For similar reasons, the identification of theology as a practical, teleologically conceived discipline was typical of Reformed covenant theology in the seventeenth century.[51] Even more importantly, this language of theology as *praxis* or as *scientia practica*, which tended to become less and less acceptable to Reformed theology (with the important exception of the covenant or federal theologians), became the norm for the Remonstrant writers, notably, Episcopius and Limborch. "There is nothing in all of theology," wrote Episcopius, "that is not directed toward action."[52] Following Arminius, Remonstrant theology in the seventeenth century stood firm against a speculative, deductive approach to doctrine and consistently argued that theology, considered as a practical discipline, directed Christians toward both the proximate goal of moral goodness in this life and the ultimate (and ultimately related) goal of union with God, the highest good, in the next.

As H. E. Weber pointed out, the analytical model of Keckermann, drawn out of the Melanchthonian Reformed theology of Heidelberg and subjected to critical scrutiny by Arminius' contemporary at Leiden, Lucas Trelcatius the Younger, gave way, on the Reformed side, to concerns for the "scientific" character of theology, but remained normative among Lutherans who were concerned to emphasize the practical character of theology.[53] After Trelcatius, the sole major Reformed proponent of the analytical method appears to

---

[51] Cf. Cocceius, *Summa theologiae*, I.ii and *Aphorisma ... prolixiores*, disp. I with the comments on Burmann, Heidanus, and Heidegger in *PRRD*, I, pp. 219, 222.

[52] Episcopius, *Inst. theol.*, I.ii (p. 5, col. 1); cf. Limborch, *Theol. christiana*, I.i.5–6.

[53] H. E. Weber, *Der Einfluss der protestantischen Schulphilosophie*, pp. 41–43.

have been Ludwig Crocius of Bremen.[54] Arminius' adoption of the method, therefore, after both Keckermann and Trelcatius and only a few years before Crocius, comes close to the end of the Reformed use of an analytical approach and at the time that the method was passing, via German Reformed theology, into the Lutheran camp. This point is doubly significant in view of Arminius' high appreciation of Melanchthonian Lutheranism as represented by Hemmingsen. Arminius clearly favored a methodological as well as a doctrinal trajectory that looked beyond the bounds of developing Reformed orthodoxy for its models and its reinforcement—even when the point at issue had originated among the Reformed.

It is not surprising, therefore, that Arminius predicated much of his theological enterprise on an irenic approach to the great theological problems of the day. Theological disagreements, disputed at length in the detailed pages of dogmatic systems, ought not to be made into points of confessional divergence. Thus, Arminius notes that he implies no necessary disagreement in doctrine with theological systems that are organized according to a pattern different from his own. He finds congenial any system that agrees with the truth of Scripture "at least in the chief and fundamental matters."[55] Although he does not elaborate on the point in his *Private Disputations*, Arminius appears to have in mind a distinction made popular among the Lutherans of the early seventeenth century by Nicolaus Hunnius (1585–1643) between fundamental and nonfundamental articles of faith and later used by the great irenicist of the seventeenth century, Georg Calixt (1586–1656), as a basis for the settlement of differences between Christians who disagreed only on nonfundamental articles.[56] Years before Calixt raised the issue, Arminius had argued that

> a distinction ought to be made between the different topics contained in the [Belgic] Confession. For while some of them address the foundation of salvation and are fundamental articles of the Christian religion, others of them are built up as a superstructure on that foundation and are not, of themselves, absolutely necessary to salvation.[57]

The former are necessarily defended by all the Reformed, the latter may be a subject of disagreement.

Arminius' plea for confessional revision based on a distinction between fundamental and nonfundamental articles went unheeded by his contemporaries, who were unwilling to identify any of the articles of the Confession as nonfundamental. They did, however, recog-

---

[54] Cf. ibid., p. 43.
[55] *Disp. priv.*, II.iv.
[56] Dorner, *History*, II, pp. 185–203.
[57] *Dec. sent.*, p. 130 (*Works*, I, pp. 713–15).

nize that such a distinction could be made in the larger context of theological system. In the course of the seventeenth century, a discussion of fundamental articles, their identification, and their relationship to other, nonfundamental articles of faith became a standard topic in the Reformed theological prolegomena.[58] Arminius' arguments for clearer identification of fundamentals were, quite probably, an impetus to the addition of this topic to the prolegomena—just as Calixt's somewhat later use of the distinction brought about increased discussion of the issue among Lutherans.[59]

The practical or resolutive approach to theology also creates in Arminius' thought a close association between the theological and the religious that places him firmly into the tradition of the Reformers as well as that of the medieval scholastics. As noted earlier, the Reformers had not viewed their systematic essays so much as essays in theology as essays in religion: witness Calvin's *Institutes of the Christian Religion* and Bullinger's *Compendium of Christian Religion*. Arminius understands the practical character of theology as directing the mind not only to knowledge but also to worship. We are not only given to know that God desires worship but that right worship is not offered in vain: God promises "an exceedingly great reward" to those who worship obediently. Therefore, worship must also "be instituted according to his command."[60] These considerations lead Arminius— like many of the orthodox or scholastic Reformed theologians of the seventeenth century—to place a *locus* on religion between the basic definitions of theology and the presentation of the individual doctrines of the theological system.[61]

---

[58] Cf. *PRRD*, I, pp. 277–95. Junius had raised the issue of agreement on fundamental scriptural doctrines in his *Eirenicon*, but had not attempted to delineate the limits of fundamentals—nor had he implied that some confessional doctrines might not be fundamentals: see *Eirenicum de pace ecclesiae catholicae*, in *Opuscula*, pp. 439–40, and cf. the citations in Brandt, *History*, II, pp. 22–23.

[59] Cf. Dorner, *History*, II, pp. 185–203.

[60] *De obiecto*, p. 30 (*Works*, I, pp. 328–29).

[61] *Disp. priv.*, IV–V; cf. Polanus, *Syntagma*, IX; Ames, *Medulla*, II.iv; Marckius, *Compendium*, III; and *PRRD*, I, pp. 112–21.

5

The Object
and Goal of Theology

As already indicated in the discussion of Arminius' views on the idea, method, and practical character of theology, the way in which God is defined as both object and goal of the theological enterprise is crucial to the construction of Arminius' entire system. In introducing the divine object of theology, Arminius not only spoke of the nature of God but also of the acts of God in creation and of the will of God in relation to worship. This broadening of the discussion does not represent a digression but rather a clarification of the way in which God is the object of theology—that is, not only according to his nature but also according to his acts and his will.[1] It is essential, therefore, that theology develop its understanding of its divine object not only into a doctrine of the nature of God but also into a doctrine of the divine acts of creation and providence and a doctrine of the divine will expressed in covenant. Each of these derived topics—the acts and will of God—point again to the practical character of theology. The doctrine of creation reveals the foundation of God's sovereignty as his creative act and points, therefore, toward the necessity of religion. The doctrine of providence teaches of the "holy, just and wise care and oversight" exercised by God over creation—including the divine governance of man's worship and obedience. The doctrine of God's covenanting will further underlines the necessity of worship and obedience inasmuch as it teaches that God is "the fountain of good and the goal of blessedness, the creator and at the same time the glorifier of his worshippers."[2] Elsewhere Arminius will identify the object of theology as God the Creator and Recreator.[3]

[1] *De obiecto*, p. 30 (*Works*, I, p. 329).
[2] Ibid., p. 31 (*Works*, I, pp. 329–30).
[3] *Disp. priv.*, XXIV.ii.

Here again we have a reflection of Junius but also a reflection of elements of the medieval discussion of the object of theology not mediated by Junius to later Reformed theology. Junius had transmitted to Protestantism the definition of the object or *materia* of theology taught by Thomas Aquinas—God and divine things (*divinarum rerum*)—and had given it a Scotist or nominalist twist by defining the divine things or works as "whatever is ordained of God." Junius had also further defined theology as the discipline concerning God—his nature, his works, and whatever is his due.[4] These views are reflected in Arminius' definition; but Arminius adds a specifically practical thrust, directing the gaze of the theologian toward final blessedness and identifying the object of theology as God the Creator and the Glorifier. No citation of sources is provided by Arminius, and it is clear that he did not elicit this definition from Junius or from the Reformers—he could have found the emphasis on the *Deus salvator et glorificator* in the writings of medieval teachers like Giles of Rome and Gregory of Rimini.[5]

Arminius next argues that the theology he has just defined—a theology accommodated to human finitude that understands God, his acts, and his will to be its object—can be no more than "a legal theology accommodated to man's primeval state."[6] Man in his "original integrity" was capable of knowing of the nature, the creative and providential acts, and the will of God and was capable of worshiping God rightly and obediently and "from a consciousness of his integrity" capable of confident repose in the goodness and righteousness of God. Following the fall of mankind into sin, this legal theology is insufficient to establish either right knowledge or right worship of God and, therefore, is incapable of serving a salvific purpose.[7] Legal theology is therefore superseded by a theology that embodies a revelation of God's mercy, long-suffering, and gentleness and of God's will to redeem man from sin under the terms of a new covenant. Since, moreover, God is unwilling and in a sense unable to reveal his mercy and salvation without also maintaining his justice and his anger against sin, this second revelation is focused on the mediator, Christ Jesus, who undertook to satisfy the justice of God by atoning for sin. "Christian theology" that knows both God and Christ as its objects supersedes legal theology.[8]

Arminius' point again reflects both Junius and the scholastic past—and the Reformers as well. Calvin had identified the object of Chris-

---

[4] Junius, *De vera theologia*, XIII.

[5] Cf. *PRRD*, I, pp. 198–201, citing Giles of Rome, *I sent.*, prol.1, q.3; Gregory of Rimini, *I sent.*, q.4, art.2.

[6] *De obiecto*, p. 32 (*Works*, I, p. 332).

[7] Ibid., p. 33 (*Works*, I, pp. 333–34).

[8] Ibid., pp. 33–34 (*Works*, I, pp. 335–36).

tian faith as God revealed in Christ,[9] and the scholastic tradition had, almost universally, spoken either of the three states of man and their respective illuminations (nature, grace, and glory) or, more typically, of four states (original integrity, law, grace, and glory).[10] Junius had argued a distinction, based on the concept of three states and three illuminations, between theology in the state of nature before the fall and theology after the fall, enlightened by grace.[11] Arminius has simply elaborated on the concept and, following Junius, distinguished theology in this life into two forms—an antilapsarian and a postlapsarian form (legal theology) and Christian or evangelical theology. He has made no attempt here to deal with the problem of grace and salvation in Christ during the time of the Old Testament, but only to identify the new form of theology necessary after the fall.[12] His Reformed contemporaries would develop a similar distinction also by way of following out the logic of Junius' argument.[13]

This "Christian theology," even more than the legal theology of man's primal condition, fulfills the criteria for identifying the most excellent of the sciences—that its object is the best and greatest of objects and is immutable; that its object is most clearly known; and that its object completely satisfies the desire of the intellect for an object. God is truly known as the best or most good (optimus) of beings since now he is revealed not only as communicating his goodness in creation and in response to obedience but also for the sake of redeeming repentant sinners and drawing them to life eternal. He is known as the greatest of beings "because he has not only produced all things out of nothing ... but because he has also effected a triumph over sin."[14] Even so, he is known to be immutable in Christ inasmuch as the gospel manifests his "peremptory" and ultimate will—the ultimate will for salvation that shall never "be corrected by another will."[15]

"This theology offers us God in Christ so clearly and evidently for our living and knowing" that we behold in Christ "as in a glass the glory of the Lord" (2 Cor. 3:18).[16] Similarly, "the object of our theology, modified in this manner" to include Christ must ultimately satisfy all desire of the mind by quelling all human boasting and, in

[9] Calvin, Inst., III.ii.1.

[10] Cf. Altenstaig, Lexicon theologicum, s.v. "status est triplex hominis" (p. 875); Aquinas, Summa, Ia–IIae, q.103, art.3, corpus; IIIa, q.53, art.2, corpus.

[11] Junius, De vera theologia, XVII.

[12] But note his discussion of the problem of the covenants (Disp. priv., XXIX, XXX, XXXII).

[13] See PRRD, I, pp. 162–66.

[14] De obiecto, p. 35 (Works, I, p. 336).

[15] Ibid., p. 35 (Works, I, p. 337).

[16] Ibid.

Christ, and in his gospel showing forth all the hidden "treasures of wisdom and knowledge" (Col. 2:3–9).[17] If there is a union of the two objects of theology, so that knowledge of Christ is also knowledge of God, there is also a certain subordination of the one object, Christ, to the other, God: God is the principal object of Christian religion and theology, Christ is the "secondary object," "subordinately under God."[18] Christ is the means by which every "saving communication" from God is made known—and, therefore, also the means by which mankind has final access to God, both in terms of approach and in terms of the final union with and enjoyment of God.[19]

It is not clear from this or from subsequent discussion whether Arminius understands the first several *loci* of the system (God, creation, providence, and human nature in its original integrity) as "legal theology" and the next series of *loci*, those dealing with salvation in Christ, as "evangelical theology," and therefore includes both legal and evangelical theology in his own system, or whether, granting his use of the resolutive method to focus his system as a whole on the blessedness ultimately given in Christ, he understands the whole system as "evangelical theology" even in the nonchristological and nonsoteriological *loci*. In any case, his comments about God as the object of legal theology and his subsequent comments about God as the author of legal theology have a direct bearing on his discussion of the doctrines of God, creation, and providence.

The logical priority of legal over evangelical theology, like the logical priority of God as primary over Christ as secondary object of theology, points toward a logical priority of the foundational, nonsoteriological topics in Arminius' theological system over the soteriological topics. Legal theology is insufficient for the salvation of fallen humanity but it nevertheless identifies the nature of God and of God's relation to the world and thereby provides an intelligible foundation on which the evangelical theology that follows it must rest. In other words, by arguing the precedence of this basic perception of God and world over the evangelical or saving revelation, Arminius implies that the basic revelation of God and of God's relation to the world not only remains unaltered by the fall and by the gift of a new, saving revelation, but provides the basis for understanding the character of God's offer of salvation. What is done by God to save his creatures is, in fact, grounded upon the original relationship established in the act of creation.

The relationship between God and world becomes, therefore, the fundamental datum with which Arminius' analytical and practical

---

[17] Ibid., p. 35 (*Works*, I, p. 338).

[18] *Disp. priv.*, XIV.i–ii; XV.1; XXIV.i; XXXIV.i.

[19] *De obiecto*, pp. 36–37 (*Works*, I, pp. 339–41).

theology works rather than, as in the case of his Reformed contemporaries, a secondary issue predicated on the doctrine of God argued in and for itself. The issue is not that the world has attained an equal ultimacy with God but rather that the conditions established by God in the act of creation become determinative of all subsequent discussion concerning God and world. The legal theology is, thus, not merely a theology of original righteousness, but a theology of the original divine ordinance that establishes a rational ground for understanding all subsequent relationships between God and the created order. Without dislodging God from the position of *principium essendi theologiae*, the rational, legal theology establishes the world as a subordinate *principium essendi*, that is, as one of the irreducible conditions for understanding all that follows. Arminius' theology will assume the inviolability as well as the rationality of this fundamental relationship between God and world as established in creation.

Arminius' discussion of the "author" or efficient cause of theology draws out these issues by linking the discussion of the proper object of theology with the problem of the two kinds of theology, "legal" and "evangelical."[20] In both cases, Arminius begins,

> the author and the object are the same, and the one who reveals the doctrine is likewise its matter and argument: this obtains in no other of the numerous sciences. For although all of them may boast of God as their author, because he is a God of knowledge ... they do not participate in his efficient causality (*in ipso efficiente*) in an equal manner with this doctrine.... God is therefore the author of legal theology; God and his Christ or God in and through Christ is the author of evangelical theology.[21]

At the very foundation of legal theology, as the presupposition of its laws, is a knowledge of the nature of God as "wise, good, just and powerful" and a knowledge of the authority that belongs to God "by which he issues his commands" that arises from his creative act. This twofold knowledge of God was made known by direct revelation before the fall and is still revealed in the creation itself. Since God is the Creator of the universe "not by a natural and internal operation, but by one that is voluntary and external" who places his imprint on his work, he can be known from his creation but also as far transcending it. This transcendence in itself makes necessary a divine self-revelation as the basis of all genuine knowledge of God and determines not only what can be concluded about God from the creation but also what can be argued about creation, given the nature of God.[22]

---

[20] *De auctore*, p. 42 (*Works*, I, pp. 348–49).
[21] Ibid., p. 42 (*Works*, I, p. 349).
[22] *De auctore*, pp. 42–43 (*Works*, I, pp. 350–51). Arminius provides a lengthy discussion of the authorship of evangelical theology, omitted from consideration

Resolution of the question of the authorship of theology not only "raises the dignity of theology ... far above the other sciences"; it also "demonstrates that evangelical far surpasses legal theology."[23] The wisdom and goodness of God manifest in "the righteousness of God by faith" are higher than the wisdom and goodness of God manifest in "the righteousness of God by the law":

> a deeper consideration of this matter almost compels me, as a matter of firm persuasion, to call *natural* the wisdom, goodness and power of God that are presented in legal theology, and as in some sense the beginning of the movement of God (*egressus Dei*) toward his image, which is man, and as the beginning of the divine relationship with him. The others, which are manifested in the gospel, I fearlessly call *supernatural* wisdom, power and goodness, and the extreme point and the perfect completion of all revelation, because in the manifestation of the latter, God appears to have excelled himself and to have unfolded every one of his blessings.[24]

Not only does this argument reflect Junius,[25] it also presses the question of the character of Arminius' own doctrines of God, creation, and providence. On the one hand he has stated quite categorically that "legal theology" is biblical and, indeed, is established in its claims to be a product of divine revelation by Scripture.[26] This contrast between a scriptural theology of God the Creator and an equally scriptural theology of God in Christ, the Redeemer, looks very much like Calvin's *duplex cognitio Dei*.[27] On the other hand, however, Arminius goes so far as to make a further distinction between natural and supernatural theology—again like Calvin, blurring the line between a purely natural and a scriptural knowledge of God the Creator—and implying thereby that the first several *loci* of his system are constructed out of an amalgam of natural reasoning and scriptural considerations.

Inasmuch as God is both the object and the author of theology, he must also be the end or goal. Arminius notes that the end of any movement must be proportionate to its origin or author:

> since the author is the first and highest Being (*primum & summum Ens*), it is of necessity that he be the first and highest Good (*primum & summum bonum*): he is therefore the ultimate End of all things. And since he, the highest Being and highest Good subjects and extends

---

here in view of the limitation of the topic of the present essay to God, creation, and providence.

[23] *De auctore*, p. 47 (*Works*, I, p. 359).
[24] Ibid., p. 48 (*Works*, I, p. 360).
[25] *De vera theologia*, IX, XI.
[26] *De auctore*, p. 42 (*Works*, I, p. 349).
[27] Calvin, *Inst.*, I.ii.1.

himself as an object to some power or faculty of a rational creature, that by its action or motion it may be engaged and occupied with him, and furthermore united with him—it cannot possibly be that the creature, after having entered into a relation with the object, should pass over it and extend itself further for the sake of acquiring a greater good.[28]

In order to attain such a goal, the creature who cannot go beyond it ought also not fall short of it: attainment implies a union limited only by "the capacity of the creature."[29]

Final union with God, accomplished in God and Christ and consisting in "the vision and enjoyment of both" by the redeemed, "to the glory of both" Christ and God must be understood eschatologically as the end of all "intermediate and deputed administration of creatures such as God is accustomed to use in the communication of his benefits."[30] God will then be "all in all" and will "communicate his own good, even himself, immediately to his creatures."[31] The end or goal of theology may, therefore, also be identified as a "possession" or "communion of blessings," which is to say, as the attainment of blessedness or beatitude.[32] "The cause of blessedness is God himself, uniting himself with man, that is, giving himself to be seen, loved, possessed, and thus enjoyed by man."[33]

"The end of theology is the blessedness of man; and that not animal or natural, but spiritual and supernatural."[34] This blessedness Arminius describes in Augustinian terms as the *fruitio* or enjoyment of God, founded on the spiritual life of man as endowed with intellect and affections and brought about in a union with God through the clear vision of God, face to face, that is possible for the redeemed intellect and affections.[35] Contrary to one recent interpretation of Arminius' thought as voluntarist, Arminius here balances the language of affections, typically associated with will in the faculty psychology of his day, with a stress on intellect or understanding.[36] Indeed, Arminius appears to stress the intellectual vision of God as the primary characteristic of blessedness and to understand the affective cleaving to God as a correspondent characteristic, dependent in some sense upon the intellectual vision.

---

[28] *De auctore*, p. 49 (*Works*, I, pp. 361–62).

[29] Ibid., p. 49 (*Works*, I, p. 362).

[30] Ibid., p. 51 (*Works*, I, pp. 364–65).

[31] Ibid., p. 51 (*Works*, I, p. 365).

[32] Ibid., p. 52 (*Works*, I, p. 367).

[33] *Disp. priv.*, III.vi.

[34] Ibid., III.i.

[35] Ibid., III.ii, iii, v.

[36] R. T. Kendall, *Calvin and English Calvinism to 1649* (New York and London: Oxford University Press, 1979), pp. 146–47.

This final union with God, Arminius argues, is not an essential union like the union of divine and human natures in Christ nor is it a formal union like the union of body and spirit. Nonetheless, it is an "objective" and "immediate" union according to which God who is manifestly "all in all" directly "unites himself to the intellect and will of his creature ... without the intervention of image, species or appearance."[37] Although this basic formula balances intellect and will, Arminius' subsequent argument gives clear priority to the intellect in the soteric logic of the vision:

> by this union, the intellect beholds in the clearest vision, as if "face to face," God himself, and all his goodness and incomparable beauty. And precisely because a good of such magnitude and known by the clearest vision cannot but be loved in and for itself (*propter se*) from this very consideration the will embraces it with a more intense love, in proportion to the mind's knowledge.[38]

The enlightenment of the intellect that draws man spiritually into final union with God leads to the "enlargement" of the will "from the inborn agreement of the will with the intellect, and the analogy implanted in both, according to which the understanding extends itself to acts of volition, in the very proportion that it understands and knows."[39] Arminius, in summary, places himself fully into the intellectualist tradition.

What is more, Arminius' argument for the priority of intellect in the final vision of God perfectly reproduces the classic intellectualist thesis of Thomas Aquinas. For Aquinas, intellect is higher or nobler than will inasmuch as the intellect does not merely address an object that is external to itself (as does the will) but, in addressing the object, also in some sense receives the object into itself and possesses in itself the form of the object. In the final vision of God, according to Aquinas, the soul has a direct vision of the divine essence that is higher and nobler than the will's love of God.[40]

The juxtaposition of an intellectualist philosophical perspective with a practical orientation in Arminius' theology represents, as noted earlier, a significant departure from the major medieval paradigms and a use of the scholastic past that is best characterized as eclectic. *Praxis* is, typically, associated with love and will, *speculatio* or *contemplatio* with intellect: the intellectualist model will, therefore, advocate a theology that is either primarily or utterly contemplative while the voluntarist model will define theology as primarily or

---

[37] *De auctore*, pp. 49–50 (*Works*, I, p. 362).

[38] Ibid., p. 50 (*Works*, I, pp. 362–63).

[39] Ibid., p. 50 (*Works*, I, p. 363).

[40] Aquinas, *Summa*, Ia, q.82, art.3; cf. *SCG*, III, 26.11, 21; cf. Copleston, *History*, II, pp. 382–83.

utterly practical. Thus Aquinas assumes that theology is primarily contemplative whereas Scotus defines theology as practical.[41] The Reformed tended toward a compromise that respected the balance of intellect and will but recognized the underlying soteriological issue as voluntaristic and, therefore, defined theology as both speculative and practical with emphasis on the practical.[42] Arminius' model for theology follows out the orientation toward *praxis* advocated by the more Scotistic and the more Ramistic of the Reformed but binds it to an intellectualism quite unparalleled among his Reformed contemporaries. This basic divergence in definition points, in turn, to the profound soteriological disagreement between Arminius and the Reformed and, consequently, toward the greater receptivity of the Arminian system to philosophical rationalism: Arminius, in contrast to his Reformed contemporaries and, indeed, in contrast to Aquinas, assumes that a practical theology can also be intellectualistic because, even in the problem of salvation, the intellect leads the will.[43] Reason, therefore, can play a greater role in the construction of theological system than it could on the assumption of a soteriological priority of will.

This synthesis of the practical with the intellectualist model, together with the alliance of revelation and reason indicated by Arminius' emphasis on the foundational character of topics originally present in "legal theology," God, creation, and providence, provides us with a preliminary indication of the thrust of Arminius' thought and a basic sense of the direction of his theology that will carry us through the doctrines of God, creation, and providence. The practical, analytical approach to theology advocated by Arminius looks to the doctrine of God as the highest good (*summum bonum*) both for the source and the goal of all things. The theological system, as Arminius has already told us, is the highest of the sciences because it sums up all knowledge—indeed, its very order and method follow out, practically and analytically, the procession of being from the being of God in the creation of the finite order and the reconciliation of finite being with the being of God, the *summum bonum*, the goal of all things. Arminius' system, then, if it follows out the promise of his prolegomena, will propose an interrelationship of the Being of God with the being of the world that is both rational and regularized, an interrelationship of the two levels of being, the eternal and the temporal that is ordained of God and cannot be undone, not by sin and surely not by the work of redemption.

---

[41] Cf. Aquinas, *Summa*, Ia, q.1, art.4 with Scotus, *Op. oxon.*, prol., q.iv, n.42.

[42] Cf. *PRRD*, I, pp. 215–26.

[43] Cf . *Disp. pub.*, XI,i,v,viii,ix,x.

PART 3

The Existence
and Nature of God

6

Knowledge of God's Existence

The scholastic Protestant doctrine of God as it developed in the late sixteenth and early seventeenth centuries stood in agreement with the teaching of the Reformers at least in its inherent biblicism. In addition, some of the Reformers, like Wolfgang Musculus (1497–1563) of Bern and Andreas Hyperius (1511–1564) of Marburg, were far more interested in the scholastic categories of existence, essence, and attributes than contemporaries like John Calvin or Heinrich Bullinger. Similarly, Melanchthon had early on seen a use for the proofs of God's existence in his *locus* on creation that stands in contrast to the interest (if not the principles) of Luther, Zwingli, Calvin, Bullinger, and most of their Protestant contemporaries. Nevertheless, there are important differences both in content and in method between the views of the Protestant scholastics and those of the Reformers. Whereas the Reformers' theology was primarily exegetical and discursive, even the *loci* drawn from Scripture by the orthodox have become methodologically stylized and thoroughly dialectical. In the doctrine of God, the materials drawn from revelation are now studiously balanced with rational argumentation and metaphysical concerns. Problems that had virtually vanished from theology in the writings of the earliest Reformers—like the proofs of God's existence and the problems of the predication and arrangement of the divine attributes—have returned in detailed treatment.

Arminius' doctrine of God is no exception to these generalizations. It is strongly biblical, particularly in the *Public Disputations*, and it is oriented toward questions of human salvation. Nonetheless, the doctrinal exposition is indebted throughout to the scholastic philosophical tradition and, as one would expect from the form of the disputation, it is accomplished logically and dialectically rather than discursively. In addition, Arminius' doctrine of God follows out the logic of system established by the scholastic distinctions and divisions of the prolegomena which identified the proper object and the practical or resolvative method to be followed by theology.

Inasmuch as God is the primary "object of the Christian religion" and, as he is revealed in Christ, the genuine object of "evangelical" or saving theology,[1] Arminius can move directly from his preliminary discussions of theology and religion to his doctrine of God. Here, too, as in the orations and disputations serving as theological prolegomena, Arminius' writings bear witness to the scholastic elaboration of Protestant theology in the late sixteenth century. Although Arminius wrote no separate orations or treatises on the doctrine of God, we have more than enough material in his *Disputationes privatae* and *Disputationes publicae* from which to elicit a highly detailed and philosophically sophisticated view of the divine essence and attributes. Whereas other topics frequently receive only a sketchy thetical statement in the *Disputationes*, the doctrine of God appears developed at length and in considerable depth.

Arminius' presentation of the doctrine of God in the neatly planned-out order of the *Disputationes privatae* borrows heavily from the rationalized ordering of the great medieval systems developed in the wake of Alexander of Hales' *Summa theologica* and Thomas Aquinas' *Summa theologiae*. This use of medieval models, often without citation of sources, was typical of the age. The Reformers had provided few clues to the organization of theological system: even the most influential of early Protestant systems—like Melanchthon's *Loci communes* and Calvin's *Institutes*—were not written in a scientific spirit or with a view toward the careful interrelation and exposition of doctrine. Rather they were highly discursive and, in the case of Calvin's *Institutes*, by turns hortatory and polemical, guided as much by occasional as by enduring architectonic concerns. The obvious models for developing Protestant theological systems—particularly systems intended for classroom use, like Arminius' sets of *Disputationes*—were the scholastic systems of the thirteenth, fourteenth, and fifteenth centuries.[2]

This recourse to medieval models for the discussion of the doctrine of God was evident, already, in the works of theologians in the generation immediately preceding that of Arminius, writers whose theology was developed largely after the deaths of second-generation codifiers like Vermigli (d. 1562), Musculus (d. 1563), and Calvin (d. 1564). Zanchi's *De natura dei* and Daneau's *Christianae isagoges* are, perhaps, the clearest examples of this change in the style of Protestant

---

[1] Cf. *Disp. priv.* XIV.i with *De obiecto*, pp. 28, 33–35 (*Works*, I, pp. 324, 336–37).

[2] Cf. *PRRD*, I, pp. 73, 132–33, 199–201, 225–26, 300–302 and passim, with Muller, "Scholasticism Protestant and Catholic," pp. 194, 198–99.

theology and also the most important precedents for the use of scholastic models by thinkers of Arminius' generation. (Beza's two more or less systematic essays, the *Confessio christianae fidei* and the *Quaestionum et responsionum christianarum libellus*, play virtually no role in this development. Neither presents an elaborate doctrine of God's essence and attributes.[3]) If reasons are to be sought for this development they must certainly lie both in the scholastic training of certain of the earlier formulators, notably Musculus and Vermigli, and of a writer like Zanchi in the generation of Arminius teachers, and in the need to find useful models for the doctrine of God—in the absence of any fully elaborated discussions in the writings of the Reformers, particularly those of the first and second generations.

When, moreover, we examine the doctrine of God as set forth by Arminius and his contemporaries, the cohesion of argument as well as the neatly presented architecture of the exposition point not so much to the preliminary efforts of writers like Vermigli, Musculus, and Hyperius or even to the far more elaborate *loci de Deo* offered by Zanchi and Daneau as to the writings of the medieval scholastics, principally Aquinas, whose thought had already provided a background for the systematic efforts of Zanchi and Daneau. Thus, Arminius' doctrine of the divine existence, essence, and attributes looks primarily to the older scholastic models rather than to earlier Protestant efforts. He shares little with Zanchi in matters of organization, somewhat more with Daneau, but together with Zanchi and Daneau, a great deal with the late medieval tradition and, indeed, with ongoing sixteenth-century discussion of scholastic categories.

Specifically, the rationale for organization of Arminius' doctrine of God, stated at the beginning of the fourteenth and fifteenth public disputations, manifests a concern for architectonic issues similar to the rationale stated by Aquinas and other medieval doctors at the beginning of their doctrine of God.

I. The object of the Christian religion is that towards which the faith and worship of a religious man ought to tend. This object is God and his Christ: God principally, Christ subordinately, under God; God per se, Christ as God has constituted him the object of this religion.

II. In God, who is the primary object of the Christian religion, three things come in order under our consideration: First, the nature of God;

---

[3] Cf. Beza, *Confessio*, I–II, where Beza presents his entire doctrine of God as one and three together with providence and angels in a single page—six short articles, all told; with the *Quaestionum* in *Tractationes theologicae*, I, pp. 681–82 where Beza discusses the divine will with specific reference to the distinction between positive willing and divine permission and to Beza's own strong desire to show that God does not will evil. Other attributes are not discussed.

of which the excellence and goodness is such that religion can honor-
ably and usefully be performed to it; Second, the acts of God (*actiones
Dei*), on account of which religion ought to be performed to him;
Third, the will of God, by which he wills religion to be performed to
himself.[4]

The practical impulse found here was, of course, largely absent from
Aquinas' model: it arises out of the analytic or resolvative approach
of Arminius' projected system and stands, as we have already noted,
in some relation to the Scotist perspective on the nature of theology
as primarily practical. The identification of God as primary object
followed by the discussion of the divine nature and its attributes
certainly reflects medieval models, including the model offered by
Aquinas.

Similarly, Arminius' enunciation of the parts of the topic at the
outset of the discussion of the nature of God mirrors the scholastic
model: "Concerning God, the primary object of theology, two things
must be known: (1) his nature or what (*quid*) God is and also of what
kind of being (*qualis*) God is; and (2) who God is (*quis sit*), or to whom
this nature must be attributed."[5] Thus, Aquinas identifies three topics
belonging to the doctrine of the divine essence: "(1) whether God
exists?; (2) the manner of his existence or, rather, what is not the
manner of his existence; (3) whatever concerns his operations—
namely, his knowledge, will, power."[6] Not only does Arminius ap-
prove the basic pattern of essence and attributes followed by Trinity
and creation, he also subdivides the topic of God into the proofs
(setting existence prior to essence in the order of discussion), the
essence or nature of God, and lastly the divine attributes (including
the divine life, and the knowledge or understanding, will, and power
of God in that order).[7] Even more like the pattern of Aquinas' *Summa*
is Arminius' movement, after his initial enunciation of the order of
argument, to the proofs of God's existence as a necessary prologue to
discussion of the divine nature. The resemblance is not exact, the use
of the medieval model is not slavish, but the parallel with Aquinas'

---

[4] *Disp. priv.*, XIV.i–ii: "Religionis Christianae objectum est, in quod fides & cultus
hominis religiosi tendere debet. Illud objectum est Deus & Christus ejus. Deus
principaliter, Christus subordinate sub Deo; Deus per se, Christus ut a Deo
Religionis illius objectum constitutus. (ii) In Deo primario Christianae Religionis
objecto tria ordine consideranda. Primo, Natura Dei, cuius es est excellentia &
bonitas, ut Religio illi honeste & utiliter praestari possit. Secundo, Actiones Dei
propter quas illi Religio praestari debeat. Tertio, Voluntas Dei, qua vult sibi praestari
Religionem."

[5] *Disp. priv.*, XV.i: "De Deo primario Theologiae objecto duo cognoscenda, tum
natura ejus, seu quid, vel potius qualis sit Deus; tum quis sit, sive cui ista natura
tribuenda sit."

[6] *Summa theologiae*, Ia, q.2.

[7] Cf. *Disp. priv.*, XV.i with XVII, XVIII, and XXII.

Summa is far more clear than any parallel that might be constructed between the work of Arminius and that of Calvin, Bullinger, Musculus, Melanchthon, or any other of the earlier systematizers of Protestant theology. Of Arminius' Reformed predecessors, only Daneau evidences the neat architecture of the medieval model—and he, too, clearly draws on Aquinas. Examination of Arminius' proofs and their relation to his doctrine of God manifests, moreover, a reflection not merely of points made in Aquinas' *Summa*—as if Arminius had read it and used it in isolation from other scholastic materials—but also of the later development of approaches to the proofs and to the doctrine of God that had used and modified the basic Thomist perspective. Significant also is the fact that this movement away from the methods and models of the Reformation toward those of the Middle Ages is *not* something that sets Arminius apart from his Reformed contemporaries and adversaries—rather it is evidence of a ground held in common.

Arminius thus echoes the interest of Protestant theologians of his generation in his exposition of the scholastic proofs of the existence of God. As early as the 1536 edition of Melanchthon's *Loci communes*, Protestant theologians had returned to consideration of the proofs—in Melanchthon's case as a part of his doctrine of creation designed to declare the relationship of the transcendent Creator with the created order.[8] This use of the proofs carried over into the thought of Melanchthon's eminent Reformed pupil, Zacharias Ursinus, who also saw the usefulness of the proofs in his doctrine of God: not only can the proofs indicate the relation of Creator and creature, they can also provide a rational preface to the doctrine of God.[9] Ursinus' return of the proofs to the doctrine of God found echoes in several of the major Reformed systems of the late sixteenth and early seventeenth centuries, notably the *Christianae isagoges* of Arminius' teacher, Lambert Daneau, and the *Syntagma theologiae christianae* of Amandus

---

[8] Philip Melanchthon, *Loci communes theologici* (1535) in *Opera*, 21, col. 369 and *Loci theologici* (1543) in *Opera*, 21, cols. 641–43. Cf. David B. Burrell, *Knowing the Unknowable God: Ibn-Sina, Maimonides, Aquinas* (Notre Dame: University of Notre Dame Press, 1986), pp. 5–6, on the underlying logic of the proofs, as they argue the relationship of God and world. This use of the proofs or arguments based on them to frame the doctrine of creation is present in Aquinas: see *SCG*, II.6 and cf. Robert L. Patterson, *The Conception of God in the Philosophy of Aquinas* (London: George Allen and Unwin, 1933), pp. 371–77.

[9] Ursinus, *Expl. cat.*, cols. 111–13, 123–24 (*Commentary*, pp. 121–23, 142–43). The Williard translation is quite accurate but, due to the problems of the text-history of Ursinus' posthumously published lectures, occasionally contains material not found in early editions of the *Explicationes catecheseos*. Thus, the two lengthy "addenda" (p. 122) to the fifth and sixth proofs are not found in the Reuter edition of Ursinus and, most probably, are later additions to the text.

Polanus.[10] There were also quite a few Protestant philosophers who, in the spirit of renewed Aristotelianism characteristic of the second half of the sixteenth century, developed the proofs as purely philosophical arguments.[11]

Nonetheless, it must not be inferred from these remarks that the proofs of the existence of God had found a place in the systems of a majority of Reformed theologians by the end of the sixteenth century. No mention of the proofs is made by Vermigli, Beza, Perkins, Gomarus, or Trelcatius—although Gomarus and the elder Trelcatius follow out the pattern of Ursinus by using the arguments typically found in the a posteriori proofs to argue that, given the existence of God, both the knowledge of God and the doctrines of creation and providence must logically follow.[12] In addition, even those Reformed theologians of Arminius' time who used the proofs expressed a somewhat ambivalent view of their use: Polanus sets the proofs at the beginning of his doctrine of God as a confutation of the atheists but establishes no integral relationship between the teaching of the proofs and his *locus de Deo*.[13]

It is worth raising briefly the question of the reason for the absence of the proofs from the writings of the early Reformers and the gradual return of the proofs to Protestant theology over the course of the sixteenth century. The reason most probably relates both to literary genre and to philosophy. In the first place, the works written by the earliest Reformers were largely exegetical, polemical, and confessional rather than systematic in genre. The proofs belong, typically, either to the preliminary portions of theological system or to philosophical treatises—and the fact is that the proofs did begin to reappear as early as 1536 in Melanchthon's systematic essay, the *Loci communes*. In the second place many of the early Reformers, at least those who noted some antagonism toward the proofs, manifest either Scotist or nominalist tendencies in their theology. This is true of Luther, Calvin, and Musculus. Inasmuch as the a posteriori proofs tend to belong to the Thomistic side of medieval thought and were questioned or refuted by Scotists and nominalists, it is hardly surprising that these theologians did not use proofs positively.

On the Reformed side, at least, elements of Thomist theology and training were present quite early: Bucer and Vermigli were Thomists. Neither wrote proofs of the existence of God, but neither wrote a fully

---

[10] Polanus, *Syntagma*, II.iv; Daneau, *Chr. isag.*, I.iii.

[11] Platt, *Reformed Thought*, pp. 155, 159, noting Jacchaeus and Timpler.

[12] Cf. Gomarus, *Disputationes*, I.xxix–xxxv and *Concilatio doctrinae orthodoxae de providentia Dei*, in *Opera*, III, pp. 158–59; Lucas Trelcatius senior, *Compendium locorum communium s. theologiae*, in *Opuscula*, p. 112; and see Platt, *Reformed Thought*, pp. 127–30, 143–48.

[13] Polanus, *Syntagma*, II.iv.

developed system of theology. In the third generation of Reformed theologians, Zanchi and Daneau manifest strong Thomist tendencies—and in the case of Daneau the proofs reappear in an explicitly Thomistic form, at the beginning of a large-scale system of theology. Two reasons, then, can be tentatively advanced for the reappearance of the proofs: the development of Protestant theological system and the rise, in Reformed theology in particular, of a modified Thomism. Arminius, following out the line of Daneau, belonged to this development.

Like those of his Reformed contemporaries who gave the proofs some place in theological system, Arminius uses both logical or philosophical arguments and a series of purely rhetorical ones: thus he used the argument *e consensu gentium* as well as the causal, cosmological, and teleological arguments. Where he differs from the Reformed is in his view of the function of the proofs in theological system. Whereas the Reformed typically state no use for the proofs other than the confutation of atheism, Arminius seems to set forth a positive, nonapologetic, systematic use of the proofs:

> To every treatise on the nature of God must be prefixed the first and highest axiom of all religion, God exists (*Deum esse*): without which, it is foolish to inquire into the nature of God, inasmuch as something having no existence would thereby become a pure phantasm in man's thoughts.... That God exists has been impressed on every rational creature that receives his voice, and though this indication [of the divine existence] can be grasped by the knower, [the existence of God] can, notwithstanding, be demonstrated by various arguments.[14]

None of the Reformed writers went so far as to indicate such an integral relationship between the proofs and system or to imply that the system of Christian doctrine in some way regarded the proofs as foundational to its existence.

Arminius' statement is too brief to provide a basis for any final conclusions concerning the importance of reason to his system or the openness of his thought to rationalism. It does, however, in its first part, sound remarkably like the argument of the eighteenth-century Wolffian theologian Daniel Wyttenbach that natural or rational theology provided a necessary prologue to a system of supernatural or revealed doctrines inasmuch as revelation assumes but does not prove the existence of God.[15] In addition, Arminius assumes that his axioms and arguments concerning the divine existence "once understood ... are known to be true" and ought to be viewed as ingrafted or implanted concepts (*notiones insitae*), thereby granting to reason a fundamental capacity to know truths concerning God. Although the

14 *Disp. priv.*, XIV.iii–iv.
15 Wyttenbach, *Tentamen theol.*, prol., 7–9.

absence of any statements concerning the limitation placed on the powers of reason by sin can be attributed as easily to the brevity of the argument as to purposeful omission, the tendency of Arminius' argument here is to open a large place for reason and philosophy in theological system and to carry the intellectualism of his prolegomena forward into the system itself. The second part of Arminius' statement, acknowledging both a general sense of the divine and the possibility of demonstrating the existence of God, once again resembles Aquinas' point.[16]

The problem of innate or implanted ideas was, of course, one of the root problems of seventeenth-century rationalism. It is one thing to argue that certain truths about nature are "known through themselves" or are "self-evident" (*per se nota*) and quite another to argue that they are innate or so fundamentally implanted that they are known not per se in the sensory apprehension of things but, in advance of any knowledge of or encounter with particulars. The humanistic recovery of Aristotle in the sixteenth century led to the rediscovery of the concept of the mind as initially *tabula rasa*, having no innate ideas.[17] In this context it is important to note that the Protestant scholastic theology of the day, including the theology of Arminius, chose not the concept of a *cognitio innata* but that of a *cognitio insita*. The Protestant view is in fact more in accord with the late medieval nominalist theory of the immediate or intuitive knowledge of particulars.[18]

Nonetheless, despite certain differences in language—specifically the use of the term *notiones insitae*—the logic and placement of Arminius' proofs in their relation to the subsequent portions of his system manifest a desire to recover the alliance of faith and reason witnessed in the logic of the argument put forth by Aquinas in the *Summa theologiae*. In other words, Arminius and his Reformed contemporaries, while respecting many of the limitations placed on rational discussion of the divine both by Scotist and nominalist thought and by the teaching of the Reformers, saw in the revived Aristotelianism and in the modified Thomism of the sixteenth century the possibility of a return to the a posteriori proofs of the existence of God, and Arminius, far more than his Reformed contemporaries, saw the proofs themselves as a way of demonstrating not only the existence of God but also the right to exercise reason and to use rational argumentation alongside and in concert with the teachings of faith. Arminius was, surely, acquainted with the use of the proofs

---

[16] Aquinas, *Summa theologiae*, Ia, q.2, art.1, ad 1; q.2, art.2, ad 1.

[17] Cf. Copleston, *History*, III, pp. 227, 417.

[18] Ibid., III, p. 64.

in Suárez' *Disputationes metaphysicae*,[19] just as he was aware of the modification of the proofs by later scholastic debate over the relationship of the first mover to the order of finite causality and the further modification of the proofs by Melanchthon and his pupils, most importantly, by Ursinus. Indeed, the rhetorical and moral arguments used by Arminius directly reflect the list of proofs provided by Ursinus in his *Explicationes catecheseos*—such as the arguments from universal consent, from the "reproofs of conscience," from the civil order, and from the prediction of future events, while the reference to *notiones insitae* may be a critical reflection of Melanchthon's doctrine of innate principles.[20] In addition, Arminius' emphasis on the universal natural knowledge of God implanted in human beings, together with his sense of the rudimentary connection between this knowledge and man's recognition, as a dependent being, that God must be worshiped, appears to be a direct reflection of Suárez.[21]

Platt not only confirms the connection between Arminius and these earlier thinkers in his exhaustive analysis of the proofs, he also establishes a connection between Arminius' rearrangement of the arguments and the theological speculations of Conrad Vorstius, the theologian and metaphysician who was chosen to succeed Arminius at Leiden, but whose theology proved so objectionable to the Reformed faculty that he never occupied the chair. Platt argues convincingly that Arminius had access to Vorstius' theology and that Arminius' modifications of the proofs rest on arguments in Vorstius' *Tractatus de Deo*.[22] The relationship between the published documents, however, is quite difficult to establish with certainty inasmuch as Arminius' disputations were published at Leiden after 1604, before the appearance of Vorstius' treatise. The printed form of Vorstius' proofs, probably in the edition of 1606, was in Arminius' library and is far more detailed than Arminius' exposition. We have, thus, no clear evidence that Arminius attempted to integrate either the entirety or the more distinctive elements of Vorstius' thought into his own doctrine of the existence and nature of God. The absence of Vorstian ideas (or of reaction to them) from the remainder of Arminius' disputations on the doctrine of God may indicate that Vorstius was

---

[19] Suárez, *Disp. metaph.*, XXIX.

[20] *Expl. cat.*, cols. 111–13 (*Commentary*, pp. 121–23); Copleston, *History*, III, p. 227.

[21] Suárez, *Disp. metaph.* XXIX.ii.5; cf. Loemker, *Struggle for Synthesis*, pp. 71–72 and 262, n. 32 where Loemker notes a parallel between Suárez and Herbert of Cherbury.

[22] Platt, *Reformed Thought*, pp. 148–57, and cf. G. J. Hoenderdaal, "Arminius en Episcopius," *Nederlands Archief voor Kerkgeschiedenes* 60 (1980): 212, who argues a common background of the two documents. Arminius' disputation on the proofs is from 1604.

the mediator of a discussion rather than a major theological influence.

Arminius' first three arguments begin with self-evident axioms: "Nothing is or can be from itself.... Every efficient primary cause is better or more excellent than its effect.... No finite force can make something out of nothing; and the first nature (*naturam primam*) has been made out of nothing."[23] These are the axioms that Arminius views as so fundamental that "once understood, they are known to be true." This self-evident character of the first three arguments sets them apart, moreover, from the remaining seven. These are "theoretical" arguments while the remainder are most probably viewed as "practical"—although he uses the term "practical" only with reference to the fourth argument, the argument based on conscience.

Each of these three axioms, of its own internal logic, points directly toward the existence of God. It is evident that "nothing is or can be from itself" inasmuch as the contrary axiom would demand that something be and not be at the same time, "both prior and posterior to itself," or be both its own cause and effect. In other words, a denial of Arminius' first axiom would be a violation of the law of non-contradiction. "Therefore," declares Arminius, "some one being must necessarily be pre-existent, from whom, as from the primary and supreme cause, all other things derive their origin: but this is God."[24]

The second and third axioms are related and, significantly, do not present a logic as convincing as that of the first axiom and argument. Indeed, Arminius' comments here recall the inconclusive debates of the thirteenth-century scholastics over the problem of the "eternity of the world."[25] Since "every primary efficient cause is better or more excellent than its effect," and since "all created minds are in the order of effects," there must be a supreme mind that is the origin of all created minds. This supreme mind is none other than God.[26] The point is easily made—as it was by Occam and the nominalists of the late Middle Ages—that causes and effects are known by experience and that, therefore, the logical shift from an order of experienced effects to an order of hypothetical causality beyond experience is illegitimate. By the same token, an infinite regress of causes and effects is also possible. Perhaps because of the weight of these two arguments

---

[23] *Disp. priv.*, XIV.v, vi, vii: "Nihil esse aut esse posse a se ipso.... Omnem causam efficientem primariam suo effecto praestantiorem esse.... Nullam vim finitam aliquid facere ex nihilo, & naturam primam esse ex nihilo factam," i.e., the first *created* nature.

[24] *Disp. priv.*, XIV.v: "Ergo oportet unum aliquod ens necessario praeexistens, unde ut a causa prima & suprema ortum ducunt omnia reliqua. At hoc est Deus."

[25] See below, 5.1.

[26] *Disp. priv.*, XIV.vi.

against the proof, Arminius does not introduce the Aristotelian argument for a first mover as one of his proofs, but only notes it at the every end of his disputation as a corollary for further discussion.[27]

As Platt has shown, the argument for the existence of a divine first mover was debated in Arminius' own day and the primary model for Arminius' own statement of the proofs, Conrad Vorstius' *De Deo*, had included an important caveat concerning this proof. Vorstius knew of the Scotist objections raised by J. C. Scaliger (1484–1558) to the effect that a first mover could well be the angelic intelligence moving the highest and first heavenly sphere. God, as beyond the celestial spheres and beyond all motion, is not reached by the logic of the argument. Platt also notes the reliance of Arminius' colleague, the philosopher Gilbert Jacchaeus, on Suárez' similar rejection of the argument from motion.[28] Thus, Arminius' phrasing of his corollary—"On account of the dissentions of very learned men, we allow this question to be discussed, 'From the motion which is apparent in the world, and from the fact that whatever is moved is moved by another, can it be concluded that God exists?'"—indicates recognition of the contemporary debate over the proof.[29] We may also infer that Arminius' statement of the argument as a corollary, with no attempt to reestablish its status as a proof, indicates a critical, perhaps Scotist or nominalist tendency at this point in his thought or, at very least, a reading of arguments like those put forth by Suárez to the effect that the basic premise, "whatever is moved is moved by another," cannot be proven universally valid inasmuch as it cannot rise above the physical to the spiritual or immaterial order.[30] This hesitance concerning the usefulness of the proof from motion serves, in addition, to show just how far from the original five ways of Aquinas the modified Thomism of the late sixteenth century had come: it was, after all, the proof from motion that Aquinas had referred to as the *manifestior via*.[31]

---

[27] *Disp. priv.*, XIV, ad fin and cf. Maurer, *Medieval Philosophy*, pp. 269–70, for a summary of Occam's critique of the proofs.

[28] Platt, *Reformed Thought*, pp. 154–55; on Suárez, see Copleston, *History*, III, pp. 362–64.

[29] *Disp. priv.*, XIV, corollarium 1; cf. Platt, *Reformed Thought*, p. 155.

[30] Suárez, *Disp. metaph.*, XXIX.i.7; and cf. John P. Doyle, "The Suárezian Proof for God's Existence," in *History of Philosophy in the Making*, ed. Linus J. Thro (Lantham, Md.: University Press of America, 1982), pp. 105–6 with John Owens, *St. Thomas Aquinas on the Existence of God: Collected Papers of John Owens, C.Ss.R.*, ed. John R. Catan (Albany: State University of New York Press, 1980), pp. 163–64.

[31] Cf. Aquinas, *Summa*, Ia, q.2, art.3, corpus. It is worth noting that the "five ways" of the *Summa theologiae* were not viewed by Aquinas either as his own creation or as the sole usable proofs. He recognized them as common property of gentile philosophers and Christian teachers and could enumerate as many as eleven patterns: see Owens, *St. Thomas Aquinas on the Existence of God*, pp. 133–34;

This tension over the validity of causal argumentation points directly toward the logical difficulty embedded in the reasoning of Arminius' third proof:

> The third axiom is, No finite force can make something out of nothing; and the first nature has been made out of nothing. Otherwise, [this first nature] neither could nor ought to be changed by an efficient [cause]. And thus nothing could be made from it. From this it follows, either that all things that exist are from eternity and are primary beings (*entia prima*), or that there is one primary being (*ens primum*); and this is God.[32]

Arminius' language evidences a fairly deep acquaintance with the concepts and problems of traditional Christian Aristotelianism. In the first place the concept of primary and secondary, efficient and material causality that runs through these arguments stands firmly noted in Aristotelian physics and metaphysics. Even more than this widely used Aristotelianism (which was, after all, accepted as part of the basic sixteenth-century worldview even by the anti-Aristotelian Calvin[33]), Arminius' identification of a primary matter made from nothing indicates reliance on the Western Aristotelian tradition. Aristotle had, against Plato, argued for a material substratum of pure potentiality out of which things are drawn by the informing, telic actuality of the primary Being or First Mover.[34]

Arminius' use of these Aristotelian categories of *materia prima*, of potency and actuality, and of primary Being as the pre- or self-existent and necessary ground of finite being enmeshed him in the underlying problem of the Christian Aristotelian proofs—the problem of the eternity of the world. Aristotle's Prime Mover is the final cause of things, the highest actuality that draws the potential order toward itself as the ultimate goal of existence. The Prime Mover is not, conversely, to be viewed as the initial causal actor in a fundamentally chronological movement of things from creative beginning to eschatological goal. Even so, Aristotle conceived of prime matter, the pure potency lying as a substratum beneath all actualized things, as neither

Jules A. Baisnée, "St. Thomas Aquinas' Proofs of the Existence of God Presented in Their Chronological Order," in *Philosophical Studies in Honor of the Very Reverend Ignatius Smith, O.P.*, ed. John K. Ryan (Westminster, Md.: Newman, 1952), pp. 63–64. In addition there are some thirteen categories of proof rejected by Aquinas: cf. Patterson, *Conception of God*, pp. 21–39.

[32] *Disp. priv.*, XIV.vii: "Tertium axioma est: Nullam vim finitam aliquid facere ex nihilo, & naturam primam esse ex nihilo factam: secus enim ab efficiente mutari neque potuit neque debuit. Et sic ex illa nihil fieri potuit. Unde sequitur, aut omnia quae sunt esse ab aeterno & entia prima, aut unum esse ens primum; & hoc est Deus."

[33] Cf. Calvin, *Commentary on Ephesians 1:5–8*, 51, cols. 148–50.

[34] Cf. Alfred Weber, *History of Philosophy*, trans. Frank Thilly, with *Philosophy since 1860*, by Ralph Barton Perry (New York: Scribner, 1925), pp. 67–68, 82–84.

coming into being nor ceasing to be—that is, as eternal. Close examination of the standard Thomistic arguments for the existence of God as necessary Being over against the contingent order and as First and Unmoved Mover over against the world of things that have been "moved" toward actuality manifests this basic Aristotelian premiss: the proofs do not necessarily imply a beginning of the material order and they function equally well as proofs in a context in which the universe is assumed to have existed from eternity.

Arminius argues that, if *materia prima* did not arise out of nothing, which is to say, if it were eternal, it would not, presumably, be subject to change. There could be no efficient cause prior to such matter and, therefore, "nothing could be made from it."[35] These statements run directly counter to the original Thomistic argument in the proofs, which assumes that the logical and ontological priority of actuality over potency is sufficient ground for arguing causality without the addition of temporal priority. The problem addressed here by Arminius arose out of late scholastic debate over the proofs and over the problem of the eternity of the world. It is highly likely that both the debate and this particular pattern of resolution were learned by Arminius from Suárez. As we will see below, Arminius appears to have assimilated Suárez' argument against an eternal, self-existent *materia prima*, based upon the divine ability to act upon the material order.[36] Arminius recognizes that, at very least, he is left with two logical possibilities: "From this it follows, either that all things that exist are from eternity and are primary beings, or that there is one primary being; and this is God."[37] The first possibility is, of course, unacceptable to theology and, perhaps, also to experience.

The latter point is very similar to that made by Ursinus, in somewhat greater detail, in his *Explicationes catechescos*. Ursinus had, as we have already noted, taken the proofs of God's existence placed by Melanchthon into the doctrine of creation and restored them to their typical scholastic place in the introduction to the doctrine of God—but Ursinus also recognized the character of the proofs as descriptions of the relationships between God and the world and, accordingly, had retained modified forms of the proofs in his doctrine of creation as demonstrations of the creation of the world by God, the original Melanchthonian use. He notes that the denial of infinite causal regress and the argument from the excellence of the world to the excellence of its cause "prove *that* the world was created and that by

---

[35] *Disp. priv.*, XIV.vii: "naturam primam esse ex nihilo factam: secus enim ab efficiente mutari neque potuit neque debuit. Et sic ex illa nihil fieri potuit."

[36] Suárez, *Disputationes metaphysicae*, XX.i.18.

[37] *Disp. priv.*, XIV.vii: "Unde sequitur, aut omnia quae sunt esse ab aeterno & entia prima, aut unum esse ens primum; & hoc est Deus."

God, but they cannot prove *when* it was created."[38] There remain, therefore, "other questions" such as whether the world was created by God from all eternity, or in time.[39]

This and other questions cannot be answered, Ursinus argues, except by revelation of God, and such revelation is known only in the church. Thus the church has the answer while "gentile philosophers," whose a posteriori argumentation is insufficient to solve the problem, have only the questions:

> It is true, indeed, that there is a certain cause of these effects [i.e., a cause of the world], but it does not follow that these effects were produced by this cause either at this or at that time, or from all eternity, because a free agent may either act or suspend his action at pleasure.... Therefore, it cannot be proven by the will of the first mover, which is God, that [the world] was either created from all eternity, or that it had its beginning in time.[40]

The point is settled, Ursinus believes, only by revelation—specifically by a right reading of Genesis 1:1 and from the computation of the age of the earth based on the genealogies in the Pentateuch.[41] From a purely logical point of view, Arminius' result is identical to Ursinus': the rational arguments are inconclusive.

It is significant that Ursinus and Arminius simply state the problematic without attempting to argue that the eternity of the world and the eternal existence of all species of things are logically absurd. Arminius notes that we must either assume the eternity of all things as "primary beings" or we must assume the temporality of all contingent species and the eternity of a single primary or first Being. And, of course, he accepts the latter alternative. Although, once again, we are presented with far too little detail to present a definitive analysis either of the mind of Arminius on this point or of the philosophical and theological antecedents to Arminius' reasoning, the outlines of the argument as given are reminiscent of the medieval debate over the eternity of the world and, specifically, of the Thomistic and Bonaventuran solutions and the tension between them.

As in the case of previously noted parallels between early Protestant scholasticism and medieval models, it is impossible to determine whether the parallels arose because of a direct reading of the medieval sources or because of an awareness of the medieval debate generated by the study of sixteenth-century Roman Catholic authors —or because of use of both sets of sources. It is certainly true that Arminius and his Protestant contemporaries, taken as a group, cite

[38] *Expl. cat.*, col. 124 (*Commentary*, p. 142).
[39] Ibid.
[40] *Expl. cat.*, col. 124 (*Commentary*, p. 143).
[41] Ibid., col. 125 (*Commentary*, p. 145).

virtually all of the great medieval teachers from Alexander of Hales to Gabriel Biel and that the works of many medieval theologians— Thomas of Strasburg, Henry of Ghent, Gregory of Rimini, Durandus of Sancto Porciano, and Thomas Bradwardine, just to name a few— together with the reasonably well footnoted theological lexicon of Johannes Altenstaig, were readily available to Protestant writers in sixteenth-century printed editions. In any case, Arminius' discussion of the problem of the eternity of the world echoes the medieval debate, as do the extended presentations of the problem in Suárez' works.[42]

In what must remain a foremost example of the characteristically Thomistic balance of revelation and reason, in which the integrity of both ways of knowing is maintained, Aquinas had argued that reason alone, unsupported by truths drawn from revelation, can arrive by legitimate logic either at a theory of the eternity of the world or at a theory of the beginning of the world in time. The Christian philosophy of Bonaventure, which had argued the logical validity of the doctrine of creation out of nothing, could not, as far as Aquinas could see, argue the unreasonability or logical falsity of the Aristotelian and in his own time, Latin Averroist, theory of the eternity of the world— but neither could the Latin Averroist philosophy of Siger of Brabant, which held to the theory of the eternity of the world, prove the unreasonability or logical falsity of the Christian doctrine of creation out of nothing. As Aquinas argued, it was possible, in view of contrast between the necessary Being of God and the contingent being of the created order, to hold a creation *ex nihilo* from eternity—while the final choice of a theory would have to be made on the ground that the higher truth of revelation, shown by logic to be not unreasonable, must supersede those rational arguments that are contrary to what has been revealed.[43] Ursinus appears to have adopted this view explicitly, Arminius to have advocated it implicitly.

The Averroist option, clearly enough, is unacceptable to Arminius. At this point, however, no choice is made between the Thomistic and the Bonaventuran patterns. On one level, Arminius seems to acknowledge the logical acceptability both of the eternity of the world and of the theory of creation out of nothing (the Thomist solution)— but on another level, he certainly assumes that creation *ex nihilo* is the correct solution and not merely on the ground that revelation offers a higher truth than reason, but rather (following a more Bonaventuran view) on the ground that the language of creation out of nothing can be recognized as reflecting one of the *notiones insitae* or

---

[42] Suárez, *Disp. metaph.*, XX.v and *De opere sex dierum*, ii; summarized in Mahieu, *François Suárez*, pp. 426–28.

[43] Vollert, *On the Eternity of the World*, pp. 50–53, 61, 64–68.

implanted ideas that exist as fundamental intuitions in the mind. This approach to the problem will have a considerable impact on Arminius' doctrine of creation which, like many of the scholastic *loci de creatione* of the day, recognized that the logic of the proofs functioned as a statement of the relationship of transcendent Being to the created order as much as it functioned as an actual "proof."

The remaining seven arguments are a mixture of rational, rhetorical, and theological lines of reasoning—with the fifth and sixth arguments taking up and completing the logical or philosophical series by considering, respectively, the perception of perfection in finite things and the perception of order in the world, and the fourth, seventh, eighth, ninth, and tenth arguments covering theological and rhetorical issues like the existence of a conscience endued with a sense of right and wrong, the maintenance of good in the political order despite the power of evil, the existence of miracles that cannot be explained by finite causality, and the universal consent of mankind.[44]

Platt is certainly correct that Arminius' arrangement of the arguments marks an advance on earlier Protestant discussion: before Arminius the arguments had been set forth in a rather disorderly way; Arminius attempts to give order and cohesion to the arguments as a group by dividing them into a theoretical set of self-evident axiomatic demonstrations and a subsequent group of arguments that are less cohesive and do not constitute demonstrations.[45] Platt is also correct in noting the order and arrangement of arguments 5 through 10: two address natural order, the next (argument 7) addresses the human or political order, two more deal with supernatural interventions, and the tenth returns to the human sphere by noting the universal consent.[46] We therefore have two groups of three, one dealing with order (arguments 5–7) and the other dealing with perceptions of divinity (arguments 8–10).

Where I would differ with Platt is over the character of the second series of arguments. Platt sets the argument from conscience apart as a single "practical" argument intervening between the first and second sets. It is probably more fruitful to accept the theoretical/practical dichotomy as exhaustive of all possible categories: if a way of knowing is not theoretical it must be practical—if it is not known as an end or for its own sake, it is known (or ought to be known) as directed toward an end. This view of the practical coincides with the general definition provided by Arminius in his discussions of theology and its object and, what is more, it covers the teleological arguments presented by Arminius in his second series—the perfection

---

[44] *Disp. priv.*, XIV, viii–xiv; cf. *De auctore*, p. 43 (*Works*, I, pp. 351–52).
[45] Platt, *Reformed Thought*, pp. 156–57.
[46] Ibid.

and arrangement of things (argument 5) and the ordering of things toward an end (argument 6). In addition, all of the arguments following the first three are less than demonstrative: they are indications or probabilities rather than proofs.

In addition, if we take seriously the critical tendencies in scholastic Protestant thought of the late sixteenth century—the Scotistic elements present in Junius' definitions of theology and the Scotistic critique of the proof from motion as mediated to the early seventeenth century by Suárez—we may also have the reason for Arminius' relegation of arguments for the existence of God from the order of the world to the category of practical arguments. Platt wonders why the argument from final causality, Aquinas' fifth way, was not raised to the status of a full demonstration by the use of an axiom like "All natural beings act for a purpose."[47] One possible answer to the question is that the argument from final causality and, indeed, the argument from the order and arrangement of the cosmos, had been seriously threatened by nominalist critique. Ockham had shown that all such arguments presuppose the existence of God, particularly in their assumption of an order in inanimate things.[48] Arminius may, again, simply be following out a more critical tendency in scholastic thought. The logic of the proofs looks back to Aquinas and to sixteenth-century use of the proofs by writers like Ursinus, Daneau, and Suárez, while the difficulties inherent in some of the proofs noted not by Aquinas but by later medieval doctors like Scotus and Occam also have their impact—not a great enough impact to undermine the proofs and produce a nominalistic skepticism concerning usefulness, but impact enough to modify the shape of some of the arguments.

The philosophical categories present in Arminius' proofs indicate that his theology was just as indebted to the tradition of Christian Aristotelianism and, specifically, just as reliant on the language of causality as the theology of his Reformed contemporaries and opponents. As in the case of the orthodox Lutheran theologians who also manifest a profound involvement in the causal terminology of Aristotelianism, Arminius' usage does not indicate an interest in a deterministic metaphysics. As will become clear in the discussion of the divine knowledge and will, Arminius was committed to the enunciation of a theological foundation for the language of freedom and contingency that pervades his discussions of sin and salvation. Finally, the difficulties confronting the a posteriori proofs—specifically the problems in the argument from motion, in the concept of *materia prima*, and in the theory of the eternity of the world—also manifest

[47] Ibid., p. 157, taking the axiom from Arminius' pupil Episcopius: cf. ibid., p. 231.
[48] Cf. Copleston, *History*, III, p. 82.

the close relationship between the proofs and Arminius' system of doctrine, inasmuch as these problems will return, particularly in the doctrine of creation, as points of difficulty with or dissension from the Reformed model. The proofs and their problems are integral to Arminius' system. The question of Arminius' sources for these musings on the proofs is tantalizing, although (because of the brevity of his statements and the lack of reference to other thinkers in his writings) ultimately insoluble. He may simply have obliged the debate that had occurred in the classes of his Leiden colleague over the reception of Suárezian metaphysics, or he may have worked over Suárez' *Disputationes metaphysicae* on this point, as he probably did on a series of other issues—or he may have made an initial acquaintance both with this revived Aristotelianism and with Averroistic accents during his year at Padua.

Although Arminius' proofs oblige many of the points of critique leveled against Aquinas' five ways by later scholastic writers, particularly the critique of the proof of the existence of a first mover, Arminius resists the theological tendency of the critique to place God beyond the realm of the rational and to define his transcendence in terms of an unfathomable absolute power or (*potentia absoluta*). There is, perhaps, via the critique, some loss of clarity (precision concerning the causal nexus between God and world, which will have significance from Arminius' subsequent discussions of divine knowledge and will, creation, and providence. Arminius will argue the rationality and therefore the rational accessibility of the identity and nature of God in God's works, the correlation of moral goodness known in the order of things with the moral goodness of God. In other words, rather than go in the direction of the nominalist critique and fracture the *analogia entis*, Arminius will strive to maintain the analogy and the intellectualist view of God and human nature from which it springs—for the sake of maintaining the goodness of God and the moral responsibility of man—despite the weakening of the proofs and their illustration of the causal nexus between the divine and the human.

As Burrell pointed out concerning the Thomist proofs, they are part of an attempt "to articulate the distinction between God and the world in such a way as to respect the reality of each" and to articulate it as "a distinction which makes its appearance, as it were, within the world as we know it."[49] Not only does this insight illuminate the reason for the struggle in Arminius' time over the proofs and their systematic implication, it illuminates also the underlying issue addressed by the highly speculative God-language that follows immediately upon Arminius' statement of the proofs. The proofs

[49] Burrell, *Knowing the Unknowable God*, p 17.

establish the connection between God and world and thereby point toward a discussion of the divine essence and attributes that, following this most basic statement of relationship, must be capable of carrying forward and clarifying the relationship, as Burrell comments, "in such a way as to respect the reality of each." Thus, the intricacies of Arminius' God-language, particularly as they became the foundation of a distinctively Arminian or Remonstrant doctrine of God in the writings of Episcopius and Limborch, are crucial to the whole of the Arminian system understood as a theological and philosophical construction of reality—a construction notably different from the Reformed thought of the day in its view not only of predestination but also of the entire relation of God to the world and, indeed, of the character of temporal reality.

7

Knowledge
of the Divine Essence

Neither the early Reformers nor their immediate successors produced an elaborate doctrine of the divine essence and attributes. They were quite content to leave consideration of such problems to the occasional exegetical task of expounding on the character of the divine existence (Exod. 3:14) or on the meaning of individual divine attributes, such as those praised by the psalmists. A major exception to this generalization is Wolfgang Musculus.[1] The teaching of the Reformation, thus, presupposed but seldom made explicit the epistemological, logical, and linguistic problems inherent in any extended discussion of the divine essence and of the attributes or perfections predicated of God. When systematic or dogmatic theology reappeared among the Protestant writers of the second half of the sixteenth century and of the seventeenth century, explicit discussion of the problem of the divine essence and attributes also reappeared—based on the investigations of theologians and philosophers who wrote prior to the Reformation.

The medieval doctors—following out the teaching of the fathers of the church—had recognized that all knowledge of God is mediate or indirect. Anselm had argued, therefore, that the perfections of the divine existence could be understood by way of the degrees of finite perfection present in the created order, and that the divine essence itself, in its utter simplicity, could not be understood as possessing these perfections in the same way that they are present in finite things. Each attribute is identical with the entirety of the divine essence and belongs to God *essentialiter*.[2] These assumptions of the indirectness of our knowledge of God and of the divine simplicity as

---

[1] Cf. Musculus, *Loci communes*, caps. 41–55.
[2] Cf. *Monologion*, 17 with Schwane, *Histoire des Dogmes*, IV, pp. 174, 184–85.

governing our understanding of the attributes provided the scholastic teachers of the thirteenth century with the basis for an extended investigation into the problem of the divine essence and attributes—specifically of the character of God-language and of the proper manner of identifying, distinguishing, and predicating attributes of God.[3]

Arminius opens his discussion of the divine essence with the assertion, already implicit in his recognition that theology is not a discourse about God in himself but a conception of God and the things of God, that we cannot know the divine essence "in itself." Rather we come to understand God "from the analogy of the nature which is in created things" and by way of "eminence according to which God is understood to exceed infinitely the perfections of created things."[4] This approach, although it departs from the Thomistic preference for the *via negativa*, certainly mirrors both the logic of the proofs and the Thomistic concept of the *analogia entis*, and is equally in accord with medieval investigation of the problem of God-language from Anselm onward. The combination of potentially Thomistic principles with an epistemological and metaphysical trust in the principle of analogy and in the ability to discern the character of the divine from its effects may reflect Arminius' reading of Aquinas, but it was also readily available to him in the influential metaphysics of Suárez.[5]

Arminius justifies his analogical consideration of God, beginning with the fundamental problem of ascribing a "nature" to God, by recourse both to Scripture and to "the general consent of all wise men and nations." He cites, as specific evidence of his thesis, Galatians 4:8 ("when you did not know God, you were in bondage to beings that by nature are no gods"), 2 Peter 1:4 ("you may escape corruption ... and become partakers of the divine nature"), Aristotle's *Politics*, and Cicero's *On the Nature of the Gods*. Justification of the point, therefore, rests both on revelation and philosophy.[6] In Arminius' theology, as in the theology of his scholastic Protestant and Reformed Thomist predecessor, Jerome Zanchi, the term *natura Dei* indicates the whatness or quiddity of God as distinguished from the "who," the

---

[3] See the extended discussion in Schwane, *Histoire des Dogmes*, IV, pp. 194–207.

[4] *Disp. priv.*, XV.ii: "Naturam Dei cum in ipsa cognoscere non possimus ex analogia naturae quae in rebus creatis ... addito semper analogiae illi modo eminentiae secundum quem Deus intelligitur perfectiones rerum creatarum infinite excedere."

[5] Suárez, *Disp.*, XXIX.1.

[6] *Disp. pub.*, IV.1: "Naturam Deo recte tribui, tum ipsa rerum Natura & Scriptura Dei, tum sapientum populorumque consensus testatur." The citations are placed marginally. The reference to Aristotle reads *"De rep. 1.7.c.1,"* but in the absence of a work by Aristotle having this title, it is most probably a citation of the *Politics*, VII.1 (1323b, 23–25): "God is a witness to us of this truth, for he is happy and blessed, not by reason of any external good, but in himself and by reason of his own nature."

triune and personal identity of God,[7] taking the place of the term *essentia Dei* in the original Thomistic pattern of discussing first the divine essence and its operations and then the doctrine of the Trinity.[8] *Natura*, in short, is used as a synonym for *essentia*. Before Arminius, Junius had divided the doctrine of God into discussion of the *essentia Dei* and of the Trinity; after Arminius, the Leiden *Synopsis* would carry forward the preference for the nomenclature, *de natura Dei*.[9]

Both revelation and reason testify that the divine nature is not known in the way that we know other natures. In an argument that sets aside the ontological proof of the existence of God (which was omitted without mention from Arminius' discussion of the proofs) Arminius denies the possibility of any a priori knowledge of God. God cannot be known a priori since the divine nature "is the first of all things, and was alone for infinite ages before all things."[10] As he indicated previously in the definitions and limitations of human theology, Arminius here asserts the problem of the diastasis between divine self-knowledge and human knowledge of God: the divine nature "is adequately known only by God, and God by it; because God is the same as it is."[11] Our knowledge of God arises by derivation: we participate in the being and goodness of God inasmuch as our "being" and "well-being" are gifts of God and we are derived from God by "an external emanation."[12] Because of our finitude, however, this emanation or derivation of being can only yield a "slight measure" of knowledge, on a scale "infinitely below what it is in itself."[13] (This language of "emanation" or of the "emanation of being" is characteristic of the medieval scholastic and, specifically, Thomistic accommodation of the language of classical philosophy to Christian theology. The Christian doctrine of creation assumes the ontological distinction between God and world: the Being of God is eternal and necessary; the being of the world had a beginning and is contingent. This distinction pressed medieval theologians like Aquinas to adapt the

---

[7] *Disp. priv.*, XV.1; cf. Zanchi, *De natura Dei*, I.i. Zanchi, however, seems to have reversed the basic order and to have placed Trinity first.

[8] Cf. Aquinas, *Summa*, Ia, q.2, prol. with q.27, prol.

[9] Cf. Junius, *Theses theologicae* (Leiden), VIII with *Synopsis purioris*, VI.

[10] *Disp. pub.*, IV.ii.

[11] Ibid.: "a Deo solo adaequate cognoscitur, & per ipsam Deus: quia idem Deus quod illa."

[12] *Disp. priv.*, XV.vii: "dicimus essentiam Dei unam esse, & Deum unum secundum illam, & propterea bonum, imo summum bonum; ex cuius participatione omnia tum quod sint, tum quod bona sint, habeant"; cf. *Disp. pub.*, IV.ii: "A nobis cognoscitur quadantenus, sed infinite inferius eo quod ipsa est: quia nos ab illa per emanationem externam." Arminius' approach, particularly his emphasis on participation in God, is reminiscent of Aquinas: see further below, chap. 8.

[13] *Disp. pub.*, IV.ii.

classical language of emanation so that it no longer implied a self-
impartation of the ultimate Being that resulted in a secondary order
of finite being, but, instead, implied the impartation of the power or
capacity for being.[14] Arminius has clearly drawn on this language and
made it his own. It will reappear in his discussions of the goodness
and creative power of God.)

Again echoing the scholastic paradigm for understanding the
various kinds of theology and the several modes of communication
of divine knowledge, Arminius recognizes two basic ways that the
divine nature can be known (still granting the problem of finitude):
"immediately (*immediata*) through the clear vision (*visionem claram*)
of it as it is" and "mediately (*mediata*) through analogical images and
signs."[15] As in the similar arguments presented in Arminius'
prolegomena on theology, the argument here stands in a direct and
positive relationship to the foundational efforts of Arminius'
predecessor at Leiden, Junius—and, therefore, very much in
agreement with the developing tradition of Reformed orthodoxy.[16]
The immediate knowledge of God is identified by Scripture as the
"face to face" vision of God and is possible only for the blessed in
heaven.[17] For believers on earth and, therefore, for Christian theology as discussed and debated by believers, only a mediate or mediated
knowledge is possible.

Mediate or mediated knowledge of God is analogical because it
presents only a likeness of the divine—an image or sign of the nature
of God—through the various instrumentalities of the finite order.
These instrumentalities not only make possible our knowledge of
God, they also determine and identify the kinds of revealed knowledge that we possess. Mediate knowledge of God, thus, arises both
from "the external acts of God and his works through them (Psalm
19:1–8; Romans 1:20)" and from "his word (Romans 10:14–17) which,
that part in which it proposes Christ, 'who is the image of invisible
God' ... gives such a further increase to our knowledge that, 'we all,
with open face beholding as in a glass the glory of God, are changed
into the same image from glory to glory' (Colossians 1:15; 2 Cor.
3:18)."[18] We see here a reflection both of the famous language of
Calvin and other Reformed writers concerning the *duplex cognitio Dei*
or twofold knowledge of God and of language of Protestant orthodoxy

[14] Cf. Aquinas, *Summa*, Ia, q.45, art.1.

[15] *Disp. pub.*, IV.iii: "Cognoscitur autem a nobis vel immediate per visionem
claram ejus, sicuti est: haec facie ad faciem dicitur; & beatorum propria est in coelis:
vel mediate per imagines analogicas & signa, quae sunt tum actiones Dei externae &
opera illis, tum verbum ipsius."

[16] Cf. Junius, *De vera theologia*, v; and *PRRD*, I, pp. 134–35, 156–59.

[17] *Disp. pub.*, IV.iii.

[18] Ibid.

after Junius of "our theology" as a reflected or ectypal theology of pilgrims. Indeed, Arminius specifically identifies this redemptive theology that beholds the divine glory "as in a glass"—in "an enigma" or "darkly"—as the theology of *viatores* or pilgrims.[19] The continued emphasis on the *analogia entis*, however, points away from the potentially Scotistic or nominalistic approach of Calvin and of Junius toward the Thomistic model.

Arminius understands the knowledge of God, then, not merely as natural and supernatural but also and primarily as a *duplex cognitio* concerning God the Creator and God the Redeemer. Both of these forms of revelation are, moreover, known according to a finite, temporal, and penultimate mode of knowing, a pilgrim-theology. These reflections on the form and character of our knowledge of God point, in turn, toward a profound difficulty encountered by all formulations of the doctrine of God. Neither through the revelation of God in his works of creation nor in the special, redemptive revelation of God in Christ do we know God as he is in himself. In all cases, we know God mediately, indirectly, and in a sense improperly inasmuch as this mediated, indirect knowledge is incapable of presenting its divine object as it is ultimately capable of being known. The divine perfection and ultimacy cannot be properly conveyed in imperfect and less than ultimate language.

From the transcendent perfection of God as first and chief Being, Arminius infers, therefore, that attributes cannot be predicated of God in the way that they are predicated of created things: "to the essence of God no attributes can be added, whether distinguished from it really or rationally, as a pure mental construct."[20] In other words, the standard patterns of distinction between essence and attribute, substance and accidents do not apply to God. Arminius' identification of the three basic kinds of distinction, together with his passing on immediately in his next proposition to the concept of divine simplicity, reflects the problem of the predication of attributes noted for the first time in the thirteenth century by Alexander of Hales, Thomas Aquinas, and Henry of Ghent.[21] This reflection, like the other reflections of medieval scholastic theology that we have found in Arminius' thought, has never to my knowledge been noted by scholars in their discussions of Arminius. Nonetheless, it ought not to come as a surprise that a Protestant professor engaging in the task of basic system building should encounter the same problems as the scholastic doctors of the thirteenth century who, for the first time in the

---

[19] Ibid.; cf. Calvin, *Inst.*, I.ii.1 for the "*duplex cognitio Dei*" and note Muller, "Duplex cognitio Dei in the Theology of Early Reformed Orthodoxy," pp. 54–60. On the *theologia viatorum*, see PRRD, I, pp. 124, 126–28, 153–66.

[20] *Disp. priv.*, XV.vi: "vel re vel ratione & puro mentis conceptu."

[21] Cf. Schwane, *Histoire des Dogmes*, IV, pp. 194–99.

history of the West had made a distinction between the interpretation of *sacra pagina* and the construction of theological *scientia* in the light of the demands of rigorously logical and rational discourse.

In the first decade of the seventeenth century, when Arminius lectured on the divine attributes, Protestant orthodoxy was still in its period of formation and neither the Reformed nor the Lutheran orthodox had yet settled on a particular pattern of exposition. Some of the early Reformed orthodox, like Polanus, argued the distinction between incommunicable and communicable attributes that would become, later in the seventeenth century, the standard pattern in Reformed dogmatics.[22] Even so, the Lutherans were already moving toward the approach to divine attributes by way of negation (*via negationis*), by way of eminence (*via eminentiae*), and by way of causality (*via causalitatis*) that would ultimately become characteristic of scholastic Lutheran theology.[23] But on either side, a majority of writers were still groping with the question of predication that had occupied the mind of thirteenth- and fourteenth-century scholasticism and, granting an answer to that primary issue, the establishment of a suitable pattern for the organization of the doctrinal locus on the divine attributes. Arminius, then, had few firm precedents in Protestant theology for his exposition of the divine attributes and, in fact belongs to the generation of Protestants in which the basic work of exposition and patterning of discussion was to be done.

The Reformers had tended not to discuss the divine attributes at length, and those who did, like Musculus, Hyperius, and, to a lesser degree, Bullinger, did not deal with the more philosophical and logical problems of predication and organization of the *locus*. Even Ursinus, whose *Loci theologici* have moved a long way toward fully scholastic method, merely enumerates the attributes.[24] Zanchi too, despite his extensive training in scholastic theology, attempts no cohesive organization or deductive patterning of the attributes.[25]

Arminius' approach to the attributes by way of affirmation and causality, negation, and supereminence does not, therefore, draw on the writings of the Reformers. It does, however, look directly to the presentation of the problem of the attributes by his predecessor at Leiden, Franciscus Junius. Junius had chosen a pattern that began with negation of creaturely imperfection, moved on to an analogical argument resting on the *imago Dei*, and then, in recognition of the fact that God is at once unlike the finite order and eminently more

[22] Cf. *RD*, pp. 60–62.

[23] Cf. *DTEL*, pp. 117–18, 122–24 with Chemnitz, *Loci theologici*, locus de Deo in genere, cap. 3 (1653, p. 27).

[24] Ursinus, *Loci theologici*, cols. 471–88.

[25] Zanchi, *De natura Dei*, in *Opera*, II.

noble than his creatures, to a language of divine supereminence (*supereminentia*). In this latter discussion, Junius attempted to come to terms, linguistically, with the final breakdown of analogy between the absolute perfection of God and the limited perfection of creatures.[26]

Junius may have drawn, here, on Scotist models. Just as his definition of an ectypal *theologia nostra* set under the divine archetype bears some resemblance to the Scotist distinction between an unknowable divine *theologia in se* and "our theology" in its finitude and limitation, so also does this sense of the difficulty of analogical language and the tendency toward a categorization of attributes by way of causality, negation, and eminence reflect Scotist usage.[27] Indeed, the way in which Junius and Arminius after him employ this model manifests a consistent worry over the limitations of analogical language and an equally consistent emphasis on the transcendence of the divine essence.

Arminius is also quite aware of various directions being taken by his contemporaries in the attempt to develop the language of the divine attributes. On the one hand, he seems to refer obliquely to the distinction between communicable and incommunicable attributes inasmuch as he explicitly notes that there are no communicable attributes. On the other hand he is, perhaps painfully, aware of the gravitation of Lutheran orthodoxy toward the paradigm of *via eminentiae*, *via negativa*, and *via causalitatis*. The Lutherans had rejected the Reformed language of communicable and incommunicable attributes on the ground that it was christologically deficient: in the Lutheran Christology, no divine attribute could be understood as incapable of communication from the divine Person of Christ to his human nature.[28]

Nonetheless, Arminius does not accept the christological argument behind the Lutheran paradigm, as is evident both from his Christology[29] and from his comment that "these modes of supereminence (*modi supereminentiae*) are not communicable to any thing, simply by reason of what they are"—that is, supereminent. The supereminence of the divine attributes, in fact, presses them beyond the normal bounds of analogy. They are, moreover, "proper to God as his essence itself" and could not be communicated without a full communication of the divine essence itself—and, of course, this is

---

[26] Junius, *Theses theologicae*, VIII.ii, 18, 27, 41.

[27] Cf. Minges, II, pp. 44–45 with Raymond, "Duns Scot," col. 1875.

[28] Cf. *DTEL*, pp. 315, 330–34 with Preus, *Theology of Post-Reformation Lutheranism*, I, pp. 168–69, and note *RD*, pp. 60–62.

[29] *Disp. priv.*, XXXIV.vi: the *communicatio idiomata* or communion of proper qualities in the person of Christ "was not real (*realis*), as though some things which are proper to the truth of this union, indicate conjunction of both natures."

impossible. To speak of such a communication is to "wish to destroy [the divine essence] after despoiling it of its peculiar modes of being."[30] Arminius fully recognizes the implications of his argument for debate with the Lutherans inasmuch as he concludes his thesis with the comment, "Therefore, Christ, according to his humanity, is not in every place."[31] Here he stands in strong agreement with the Reformed Christology.[32]

His argument, however, is somewhat different from the arguments proposed by those few among the Reformed who also rejected the distinction of attributes into categories of communicable and incommunicable. Alting, for example, rejected the distinction for reasons virtually the opposite of those of Arminius: some communicable attributes clearly have an analogy in man and others are known by their effects in the created order, but the idea of incommunicable properties, comments Alting, is obscure and ambiguous. The implication of his argument is that all attributes are known by some analogy —and to say, in effect, that some are nonanalogical is to make discussion impossible. The division into negative and affirmative attributes is, therefore, preferable.[33]

Rather than predicate attributes of God as if they were accidents somehow distinguishable from the substance or essence of God, Arminius states that predication is possible only in a supereminent way (modus supereminentiae),

> according to which it is understood to comprise within itself and to exceed all the perfections of all things, as may be explained in the phrase, that the essence is without beginning and without cause (anarchos kai anaitios). Hence it follows that this [essence] is simple and infinite; from this, that it is eternal, immeasurable; and lastly that it is unchangeable, impassible, and incorruptible.[34]

Arminius' language appears, again, to reflect Aquinas.[35] Since no term or accident can be directly predicated of God, but only assumed

---

[30] Disp. priv., XV,x.

[31] Disp. pub., IV.xix.

[32] Cf. Mastricht, as cited in RD, p. 62.

[33] Alting, Methodus theologiae, III (in Opera, V, p. 76, col. 2).

[34] Disp. priv., XV.vi–vii.: "Essentiae Dei nullum attributum vel re vel ratione et puro mentis conceptu ab illa distinctum, addi potest, sed tantum modus supereminentiae, secundum quem omnes omnium rerum perfectiones in se complecti et excedere intelligitur tribui potest; qui uno verbo exprimi potest, quod essentia sit anarchos kai anaitios. (vii) Unde sequitur illam esse simplicem et infinitam; inde aeternam et immensam: denique immutabilem, impatibilem, incorruptibilem."

[35] Cf. Aquinas, SCG, I.30.2: "Quia enim omnem perfectionem creaturae est in Deo invenire sed per alium modum eminentiorum.... Quae vero huiusmodi

to be said of God because of the analogy between the good Creator and all that is good in the created order, Arminius advocates an indirect, analogical predication by way of eminence. Indeed, all that Arminius predicates directly of the divine essence is a mode or manner of being supereminent—and, from this assumption of supereminence of the divine Being, he can infer the supereminence of God in all perfections.

Whereas the *Disputationes privatae* only sketch out the problem of predication and discuss only the *via eminentiae*, the *Disputationes publicae* take up the problem of predication at considerably greater length and develop a full paradigm of *via negationis, via eminentiae*, and *via causalitatis*. It is also clear, at this point, that the two series of disputations are interrelated and that the *Disputationes privatae* are the later set, written with specific reference to the *Disputationes publicae* and with the intention of avoiding excessive duplication of argument.[36]

The mediate or analogical knowledge of God, resting both on the works of God in nature and on the revelation given in Scripture, follows two basic patterns according to Arminius—the way of affirmation or causality and the way of negation or removal. In one of his few direct citations of medieval writers, Arminius notes that Thomas Aquinas defined the affirmative way of the knowledge of God as "the mode of causality" by which "the simple perfections which are in creatures, as being productions of God, are attributed analogically to God according to some similitude."[37] This affirmative or causal pattern, moreover, passes over logically and directly into the *modus supereminentiae*: since no effect can exceed its cause and, in the case of God, the first cause, can make not even a distant approach, the perfections that are predicated causally of God must be understood as "infinitely more perfect in God" than in creatures.[38]

This supereminence of the divine perfections draws directly, also, on the logic of the second basic way of understanding the divine attributes, the *via negationis*. The negative way understands the divine attributes as they arise from the removal or negation of all "the rela-

---

perfectiones exprimunt cum supereminentiae modo quo Deo conveniunt, de solo Deo dicuntur."

[36] Cf. *Disp. priv.*, XV.vii, where Arminius notes, at the end of his thesis that the divine essence is eternal, etc. "in the manner in which it has been proved by us in our public thesis on this subject"—demonstrating Bangs' point concerning the later date of the *Disputationes privatae* (1603ff. rather than the 1598ff. supposed by Nichols): see *Works* (1986), I, pp. xviii, 131 and II, p. 318.

[37] *Disp. pub.*, IV.iv. Aquinas is also cited rather frequently in the *Conference* with Junius—as the author of one of the major options for formulating the doctrine of predestination: cf. *Amica collatio*, pp. 553, 570, 573, 575, 582, 585, 609 (*Works*, III, pp. 152, 176–77, 181, 184, 195, 199, 234).

[38] *Disp. pub.*, IV.iv.

tive perfections and all the imperfections that pertain to creatures, as having been produced out of nothing" from the concept of God. In the case of the removal of finite or relative aspects from the relative or "circumscribed" perfections of creatures, the negative way is in fact a form of argument from supereminence.[39] Arminius thus echoes the threefold patten of predication favored by the Lutheran orthodox even as he reduces it to two primary patterns of argumentation, with the logic of eminence or supereminence standing in the background as the underlying logic and problematic of all discussion of divine attributes.

Underlying this problem of predication is the problem of divine simplicity. Beginning with Albert the Great, the scholastics had recognized that the supereminence or ultimacy of God could only be properly acknowledged in theology if the divine Being were conceived as prior to all things not merely in a physical and temporal sense but also in a metaphysical and logical sense.[40] If God were conceived as a sum of attributes, as a logically composite being, then those attributes or the *ideas* of them would be more ultimate than God—and such concepts as the idea of the Good or the idea of Truth would stand above and over against God and would both govern the divine will and limit the divine freedom. In order to avoid this difficulty, the scholastics inferred from the divine preeminence the concept of divine simplicity, the freedom of God from all composition.[41] This solution, however, brought with it its own difficulties. Preservation of divine unity and ultimacy through recourse to the concept of essential simplicity led to a deep concern over the problem of predication. As the nominalist teachers of the later Middle Ages recognized, utter simplicity rules out the existence of attributes in God. Indeed, Occam went so far as to argue against the usage *attributa Dei* and in favor of *nomina Dei* on the ground that any terms applied to God are human concepts or words and not distinctions of any sort in the divine essence.[42] Arminius will encounter these issues as soon as he moves from the basic discussions of the patterns of identifying and predicating attributes and of the divine nature in its essence and like to the enumeration and analysis of particular attributes.[43]

[39] Ibid.
[40] Schwane, *Histoire des Dogmes*, IV, p. 194.
[41] Ibid.
[42] Occam, *Quodlibet* III, q.11, cited in Vignaux, "Nominalisme," *DTC* 11/1, cols. 757–58.
[43] Cf. *Disp. pub.*, IV.xi with *Disp. priv.*, XV.vii.

8

The Nature
and Attributes of God

Arminius' discussion of the nature and attributes of God is both an elaborate typology of the divine attributes built upon the basic discussion of predication and identification and a unified theological essay that develops the practical or resolvative premise of his entire system. In the first place, the language of negation provides an avenue for discussion of the essential attributes, while the language of affirmation and causal preeminence yields up the divine life and its perfections. Arminius proposes, therefore, an initial division of his *locus de natura Dei* into the categories of *essentia* and *vita*. Under *essentia*, he discusses simplicity and infinity; under *vita*, he discusses understanding and will. Simplicity and infinity yield, logically, eternity, immensity, omnipresence, impassibility, immutability, and incorruptibility. Understanding (*intellectus*) implies knowledge (*scientia*) and, by extension, wisdom (*sapientia*)—and will carries with it all of the affective and relational attributes like goodness, love, mercy, and so forth. Arminius' disputations do not contain any of the diagrams so frequently found in sixteenth- and seventeenth-century theological works, but the structure of his presentation certainly mirrors the Agricolan and Ramist method of logical bifurcation and could easily be drawn out in such a diagram.

In the second place, Arminius' doctrine of God is fashioned with a consistent emphasis on the relationship of God to things *ad extra* under the categories of understanding and will—with a specific focus on God as *summum bonum* and final cause of all things. Arminius, thus, presents his doctrine of God in truly principial fashion, as the ground and as a reflection of his entire theology. His Protestant contemporaries had, after all, identified two *principia* or foundations of theological system: Scripture, the cognitive foundation (*principium cognoscendi*) and God, the essential foundation (*principium essendi*).[1] The divine Being, in its knowledge and will, must be the archetype for all finite being: if there is goodness in the created order, it is there by derivation from and participation in the divine goodness; if there is freedom, sin, and salvation in the created order, so also must the divine knowing and willing provide some ultimate explanation for the possibility, existence, and order of such things. Here, and again in the doctrine of creation, we will encounter the foundational principles for Arminius' departures from the Reformed theology of his day.

The basic rule that discussion of the divine attributes proceeds by analogy and with recognition of the divine preeminence provides Arminius with his point of entrance into his doctrine of the nature of God.[2] From a procedural and a structural point of view, Arminius' emphasis on preeminence or the *via eminentiae* leads him to a positive use of analogy and an emphasis on the affirmative or causal logic of the Thomistic "five ways." There is, in other words, a substantive and organic relation between Arminius' proofs of the existence of God and his doctrine of the divine nature. This approach is consistently more rationalistic than the approach noted in the systems of his Reformed and Lutheran contemporaries. Entrance into the doctrine of the divine nature by way of eminence, affirmation, and causality leads Arminius to seek out not merely analogies from finite nature but analogies from the highest knowable forms of finite nature.

Beyond the analogies drawn generally from nature, Arminius points, therefore, toward those drawn specifically from man who is "created after the image of God." From the general analogy of nature and the specific analogy of man, Arminius concludes that existence (*esse*) and life (*vita*) must be the two fundamental categories belonging to discussion of the essence (*essentia*) of God. Some theologians argue that the basic categories are being, life, feeling, and understanding, but feeling and understanding are best conceived as aspects of life—so that being and life remain the two fundamental categories or, as Arminius calls them, "moments" (*momenta*) or "substantialities" (*substantialia*) of the divine nature.[3] Thus Arminius can say in his initial structuring of the doctrine of God that the

> essence of God is the first moment of the divine nature, by which God is purely and simply understood to be (*esse*).... Life is that which comes under our consideration, in the second moment of the divine nature.[4]

---

[1] Cf. *PRRD*, I, pp. 295–304.

[2] Cf. *Disp. priv.*, XV.ii; *Disp. pub.*, IV.v–vi.

[3] *Disp. priv.*, XV.iii; *Disp. pub.*, IV.v.

[4] *Disp. priv.*, XV.iv: "Essentiam Dei primum naturae divinae momentum esse dicimus, quo Deus pure & simpliciter esse intelligitur" and XVI.i: "Vitam, quae in secundo momento naturae divina consideranda venit"; cf. *Disp. pub.*, IV.vii, xxv.

Being is the moment or substantial ground that constitutes "the perfection of all created things" while life is the moment or substantial ground that constitutes the perfection of higher creatures only.[5]

The terms used by Arminius, *momentum* and *substantialia*, rendered "moment" and "substantialities," are both somewhat obscure and both are difficult to render into English. Nichols' translation of *momentum* as "cause of motion"[6] or as "impulse"[7] simply cannot stand. Arminius himself tells us, in agreement with the scholastic and Aristotelian tradition, that there is no change or motion in God—not even in the inward operations of the divine essence.[8] In addition, Arminius uses the term *momentum* not only in this fundamental, substantial, or essential sense, as a reference to the Being and life of God, but also in a discussion of the divine affections as belonging to the volitional *momentum* of the divine nature, that is, to the divine will.[9] Arminius does not follow the classical usage, where *momentum* indicates movement or motion—instead he probably follows the later usage as noted in Altenstaig's *Lexicon theologicum* (1619), where *momentum* indicates an instant, a point of imperceptible duration. Arminius' intention is, surely, to indicate an irreducible instant and, in some sense, a foundation or ground, prior to all internal acts of the divine nature, for both sets of attributes, the negative or essential attributes and the positive attributes or operations of divine life.[10]

This conclusion is borne out in his use of *substantialia*. Had he meant "substance" as Nichols renders the term, Arminius could have used *substantia*—but it is quite clear that substance is a term that refers to an entire essence (*essentia*) when that essence is identified in an actual existent.[11] Granting this to be the normal theological use of *substantia*, it is quite clear that "being" or "essence" cannot be one substance and "life" another; certainly not in God, who is defined as a single essence or substance. Rather, Arminius hopes to identify in the nature or substance of God two aspects of substance or substantial categories in which the two basic sets—negative and positive—of divine attributes are grounded.

---

[5] *Disp. pub.*, IV.v: "Porro in tota rerum Natura & Scriptura duo tantum reperiuntur substantialia, quibus omnis rerum perfectio continetur: Essentia & Vita; illa omnium creaturarum existentium, haec non nullarum tantum & perfectissimarum."

[6] *Disp. pub.*, IV.v, vii, in *Works*, II, pp. 113–14 and see the fn., p. 113.

[7] *Disp. priv.*, XV.iii; XVI.i, in *Works*, II, pp. 338–39.

[8] *Disp. pub.*, IV.xviii.

[9] *Disp. pub.*, IV.lxiv.

[10] Cf. his use of *momentum* as an "instant" in *Examen modestum*, pp. 732–33 (*Works*, III, pp. 416, 418) and *Disp. priv.*, XX.v.

[11] Cf. Altenstaig, *Lexicon theologicum*, s.v. "*substantia*" (pp. 879–80).

Being and life, therefore, provide the limits for human consideration of the divine nature. The mind, argues Arminius, is incapable of
rising beyond its creaturely status to the comprehension of any substance or substantial ground other than these two constitutive perfections of the world order. The mind "is itself circumscribed by the
limits of created nature, of which it is *a part*; it is therefore incapable
of passing beyond the circle of *the whole*."[12] In other words, as Aquinas
assumed, all knowledge is a posteriori, from the experience of the
world: the two fundamental "moments" of the divine nature, being
and life, are known analogically from the created order as are all
other perfections of God. They are the fundamental categories of our
God-language because they are recognized, analogically, from the
fundamental categories of our language about the world. "In the
entire nature of things and in the Scriptures themselves, only two
substantial grounds (*substantialia*) are found in which the perfection of
all things is contained: essence (*essentia*) and life (*vita*)."[13]

This language of "two moments" of a given nature, quite strange to
the modern reader and quite foreign to the basically biblical and
exegetical statements of the doctrine of God found in the writings of
the early Reformers, is fully intelligible in the scholastic context.
Arminius is making a distinction that is, more typically, stated in the
terms *actus primus* and *actus secundus*, primary and secondary actuality.
When a thing is in its primary actuality (*in actu primo*) it is in actual
existence, in possession of all its faculties, but not active or operative
in its faculties. The mind, when it is not engaged in thought but is
nonetheless capable of thinking, is *in actu primo*—but when the
activity of thinking begins, the mind passes over into its secondary or
operational actuality, the *actus secundus*. In God, of course, the
distinction between primary and secondary actuality is a purely
rational distinction, contrived for the sake of clarifying discussion of
the divine essence: *actus primus* is a condition of potency, of the latent
but unused power of operation; *actus secundus* is a condition of full
actuality—but, of course, there is no potency but only actuality in God.
In Arminius' terms, there is no "first moment," of being in God
without the "second moment," life. The being and life of God are
identical: God "is the life of himself"—"the life of God is most simple,
so that it is not distinguished from his essence as one thing from
another."[14]

In other words, although a rational distinction can be made between
two fundamental *momenta* of the divine nature, the simplicity and
eternity of God and the fully actualized and uncaused nature of the

12 *Disp. pub.*, IV.v.
13 Ibid.
14 *Disp. priv.*, XVI.ii, iii; cf. *Disp. pub.*, IV.xxviii.

divine essence prevent Arminius from pressing the distinction of "moments" into the divine nature in such a way as to separate essence and life or to make life the result of a movement of essence from passivity into activity or from potency to actuality. This problematic of the language may be the reason that Arminius uses the term *momentum* rather than the more typical *actus*. Indeed, virtually none of the Protestant scholastics use the distinction between *actus primus* and *actus secundus* as a way of identifying the fundamental being of God as distinct from attributes such as life. Some note the difficulty of the language, but by far the greater number avoid the language entirely on the ground that God is *actus simplicissimus* and *actus purus* and speak of attributes that are in their actuality incommunicable or communicable, immanent or operative. The concept of fully actualized, communicable, or operative attributes, thus, stands instead of a concept of secondary or operative actuality.[15]

The issue between Arminius and his Reformed colleagues is clear when the distinction between *actus primus* and *actus secundus* is applied to will: as Altenstaig points out, *actus primus* indicates, in this case, a power of the soul prior to its actual operation—something that is in the soul habitually. Thus "to will" or "to be willing" (*velle*) is the primary actuality of will (*voluntas*) that precedes the secondary actuality of actual volition (*volitio actualis*), the act of will directed toward a particular object.[16] If God is utterly simple, the fact of God having a will and the divine willing must be identical. What is more, such a distinction in addition to impinging on divine simplicity could also become the basis of a distinction between what God intends in his will and what is actually effected by his will—a distinction that the Reformed deny but Arminius affirms, echoing, significantly enough, Suárez.[17]

This reading of the term *momentum*, moreover, allows us to maintain the identity of *natura* and *essentia* as noted at a previous point in the discussion.[18] When Arminius identifies the essence as the first *momentum* of the divine nature, he is not claiming that essence is somehow distinguishable from nature and a category of being somehow secondary to nature (as would be the case if the term *momentum* indicated an "impulse" of the nature). Instead he is asserting the fundamental identity of essence and nature and, in addition, the use of *essentia* as a term for the *natura Dei* considered in and

[15] Cf. Zanchi, *De natura Dei*, II.iv.1; Gomarus, *Disp.*, II.xxxix–xl; Burmann, *Synopsis theol.*, I.xx.2–3; and note Walaeus, *Loci communes*, III.8 (p. 170), where the order parallels Arminius' view of divine knowledge, will, and power but any notion even of logical sequence or ordering is denied; cf. *RD*, pp. 68–69.

[16] Altenstaig, *Lexicon theologicum*, s.v. "Actus primus" (pp. 16–17).

[17] See below, chap. 10.

[18] See above, chap. 7.

of itself, in its primary actuality, apart from any operation. (Although it must be granted that, given the essential identity of all of the attributes, the removal of *vita* from this primary category is, at best, something done for convenience in discussion.)

At a stage in the development of Protestant theology when the major teachers were searching the theological systems both of their predecessors and of their contemporaries for usable models, Arminius' basic bifurcation into attributes of essence and of life is quite significant. The intellectualist model offered by Aquinas had first set forth essential attributes (simplicity, perfection, goodness, infinity, omnipresence, immutability, eternity, unity)[19] and then, after discussing the names of God,[20] had set forth the operations of the divine essence looking first to the divine knowledge, under which he placed discussions of the ideas in God, of the truth and of the life of God,[21] and second to the divine will, under which he placed discussions of love, justice and mercy, providence and predestination.[22]

There is, thus, a basic resemblance between the logic of Arminius' ordering of the attributes and Aquinas' logic. What we find in the *Summa* is a fundamental distinction between the existence and essence of God on the one hand and the operations of the divine essence on the other. This argument could easily be directed toward a distinction between the divine essence as existent and conceived *in actu primo* and the divine essence as operative and conceived *in actu secundo*, such as appears in Arminius' ordering, in his primary division of the discussion of the divine nature into the examination of its being and its life. In addition, Aquinas had himself conceived of life as the precondition of knowledge and had, therefore, inverted the order of logical and ontological priority in moving from knowledge as operation of the divine essence to the discussion of life as implied by knowing: "because to understand is a kind of life, after treating of the divine knowledge, we consider the divine life."[23] Similarly, in the *Contra gentiles*, despite his placement of the *vita Dei* in the penultimate position in the list of attributes, immediately before the discussion of divine blessedness, Aquinas clearly indicates the ontological priority of life over intellect and will: there can be no knowing or willing, he argues, without life. Aquinas has already demonstrated that God knows and wills; therefore God must be living.[24]

[19] Aquinas, *Summa*, Ia, pp. 3–11.

[20] Ibid., p. 13.

[21] Ibid., pp. 14–18.

[22] Ibid., pp. 19–24; and cf. the discussion of the logic of Aquinas' ordering in Garrigou-Lagrange, *God: His Existence and His Nature*, II, pp. 33–41.

[23] Aquinas, *Summa*, Ia, q.14, prol.

[24] *SCG*, I.97.2.

It is worth raising the question, here, of the influence of Daneau on Arminius. Granting that Arminius owned and obviously read both of Aquinas' *Summas*, this distinction between the essence or substance of God *secundum se* and the essence in its *operationes* could have been drawn directly from Aquinas. Arminius might also, however, have had it impressed upon his mind at a fairly early stage by Daneau who not only cited the distinction directly from Aquinas but used it even more clearly than Aquinas himself in an architectonic principle in the discussion of the divine attributes.[25] Daneau's arrangement of the individual attributes is different from that of Arminius, but the pattern of movement from the essential attributes to the operations is strongly asserted as is the identification of the operations as consisting in the activities of *scientia, voluntas,* and *potentia*.[26] Daneau did not elaborate, however, on the operations—so that the Thomistic detail found in Arminius' theology ultimately must look to Aquinas, even if at the suggestion of Daneau.

Differences between Arminius' approach and the model developed by Aquinas should probably be understood less as a function of Arminius' Protestantism than as a result of scholastic discussion of the doctrine after Aquinas, up to and including the discussion of divine attributes in Suárez' *Disputationes metaphysicae*. Thus, the neat division of the attributes, according to faculty psychology, into attributes of intellect and attributes of will became, in the theology of the fourteenth-century Dominican, Hervaeus Natalis (much as it would become in the Protestant scholastic theology of Arminius) a basis for the rational deduction of the remaining divine attributes, now viewed as derivable from intellect or from will.[27] Hervaeus, in turn, may have developed his arguments as a Thomistic alternative to the doctrine of the divine attributes proposed by Duns Scotus. Scotus had not only divided the attributes into a primary category of essential predications and a secondary category consisting in attributes of intellect and attributes of will, but he had also indicated that intellect and will could be understood as the basic activities of the life of God.[28]

In view of the occasional hints of Scotistic argumentation in the thought of Arminius and his Reformed contemporaries, it is of interest that the discussion of divine attributes as an order or movement flowing forth from the divine essence in two "moments" (*instantes*)

---

[25] Daneau, *Christianae isagoges*, I.7 (p. 14r).

[26] Ibid., p. 14v.

[27] Hervaeus Natalis, *IV sent.*, I, d.d.2, q.1, as cited in Chossat, "Dieu. Sa nature selon les scholastiques," *DTC* 4/1, cols. 1157–58. [Hervaeus Natalis (d. 1323) is frequently referred to in the French form of his name, Hervé Nédellec or Hervé de Nédellec, less frequently in the Latin form, Hervaeus Britto.]

[28] Cf. Raymond, "Duns Scot," *DTC* 4/2, cols. 1875–76.

was also characteristic of Scotus' doctrine of the divine attributes. It was Scotus, of all the medieval doctors, who raised and pressed the issue of the order of the divine attributes as they "flow forth from the essence" of God (*quasi ab essentia fluunt*).[29] According to Scotus the divine essence, understood as in possession of its essential attributes (*essentialia*) including intellect and will, is the first moment or origin of *progressus* toward the second moment or operative actuality of intellect and will (*actus intelligendi* and *actus volendi*).[30] Arminius' adoption of the language of *momenta*, taken together with his emphasis on the flow and order of the attributes, may, therefore, indicate a borrowing from Scotist thought that led to the modification of the basically Thomistic division of the attributes. This is not to say that Arminius necessarily read Hervaeus—he did have direct access to Scotus in his own library—rather it is simply to point out that Arminius' reception of medieval scholastic models involved not merely the study of one great representative figure like Aquinas but, beyond that, the appropriation of a tradition of discussion that, by his time, had modified and developed the arguments of its inaugurators in considerable variety and depth. From this point of view, Arminius' reading of Suárez was crucial, inasmuch as Suárez was a master of the tradition who, true to the inclinations of the founder of his order, held Aquinas and later Dominicans in high esteem but who also constructed his own thought out of the juxtaposition and comparative evaluation of the opinions of Thomists, Scotists, and a variety of other late medieval schools of thought.[31]

In addition, Arminius did have some precedent for this patterning in Junius' *Theses theologicae*, although Junius makes no mention of *momenta, actus*, or *operationes* in God. The negative path of argument had enabled Junius to identify such attributes as simplicity, infinity, unity, immensity and omnipresence, eternity, unicity, and immutability—a list almost identical with Arminius' list of essential attributes.[32] When Junius moves on to discuss the affirmative attributes resting on creaturely analogy and preeminently on the *imago Dei* in man, he first notes that God is living, both as stated directly in Scripture (Gen. 10:14; Rom. 9:26; Ps. 36:10; 1 John 5:20) and as argued philosophically and enshrined in Boethius' definition of eternity as the simultaneous and perfect possession of endless life.[33] From the fundamental concept of divine life, Junius deduces first, by way of analogy with spiritual creatures, the intelligence (*intelligentia*) and

---

[29] Scotus, *I sent.*, d.35, q.3, as cited in Vignaux, "Nominalisme," col. 758.

[30] Cf. Vignaux, "Nominalisme," *DTC* 11/1, col. 758, citing Scotus, *I sent.*, d.9, q.3.

[31] Cf. Vollert, "Introduction," in Suárez, *On the Various Kinds of Distinction*, pp. 10–11.

[32] Junius, *Theses theologicae*, VIII.19–26.

[33] Ibid., VIII.28.

understanding (*intellectus*) of God and second, by way of analogy with living creatures generally, the will (*voluntas*) and omnipotence (*omnipotentia*) of God.[34] This deduction of understanding, will, and power from life is precisely the pattern of Arminius' disputations.

Junius and Arminius may simply have drawn on the modified Thomist paradigm, moving from the *via negativa* and the strictly essential attributes to the attributes of divine operation, but attempting at the same time to draw out the internal logic of Aquinas' identification of life as the precondition for knowledge and, by extension, will and power as well. In Junius, the discussions of the attributes of the living God—intellect, will, and power—and of the *vita Dei* itself, are merely rearranged for the sake of cohesion. In Arminius' thought, now a step beyond Junius', an attempt is made to argue essence and life as larger categories, corresponding strictly to the negative and affirmative paths of identifying the attributes. Arminius can be viewed, then, as consciously charting out the logical development of a "Leiden theology" in the era of early orthodoxy, with reference to the doctrine of the divine attributes just as we saw earlier, with reference to the concept of theology. In addition, Arminius' rationalization of the Thomist pattern of divine attributes parallels and reflects the medieval development of the doctrine in the hands of Duns Scotus, Hervaeus Natalis, and other writers of the fourteenth century.

This reflection, in turn, manifests the methodological and stylistic kinship between Arminius and his scholastic Reformed contemporaries. They, too, developed their theological systems in reliance on the models that had been created, earlier in the century, by major Protestant codifiers like Ursinus, Daneau, Zanchi, and Junius; and they too elaborated and modified these systematic models not only by reflection on the Protestant exegetical tradition but also by close reference to the systematizing efforts of the medieval scholastics. This recourse to medieval models was particularly crucial for the Protestant formulation of doctrinal topics not addressed at length or, indeed, not addressed at all by the Reformers.[35]

It is significant, also, that this rationalization of the Thomist pattern, subsuming intellect and will under the broader category of divine life, was adopted by Suárez in his *Disputationes metaphysicae* of 1597.[36] Since Junius does not follow this pattern in his Heidelberg theses but only in the theses that he developed for his courses at Leiden, he must have conceived of it after 1592.[37] The influence of

---

[34] Ibid., VIII.29–30, 35.

[35] Cf. *PRRD*, I, pp. 73–74, 126–38, 199–201.

[36] Suárez, *Disp. metaph.*, XXX. vi.19; xiv.6, 9–11; xvi.1–2.

[37] Junius, *Theses theologicae* (Heidelberg), 11–12; cf. *Theses theologicae* (Leiden), VIII.29–30, 35.

Suárez on Junius is, therefore, possible although Suárezian thought appears to have surfaced at Leiden only in 1603, the year after Junius' death.[38] Junius' patterning of the doctrine may simply reflect late medieval Thomist argumentation; Arminius' reshaping of the doctrine, however, more probably reflects some influence of Suárez in addition to the clear influence of Junius, particularly in view of the similarities between Suárez' argument and that of Arminius and in view of the interest in Suárezian metaphysics at Leiden in the early seventeenth century.

In view of Gomarus' complaint against Arminius' use of scholastic categories like contingency, necessity, and so forth,[39] it is worth noting that Gomarus' discussion of the divine attributes is far less elaborate and speculative than Arminius' presentation but that it also follows the Thomistic or Suárezian model of establishing a bifurcation between essence and life and also organizes the attributes according to a distinction between primary or negative and secondary or affirmative attributes, very much like that proposed initially by Arminius in his discussion of the problem of predication, but argued more briefly and less speculatively.[40] In addition, Gomarus adds to his doctrine of God an extended discussion of the divine names that gives his theology a more strongly exegetical and biblical cast than is apparent in Arminius' doctrine of God.[41]

This particular pattern for organizing the divine attributes, moreover, continues in the theology of the famous "Leiden *Synopsis*" or *Synopsis purioris theologiae* written conjointly as a series of disputations by the theological faculty at Leiden and published in 1626. Arminius' language of *momenta* does not appear, but the basic distinction of the attributes into a first genus of essential attributes and a second genus of relational or operational attributes belonging to the divine life provides the locus *de natura Dei* with its basic structure. The *Synopsis*, equally so, divides the *vita Dei* into the basic categories of intellect and will.[42] Unlike Arminius or Gomarus, the *Synopsis* applies the term "incommunicable" to the essential attributes and the term "communicable" to the attributes of the divine life, despite the recognized problem with those terms.[43] If this latter difference needs explanation, it ought probably to be seen as belonging to the solidification of Reformed orthodoxy into standard patterns rather than as a

---

[38] See Dibon, *L'Enseignement philosophique*, pp. 66–67.

[39] Sepp, *Het Godgeleerd*, pp. 108–9; Dibon, *L'Enseignement philosophique*, p. 66.

[40] Gomarus, *Disp. theol.*, III.xxvi–xxviii, xxxix.

[41] Ibid., IV.

[42] *Synopsis purioris*, VI.xxii, xxiv, xxx, xxxii.

[43] Ibid., VI.xxii–xxiii.

polemical rejection of the alternative language found in Junius and Arminius.

Whereas the Reformed writers of the seventeenth century—with notable exceptions, like the semi-Cartesian federalist, Heidanus—tended away from the classification of attributes into those of essence and those of life, the Arminian or Remonstrant writers seem to have gravitated toward the paradigm and, indeed, toward the intellectualist form of the paradigm, where the divine life is understood as consisting in intellect and will, with intellect prior to will.[44] Both Episcopius and Limborch constructed their doctrines of God with close reference to the model presented in Arminius' *Disputationes*. Episcopius even maintains the usage of *natura Dei* as the basic category which must be considered in two ways, insofar as it exists (*ut est*), that is, as essence, and insofar as it lives (*ut vivit*) as the *vita Dei*. In addition, Episcopius not only uses Arminius' term *momentum*, he clearly follows out the interpretation that we have given to the term by identifying the doctrine of divine essence as the rudimentary consideration of God as such (*nuda ac per se*) and the divine life as that which provides the essence with actuosity (*quae essentiam actuosam facit*). The divine essence is, thus, to be understood as the *primum naturae divinae momentum* and the life of God as the *secundum naturae divinae momentum*.[45] Limborch follows the same pattern, with an almost identical definition of the *vita Dei* as the divine essence in its actuosity, although without reference to the term *momentum*.[46] Arminius here again can be identified as the author of a crucial trajectory in Remonstrant theological system. It is worth noting that this pattern of the attributes is nowhere evident in Vorstius' *De Deo*, which moves from the *natura Dei* to the attributes of omnipotence, omniscience, wisdom, will, and dominion, in that order. Vorstius, above all, does not make the basic distinction between essence and life or the further distinction of life into intellect and will.[47]

As a primary characteristic of the divine essence Arminius looks to spirituality. The *Disputationes privatae* do not draw on the biblical text, "God is Spirit" (John 4:24) but rather mount a rational argument from the analogy of the created order:

As the whole nature of things is distributed according to their essence into body and spirit, we affirm that [the divine essence] is spiritual, and from this that God is a spirit, since it is impossible for the first and highest being (*primum & summum Ens*) to be corporeal. From this one

[44] Heidanus, *Corpus theol.*, II (p. 68). Heidanus' language is virtually identical to Episcopius'.

[45] Episcopius, *Inst. theol.*, IV.ii.2, 25 (pp. 280, col. 2; 296, col. 1).

[46] Limborch, *Theologia christiana*, II.vii.1.

[47] Vorstius, *De Deo*, caps. III–VII, especially pp. 22, 29, 222–25, 307.

cannot do otherwise than justly admire the transcendent power and
fullness of God, by which he is able to create even things corporeal that
have nothing analogous to himself.[48]

The argument depends, as most probably would have been made
clear immediately in the classroom disputation, on the assumptions
that the spiritual is superior to the material and that a cause must be
superior to its effect. Indeed, this is precisely the argument found in
the corresponding public disputation: "spiritual ... denotes
perfection" while "corporeal" indicates a privation of or declension
from the perfection of spirit.[49] This spiritual essence is the "first
moment of the divine nature, by which God is understood to be," or
more simply still, "the essence of God is that by which God is."[50]
Episcopius, once again, follows out Arminius' pattern precisely,
beginning his discussion with a rational argument concerning the
relation of spirituality to perfection, materiality to imperfection, but
adding a lengthy elaboration of the thesis, complete with exegetical
argumentation.[51]

The divine essence, in other words, is identical with the divine
existence: the *essentia* or whatness of God is, simply, *esse*, to be. In the
most rudimentary sense—foundational to what later will be said of
the identity of all the divine attributes with the divine essence—it is
not the essence of God to be any particular attribute. Rather it is the
essence of God simply to be. This concept of the identity of essence
and existence in God alone, mediated from Avicenna to the Latin
West by William of Auvergne, became in the philosophy and theology of Thomas Aquinas the cornerstone of the identification of God
as *actus purus* and as utterly simple, in other words, the cornerstone of
the entire doctrine of the essence and attributes of God and of the
conception of God's relation to the created order.[52] In Burrell's words,
"this identification forbids us from considering God's essence in the
line of properties, and invites us to recognize the limits of our own
conceptual powers" at the same time that it "makes a strong plea to
raise one's intellectual vision beyond essences" as they are normally
understood in and from the finite order "to 'pure act.'"[53] Arminius
has not only accepted this line of argument, he has also accepted one
of its basic implications—that the identity of God as *esse*, to be, is the
ground of the created order and of the necessary divine relation to it.
God alone is Being itself and, therefore, God alone can confer being.

[48] *Disp. priv.*, XV.v.

[49] *Disp. pub.*, IV.viii.

[50] Ibid., IV.vii: "Essentia Dei est, qua Deus est, vel primum Naturae divinae
momentum, quo Deus esse intelligitur."

[51] Episcopius, *Inst. theol.*, IV.iii (p. 282, col. 102).

[52] Copleston, *History*, II, pp. 219, 360–62.

[53] Burrell, *Knowing the Unknowable God*, pp. 48–49.

The essence and existence of creatures are really distinct; it does not belong intrinsically to creatures to exist. Rather, their *esse* rests on their participation in God.[54] Or, to put the point somewhat differently, the potency of the Being who is pure act and whose essence it is simply to be is a potency *ad extra* for the being of the created, contingent order.[55] It is this basic Thomistic definition that leads Arminius, as it did Aquinas, to a doctrine of God that is, in its primary structural implication, a paradigm of the emanation of *esse* from the divine and of the interrelatedness of the divine with the created order.[56] The difficulty that Arminius will have, and toward the resolution of which his language obviously strains, is the consistent affirmation of divine actuality and simplicity while at the same time arguing that the emanation of *esse* is a movement grounded in the ultimate identity of essence and existence, the *essentia* and *esse*, of God.

The second "moment" of God, the divine life, is defined as "an act or actuality (*actus*) flowing from the essence (*ab essentia*) of God, by which it is understood to be actualized or have actuosity in itself (*in se actuosa esse*)."[57] Arminius next proceeds to expand this definition in a highly sophisticated argument laden with philosophical considerations as well as profoundly indebted to the older scholasticism:

> We call [life] an act flowing from his essence, since, as our nature conceives of essence and life in the nature of God under distinct forms, and of the former as prior to the latter, we ought not to conceive of life as an actuality approaching the essence as to a unity—which, when added to the unity renders it binary, but as an actuality (*actus*) flowing from the essence in its self-extension toward its own perfection, just as a [mathematical] point by its own flowing moves itself forward in length.[58]

[54] *Disp. priv.*, XV. viii.

[55] Cf. *Disp. priv.*, XV.iv with *Disp. pub.*, IV.v, vii, xxv and *Disp. priv.*, XXV. iii–iv.

[56] Cf. Burrell, *Knowing the Unknowable God*, pp. 28–29, 93–95 with Weisheipl, *Friar Thomas D'Aquino: His Life, Thought, and Work* (Garden City: Doubleday, 1974), p. 230. On Aquinas' doctrine of participation, see L. B. Geiger, *La participation dans la philosophie de S. Thomas d'Aquin* (Paris: J. Vrin, 1942) and Chossat, "Dieu. Sa nature selon les scolastiques," *DTC*. 4/1, cols. 1236–38. Where Chossat labors to argue the continuity of Aquinas' view of participation with earlier, Platonizing approaches to the doctrine, Geiger argues the unique contribution of Aquinas' synthesis of the concept of participation with the themes of his Aristotelian philosophy—a doctrine of participation that avoids extreme realism and the related problem of a natural emanation of being from the One (see Geiger, *La Participation*, pp. 28–35, 45–51, 77–84, 451–56). Arminius' comments clearly partake of the Thomistic approach to the concept.

[57] *Disp. pub.*, IV.xxv: "Vita Dei, quae in secundo momento naturae divinae consideranda venit, est Actus ab essentia Dei fluens, quo illa in se actuosa esse significatur."

[58] Ibid., IV.xxvi: "Actum ab essentia fluentem dicimus: quia quum intellectus noster in natura Dei esentiam & vitam sub formis distinctis concipiat, & illam prius

More simply, essence is God *in actu primo*; life is God—or, indeed, is the divine essence—*in actu secundo*. The divine life is, in other words, the living of the divine essence.[59] Any other view of these basic concepts would imply a twofold or doubled divinity.

The inherent problem in distinguishing primary from secondary actuality in God comes to the fore briefly as Arminius identifies the relation of divine life to things *ad extra*. The *vita Dei* itself can be distinguished into primary and secondary actuality:

> since life is understood either in secondary actuality (*in actu secundo*) and is called activity (*operationem*), or in its primary, principal and fundamental actuality (*in actu primo principali & radicali*) as the very nature and form of a living thing; we attribute the latter, of itself, primarily and adequately to God: so that he is his own life not having it by union with another thing (inasmuch as that is characteristic of imperfection), but having existence that is identical with life: living in primary actuality and bestowing life in his secondary actuality [or operation].[60]

The basic definition of the life of God *in actu primo* and *in actu secundo* is taken virtually verbatim from Suárez.[61] The Reformed, for the reasons noted above, either ignore or deny this distinction—noting that in human beings, life is the *actus secundus* of the nature or essence, while in God, who is entirely simple, life is God's *ipsissima essentia*.[62]

"The life of God is, therefore, most simple, inasmuch as it is not distinguished as a thing (*ut re*) from the essence."[63] The distinction is made only for the sake of human comprehension of the relation of God to created life as a relation that flows forth from the very Being of God. God's life, then "may in some way be described as an actuality flowing from the essence of God, by which it is understood to be actualized in itself: first by a reflexive action (*actione reflexa*) in God himself, and then on other objects, on account of the most abundant copiousness and the most perfect activity of life in God."[64] In

---

hac: cavendum ne haec ut actus ad illam accedens concipiatur, unitatis instar quae unitati addita facit binarium: sed ut actus ab illa fluens promovente se ad sui perfectionem, quemadmodum punctus suo fluxu se promovet in longitudinem."

[59] Ibid., IV.xxvii.

[60] *Disp. priv.*, XVI.ii: "vita sumatur aut in actu secundo, et sic dicit operationem; aut in actu primo principali et radicali, et sic est ipsa natura et forma rei viventis."

[61] *Disp. metaph.* XXX, sec. xiv.6: "Vita enim aut sumitur in actu secundo, et sic dicit operationem, aut in actu primo principali et radicali, et sic est ipsa natura seu substantia rei viventis."

[62] *RD*, p. 69.

[63] *Disp. priv.*, XVI.iii.

[64] Ibid.

addition, because of its abundance and perfection both *ad intra* and *ad extra*, the *vita Dei* must be understood as the goal of all things, worthy of being loved in and of itself, the *fruitio* or enjoyment "by which God is said to be blessed in himself."[65]

This emphasis, too, carries over strongly into the theology of Episcopius, who identifies the life of God as "the foundation of all ultimate enjoyment and the ground of all activity" (i.e., the foundation of the love of God for himself as the highest goal of all things and of the movement of God's will *extra se*) so that the *vita Dei*, "mediated by the divine *potentia*, is the cause of all things."[66] In both cases, the divine life is understood as the activity in and flowing forth from God that establishes the relationship between God and all things.

The strong emphasis on absolute divine transcendence evident both in Arminius' conception of divine unity and his conception of divine goodness—the denials of immanence and communicability of essence and essential attributes—is counterbalanced by Arminius' emphasis on the divine life and its attributes of understanding, will, and power as movements or extensions of God toward finite objects. Indeed, this counterbalancing of incommunicable, negatively conceived, and nonrelational divine essence with the creative self-extension, toward the world order, of the divine life and its operations most probably holds the key to Arminius' unique argument for essence and life as two *momenta* of the divine nature and for the divine life itself as distinguishable into two *actus*. It is the divine life that is, for Arminius, the ground of all relations *ad extra*.

This fundamental language of essence or being and life provides Arminius with the formal pattern for the arrangement of the attributes in his system once they are enunciated either affirmatively or negatively. Thus, a series of attributes, including simplicity, infinity, eternity, and most of the attributes identified either as negative or, in the typical Reformed systems, as incommunicable, are deduced from the concept of divine essence or being—and a second series, including principally knowledge, will, and power, attributes identified frequently as positive or communicable, is derived from the concept of divine life. The logic of both series demonstrates a high level of argument in Arminius' systematic efforts and places him quite clearly at the forefront of the scholastic development of Protestantism in his day. The two series of attributes appear as more closely argued than the corresponding sections either of Gomarus' *Disputationes* or Trelcatius' brief *Institutio*.[67]

[65] Ibid., XVI.iv.

[66] Episcopius, *Inst. theol.*, IV.ii.25 (p. 296, col. 2).

[67] Cf. Gomarus, *Disputationes*, III–IV and Trelcatius, *Scholastica et methodica locorum communium institutio*, I.iii. 152. *Disp. pub.*, IV.ix, citing Isa. 43:10; 44:8, 24; 46:9; Rev. 1:8; Rom. 9:35–36; 1 Cor. 8:4–6; Rom. 9:5.

Whereas the first argument, in which Arminius identifies being and life as the two fundamental movements or actualities of the divine nature, is a positive argument according to the *via eminentiae*, the second argument, in which he moves to develop the series of essential attributes, is a negative one that assumes, initially, the removal of corporeality and its attendant liabilities from the concept of God together with the removal of the limitations of all lower forms of spiritual existence.

> As we ought to enunciate negatively the mode by which the essence of God pre-eminently both is and is spiritual, above the excellence of all essences, even those which are spiritual; so this may be done first and immediately in a single phrase: he is *anarchos kai anaitios*, without beginning and without cause (*principii & causae expers*) either internal or external.[68]

This negative logic, removing beginning and cause from God, corresponds, moreover, to the causal and analogical direction of the proofs:

> For since there cannot be any *progressus in infinitum* (for if there could, there would be no essence and no knowledge), there must be one existence (*esse*), above and before which no other can exist. Such must, necessarily be the *esse* of God: truly, whatever receives this attribution must be God himself.[69]

The ultimate, uncaused nature of the divine essence leads directly to the identification of God as simple and infinite. In other words, in Arminius' thought, as in the thought of the medieval scholastics and his Protestant scholastic contemporaries, simplicity and infinity are necessary correlates of the absolute preeminence and perfection of God as the uncaused cause of all things.[70] Simplicity is not so much an attribute of God as a characterization of "God's ontological constitution" that follows directly from the fact that God is utterly without beginning or cause, inasmuch as it indicates that God is "devoid of all composition, and of component parts, whether sensible (*sensibilium*) or intelligible (*intelligibilium*)"; absence of composition indicates absence of "external cause"; absence of component parts indicates absence of "internal cause."[71]

> The essence of God therefore neither consists of material, integral and quantitative parts, of matter and form, of genus and differentia, of subject and accident, or of form and thing formed.... Whatever is abso-

[68] *Disp. pub.*, IV.ix.
[69] Ibid.
[70] *Disp. pub.*, IV.x; cf. Aquinas, *Summa*, Ia, q.3, art.8.
[71] *Disp. pub.*, IV.xi; cf. Burrell, *Knowing the Unknowable God*, p. 46 on simplicity as the characterization of "God's ontological constitution" rather than a predicate in the usual sense.

lutely predicated of God is understood essentially and not accidentally; and those things (whether many or diverse) that are predicated of God are, in God, not many but one.[72]

In the simplicity of the divine essence, therefore, the divine attributes are identical with the divine essence and are essentially identical with one another. We are thrown back, by this doctrine, on the problem of predication. It is in fact the notion of divine simplicity, understood as the bulwark of divine ultimacy and preeminence, that actually forces the problem of predication in the first place. Although Arminius states the concept of simplicity as a conclusion after ruling out the applicability to God of the three basic patterns for distinguishing attributes or predicates from a substance,[73] we now see that simplicity is a governing concept that controls the basic language of the predication of attributes. Thus, a real distinction between attributes and essence—viewing them as distinct from one another as one thing from another thing—would indicate composition in God, which is unacceptable. Nor can the attributes be distinct as subsistent relations in the divine essence. Such a view would impinge on the domain of trinitarian definitions. And if the distinction of attributes is only "a mere conception of mind" with no relation to the reality of God,[74] it becomes a worthless conundrum.

This problem was certainly not new in the late sixteenth century. It was, however, relatively new to Protestantism. Not a hint of the problem of predication can be found in the dogmatic works of Calvin, Bullinger, Musculus, or Vermigli.[75] Nor did Ursinus, Zanchi, or Daneau dwell on the issue at any length. When the problem arose in the exposition of extended Protestant dogmatic system in the late sixteenth and early seventeenth centuries, Arminius and his contemporaries were pressed to examine the medieval scholastic language of the divine attributes and their distinction as found in the writings of the scholastics themselves and, indeed, in more recent Roman Catholic works, like Suárez' *Disputationes metaphysicae*.

Following this traditional scholastic argumentation, Arminius draws a way of understanding the distinction and predication of attributes out of the language of divine simplicity. For although they are essentially one and identical, they are indeed "distinguished" as being "many and diverse" not, of course, *essentialiter* or *realiter*, but "in our mode of considering them which is composite."[76] The human way of

[72] *Disp. pub.*, IV.xi.
[73] *Disp. priv.*, XV.vi.
[74] Ibid.
[75] Cf. Calvin, *Inst.*, I.xiii.1; Bullinger, *Compendium*, iii; Musculus, *Loci communes*, i, xli–xlii; Vermigli, *Loci communes*, I.xii.2.
[76] *Disp. pub.*, IV.xi: "nostro tantum considerationis modo, qui compositus est."

understanding things is by composition: the human mind understands what a thing is by compiling a list of its properties and understanding it as compounded of those properties. Even so, the human mind seeks to understand God by compiling a list of divine attributes. The question immediately arises whether this understanding is a "mere conception of mind"—a product of reason reasoning (*ratio ratiocinans*) in a vacuum. Arminius must move past the problem: attributes may not be essentially distinct in God, but our distinction of attributes, based on both reason and revelation, must give genuine insight into the reality of God. Our consideration of attributes under the rule of divine simplicity is, Arminius concludes, "not inappropriate" inasmuch as the attributes "are indeed distinguished by a formal reason."[77]

The answer is not set out at length: Arminius mentions the formal distinction of attributes, does not attempt to explain the term, certainly not to point out its history, and then passes on to his next topic. Yet he has made a major doctrinal decision and has exchanged his Thomistic accent for a Scotist one. The so-called formal distinction, *distinctio formalis a parte rei*, indicates a distinction among aspects or forms in and of a thing. Such aspects or forms are not distinct from the thing itself but are essentially identical to it—but they are objectively distinct from one another, again, not essentially as things from other things, but as "different, but not separable formalities of one and the same object."[78] Thomists rejected the idea of a formal distinction, arguing it to be nothing more or less than a poorly defined rational distinction. The Reformed of the seventeenth century rejected it also, tending to lodge the distinction of attributes not in God but in the working of God *ad extra*, in his self-revelation.[79] The formal distinction of perfections in God was noted, in the late sixteenth century, by Suárez in order to distinguish the attributes individually and, at the same time declare their identity with the divine essence.[80]

Once again, it is significant that Arminius, in his modification of an essentially Thomistic position, has moved in the direction taken by Suárez. And although Suárez had preferred the term "modal" to "formal" in his definition of the distinction, Arminius' usage and fundamental philosophical motivation parallel Suárez closely. Suárez had recognized that neither the original arguments of Aristotle nor the reasonings of Aquinas had led to the notion of a "formal

---

[77] Ibid.

[78] Cf. the discussion in Copleston, *History*, II, pp. 508–13, 529.

[79] Cf. Burmann, *Synopsis theol.*, III.xix.11. The distinction of attributes *in* God is, therefore, by reason of analysis (*ratio ratiocinata*) and not a real or formal distinction that would imply division in the Godhead: see *RD*, pp. 59–60.

[80] Suárez, *Disp. metaph.*, XXX.vi.3, 19.

distinction" but also that neither Aristotle nor Aquinas had addressed the issue singled out by Scotus.[81] "Whatever extends beyond the essential definition of a thing," Suárez argued, "is in some sense really distinct from it; but many elements extend beyond the essence of a thing without being themselves things distinct from the thing in question; therefore it is a distinction in the real order that is less than a real distinction."[82] Arminius' entire exposition of the attributes— including the basic identification of two *momenta* of the divine essence—points toward an insistence on distinctions existing or sub- sisting in reality, "in the real order," in God that indicate the order and flow of the divine life and activity without disrupting the essen- tial simplicity of God.

From the identity of the divine essence as uncaused cause, Armin- ius also deduces the divine infinity. Of course, he believes this doctrine, like the preceding two attributions, to be fully biblical. God is "devoid of all limitation and boundary" as Psalm 145:3 and Isaiah 43:10 testify. The primary issue, however, is the relation of the divine boundlessness to the uncaused nature of God. Thus, the infinite essence of God

is devoid of all limitation and boundary, whether above or below, before or after: not above, since he receives his existence (*esse*) from no one; nor below, since [his] self-identical form is not limited to the capacity of any material substance (*materiae*) that might receive it; nor before, since it is from no efficient [cause]; nor after, since it does not exist for the sake of an end other [than itself].[83]

Of course, the divine essence has limits of a sort—as Arminius argues, at length, in his discussions of the divine will and power—but these are limits set by the nature of the divine Being itself. Thus Arminius can say, briefly, that God's "essence is terminated inwardly by its own property, according to which it is what it is and nothing else."[84] Thus God cannot be less than good, cannot cease to live, can- not become complex or compound, cannot be other than Father, Son, and Spirit. God is and must be God. Nevertheless, such limitation does not threaten the concept of divine infinity; rather, it defines and reinforces the concept.[85]

The other attributes commonly identified as incommunicable or negative are, in fact, according to Arminius, conclusions about the

---

[81] Suárez, *Disp. metaph.*, VII.13–14; cf. the translation, Francis Suárez, *On the Various Kinds of Distinctions*, trans. with an intro. by Cyril Vollert (Milwaukee: Marquette University Press, 1947), pp. 24–26.

[82] Ibid., VII.15; trans. Vollert, p. 26.

[83] *Disp. pub.*, IV.xii.

[84] *Disp. pub.*, IV.xii.

[85] *Disp. pub.*, IV.xii.

divine essence that follow logically from the doctrines of divine simplicity and infinity:

> From the simplicity and infinity of the divine essence arise infinity
> with regard to *time*, which is called eternity; and with regard to *place*,
> which is called immensity.[86]

The remaining attributes of impassibility, immutability, and incorruptibility are appended to Arminius' thesis immediately following immensity, but the logic of their derivation is not argued directly. It is clear, however, from the subsequent discussion, that these three attributes look back to the problem of causality: for God truly to be uncaused, God must be impassible, immutable, and incorruptible.[87] Here again, as in the initial choice to adopt a classification of the attributes into perfections of eminence and perfections by way of negation, we see a Scotist or even nominalist tendency in Arminius' thought. Whereas Thomists of the late Middle Ages and sixteenth century, like Capreolus and Bañez, had chosen *aseitas* as the primary divine attribute, the Scotists had typically pointed to the infinity of God as the ground of the divine possession of all perfections.[88] Nominalist theologians, typically, grounded their doctrine of the *nomina Dei* in the divine simplicity.[89]

The derivation of eternity from simplicity and infinity and its definition as "infinity with regard to time," therefore, points us once again toward the multiple roots and the eclectic character of Arminius' scholasticism. The problem of this derivation, as Aquinas had implied in his discussion of eternity, is the qualitative difference between eternity and an infinite lapse of time. The point is important and it will come back to haunt Arminius in his discussion of creation. The eternity of divine duration is, indeed, governed by divine simplicity and unity inasmuch as the divine eternity is not only free from the limitation of endings and beginnings but also free from the limitation of succession, that is, of temporal sequence as well as logical sequence. If the world were "eternal" in the sense of being infinite in duration, it would lack beginning and end, but it would not experience the simultaneous existence of all finite beings. It would still be in time.[90] Aquinas therefore states that "eternity is the measure of a permanent being; while time is the measure of movement ... eternity is simultaneously whole, but ... time is not so."[91]

[86] *Disp. pub.*, IV.xii.
[87] Cf. ibid., ad fin with ibid., IV.xvii–xviii.
[88] Toussaint, "Attributs divins," *DTC* 1/2, col. 2229.
[89] Vignaux, "Nominalisme," *DTC* 11/1, cols. 755–56.
[90] See Wippel, *Metaphysical Thought of Godfrey of Fontaines*, p. 164.
[91] Aquinas, *Summa*, Ia, q.10, art.4, corpus.

Aquinas, accordingly, does not derive eternity from infinity but rather from immutability: "the idea of eternity follows immutability, as the idea of time follows movement."[92] Infinity of time, which indicates an infinity of movement, is quite antithetical to the divine eternity—and, of course, as Augustine had long before established, time is of its very nature mutation—so that there is logical coordination of eternity with an absence of movement.[93] Suárez, however, departs from Aquinas on precisely this point and provides some precedent for Arminius' views: he parallels eternity to immensity, defining the former as infinitely exceeding all time and the latter as infinitely exceeding all place—so that God may be understood as existing before "real time" in all "imaginary time" at least for the sake of declaring the character of the divine infinity. Equally so, God is infinite—that is, immense—with regard both to actual and to imaginary space.[94] Suárez does, however, recognize the need to distinguish between the divine eternity and the infinite duration of spiritually mutable creatures such as angels. He returns, therefore, to the point that the infinite divine duration is utterly free of succession in its perfect immutability.[95]

These considerations do, in fact, appear in Arminius' definition. Since God's Being is infinite, it has no beginning or end—and since his Being is utterly simple, never in potency, always in actuality, it experiences no motion or succession.[96]

> According to this [mode], therefore, the essence of God is always universal, the whole, the fullness of his essence, without separation (*indistanter*), fixedly, and at every instant present with the essence, resembling a point in time devoid of intelligible parts and not flowing forth but ever remaining in itself.[97]

Eternity, then, is the correlate of the divine infinitude with regard to the limitation of time or duration: God is recognized as eternal by the negation or removal of the concept of temporality from our view of the divine Being. Arminius specifically identifies eternity as an infinitude of being without beginning or end, without succession or movement from past to future—and above all, a perfection of being such that God is always fully actualized and not in motion from potency to act.[98] The latter point draws directly on the basic identification of the nature of God as consisting in the two *momenta*, being and

---

[92] Ibid., Ia, q.10, art.2, corpus.
[93] Augustine, *Confessions*, XI.30–31.
[94] Suárez, *Disp. metaph.*, XXX.vii.38.
[95] Ibid., XXX.viii–ix; cf. Mahieu, *François Suárez*, p. 214.
[96] Suárez, *Disp. metaph.*, XXX.vii.38.
[97] *Disp. pub.*, IV.xiv.
[98] Ibid.

life: God is not a being who comes to life but the Being who is life and the life that is, existing always in utter simplicity. As implied previously, these arguments point toward Scotist and even nominalist antecedents—or, at least, toward modifications in the Thomist model inspired by debate and dialogue with the Scotist and nominalist positions. Once again, Arminius needed to look no farther than Suárez for a summary of these views or, indeed, in the case of the derivation of eternity from infinity, to the thought of several Reformed writers of his generation.[99]

Arminius draws upon and modifies the Boethian definition of eternity that had so influenced the medieval scholastic conception of God. Boethius had defined eternity as "the simultaneous and perfect possession of endless life"; Arminius offers as a modified definition, "endless, complete and simultaneous perfect possession of essence."[100] The modification is just, Arminius argues, because essence comes to be considered in the first movement of the divine nature, before life; and because eternity does not belong to essence through life, but to life through essence.[101] The primary, not the secondary or operative, divine actuality now provides the basis for definition of the divine attributes. The problem in Boethius' definition, the limitation of the term *vita* in its accustomed usage, was noted by the medieval doctors. Scotus, for example, accepts the definition when *vita* is understood as "actualized, perfect existence."[102] The same problem had been noted by Aquinas in his second objection to the Boethian definition:

> eternity signifies a certain kind of duration. But duration regards existence rather than *life*. Therefore the word life ought not to come into the definition of eternity; but rather the word *existence*.[103]

Aquinas nonetheless retains the word *vita* in his definition—significantly, for much the same reason that Arminius rejects it: "what is truly eternal, is not only being, but also living; and life extends to operation, which is not true of being."[104] Arminius' deduction of eternity from infinity rather than from immutability had important implications for later Arminian theology, where the notion of eternity as "duration without beginning or end" and as not necessarily

[99] Cf. Polanus as cited in *RD*, p. 65 with Suárez, *Disp. metaph.*, XXX.xiv. 1–16 and note how immutability and eternity are coordinate inferences from infinity in ibid., XXX.viii.1, 10; ix.55.

[100] *Disp. pub.*, IV.xiv.

[101] Ibid.

[102] Cf. Minges, II, p. 83.

[103] Aquinas, *Summa*, Ia, q.10, art.1, obj.2.

[104] Ibid., Ia, q.10, art.1, ad obj.2.

contrary to a succession of moments was elaborated by both Episcopius and Limborch, with considerable impact on their view of the relationship of God to the world.[105] Indeed, if as Episcopius argued, the reality of past, present, and future depends on the acknowledgment of the changeless duration of God and, therefore, of the reality of succession to God extrinsically considered,[106] then a way is opened to argue not only the relation but also the interrelation of God with the world and, perhaps, even of a certain temporal determinedness of the divine.[107]

Arminius' concept of divine eternity has direct implications for his language of the attributes in general:

> Whatever [properties] are predicated absolutely of God, belong to him from all eternity and all together; it is certain that those things which do not belong to him from all eternity, are predicated of him not absolutely, but by relation to creatures, such as Creator, Ruler and Judge of all things.[108]

The divine perfections, therefore, belong to God absolutely and eternally—and any term predicated of God from a temporal perspective and in a relative sense does not belong to the essential attributes of God. In other words, the essential attributes of God must respect the divine eternity as a governing concept or heuristic principle inasmuch as God must be conceived of as possessing his essential attributes prior to and apart from the act of creation in which both world and time came into existence.

These two kinds of attribution, the absolute and the relative, as identified by the concept of divine eternity, lead Arminius to his discussion of immensity (*immensitas*) and omnipresence (*omnipraesentia*).

> Immensity is a pre-eminent mode of the essence of God, by which it is void of place according to space and limits ... from this immensity follows ... the omnipresence or ubiquity of the essence of God, according to which it is entirely wherever any creature or any place is.[109]

Immensity, like eternity, was derived from the infinity of God,[110] but

---

[105] Episcopius, *Inst. theol.*, IV.ii.9 (pp. 287, cols. 2–289, col. 1) and Limborch, *Theologia christiana*, II.v.i, v.

[106] Episcopius, *Inst. theol.*, IV.ii.9 (p. 288, col. 1).

[107] Note that this was precisely the critique leveled by the Reformed against the Arminians and Vorstius and by Thomists against Molina and Suárez for their advocacy of the *scientia media*: see *RD*, pp. 65, 79–81; Garrigou-Lagrange, "Thomisme," *DTC* 15/1, col. 870.

[108] *Disp. pub.*, III.xiv.

[109] Ibid., IV.xv–xvi.

[110] Ibid., IV.xiii.

is placed second by Arminius in view of its temporal corollary—a corollary defined not only by the relation of God to created space but also by the temporal character of created space. Space, in other words, is not viewed by the scholastic mind as eternal: rather it is a predicate of material substances which, by definition, have a beginning in time. Eternity, therefore, governs the language of immensity: only in relation to time may God be called omnipresent. We are once again thrown back on Scotist antecedents: Aquinas discussed omnipresence prior to eternity and did not raise the distinction between immensity and omnipresence.[111] Scotus, by way of critique, had argued that previous definitions of omnipresence rested on an unacceptable analogy between God and creatures and that the divine presence ought to be defined primarily in terms of the immutability and ultimacy of God prior to any activity or relation to creatures. This modification of definition, like the others we have noted, could have been mediated to Arminius by Suárez.[112]

Just as it is conceived of as devoid of time and space, the divine essence is also regarded as impassible, that is, as "devoid of all suffering," not in the sense that God is without relation to the created order or without affections of will like love and mercy that are somehow remotely analogous to human emotions, but rather in the sense that "nothing can act against" God and that God "cannot receive the action of any thing."[113] God is, as already recognized, uncaused and simple. Only a being that has been or can be caused—is or can be an effect—can be acted against; and only a being that is composite or potentially composite can "receive an act" from without and have an attribute or part added thereby to its essence. Therefore, God must also be recognized as immutable or devoid of change. Since God is uncaused and beyond the power of all creaturely causes, God cannot be subject to alteration, to generation or corruption, to increase or to decrease. Since God is immense and omnipresent, and since also God is his own eternally actualized goal and good, he is not subject to movement from place to place or from one condition to another.[114] Similarly, God is incorruptible inasmuch as he is not subject to motion from potency to actuality: "it belongs to God, and to him alone, to be quiescent (*quietum*) in operation."[115]

The last two essential attributes in Arminius' derivation are unity and goodness, respectively. Their placement at the end of the order, at least in the case of unity, may reflect Aquinas—while the language,

---

[111] I.e., Aquinas, *Summa*, Ia, pp.8 (omnipresence) and 10 (eternity).

[112] Scotus, *I sent.*, I, d.37; II, d.2, q.5; cf. Suárez, *De Deo*, I.ii.2 and *Disp. metaph.*, XXX.vii; Mahieu, *François Suárez*, pp. 211–14.

[113] *Disp. pub.*, IV.xvii.

[114] Ibid., IV.xviii.

[115] Ibid.

if not the placement, of Arminius' doctrine of the divine goodness also appears to have strong affinities with Aquinas.[116] Specifically, Aquinas expresses the identity of being and goodness with the qualification that although "a thing is good so far as it is being," good nonetheless "presents the aspect of desirableness, which being does not present."[117] The good, therefore, represents the affective aspect of being—it is the reason that being is the proper object of knowing and willing. Indeed, it appears to be this Thomistic definition of goodness that leads Arminius to discuss it last in order, together with the divine unity, prior to his discussion of the attributes of divine life, intellect, and will. The oneness and the goodness of God define and qualify the language about God's knowledge and will.

Arminius defines unity and goodness as "general affections of being" and therefore appends discussion of the divine unity and goodness to his discussion of the essential attributes. These "affections of being" must, of course, be understood in terms of "the mode of pre-eminence, according to the rule of the simplicity and infinity of [the divine] essence."[118] By unity we understand that God is undivided and "altogether indivisible with regard to number, species, genus, parts, modes, etc." Even so, God's essence is divided from things and incapable of "entering into composition with any other thing."[119] Despite some of our previous observations about order and derivation, the definition accords well with the definitions in Aquinas' *Summa*, where the derivation of divine unity from simplicity and infinity manifests a point of contact with later Scotist and nominalist teaching.[120] Indeed, it may well be this point of contact that permitted Arminius to draw out his doctrine of the essential attributes in terms of the critical insights of late medieval Scotist and nominalist teaching while at the same time retaining the Thomistic and intellectualistic premises of his doctrine of God and God's relation to the world.

(In an exegetical shift reminiscent of the doctrine of the Reformers, Arminius declares that the language of divine unity is implied in the biblical language of divine holiness. God, as holy, is set apart and "divided from all others." Since God is one and set apart, it follows that "God is neither the soul of the world, nor the form of the universe; neither an inhering form [*forma inhaerens*] nor a bodily one."[121] In other words, Arminius expresses a radical opposition to all

---

[116] Cf. Aquinas, *Summa*, Ia, pp.6 and 11.

[117] Ibid., Ia, q.5, art.1, corpus.

[118] *Disp. pub.*, IV.xx.

[119] Ibid., IV.xxii.

[120] Cf. Aquinas, *Summa*, Ia, q.11, art.3, corpus.

[121] *Disp. pub.*, IV.xxii.

notions of divine immanence in favor not only of a philosophical
concept of transcendence but also of a religious concept of otherness.
His point stands, however, in relative isolation from the general
direction of his argument which had drawn little upon exegesis and
much on the traditional discussion of divine attributes. The point is
also rather different from that made by the Reformed orthodox, who
tend to define holiness as a moral attribute associated with God's
righteousness and absolute perfection.[122])

Although Arminius' initial discussion of the divine goodness as an
essential attribute is comparatively brief, it provides the foundation
for virtually all that Arminius says about the relation of the divine
intellect and will and about the relation of God, as knowing and willing, to the created order. Here, too, his Thomistic inclinations are
apparent. Indeed, the intellectualistic presuppositions of his teaching
inherited from Aquinas are probably the reason that Arminius
departed from Aquinas' own prior placement of divine goodness last
among the essential attributes as the chief object and, therefore, the
immediate, governing category prior to his discussion of the divine
intellect and will. Arminius' definition does, in fact, point in two
directions—back toward the initial language about the divine essence
and forward toward subsequent discussion of the relationship of God
to finite things:

> The goodness of the divine essence is that according to which it is,
> essentially in itself, the supreme and true Good; from a participation
> in which all other things exist and are good; and to which all other
> things are to be referred as to their supreme end. For this reason it is
> called communicable.[123]

The basic definitions are clearly reminiscent of Aquinas. It is characteristic of Aquinas' thought to understand goodness as identical with
being and as self-diffusive or communicable in two ways: in the first
place all things have their being and goodness "by participation,"
having received it from God; in the second place, this communication of goodness is a matter of final, not of first efficient causality. The
goal of creation is the communication of goodness *ad extra*, to finite
things, for the sake of the ultimate manifestation of God's goodness.[124] This is precisely Arminius' point.

[122] *RD*, pp. 92–96.

[123] *Disp. pub.*, IV.xxiii, citing Matt. 19:17; James 1:17; I Cor. 10:31 in margin:
"Bonitas essentiae Dei & secundum quam ipsa summum & ipsum bonum est,
essentialiter in se ipsa, ex cuius participatione omnia alia sunt, & bona sunt: & ad
quam omnia alia tanquam ad summum finem sunt referenda. Hac ratione dicitur
communicabilis."

[124] Cf. Aquinas, *SCG*, I.40.3: "Deus est bonus per essentiam, omnia vero alia per
participationem" with ibid., II.15.5: "Deus autem est ens per essentiam suam: quia

The priority of essence and therefore of the essential attributes over life leads to the use of the essential attributes as governing concepts that determine the meaning of the life of God and of all the attributes belonging to it. The attributes of the primary movement or actuality of the divine nature are, thus, to be used to interpret the attributes of the secondary movement or actuality of the divine nature.[125] Thus, the life of God is infinite, simple, eternal, and immutable—and so also the understanding, will, and power of God.[126] Even so, the attribution of affections like love, hate, grace, goodness, righteousness, patience, and so forth must oblige the basic definition of simplicity, eternity, and immutability of essence.[127] It is worth noting that the question of an ordering of attributes arose in the later development of medieval scholasticism and that the specific issue of "primary attributes" as interpretive of the order belongs to the fifteenth century.[128]

The logic of Arminius' exposition of the essential attributes is strongly reminiscent of Aquinas in its underlying assumptions that the articles of faith will not be unreasonable and that reason, in its right exercise, can be eminently faithful. Certain elements, however, such as the interest in ordering the attributes and in distinguishing primary from secondary attributes, presuppose theological developments in later medieval scholasticism and, indeed, developments as are found, in Arminius' own time, in Suárezian metaphysics. Arminius seems, moreover, to move farther than Aquinas toward a rationalist theology: in the first place, the emphasis on the causal, affirmative path and the logic of preeminence grants more power to the positive efforts of reason than does Aquinas' insistence on reason's ability to infer only "what God is not"; and in the second place, Arminius manifests a far greater interest than Aquinas in deducing all of the essential attributes from a set of primary inferences about the divine essence. Indeed, although Aquinas considers understanding or knowledge a characteristic of living beings, he does not attempt to subsume the *scientia* or *intellectus Dei* under the *vita Dei*—rather he presents the life of God after he argues the knowledge of God,[129] and makes no attempt at a deductive presentation of the attributes.

---

ipsum esse. Omne autem aliud ens est ens per participationem" and cf. *Summa*, Ia, q.44, art.4; q.65, art. 2; q.5, art.4; and q.6, art.4 with and *Compendium theologiae*, I. 109, Copleston, *History*, II, pp. 365–66 and Patterson, *Conception of God*, pp. 261–64.

[125] *Disp. pub.*, IV.xxiv.

[126] Ibid., IV.xxvii, xxxiii–xxxiv, li–lii, lxxxiii.

[127] Ibid., IV.lxxiii.

[128] Cf. Toussaint, "Attributs divins," *DTC* 1/2, col. 2228.

[129] Cf. Aquinas, *Summa*, Ia, q.14 (knowledge) with q.18 (life).

PART 4

The Divine Knowledge and Will

9

The Divine Knowledge

Faculty psychology, with its characteristic distinction of spiritual life into the faculties of intellect and will, or, more precisely, of the soul into four faculties—intellect, will, sensitive power, and vegetative power—had its roots in Aristotle and became, in the thirteenth-century development of a Christian Aristotelianism, the dominant view of spiritual or rational existence.[1] This model, which was so useful in describing the characteristics of created life, was equally useful in presenting the characteristics of purely spiritual being. The vegetative and sensitive powers, as related to the physical order, could be set aside, leaving intellect and will as the characteristics or faculties of spiritual being. Inasmuch as this model continued to be viewed as correct throughout the era of the Reformation,[2] it is not at all surprising that Protestant theologians in the era of early orthodoxy, including Arminius, developed it once again in considerable speculative depth and returned to the scholastic question of the relationship of intellect and will in their doctrine of God.

In passing from his discussion of the essential attributes and the divine life to his discussion of the understanding, will, and power of God, Arminius presents a basic definition that he will develop at considerable length in three major divisions of his discussion:[3]

> the life of God is actualized (*actuosa*) in three faculties: in understanding (*intellectu*), will (*voluntate*) and power (*potentia*) properly so called; in intellect or understanding inwardly considering its object ...; in the will inwardly willing its first, highest, and proper object, and extrinsically the rest; in power operating only extrinsically, which is

[1] Cf. Copleston, *History of Philosophy*, I, pp. 328–29; II, pp. 289, 376–83, 538–41; III, p. 100.

[2] Cf. Calvin, *Inst.*, I.xv.6–7.

[3] Cf. *Disp. pub.*, IV. (1) xxx–xlvi; (2) xlvii–lxxvii; (3) lxxvii–lxxxvi with *Disp. priv.*, XVII, XVIII–XXI, XXII.

the reason for its being termed *potentia*, inasmuch as it is capable of working in all its objects prior to an object's own act.[4]

The faculties and operations of the *vita Dei*, therefore, are arranged in terms of the relationship of God to himself and to all things *ad extra*. The *intellectus Dei*, as the highest faculty, stands behind and regulates both *voluntas* and *potentia* and remains always an *ad intra* operation, knowing externals but not issuing forth to address things *ad extra*. The will, operating below the intellect, wills first and foremost the ultimate divine good known to the *intellectus Dei* and wills secondarily all other goods. The *potentia Dei* operates below the will to bring about the existence of things *ad extra*—so that the will operates both *ad intra* and *ad extra*, while the power of God is exerted *ad extra* only. God, after all, is fully actualized—not in potency—and, therefore, cannot exercise *potentia* inwardly. The way in which the *potentia Dei* operates, moreover, is to bestow on objects the potential or potency for their own being, so that it logically precedes the acts or operations of its objects. This basic pattern of operation of the divine faculties provides the foundation for everything that follows in Arminius' doctrines of God, creation, and providence, both the order of divine operation and the concurrence of God with the independent activity of creatures.

By formulating his definition in this manner—referring the divine knowing entirely to intellect or understanding—Arminius omits a category of knowing that was of fundamental importance to his Reformed contemporaries: the wisdom of God or *sapientia Dei*. Knowledge (*scientia*) and understanding (*intellectus, intelligentia*) are referred to as knowledge of causes and effects and knowledge of first principles, respectively. Scholastic usage typically reserves *sapientia*, wisdom, for the knowledge of purposes and goals. The omission of a discussion of *sapientia* from the doctrine of divine attributes is curious in view of Arminius' clearly enunciated practical, analytical, or resolvative model according to which the whole system is ordered toward its end—and also in view of Arminius' reliance on the concept of divine wisdom in his subsequent discussion of creation and providence. *Sapientia*, had it been given a formal place in Arminius' doctrine of God, would most certainly have been placed with *scientia* under the larger category of the *intellectus Dei*. Indeed, Arminius' discussion of the kinds of knowledge belonging to the divine intellect does contain hints of the concept of divine *sapientia*.

The length and detail of these discussions, particularly of the discussions of the divine understanding and will, are surely an indication of their importance to Arminius' fundamental assumptions concerning the shape of theological system as a whole. A similar em-

---

[4] *Disp. pub.*, IV.xxix.

phasis on the problem of the divine will in the thought of Beza and Zanchi has been noted as characteristic of their increasing reliance on patterns of scholastic argumentation and as evidence of the increasingly logical and rational approach to theology found in the era of early orthodoxy.[5] Rather than understanding this interest in the *voluntas Dei* and the distinctions among various aspects of divine willing as a purely speculative or deterministic development in Reformed Protestantism, we ought to view it as a renewed reflection on the heritage of the topic and on the importance of its right statement to the whole of theology, whether the system or theologian in question follows a doctrine of strict predestinarianism or not. Once again we must refer, therefore, to the writings of the medieval doctors, where the concept of *voluntas Dei* in its relation to the divine understanding and goodness and in relation to the freedom and contingency of the created order was a topic of intense discussion, particularly in the case of thinkers like Scotus and Occam, who can hardly be classed as determinists. The substantive relationship of Arminius' thought both to the teaching of Zanchi and Beza and to that of Scotus and Occam, his balancing of themes and issues from the newer and from the older scholasticism, is evidence of his extended knowledge of these sources despite the absence of direct citation.

Arminius' intellectualism is evident from the first in his definition of the *scientia Dei* as the faculty of the divine life that is "first in nature and in order."[6] The divine will, in other words, as "the second faculty" of the divine life, is not merely placed second in order for the sake of discussion: it is placed second because it "follows the divine intellect and is *produced from it.*"[7] It is, thus, by the divine will that God is inwardly directed (*fertur*) "toward a *known* good."[8] (Nor is Arminius' intellectualism confined to his doctrine of God: he assumes the priority of the intellect over the will in human beings also, both in their primitive condition before the fall and in their fallen condition as well.[9] This latter point stands in contrast to the Reformed who, following Calvin, were typically philosophical intellectualists and soteriological voluntarists, who placed the will over the intellect in the fallen nature of man.[10] The point also, significantly, stands in some contrast with Aquinas' teaching—insofar as it represents a more thoroughgoing intellectualism, indeed, an intellectualism tinged with rationalism. Aquinas had assumed that the

---

[5] Cf. Brian Armstrong, *Calvinism and the Amyraut Heresy* (Madison: University of Wisconsin Press, 1969), pp. 32, 131–39.

[6] *Disp. pub.*, IV.xxx.

[7] Ibid., IV.xlix, emphasis added.

[8] Ibid., emphasis added.

[9] *Disp. pub.*, XI.i, v, vii, ix, x.

[10] Cf. Calvin, *Inst.*, I.xv.7–8; II.ii.26; *RD*, pp. 241–42.

indirect character of the knowledge of God available in the temporal order rendered the knowledge of God available to the *viator* less perfect than the love of God which, even in this life, wills God directly. In Copleston's words, "in the beatific vision in heaven, ... when the soul sees the essence of God immediately, the intrinsic superiority of intellect to will reasserts itself."[11] Arminius grants a higher status to mediate knowledge of God than does Aquinas—or, perhaps, a lower status to temporal human willing—with the result that intellect remains higher than will or love in the fallen condition.)

From the tradition in general and from the scholastic theology both of the Middle Ages and of early orthodox Protestantism, Arminius draws out a doctrine of divine omniscience. The *intellectus Dei*, like all other predicates of the divine nature, partakes of the simplicity, infinity, and eternity or simultaneous wholeness of the divine essence. Although it is a faculty of the divine life, which is to say an aspect of the fundamental operation or *actus secundus* of the divine essence, it is eternally fully actualized. The *intellectus Dei*, therefore, is an eternal knowledge of "all things and every thing which now have, will have, have had, can have, or might hypothetically have, any kind of being."[12] Even so, God does not merely know things but also the order and relation of all things. Arminius extends this divine knowledge even to purely rational "things"—to concepts and relations—that exist only in the imagination.[13] It ought to go without saying that this kind of intensely speculative argumentation, though quite typical of scholastic theology and philosophy, has no parallel in the thought of the Reformers. It is also possible that this broadening of the knowledge of things to include mental or rational constructs existing only in the mind parallels and draws on a development in the metaphysics of Arminius' time toward the identification of the object of metaphysics not merely as *ens* but as both *ens* and *non ens*. Further indications of this parallel occur in Arminius' doctrine of creation.[14]

This utter omniscience can be further described as a total self-knowledge, a complete knowledge of all possibility, and an absolute knowledge of all actuality.[15] God, therefore, can be said to know himself absolutely. We have already encountered this aspect of omniscience as the *theologia archetypa*, the infinite, essential self-knowledge of God which, by definition, is identical with God himself.

---

[11] Copleston, *History*, II, p. 383.

[12] *Disp. pub.*, IV.xxx.

[13] Ibid.

[14] See Jean-François Courtine, "Le projet suárezien de la métaphysique: pour une étude de la thése suárezienne du néant," *Archives de philosophie* 42 (1979): 234–74 and see below, chap. 11.

[15] *Disp. pub.*, IV.xxxi.

Granting this infinite self-identical self-knowledge and granting also that God is the first cause of all things, God must know all possibility and all actuality (which is to say, all actualized possibility) and know these categories exhaustively:

> He knows all *possibilia*, whether they are in the capability (*potentia*) of God or of the creature; in active or passive capability; in the capability of operation, imagination, or enunciation: he knows all things that could have an existence, on any hypothesis; he knows things other than himself, whether necessary or contingent, good or bad, universal or particular, future, present or past; he knows things substantial and accidental of every kind.[16]

The divine knowledge of possibility, since it is a knowledge of what things can come into existence, is also a knowledge of the way in which all possibles could exist ideally or perfectly, without defect and a knowledge of impossibility as well. Arminius even argues an order in the divine knowledge of possibles. Thus God knows, first, "what things can exist by his own primary act." Second, in the logical order of knowing, God knows the possibilities resident in the secondary order of causality belonging to creatures. Whether a creature or order of creatures exists or will exist, God knows the capabilities of these creatures and what can occur in and through them by means of "his conservation, motion, assistance, concurrence, and permission (*conservatio, motus, auxilium, concursus, permissio*)."[17] Third, "he knows what he can do concerning the acts of creatures, consistent with himself and these acts."[18] This logic must also be applied to God's knowledge of actual things.[19] The argument could be cited directly from Aquinas.[20]

Again following Aquinas, Arminius states that God's understanding is identical with the divine essence in its simultaneous wholeness and since the divine knowledge is, first and foremost, a self-knowledge, God's knowledge is neither abstractive nor discursive, compositive or dialectical.[21] God does not know things, in other

---

[16] Ibid.

[17] *Disp. priv.*, XVII.iv.

[18] Ibid.

[19] Ibid.; cf. *Disp. pub.*, IV.xxxiv.

[20] Cf. Aquinas, *Summa*, Ia, q.14, art.9 with Gilson, *Christian Philosophy of St. Thomas Aquinas*, pp. 113–14, Patterson, *Conception of God*, pp. 294–95; and Rousselot, *Intellectualism of Saint Thomas*, p. 65.

[21] *Disp. pub.*, IV.xxxii.1: "Intellegere Dei est ipsius esse et essentia"; cf. *Disp. priv.*, XVII.iii; and note Aquinas, *SCG*, I.45.2: "Intellegere ergo Dei est divina essentia, et divinum esse, et ipsius Deus"; ibid., 46.6: "Intellegere Dei est eius essentia." Note also that Arminius' brief statements of the character of divine knowledge as simultaneous, neither abstractive nor discursive, neither compositive nor

words, by first apprehending the idea or intelligible species of the individual thing and then applying it to or finding it in the thing—nor does God know by the application of a knowledge of previously apprehended things to other things, newly apprehended. Rather, God knows all things by a simple, infinite, immediate apprehension.[22] This general argument leads Arminius to five theses concerning the *intellectus Dei*: (1) "God knows all things from eternity and nothing *de novo*"; (2) "he knows all things immeasurably, apart from the augmentation or diminution of the things known or of his knowledge"; (3) "he knows all things immutably, his knowledge not being varied to the infinite changes of things known"; (4) "he knows all things by a single undivided act"; (5) when "sleep, drowsiness and oblivion are attributed to God" in Scripture, these attributions refer to temporal postponements of rewards and punishments and not to limitations of divine knowledge.[23]

The identity of the *intellectus Dei* with the divine essence and the eternal divine knowledge of all things are, moreover, merely two sides of the same issue. Since the *intellectus Dei* is the divine Being and essence, it is an "entire" and "adequate"—that is, infinite and perfect—knowledge of all that is in God. God not only "understands all things through his essence" but also knows them "entirely" and "excellently as they are in himself and in his understanding," which is to say that God does not know things other than himself through the perception of "intelligible species"—knowable things—that are external to him prior to his knowing. Nor does God know things by knowing their likeness.[24]

The point is, once more, identical with Aquinas: "From the fact that God understands himself primarily and essentially, we must posit that he knows in himself things other than himself," not, however, because they are intelligible species prior to his knowing—since that kind of knowing would indicate a potency in God—but because he knows all things in his own essence. Equally so, God does not know things by knowing their likenesses.[25] As both the order of

---

dialectical also follows out the pattern of Aquinas' *SCG*, I.45–48: cf. *Disp. pub.*, IV.xxxiii.; and Gilson, *Christian Philosophy of St. Thomas Aquinas*, p. 111.

[22] *Disp. pub.*, IV.xxxii–xxxiii; cf. Aquinas, *SCG*, I.48, 55, 57, 58; and Patterson, *Conception of God*, p. 302.

[23] *Disp. pub.*, IV.xxxiii.

[24] Ibid., IV.xxxii: "Seipsum novit ... alia etiam tota, sed excellenter ut in ipso sunt et eius intellectu" and ibid.: "Novit Deus omnia quae novit, non per species intelligibiles, non per similitudinem ... sed per suam ipsius essentiam." See also xxxiii.

[25] *SCG*, I.49.1: "Et hoc autem quod seipsum cognoscit primo et per se, quod alia a se in seipso cognoscat ponere opportet"; I.46.1: "intellectus divinus nulla alia specie intelligibili intelligat quam sua essentia"; I.46.5: "Species intelligibilis similitudo est

argument and the strong verbal resemblances indicate, Arminius constructed this section of his doctrine of the *intellectus Dei* with a consistent reference to Aquinas' *Summa contra gentiles*. Arminius can hardly be said to have reproduced the *Summa* on a large scale. Rather he appears to have have elicited key ideas from chapters and used them as the material of a thesis for classroom disputation. (Arminius does not, it should be noted, take from Aquinas the notion of eternity as an eternal present or the Boethian concept of foreknowledge as an eternally present, direct, and simultaneous knowing of all temporal objects, perhaps because this notion is unnecessary to the central Thomist affirmation of infinite divine knowledge as grounded in the divine essence.[26] The exclusion of this idea from the doctrine of God has, moreover, a major impact on Arminius' view of creation and providence.[27])

Contrary to the kind of logic found so frequently in twentieth-century musings on divine omniscience, Arminius assumes that the character or mode of divine knowing provides no impediment to the divine knowledge of beings that exist and know in other ways.[28] Indeed, Arminius appears to know of this kind of objection to traditional theism and to propose an answer to it. Not only does Arminius insist that God knows all things, whether substance or accident, externally existent or purely rational, he also insists that God knows the relations between things. What is more, God's knowledge is particular, not merely universal or general. And it is a complete knowledge of the conditions of all things: God knows "things in their causes, in themselves, in his own essence—presently in themselves, antecedently in their causes, and pre-eminently in himself."[29] Thus, while God does not know temporal things in a temporal way, he eternally and utterly knows them as they are in their own temporality:

> The understanding of God is certain and infallible, so that he sees even future contingencies certainly and infallibly, whether he sees them in their causes or in themselves. But this infallibility depends on the infinity of the essence of God, and not on his unchangeable will.[30]

A distinction must be made, therefore, between certainty of knowledge and necessity of existence. The former is in the knower and has no direct relation to issues of causality; the latter is in the object

---

alicuius intellecti. ... Nec etiam potest esse in intellectu divino species alia praeter essentiam ipsius quae sit alterius rei similitudo."

[26] Cf. Aquinas, *Summa*, Ia, q.10, arts.1–2; q.14, art.13, ad obj. 3.

[27] See below, chaps. 11–12.

[28] Cf., e.g., Norman Kretzmann, "Omniscience and Immutability," *Philosophy of Religion*, ed. Stephen Cahn (New York: Harper and Row, 1970), pp. 89–103.

[29] *Disp. pub.*, IV.xxxii, thesis 4.

[30] *Disp. priv.*, XVII.v.

known, arises directly from causality and can be in the object whether the object is known with certainty, with uncertainty, or is unknown. Thus,

> the understanding of God, however certain, does not impose necessity on things, but rather establishes contingency in them. For as he knows the thing and the manner of the thing, if the mode of the thing is contingent, he must know it as such, and therefore it remains contingent with respect to divine knowledge.[31]

To argue otherwise would be to impose both a limit and a contradiction on the divine knowing—since an equation of certainty with causal necessity would mean that a certain knowledge of a contingent thing would render the thing necessary, implying an alteration of the mode of the thing known and/or a divine inability to have knowledge of contingent things![32]

Even though God knows all things "by one infinite intuition" or immediate apprehension and not by the exercise of a disposition to know but rather as an eternally and perfectly actualized knowing that is simple, having in itself no succession either temporal or logical, some distinction can be made between modes of divine knowing inasmuch as God may be said to know of all possibilities in a manner different from the way in which he knows all actuality or to know all necessary things in a manner different from the way in which he knows contingencies. Such distinctions arise, of course, not from consideration of God, but from consideration of the objects of divine knowledge—so that the *scientia Dei* can be distinguished into various categories for the sake of discussion.[33]

On the basis of these considerations, Arminius makes two distinctions: the knowledge of God can be understood as either "theoretical" or "practical" or as either a "knowledge of simple intelligence" (*scientia simplicis intelligentiae*) or a "knowledge of vision" (*scientia visionis*). Thus,

> *theoretical knowledge* is that by which things are understood in terms of (*sub ratione*) being and truth. *Practical knowledge* is that by which things are considered in terms of (*sub ratione*) the good, and as objects of the will and power [of God].[34]

This brief reference to "practical knowledge" (*scientia practica*) in God, paralleled by an equally brief comment in a subsequent thesis,[35] is the closest that Arminius comes in his doctrine of God to a discussion of

[31] Ibid., XVII.vii; cf. *Disp. pub.*, IV.xxxviii.
[32] Cf. *Disp. pub.*, IV.xxxviii.
[33] *Disp. pub.*, IV.xl.
[34] Ibid., IV.xli; cf. *Disp. priv.*, XVII.viii.
[35] *Disp. pub.*, IV.xlv.

the *sapientia Dei* or wisdom of God—a concept of considerable importance to his doctrines of creation and providence. *Sapientia* is typically defined by the scholastics in the Aristotelian sense of knowledge ordered toward a goal—that is, practical knowledge.[36]

The second distinction, between knowledge of simple intelligence and knowledge of vision, returns us to the issue of possibility and actuality. For God, in knowing the entire range of possibility, knows also which of those possibilities will come into being and which will not. The *scientia simplicis intelligentiae* is the knowledge by which God "knows himself, all possible things, and the nature and essence of all entities."[37] This knowledge is also called *scientia necessaria* and is described as "indefinite" or "indeterminate." It is "simple" or "simply necessary" inasmuch as it rests upon the perfection and pre-eminence of the divine knowing: the divine knowledge, in its widest sense, *must* be an unlimited knowledge of all possibility, exclusive of any determination of actual objects either by the divine will or by the free or contingent actions of the objects themselves. It is a knowledge of "simple intelligence" inasmuch as the divine intelligence, that is to say, the divine Knower himself, is utterly simple and without succession in his absolute (and absolutely necessary) knowledge of himself and of all possibility.[38]

This necessary or simple knowledge is also called natural knowledge (*scientia naturalis*) because it is in God according to the infinitude of the divine nature and "indefinite" or "indeterminate" because it rests on the natural knowledge that God has of all possibility, prior to the free, creative activity of the divine will. It is an indefinite and indeterminate knowledge, then, because it arises out of the nature of God without reference to actual, that is, to definite and determinate objects.[39] Nonetheless, the *scientia naturalis* directs the actions of divine will and power. Here, Arminius propounds, once more, an essentially Thomistic definition:

> The *scientia Dei* that is called practical, of simple intelligence, and natural or necessary is the cause of all things through a mode of prescribing and directing, to which is added the action of the will and power.[40]

When we come to discuss the *scientia media*, we will see Arminius qualify this point—but in the basic definition, he follows out the Thomist and intellectualist view that God's knowledge is the cause of things.

[36] Cf. *PRRD*, I, pp. 205–15.
[37] *Disp. priv.*, XVII.ix.
[38] Cf. ibid., XVII.x with *Disp. pub.*, IV.xlii.
[39] Cf. *Disp. pub.*, IV.xlii–xlii with *Disp. priv.*, XVII.x.
[40] *Disp. pub.*, IV.xlv.

The *scientia visionis* is the knowledge of divine vision of actual objects or entities. It is therefore identified as definite and determinate knowledge.[41] Arminius notes that the "scholastics" relate this knowledge of vision to the divine willing: whereas the simple or natural knowledge of possibility is logically prior to the free acts of the divine will, the visionary and determined knowledge of actual objects follows "every free act of the divine will."[42] This knowledge is, therefore, also called "free knowledge" (*scientia libera*) by the scholastics because it rests on the free exercise of the divine will. Whereas the *scientia simplicis intelligentiae* is simply or absolutely necessary, the *scientia libera* or *scientia visionis* is relatively or "hypothetically" necessary, "for when any object whatsoever is set forth, it must of necessity fall within the knowledge of God" but actual objects exist *ex hypothesi* on the divine determination that they exist, and the knowledge of them as existent things is a knowledge relative to the divine will.[43]

The *scientia visionis*, understood as a knowledge of definite objects, is what is typically called the divine foreknowledge (*praescientia*). As he noted previously in his general definition of omniscience, Arminius now notes specifically of the divine foreknowledge that it does not impose necessity on things. Foreknowledge follows the divine will but is not identical with it—its certainty rests upon the divine apprehension of the object, not upon the divine will concerning the object. Arminius can say, therefore, "that things do not exist because God knows them as existing in the future, but that he knows future things because they are future."[44] Arminius appears to follow the argument, first set forth by Boethius and later adopted by a majority of the medieval scholastics, that God, as eternal, sees things as they are: his knowledge does not precede the objects in time and recognize them as about to come into existence; rather it knows objects as they are in time from beyond time. What is future to me God knows as future to me because he simultaneously knows all things, whether they are past, or present, or future in relation to me.[45]

This point—that God "knows future things because they are future"—represents a departure from the typical intellectualist view of the divine nature, at least as it was defined by Aquinas. We find in the *Summa* precisely the opposite statement: "if things are in the future, it follows that God knows them; but not that the futurity of

---

[41] Ibid., IV.xlii; *Disp. priv.*, XVII.ix.

[42] *Disp. priv.*, XVII.x.

[43] Ibid.

[44] *Disp. pub.*, IV.xliv; cf. *Disp. priv.*, XXVIII.xiv.

[45] Cf. Boethius, *De consolatione*, V.

things is the cause why God knows them."[46] Indeed, Aquinas can argue that "God causes things by His intellect, since His being is His act of understanding; and hence His knowledge must be the cause of things in so far as His will is joined to it."[47] At least by way of contrast, the Arminian view implies a less than total conjunction between the divine intellect and the divine will: for although Arminius, like Aquinas, subordinates will to intellect, unlike Aquinas, he obviously allows that God knows some existent things that he does not directly will. Aquinas, it should be noted, does not here make a distinction between positive and permissive willing.

Although these basic definitions of *scientia necessaria* and *scientia libera*, *scientia simplicis intelligentiae* and *scientia visionis* are in agreement with the usage of Arminius' Reformed contemporaries, they are nuanced in a rather different direction. Whereas Arminius places both aspects of the divine knowing firmly under the Boethian argument that certainty of knowledge does not impose necessity, and whereas he relativizes the language of *scientia libera* by separating it clearly from the free activity of the divine will and resting its certainty on the object alone, the Reformed draw out the implications of placing the divine causality in between the necessary or simple knowledge and the free or visionary knowledge of God. Polanus argues, for example, that God knows the objects of his *scientia visionis* because he knows himself as capable of bringing them into being and, in addition, as actually willing them to be.[48] God knows determinately as existent those things that he wills to exist. By implication, the *scientia visionis* is utterly coextensive with actuality, since only those things that God either positively or permissively wills to exist do in fact exist.

Heppe's summary of the Reformed point is precise and correct:

> "Knowledge of vision" and "knowledge of simple intelligence" are so distinguished from each other that the former is a proper awareness by which God's vision pierces everything that is not Himself, since He can and does will to effect all that exists and takes place outside of Himself. Whereas the latter is not knowledge (*scientia*) properly so called but an *intelligentia* by which God reviews the realm of His absolute freedom; in which lie countless possibilities, which however He will not allow to be realized.[49]

In such a view, there is no room between the simple or necessary knowledge and the visionary or free knowledge for a third category of

---

[46] Aquinas, *Summa*, Ia, q.14, art.8, ad obj.1.

[47] Ibid., art. 8, corpus.

[48] Polanus, *Syntagma*, II.xviii; cf. *RD*, p. 74.

[49] *RD*, p. 74.

knowing—the entire range of all knowledge is exhausted by the two categories.

Up to this point we have noted a series of differences between Arminius' theological system and the systems of his Reformed contemporaries, but none of them were on issues crucial to the development of Arminius' views on predestination, free will, and the order of salvation. None of the points of difference concerning the nature of theology or the doctrine of God correlates with or provides a metaphysical basis for the controverted articles of Arminius' *Declaratio sententiae*. In addition, virtually all of these points of difference can be juxtaposed with points of similarity and continuity with Reformed teaching stated in the same doctrinal context as the difference: although Arminius views theology as essentially practical, he is at one with the Reformed in his identification of archetypal theology and its relation to the forms of ectypal theology; he does not accept the communicable/incommunicable classification of attributes, but he adheres strictly to the christological implications of Reformed teaching on this point—and so forth. Now, however, in the doctrine of the divine understanding or knowledge, we finally have a point of difference with Reformed teaching that bears directly on the substance of later debate. Indeed, Arminius' conception of the *scientia media* is foundational to his revision of the doctrine of predestination and to his soteriological synergism.

Junius had noted, quite briefly, the distinction between *scientia simplicis intelligentiae* and *scientia visionis*. God knows all things, both contingent and necessary, whether past, present, or future, and knows them perfectly. God also knows things that are not but are *in potentia* both in potency and therefore possible under his will and under the will of creatures. His knowledge of actual things rests on the determination of his will.[50] Junius makes no mention of *scientia media*—demonstrating, if nothing else, that his theses on the *scientia Dei* were written in the early 1590s before the concept of *scientia media* became a focus of Protestant theological debate.

The theologians of the early seventeenth century, however, were profoundly interested in the concept. On the Reformed side, reaction was at first mixed: Gomarus, Walaeus, and Crocius viewed the concept as useful in explaining God's permissive concurrence in the evil acts of human beings,[51] but were not at all concerned to argue, in general, for a conditional divine foreknowledge of future contingents. In general, Reformed writers held that God, in his ordination of all things, had ordained some things to occur necessarily and others contingently. Since the existence of contingents thus depended

---

[50] Junius, *Theses theologicae*, IX.4.
[51] *RD*, p. 79.

directly on the divine will, the divine foreknowledge of future contingents could be explained as belonging to the *scientia libera seu visionis*, without recourse to any concept of a *scientia media*.[52] The Reformed orthodox may be argued, therefore, to have adopted a Scotistic solution to a Thomist problem: God knows the existence of future contingents either because he has decreed their existence or because he eternally concurs in the free acts of the creature.[53] (By way of repudiating the Reformed view, Arminius would not only adopt a concept of *scientia media*, he would also argue an alternative view of concurrence.[54])

The problem of middle knowledge, however, would not go away. The concept was elaborated not only by the Jesuits but also by the Socinians and the notorious Conrad Vorstius as a way of arguing the place of human freedom in the work of salvation. The Socinians had even moved toward a concept of the limited foreknowledge of future contingents—restricting the knowledge to the range of contingent possibilities and excluding the actual result as future.[55] Walaeus eventually developed a counter-argument at length by recognizing *scientia media* as a valid description of a divine hypothetical knowledge of unrealized future possibilities: God knows, for example, that Tyre and Sidon would have repented if they had seen mighty works like those done by Jesus in Chorazin and Bethsaida (Matt. 11:21). There is, therefore, in God a certainty regarding hypothetically known future contingencies, a knowledge that stands prior to God's decretive will and prior, therefore, to the *scientia visionis*. Walaeus notes, however, that this hypothetical knowing is not necessarily to be understood as a third kind of knowledge separate from the *scientia simplicis intelligentiae*.[56]

Arminius argues precisely the point that the definitions offered by his Reformed contemporaries have purposely excluded. After his basic set of definitions, Arminius presents the thesis that

> the Scholastics say besides, that one kind of God's knowledge is natural and necessary, another free, and a third intermediate (*mediam*). (1) Natural or necessary knowledge is that by which God understands himself and all possibles; (2) free knowledge is that by which he knows all other beings; (3) middle knowledge is that by which he knows that "if this occurs, that will happen." The first precedes every free act of the divine will. The second follows the free act of the divine will. This

---

[52] Ibid., pp. 79–80.

[53] Cf. Raymond, *DTC* 4/2, "Duns Scot," col. 1880, citing *I sent.*, d.39, nota 23.

[54] Below, chap. 12.

[55] Cf. Fausto Socinus, *Praelectiones theologicae*, caps. 8–11 in *Bibliotheca fratrum polonorum*, vol. 1 with Johann Crell, *Liber de deo eiusque attributis*, cap. 24, in ibid., vol. 4; and see Otto Zöckler, "Socin und Socinianismus," *RE* 18, p. 471.

[56] Walaeus, *Loci communes*, p. 175.

latter act indeed is preceded by the free will, but sees any future thing as a consequence of it.... middle [knowledge] must intervene in things that depend on the freedom of creaturely choice.[57]

Thus the *scientia media* intervenes between the natural or necessary and the free or visionary knowledge as a knowledge of contingent events that lie outside of the realm of positive divine willing, in the realm of secondary causality. Significantly, Arminius does not identify the "scholastics" from whose works he has taken his definitions.

Arminius recognizes that the distinction of several kinds of knowledge in an omniscient God is somewhat problematic. Strictly speaking, all of God's knowledge is necessary: God knows all things because of the infinity of his essence. Even the *scientia libera* cannot be viewed as a result—not even as a result of the divine will offering a willed object to the divine intellect.[58] Arminius, after all, has argued the intellectualist position: the divine intellect governs the divine willing, not vice versa. Any object—even objects presented hypothetically or contingently—are known because of the infinite understanding of the divine essence which, as infinite, must know all things.

Arminius does not develop his definition of *scientia media* at any great length, but his very definition of the concept raises a serious question about the extent of divine knowledge and its possible limitation. The definition inserts an element of conditionality into the *scientia Dei*: "*if* this happens, that will take place." Arminius seems to be saying that, according to the *scientia media*, God has a conditional knowledge of future contingents. God does not, in other words, know a future contingent absolutely as something that will happen. Rather, God knows the future contingent relatively or hypothetically as a potential result of a prior creaturely act. The *scientia media*, in other words, seems to introduce into the divine mind an element of potency or knowledge of possibility that is actualized by something external to God.[59] At least this is the implication of the conditional element in the definition—and, indeed, of the creation of a category of knowing in between the pure, precreative knowledge of possibles and the absolutely certain postcreative knowledge of positively willed actuality. Is the *scientia media* merely a knowledge of the results of divine permissive willing (in which case it would be a certain and definite knowledge)—or is it also a knowledge of events that take place *outside* of the divine willing, whether positive or permissive (in which case it would be an uncertain and indeterminate knowledge)?

[57] *Disp. pub.*, IV.xliii, xlv ad fin.
[58] *Disp. pub.*, IV.xliii.
[59] Cf. *Amica collatio*, p. 492 (*Works*, III, pp. 65–66).

Whereas the Reformed had subsumed knowledge of all contingent events, including those only indirectly or permissively willed, under the *scientia visionis*, Arminius allows a separate category. It is crucial to ask where this category comes from as well as what its implications are for the doctrine of God and for the theological system in general. Arminius identifies the three categories of *scientia Dei* as taken from the scholastics, which was the typical Protestant designation not of contemporary Protestants who followed a scholastic method but of medieval scholastics. The problem, here, is that the concept of a *scientia media* does not come from the medieval scholastics whose theological and philosophical systems have been identified here as resources used in the development of Protestant orthodoxy. Rather it arose out of a sixteenth-century Roman Catholic debate and, specifically, the encounter between Driedo, Molina, and Suárez and the predestinarianism of Bañez and of the Thomistic tradition in general. The term *scientia media*, brought into prominence by Molina, most probably was invented by his teacher, Fonseca.[60]

Aquinas had, for example, raised the question of whether God is capable of knowing future contingents. On the negative side, he pointed out that all divine knowledge is in some sense necessary. Granting that the proposition "If God knew that this thing will be, it will be" is a true proposition, then "the antecedent conditional," that is, "If God knew that this thing will be," is "absolutely necessary" inasmuch as it is a statement about God's eternity. The consequent, therefore, follows as a necessity given the necessity of the antecedent. Everything that God knows, even those things presented in the form of true conditional propositions, is necessary—and God knows no contingent things.[61] More simply, everything that God knows, God knows necessarily:

> But no future contingent thing must necessarily be. Therefore no contingent future thing is known by God.[62]

In other words, either God knows everything and there are no contingents, or there are contingents and God's knowledge is limited.

Of course, neither of these options is acceptable. As an alternative, Aquinas has recourse to the Boethian definition of eternity as simultaneous life (although he denies the Boethian argument that knowledge, as such, is not causal).[63] Certainty does not imply necessity.

---

[60] Cf. Robert Merrihew Adams, "Middle Knowledge and the Problem of Evil," in *The Virtue of Faith and Other Essays in Philosophical Theology* (New York: Oxford, 1987), p. 91, n. 2, with Vansteenberghe, "Molinisme," *DTC* 10/2, col. 2096.

[61] Aquinas, *Summa*, Ia, q.14, art.13, obj.2.

[62] Ibid., obj.3.

[63] Ibid., q.14, art.8.

Thus God "knows all contingent things not only as they are in their causes, but also as each one of them is actually in itself." Moreover, God knows contingent things as actualities in the simultaneous wholeness of his eternity, without temporal succession: "Hence it is manifest that contingent things are infallibly known by God, inasmuch as they are subject to the divine sight in their presentiality; and yet they are future contingent things in relation to their own causes."[64] The Reformed view, cited above, agrees generally with Aquinas in making a distinction between the eternal simultaneity of the divine knowing and the fact of futurity as a fact belonging restrictively to the temporal order, and then in inferring that God certainly and absolutely knows contingent things according to the *scientia visionis*—although the Reformed, like Arminius, generally assume that knowledge is *not* causal.

Aquinas can reply to his objections with a similar division of the issue: "things known by God are contingent on account of their proximate causes, while the knowledge of God, which is the first cause, is necessary."[65] On the argument based upon the antecedent condition of divine knowledge, Aquinas first distinguishes between the necessity and contingency of things and the purely logical necessity and contingency of propositions: the former does not follow from the latter. The basic issue is that "what is known by God must be necessary according to the mode in which they are subject to the divine knowledge, ... but not absolutely as considered in their own causes."[66] Arminius also argues that the necessity of divine knowledge arises in the infinity of God but, unlike Aquinas, who simply assumes that God can unconditionally and absolutely know contingent things, Arminius assumes that such knowledge is not causal and adds the category of *scientia media*. (Aquinas' assumption that knowledge in God is in fact causal, as the intellect of the first cause who establishes the entire order of secondary causality,[67] would, presumably, rule out any notion of a *scientia media*.)

This problem, resident in Thomist theology, had become a focus of discussion at the University of Louvain after the publication of John Driedo's *De concordia liberi arbitrii et praedestinationis divinae* in 1537. Driedo argued that divine grace and human freedom ought not to be severed in the work of salvation and, indeed, that "the right use of free will, foreknown by God, ought to be a basis for election to the grace of justification" and that, therefore, predestination could be defined as the divine decree "to call and to aid human beings in such

[64] Ibid., q.14, art.13, corpus.
[65] Ibid., q.14, art.13, ad obj.1.
[66] Ibid., ad obj.3.
[67] Ibid., q.14, art.8, corpus.

a way as to bring about their obedience."[68] Driedo found it necessary to distinguish between the prior divine intention to save all human beings which establishes the priority of grace and rests all salvific acts of human beings on the effective movement of God as first cause and the divine foreknowledge of the success or failure of that grace, inasmuch as those who are called do not respond equally to the divine offer of salvation. The ultimate ground of predestination is the divine good pleasure, but this ultimate ground cannot conflict with the divine demand that human beings freely choose to live rightly.[69] Driedo's views were carried forward by his students at Louvain and were, beginning in 1556, adopted by the Jesuit teacher, Fonseca, as the basis for his refutation of Calvin's teaching, *De praedestinatione, libero arbitrio et gratia contra Calvinum* (Paris, 1556). By 1565, Fonseca had provided a full description of the concept of a divine *scientia media*, prior to the divine decrees and, therefore, having the character of a noncausal knowing, distinct from the categories of *scientia necessaria* and *scientia libera*.[70]

It was precisely this ultimately causal character of the divine intellect—that God knows all possibilities and, granting the priority of intellect over will, knowingly ordains which possibilities he will actualize—that Molina strove to overcome in his debate with the somewhat radicalized Augustinianism of Bañez and with the Dominican interpreters of Thomas Aquinas. Whereas Thomism generally and Bañez in particular "began with metaphysical principles," with God "as first cause and prime mover," Molina began with the problem of the free consent of the will and assumed as his task the explanation of "divine foreknowledge and the action of grace in such a way that the freedom of the will is not explained away or tacitly denied."[71] Molina's *Concordia liberi arbitrii cum gratiae donis, divina praescientia, providentia, praedestinatione et reprobatione*, published in 1588, argued that God's foreknowledge of future contingents must be understood not as a knowledge of contingencies created or ordered as such by the direct action of the divine will (and therefore a category of *scientia libera*) but as a knowledge of contingencies standing prior to "any free act of his will" and resting on a clear and certain knowledge of the act of the creature.[72]

[68] Driedo, *De concordia*, as cited in Vansteenberghe, "Molinisme," *DTC* 10/2, col. 2096.

[69] Dumont, *Liberté humaine*, pp. 99–101, citing Driedo, *De concordia*, I.iv and II.iii.

[70] Cf. Vansteenberghe, "Molinisme," *DTC* 10/2, col. 2096 with Dumont, *Liberté humaine*, pp. 127–28.

[71] Copleston, *History of Philosophy*, III, p. 342.

[72] Luis de Molina, *Concordia liberi arbitrii cum gratiae donis, divina praescientia, providentia, praedestinatione et reprobatione*, ed. Johann Rabeneck (Onia and Madrid: Collegium Maximum Societatis Iesu, 1953), VII, q.23, arts.4–5, disp. 1, memb. ult (14).9: "Tertium est praescientia illa media inter scientiam Dei liberam et mere

Thus, Molina argues the existence of a divine knowledge or fore-knowledge

> mediate between the free and the purely natural knowledge of God by which ... God knew, before any free act of his will, what would come to pass conditionally (*ex hypothesi*) by the agency of the created will in the order of things, granting that he had decided to place these angels or men in a particular situation; if, moreover, the created will were able to do the contrary, by [this foreknowledge] he would know the contrary.[73]

This divine knowledge, therefore, rests entirely upon the acts of creatures. No divine determination enters into the *scientia media*. Thus, God is capable of foreknowing the way a given creature will act, given certain conditions—and capable, therefore, of acting upon this foreknowledge of future contingents by establishing those conditions accordingly. Molina refers specifically to the statement of Origen that "a thing will happen not because God knows it as future; but because it is future, it is on that account known by God before it exists," as cited by Aquinas, and specifically disagrees with Aquinas' interpretation. Aquinas had categorically refused to view the future event as the cause of something in God or as standing outside of the divine causality.[74]

A crucial element, therefore, in the transition from Aquinas' view to the modified Thomism—on this point, radically modified—of the Jesuit theologians, was the denial of the causal nature of divine knowing. Molina insisted on the utter omniscience of God and rested the divine foreknowledge of future contingents on the "unlimited perfection of the divine intellect." In other words, God so utterly knows the entire realm of possibility that, beyond his willing some things to be and other things not to be, God also knows, simply because of his own infinite cognitive powers, the actual results of all contingent causes prior to their actualization.[75] Suárez, whose formulation of the problem Arminius also probably read, chose not to rest his argument purely upon the nature of divine cognition. Suárez argued that God, in foreknowing the nature or character of his crea-

---

naturalem qua ... ante actum liberum suae voluntatis cognovit Deus, quid in uno-quoque rerum ordine per arbitrium creatum esset futurum ex hypothesi, quod hos homines aut angelos in hoc vel illo ordine rerum collocare statueret, qua tamen cogniturus erat contrarium, si contrarium, ut potest, pro libertate arbitrii creati esset futurum."; cf. Vansteenberghe, "Molinisme," *DTC* 10/2, col. 2119.

[73] Molina, *Concordia*, p. 549.

[74] Ibid., pp. 317–18, citing Aquinas, *Summa*, Ia, q.14, art. 8, ad obj.1.

[75] Cf. Adams, "Middle Knowledge," p. 81, citing Molina, *Concordia*, q.14, art.13, disp.53.

tures, foreknows how creatures will be disposed to act in any given situation, and therefore foreknows with certainty the actual result of a future creaturely choice.[76]

Arminius nowhere cites Driedo, Molina, Suárez, or Origen and nowhere notes the contemporary Roman Catholic debate over middle knowledge. His only citation of Aquinas stands in no direct relation to the question of *scientia media*, but it is hard to rule out the influence of Molina and Suárez on his doctrine. There is even a hint of the famous Thomistic citation of Origen and its Molinist interpretation in Arminius' remark that "a thing does not come to pass (*non sit*) because it is foreknown or foretold; but it is foreknown or foretold because it is yet to be (*futura est*)."[77] It is also the case that Arminius' motivation in arguing the *scientia media* is identical with Molina's: "the middle knowledge," argues Arminius, "ought to intervene [i.e., between natural and free knowledge] in things which depend on the freedom of creaturely choice."[78] Thus the *scientia media* must precede "the free act of will with regard to intelligence"—that is, precede the act of will that grounds the *scientia libera* or *scientia visionis*, and must know future events, not because they have been willed but on the hypothesis of their future occurrence.[79] God will, therefore, be able to ordain the means of salvation on the basis of a hypothetical or consequent knowledge of the creature's free choice in a context of grace.[80]

The question naturally arises as to the actual source or antecedent for Arminius' conception of *scientia media*. Does it come from Molina or does it come from Suárez? There were, in fact, three basic views of the *scientia* and its relationship to the election of individuals held by members of the Jesuit order involved in the controversy, one represented chiefly by Molina, Toletanus, Vazquez, and Lessius, another by Suárez and Bellarmine, and the third by Aquaviva. The Molinist view argues that God has eternally determined to distribute to all mankind the grace necessary for salvation. Grace is, thus, unequally distributed but is sufficient for each individual. According to his *scientia media*, God knows how individuals will accept or resist the assistance of his grace and can destine them either to glory or to reprobation on the grounds of their free choice. Predestination,

---

[76] Suárez, *De scientia Dei futuorum contingentium*, prol.2, cap.7, nn.21–25 in *Opera*, XI, pp. 94–96; and see the exposition in Adams, "Middle Knowledge," pp. 81–82.

[77] *Disp. priv.*, XXVIII.xiv.

[78] Ibid., XVII.xii.

[79] Ibid., XVII.xi; Vansteenberghe's summary of Molina's teaching parallels Arminius' definition perfectly: see "Molinisme," *DTC* 10/2, col. 2119.

[80] Cf. *Disp. priv.*, XL.v; XLI.iii (on predestination).

therefore, is *post praevisa merita et demerita*.[81] By way of contrast, the view of Suárez and Bellarmine argues that God eternally chooses those who are his and, in accordance with this election, provides the grace sufficient for the salvation of each. The *scientia media* serves to provide God with a knowledge of the free acceptance by the elect of his grace and, equally, with a knowledge of the rejection of his sufficient but ineffectual grace by the reprobate. The grace provided is congruous with the divine end of an election *ante praevisa merita*: the Suárezian doctrine, therefore, is called "congruism" or "pure congruism."[82] The third view, attributed to Aquaviva, has been called "mitigated congruism." It argues that God eternally determines which virtuous acts will merit eternal glory. God then provides the grace sufficient to and congruous with his will and, according to his *scientia media*, knows which individuals will accept his grace: predestination is *post praevisa merita*.[83] All three views assume that the elect are saved because they cooperate with a resistible divine grace and the reprobate are lost by their own fault—but the Suárezian view, by assuming the prior divine choice of the elect, presses the idea of *scientia media* back toward the Thomist model. It comes closer to the position of Bañez than the Molinist view and, indeed, close to the Reformed teaching.[84]

Some indication of the direction of Arminius' language of *scientia media* is provided by his final discussions of the eternal decree of salvation—and further indication in the language of antecedent and consequent, absolute and conditional willing in God that belongs to Arminius' concept of the *voluntas Dei*.[85] In a short set of articles written most probably in 1608 and in the *Declaratio sententiarum* of the same year, Arminius described the eternal decree of God as consisting in four logically distinguishable decrees. The first three of these decrees set forth the general divine intention to appoint Christ as the Mediator of salvation to fallen mankind, "to receive into [his] favor those who repent and believe" in Christ; and to provide "such means for repentance and faith as are necessary, sufficient, and efficacious."[86] The fourth decree, by way of contrast, refers to particular persons and "rests on the prescience (*praescientia*) and foresight (*praevisione*) of God, by which he foreknew, from all eternity, who would ... believe by

[81] Scorraille, *François Suárez*, I, p. 355; cf. Dumont, *Liberté humaine*, pp. 127–40, 164–70 and La Servière, *Théologie de Bellarmin*, pp. 575–84, 597–601.

[82] Ibid., pp. 355–56.

[83] Ibid., p. 356.

[84] Cf. ibid., pp. 355–56.

[85] *Disp. pub.*, IV.lx–lxiii; *Disp. priv.*, XIX.iii–ix; and below, this chap., pp. 138–41.

[86] *Articuli nonnulli*, XV.1–3; cf. *Dec. sent.*, p. 119.

the aid of prevenient grace and would persevere by the aid of subsequent grace; and who would not believe and persevere."[87]

In its detail, Arminius' language of the divine decrees veers away from the Suárezian view of predestination *ante praevisa merita* and evidences some affinity for both the teaching of Driedo and Molina and the formulation of Aquaviva—although, of course, the Arminian doctrine of *scientia media*, in keeping with the Protestant doctrine of justification, would argue that God elects *post praevisam fidem* rather than *post praevisa merita*. Like Driedo and Molina, Arminius assumes a prior, general divine determination to save the human race and to provide sufficient means to this end—and, again like Molina, he assumes that God elects or rejects on the basis of a foreknowledge of human response to grace.[88] The basic outline is Molinist, then, inasmuch as the divine foreknowledge includes knowledge of the rejection as well as of the acceptance of grace. Nonetheless, like Driedo and Aquaviva, Arminius also includes in his description of the prior or antecedent decrees of God the ordination of the conditions of salvation—in Arminius' teaching, faith rather than merits.[89] Not only, moreover, can we assume that Arminius was aware of the general outlines of the Roman Catholic debate over grace, free will, and predestination, we can also infer from the catalogue of his library that he had a detailed, first-hand knowledge of the positions of Driedo and Molina and, most probably, of Suárez: he owned copies of Driedo's *De concordia liberi arbitrii et praedestinationis divinae* (Louvain, 1537), Molina's *Concordia liberi arbitrii cum gratiae donis* (Antwerp, 1595) and Suárez' *Opuscula theologica*.[90]

Arminius' reason for adopting this approach to *scientia media* arguably parallels that of Molina. In the *Conference* with Junius, Arminius singled out for discussion three views of predestination: Calvin's (and Beza's), Aquinas', and Augustine's. His preference was clearly for Aquinas' teaching, although he felt that it, like the doctrines of Calvin and Augustine, stood in the way of a full affirmation of human liberty and responsibility. Arminius specifically argues that God infallibly and certainly foreknows the fall of man into sin—but that this infallibility is "in respect only of ... foreknowledge, not in respect of any act of God's will either affirmative or negative."[91] Like Molina, Arminius sees it as a problem in Aquinas' teaching that there is no knowledge of contingencies prior to the act of divine will that establishes all things in existence. Like Molina, Arminius modified

---

[87] *Articuli nonnulli*, XV.4.
[88] Cf. *Dec. sent.*, p. 119 and *Articuli nonnulli*, XV.1–3.
[89] Cf. *Dec. sent.*, p. 119 and *Articuli nonnulli*, XV.4.
[90] *Auction Catalogue*, pp. 7–8 (titles are corrected).
[91] Cf. *Amica collatio*, p. 372 (*Works*, III, p. 180).

the Thomistic model that lay at the center of his theology. Whereas Aquinas had simply argued that God knows all things through his essence inasmuch as he "knows himself perfectly" and therefore knows also the "essence of created being" which is from him and exists by participation, Arminius held that although "God knows all things by his essence" because of their participation in his *esse*, some things are known prior to their being willed by God.[92] According to Arminius, God knows things both "in themselves" and "in their causes"—whereas Aquinas states, categorically, that God sees contingent things "even before they come into being ... as they actually exist, and not merely as they will be in the future and as virtually present in their causes, in the way we are able to know some future things."[93]

Arminius' language concerning the decree rests, in other words, on a distinction between a divine knowledge of soteriological possibility (which is universal or at least hypothetically universal from the perspective of God's offer) and a divine foreknowledge of human actuality. The latter, moreover, is known by God, apart from any direct divine causality, as a result of human choices in the contingent order. Thus, the divine will to save particular persons rests on the divine knowledge of future contingent acts—*scientia media*. Indeed, it is only by the device of the *scientia media* that Arminius can argue a genuinely universal will to save, resting on a knowledge of possibility and also argue, subsequently, a genuinely specific will to save believers only. If there were only a *scientia simplicis intelligentiae* and a *scientia visionis*, then the possibility of a universal salvation would be always known to God as a possibility lying outside of his will and the actual knowledge of those saved would be the direct result of a will to save some and not others—that is to say, the Reformed position.

Arminius' teaching on the *scientia media*, moreover, marks the decisive entrance of this concept into Protestantism—with the result that the Reformed scholastics of the seventeenth century would find it necessary to argue at length against the doctrine, while the Remonstrant writers, Episcopius and Limborch, together with Grotius and Vorstius, would elaborate and defend the position. Ritschl, it should be noted, locates the concept in Grotius and Vorstius, but neither recognizes its rootage in the Roman Catholic debates of the era nor its appropriation by Arminius, nor its subsequent history in Remonstrant theology.[94] Episcopius and Limborch develop the point in a manner identical with the teaching of Arminius: the *scientia media* is a

---

[92] Cf. Aquinas, *Compendium theologiae*, I.133 with Arminius, *Disp. priv.*, XVII. ii, xi.

[93] Arminius, *Disp. priv.*, XVII.v; Aquinas, *Compendium theologiae*, I.133.

[94] Cf. Ritschl, *Dogmengeschichte*, III, p. 352.

certain foreknowledge of future contingents, specifically of the free acts of men and angels. Episcopius in particular points to the difference between this Remonstrant definition of the concept and the Socinian view of a limited divine foreknowledge.[95]

By way of conclusion, it is also worth noting that Arminius' discussion of the divine knowledge or understanding conforms to the view of Protestant scholasticism in general and Reformed orthodoxy in particular as a modified Thomism. Arminius has followed out the intellectualism of Aquinas by viewing the divine intellect as prior to the divine will in the ordering of the attributes. On this point he has modified Aquinas far less than his Reformed contemporaries who had, in many cases, moved toward a stronger, perhaps Scotistic, emphasis on the divine will. Arminius' concept of the *scientia media* is also a conscious modification of the Thomistic intellectualism—in this case, a modification not entertained by Arminius' Reformed contemporaries, at least not in any substantive way. In sum, Arminius retains the Thomistic priority of intellect over will but sets aside the equally Thomistic assumption of the active nature of the *scientia Dei*: for Aquinas and for subsequent Thomistic thinkers, like Giles of Rome, the divine knowledge is the cause of things.[96]

Arminius must, therefore, assume the existence of contingent events lying outside the divine causality, events that are, in some sense, the cause of God's knowledge of them. Arminius' basic definition, prior to his discussion of the *scientia media*, denies this.[97] Nonetheless, inasmuch as Arminius retains his Thomistic sense of the priority of intellect over will but denies the causal nature of divine knowing, God must have a noncausal knowledge of those future contingents brought about by free acts of creatures. As Garrigou-Lagrange argues concerning Molinism, "in the eyes of Thomists, this theory leads to the admission, in God, of a *dependence* or *passivity* of knowledge with regard to an occurrence in the created order that has not arisen thorough him."[98] "If God is not *determining*," concludes Garrigou-Lagrange, "he is *determined*."[99] The point ought also to be made that the implications of the concept of *scientia media*, particularly in a philosophical and theological system that holds the priority of intellect over will, extend far beyond the rather limited issue of human freedom in the work of salvation. The determinedness of the God who foreknows future contingents lying outside of the divine willing qualifies the relationship of God to the entirety of the created

---

[95] Cf. Episcopius, *Inst. theol.*, IV.ii.17–19; Limborch, *Theologia christiana*, II.viii.8–29.
[96] Cf. Steinmetz, *Misericordia Dei*, p. 42.
[97] Cf. *Disp. priv.*, XVII.vi with *Disp. pub.*, IV.xxxvii.
[98] Garrigou-Lagrange, "Thomisme," *DTC* 15/1, col. 870.
[99] Ibid.

order. The question of the character and extent of divine knowing is, in other words, a question about the character and extent of the divine relationship to creation and, beyond that, granting the goodness and love of the Christian God, a question about the character and extent of divine providence.[100] Arminius' advocacy of the *scientia media*, thus, points directly toward his reconstruction of the doctrines of creation and providence.

---

[100] Cf. Burrell, *On Knowing the Unknowable God*, p. 80.

10

The Divine Will

The doctrine of the will (*voluntas*) and power (*potentia*) of God was a major emphasis of Reformed dogmatics from Musculus' *Loci communes* (1560) onward.[1] Beza devoted much space to a discussion of the will and power of God and Zanchi's treatment must be regarded as one of the most elaborate and exhaustive in the entire history of doctrine.[2] Arminius, therefore, entered upon a Reformed tradition that had already, prior to his time, experienced a major scholastic development of the doctrine of the will of God and its affections and power. Indeed, from Musculus and his side of the Reformed tradition there came a Scotist and nominalist tendency; from Zanchi's side, a Thomistic direction. Arminius' doctrine took shape, therefore, against a varied background and in a context where major tendencies in late medieval scholasticism were already being appropriated and modified.

The stress both on revelation and rational argument evidenced so strongly in Arminius' proofs and in his discussion of the divine nature appears again in his introductory remarks on the will of God: "not only a rational view of the essence and understanding of God, but also the Scriptures and the universal consent of mankind testify that will is correctly attributed to God."[3] Arminius seems here to reflect the typically scholastic introductory question—"whether there is a will in God" or "whether will can be predicated of God"[4]—and to

---

[1] Wolfgang Musculus, *Loci communes* (Basel, 1560), cap. 45.

[2] Theodore Beza, *Quaestionum et responsionum christianarum libellus* (Geneva, 1584), pp. 95–125 on providence, predestination, and the divine will; Jerome Zanchi, *De natura Dei*, III.iv.

[3] *Disp. pub.*, IV.xlviii.

[4] E.g., Aquinas, *Summa*, Ia, q.19, art.1; Alexander of Hales, *Summa*, I, tract.vi, q.1, cap.1; Peter Aureole, *I sent.*, dist.45–46; Henry of Ghent, *Summa*, art.45, q.1; and Suárez, *Disp.*, XXX.xvi.

provide a threefold answer. That there is a will in God, therefore, cannot be questioned; but how that will is to be conceived and how it relates to the created order are major issues to be addressed, particularly in view of the relationship of intellect and will and the placement of some contingent event in the divine intellect but outside of the divine will argued by Arminius in the preceding section of his disputations.

As in the basic discussion of the divine nature and in his presentation of the divine life, Arminius defines the divine will in terms of its primary and secondary actuality—here specifically echoing the language of scholastic faculty psychology. The will is a faculty of the divine life which both exists within the divine life as such, as a passive or quiescent disposition, and as an operation, as an active disposition or activity tending toward an object. Arminius therefore recognizes that

> the will of God is spoken of in three ways. First, the faculty of willing as such. Second, the act of willing (*actus volendi*). Third, the object willed.[5]

Therefore, the will may be defined as

> the second faculty of the life of God, flowing through the understanding from the life and extending beyond it [i.e., toward objects], by which God tends toward a known good. Toward a good, because this is an adequate object of every will. Toward a known good, not only insofar as it is a being (*qua Ens est*), but also insofar as it is good, whether in reality or only in the act of the divine understanding.[6]

In this basic definition, Arminius set himself apart from the Scotistic or nominalistic tendency that we have already identified with Musculus' contribution to Reformed theology. Musculus had specifically repudiated the analogy between divine and human willing by arguing that the faculty psychology model of will and affections could not be applied to the divine being.[7] Arminius follows the more Thomistic pattern of analogy with the faculties of the human soul and, in addition, with their arrangement or order. The discussion of divine will found in Arminius' *Disputations* is, moreover, the most extensive discussion of this doctrine to arise from the University of Leiden in his day: it goes far beyond the detail of Junius and the *Synopsis purioris* and Gomarus' published disputations actually omit the topic.[8] Walaeus, however, would develop the doctrine at length

---

[5] *Disp. priv.*, XVIII.i; cf. the similar argument in *Disp. pub.*, IV.xlvii.

[6] *Disp. priv.*, XVIII.ii; cf. *Disp. pub.*, IV.xlix.

[7] Cf. Musculus, *Loci communes*, cap.xlv.

[8] Cf. Junius, *Theses theologicae* (Heidelberg), secs. 11–12; (Leiden), IX.5; *Synopis purioris*, VI.xxxiv–xxxv.; Gomarus, *Disp. theol.*, III.

with some significant reflections on or parallels with Arminius' exposition.[9]

Arminius' definition is significant for its intellectualist dimension—inasmuch as it places the will below the intellect—and also for its omission of reference to the wisdom of God (*sapientia Dei*). In subsequent discussions of creation and providence, Arminius can argue the grounding of the divine will in the wisdom of God as well as in the divine intellect or understanding.[10] The omission here is, therefore, somewhat curious and may indicate the incomplete and occasionally provisional character of Arminius' disputations: what we have from the hands of Arminius is, after all, a fragmentary system that would have been reworked considerably for final publication. It is also the case that Arminius' discussion of particular attributes appears in the somewhat earlier *Disputationes publicae* and his discussions of creation and providence in the *Disputationes privatae*, for which he made no effort to rework the discussion of the attributes.[11]

Arminius' intellectualism is perhaps most obvious in his statement that the object of the will is not merely the good but a "known good." The object of the will is first recognized as good by an act of the understanding (*actus intellectus*): the intellect, in short, presents the will with its object. Since, of course, intellect and will are identical with the divine essence, which is the highest good, the order described here by Arminius is purely logical. God, therefore, in willing the good that he knows, first and foremost wills himself. The argument, once again, reflects the logic of Aquinas.[12] The basic Thomist position is modified, however, in Arminius' view of the function of the will: for Arminius, the intellect is not directly causal—so that God's knowledge of an object does not account for the existence of the object. Rather, according to Arminius, the will functions distinctly (but not, of course, separately) from the intellect in bringing about the known good *ad extra*.

Since the good can be understood either as the highest good or as derived goodness, the divine will can be understood as having two

[9] Walaeus, *Loci communes*, III.9 (pp. 176–81).

[10] Cf. *Disp. priv.*, XXIV.iv, viii and corollarium ii (on creation) and *Disp. priv.*, XXVII.vi, xi (on providence).

[11] Cf. *Disp. priv.*, XV.vii.

[12] Cf. Aquinas, *Summa*, Ia, q.19, art.2, ad 4: "ita velle divinum est unum et simplex, quia multa non vult nisi per unum, quod est bonitas sua"; and idem; *SCG*, I.75.7: "Deus intellectu suo intelligit se principaliter et in se intelligit alia. Igitur similiter principaliter vult se, et, volendo se, vult omnia alia"; with Arminius, *Disp. pub.*, IV.li: "ut intellectus Dei simplicissimo actu intelligit essentiam suam, & per illam omnia alia; sic voluntas Dei uno et simplici actu vult bonitatem suam & omnia in bonitate sua."

objects, a "primary, immediate" or proper object, the highest good, and a "secondary and indirect" object, a derived good, "toward which the divine will does not tend except by means of [the highest good]."[13] If this argument is accepted, then it follows for Arminius, as for Aquinas, that God primarily wills himself as the highest good and secondarily wills all things inasmuch as they derive their being from him and his goodness and insofar as they tend toward him as their highest good. God does not will evil.[14] We find no parallel discussion in Gomarus' disputations, but the later Leiden theology of Walaeus and Episcopius takes up precisely this point, identifying the primary object of the divine will as God himself and the secondary object as all things made by God, who as the source of all good is also the end of all things.[15] Where Walaeus—on the Reformed side—differs from Arminius is in his emphasis on identity of the *voluntas Dei* with the divine essence and, therefore, with the eternal decree that established all things and does so immutably.[16] Episcopius, on the Remonstrant side of the Leiden theology, takes up the basic point of the relation of the divine will to the ultimate goodness of God and, following out the line of Arminius' argument, stresses not the relation of the will to the immutable decree but rather the character of the divine goodness as determinative of God's will. Thus, for Episcopius, it is clear that God *permits* evil—but it is equally clear, granting that the divine goodness is the primary and derivative goodness of finite things the secondary object of the divine will, that God does not directly *will to permit* evil. Or, more precisely, God permits only the free function of the human will and not the power of sinning.[17] Indeed, argues Episcopius, God wills directly only the good and does so as a "necessity of nature."[18] As in Arminius' theology, the primary direction of argument is to affirm the goodness of God to the point of setting aside the Reformed assumption that God wills everything, with the result that permission, to borrow Augustine's phrase, is a "willing permission."[19]

---

[13] *Disp. priv.*, XVIII.iii.

[14] Cf. *Disp. pub.*, IV.xlix: "Malum autem, quod culpae dicitur, non vult Deus. Quia nullum bonum malo isti connexum magis vult, quam bonum cui malitia peccati adversatur, nempe bonum ipsum divinum" with Aquinas, *Summa,*Ia, q.19, art. 9, corpus: "Nullam autem bonum Deus magis vult quam suam bonitatem.... Unde malum culpae, quod privat ordinem ad bonum divinum, Deus nullo modo vult," and with Patterson, *Conception of God*, p. 333.

[15] Walaeus, *Loci communes*, III.9 (pp. 176–77).

[16] Ibid., p. 176.

[17] Episcopius, *Inst. theol.*, IV.ii.20 (p. 305, col. 1).

[18] Ibid., p. 305, col. 2.

[19] Augustine, *Enchiridion*, cap.100.

This distinction between two kinds of good and, therefore, between two objects of the divine will, primary and secondary, direct and indirect, points toward the doctrine of creation, specifically in terms of the relationship of the eternal Creator to the order of contingent things. Since this aspect of the doctrine of creation relates directly to the problem of the divine will and the way in which it identifies and relates to external objects, Arminius raises the issue in his public disputation on the will of God (which is, at this point, somewhat more elaborate than his private disputation). The highest good, which is necessarily the primary and direct object of the will of God, can be nothing other than the divine essence itself.[20] By definition, goodness is not merely a predicate of the divine essence, it is—in the simplicity of the divine essence—essentially identical with the essence itself. Goodness is the preeminent perfection of the divine essence, as, indeed, are all of the other attributes. Even so, the primary object of the divine will "was alone from all eternity, infinite ages prior to the existence of any other good; and therefore it is the only good (Prov. 8:22–24)."[21]

There is, according to Arminius, an ordering of lesser goods under the highest good that reflects the order of "movements" and secondary acts or operations in the nature of God. Finite good "does not exist with [the highest good], but from it, by the intellect and will of God."[22] The highest good is therefore the primary and direct object of the divine will and all other objects are both secondary and indirect: the highest good, which is the divine essence itself, is prior in order to the intellect and will of God, while all lesser goods are separated from the divine essence and stand under the operations of intellect and will.

Arminius recognizes that this identification of God as the primary, eternal and, indeed, eternally sufficient object of his own willing immediately raises the question of why the Godhead extends its willing to any secondary objects. In other words, if God exists eternally and "for infinite ages prior to the existence" of all finite good, what is the reason for his creative willing of lesser objects in time? The answer is that both the divine understanding and will, by seeking out the divine essence as the highest good, have as their primary object not merely being and goodness but the fullness or plenitude of being and goodness. This plenitude of its very nature is self-communicating. The divine knowledge confirms and the divine will enacts this self-communication of being and goodness, from which all good things arise—as secondary objects of the divine willing.[23] The

---

[20] *Disp. pub.*, IV.1.
[21] Ibid.
[22] Ibid.
[23] Ibid.

point is not well made, but it does reflect Aquinas' argument that

> it pertains ... to the nature of the will to communicate as far as possible
> to others the good possessed; and especially does this pertain to the
> divine will.... Thus, then, He wills both Himself to be, and other
> things to be; but Himself as the end, and other things as ordained to
> that end; inasmuch as it benefits the divine goodness that others
> should be partakers therein.[24]

The way in which Arminius argues the point not only reflects this
basic Thomist argument, but also the later elaboration of the argument by Capreolus and Suárez.[25] Capreolus had argued that the will
of God cannot be indeterminate inasmuch as it would, then, be inop-
erative—but it cannot be determined by imperfection, since that
would be counter to the very nature of God. The will of God, therefore, is subject to a "determining that cannot be outside of God"—that
is, to an internal or *ad intra* determining such as may be provided by
the adjudicating function of the intellect.[26] Thus, adds Suárez, the
divine intellect naturally and necessarily knows all things and proposes objects to the will. The will, in turn, naturally and necessarily
wills its principal object—which is to will that the intellect conceive
and dictate to the will what to produce in order to manifest the
divine goodness.[27] Here again, the basic intellectualist point was
retained in the later Leiden theology, as evidenced by Walaeus' discussion of the direction of the divine will. Since the will is a "rational
or intellectual faculty" it is directed by the intellect toward "the
known good"; so that God necessarily wills himself as the highest
good and freely wills all finite goods as they arise from and are drawn
toward his own goodness as their goal.[28]

God can, therefore, be said to will "things apart from himself by
willing his own goodness"[29] inasmuch as God both wills and loves
his essence and his essential goodness as the primary object of his
willing and loving. Since "the divine essence cannot be increased or
multiplied" except insofar as it is reflected in finite things that receive
being and goodness from it, God must be conceived of as willing "the
multitude of things in willing and loving his own essence and perfection."[30] Such would appear to be Arminius' point, made through the
words of Aquinas. The intellect is maintained as prior to will in the

[24] Aquinas, *Summa*, Ia, q.19, art.2, corpus.
[25] Cf. Suárez, *Disp.* XXX.xvi.44–48 (pp. 198–200), citing Capreolus, *Defensiones*, I,
dist.45, q.1, art.2, ad argum.
[26] Ibid., XXX.xvi.44.
[27] Ibid., XXX.xvi.47.
[28] Walaeus, *Loci communes*, III.9 (p. 176).
[29] Aquinas, *Summa*, Ia, q.19, art.2, ad obj.2.
[30] Aquinas, *SCG*, I.75.3.

assertion that intellect or understanding provides the will with its object, the divine goodness and, at the same time the will is recognized as the avenue by which the known good is communicated. Arminius' form of the argument, however, immediately raises the problem of a logical or ideational complexity or compoundedness in the divine essence—since he has not been nearly as careful as Aquinas to maintain the essential identity of intellect and will and their distinction in order only.[31]

Dorner's assessment of the Arminian teaching on the divine will as a radical extension of the nominalist *potentia absoluta* runs totally contrary to these basic tendencies of Arminius' thought. According to Dorner, Arminian theology "will not ... consider free divine sovereignty to be bound to any law in God" with the result that "the goodness as well as the righteousness of God" is "placed under his power" and that it is not because a thing is good in itself that it is willed by God "but that is good which God in fact commands and wills."[32] So arbitrary is this absolute power of God in the Arminian system, Dorner declares, that "there was nothing in God to prevent Him from giving other moral laws, if well-being had been thereby attainable."[33] Quite to the contrary, Arminius' radical intellectualism places the divine knowledge of the good prior to all acts of divine willing and identifies the human good as derived from the divine good. Indeed, the ultimate good of human beings arises, for Arminius, in the vision of God as the highest good and depends, ontologically, on the participation of the creature in the creative goodness of God: God wills first his own goodness and, second, the goodness of the creature in and through himself. Arminius' affinity for Thomism stands firmly in the way of a view such as proposed by Dorner.

The movement of the divine will toward objects *ad extra* must be understood not only in terms of the plenitude of divine goodness but also in terms of the other divine attributes. Indeed, it would be to misunderstand the character of the divine will to define it without reference to the simplicity, infinity, eternity, and immutability of the divine essence. As Arminius notes, the will of God is identical to the divine essence, "distinguished from it" only "according to formal reason."[34] Thus,

> the act by which the will of God extends toward its objects is most simple: for as the understanding of God by a most simple act understands its own essence, and, through it, all other things; so the will of

---

[31] Cf. ibid., I.45, 73, 74.
[32] Dorner, *History,* I, pp. 417–18.
[33] Ibid., p. 419.
[34] *Disp. pub.,* IV.1

God, by a single and simple act, wills its own goodness, and all things in its goodness.[35]

This point is much more clearly made than the preceding argument concerning the self-communication of divine goodness, primarily because Arminius does not attempt here either to describe the inter-relation of understanding and will in relation to goodness but, in a nearly perfect citation of Aquinas, relates understanding or intellect to essence and will to goodness.[36] The point could, of course, be just as easily drawn from Scotus, and although Scotus differs in his assumption of the priority of the will, Arminius' comment that the will is formally distinct from the divine essence may indicate a Scotist modification of his argument, perhaps, once again, mediated by Suárez. In any case, the language of Arminius' basic definition, "voluntas Dei est ipsamet Dei essentia" is more like the rather straightforward Latin of Aquinas' definition, "Est igitur voluntas Dei ipsa eius essentia" than it is like the more detailed argument of Suárez with its preference for *substantia* over *essentia*. The language of a "formal distinction," however, is foreign to Aquinas but clearly present in Suárez' definitions of the *voluntas Dei*.[37]

Arminius' doctrine here stands in substantial agreement with Reformed (and Lutheran) orthodoxy over against the views of Vorstius and the Socinians while, in a formal sense, it mediates between the two positions. The latter had denied the divine simplicity and its implication for the doctrine of the divine attributes, with the result that the will of God could be abstracted from the other attributes and conceived of as in some sense temporal and mutable.[38] Against this claim of real distinctions between the divine attributes, the Reformed had argued the Thomistic view of a distinction between the attributes that was neither a real distinction nor a merely rational distinction (*ratio ratiocinans*) but rather a distinction by reason of analysis (*ratio ratiocinata*) and, therefore, having a basis in the thing analyzed. On their way to this conclusion, moreover, the Reformed had considered and rejected the notion of an objective formal or, to

---

[35] Ibid., IV.li.

[36] Cf. Aquinas, *Summa*, Ia, q.19, art.2, ad obj.2: "Unde, cum Deus alia a se velit nisi propter finem qui est sua bonitas, ut dictum est, non sequitur quod aliquid aliud moveat voluntatem eius nisi bonitas sua. Et sic, sicut alia a se intelligit intelligendo essentiam suam, ita alia a se vult, volendo bonitatem suam." Cf. Arminius, *Disp. pub.*, IV.li: "nam ut intellectus Dei simplicissimo actu intelligit essentiam suam, & per illam omnia alia; sic voluntas Dei uno & simplici actu vult bonitatem suam & omnia in bonitate sua."

[37] Cf. Arminius, *Disp. pub.* IV.1, ad fin with Aquinas, *SCG*, I.73.2 and Suárez, *Disp. metaph.*, XXX.xvi.12–13; on Scotus, see Minges, II, pp. 122, 151; and, on the formal distinction of attributes, ibid., II, pp. 59–60.

[38] Cf. Walaeus, *Loci communes*, III.9 (p. 176) with Turretin, *Inst. theol.*, III.vii.

use another of Suárez' terms, a modal distinction.[39] Not only, therefore, is it the case that the medieval discussion of rational, formal, and real distinctions created an exhaustive paradigm, it is also the case that the Protestant scholastics, from Vorstius, to Arminius, to the Reformed and Lutheran orthodox, reproduced the older paradigm, including the view rejected by the medieval church, of real distinctions between the essence and attributes of God.[40]

In accord with his scholastic view of the divine attributes, Arminius must conclude that "the multitude of things willed (*multitudo volitorum*) is not repugnant to the simplicity of the divine will."[41] God's will is one—its secondary object is a universe of finite beings. Why is it that the multiplicity of the object is not reflected in the will, and how is it that a single will can effect a universe of things? The answer lies in the relationship of the will to the divine goodness. In willing simply and undividedly the plenitude of his own goodness, God wills the actualization of all good *ad intra* and *ad extra* inasmuch as all finite good both issues forth from and finds its goal in God, the highest good.[42] The difficulty with this position, of course, lies in the experience of freedom, contingency, and, indeed, of evil running counter to the will of God, in the finite order. The emphasis on God's willing all things in and through the goodness of the divine essence points toward an infinite, eternal, and, in some sense necessary divine willing, indeed, toward precisely the kind of causal determinism that Arminius strives to avoid.

Even so, this "act by which the will of God extends toward its objects" is also infinite, eternal, immutable, and, Arminius adds, holy. He seems to equate the infinitude of the divine will with the uncaused ultimacy of the divine essence: "it is ... infinite because it is moved to will, neither by an external cause, whether efficient or final,

---

[39] Cf. Burmann, *Synopsis theol.*, III.xix.8–9 with Turretin, *Inst. theol.*, III.v.9 and Mastricht, *Theoretico-practica theol.*, II.v.7.

[40] See Schwane, *Histoire des Dogmes*, IV, pp. 185–86, 190–207.

[41] *Disp. pub.*, IV.li: "Itaque multitudo volitorum non repugnat simplicitati voluntatis divinae"; cf. Aquinas, *SCG*, I.77.1: "Et hoc sequitur quod volitorum multitudo non repugnat unitati et simplicitati divinae substantiae."

[42] *Disp. priv.*, IV.li: "sic voluntas Dei ... vult bonitatem suam et omnia in bonitate sua"; cf. Aquinas, *SCG*, I.77.3: "Ostensum est quod Deus alia vult inquantum vult bonitatem suam." Also, Arminius, *Disp. pub.*, IV.xxiii: "Bonitas essentiae Dei et secundum quam ipsa summum et ipsa bonum est, essentialiter in se ipsa, ex cuius participatione omnia alia sunt, et bona sunt: et ad quam omnia alia tanquam ad summum finem sunt referanda"; cf. Aquinas, *Summa*, Ia, q.5, art.5, ad 3: "quia Deus est bonus, summus, refertur ad causam finalem"; q.6, art.4: "Et quia bonum convertitur cum ente, sicut et unum, ipsum per se bonum dicebat esse Deum, a quo dicuntur bona per modum participationis"; *SCG*, I.41.3: "Deus est bonus per suam essentiam, alia vero per participationem.... Est igitur ipse summum bonum."

... nor is it moved by any object other than itself."[43] The act of divine will is also eternal and immutable inasmuch as God always knows what will be and what is good: nothing from the finite order can appear new or different to God. What God knows and wills, God knows and wills perpetually, since the "immutable being" of God is the subject that both knows and wills. Thus, also, the will of God is holy,

> because God inclines toward (tendit) his object only insofar as it is good, not on account of any other thing which is added to it; and only because his understanding accounts it good, not because one of his affections [e.g., love, mercy, kindness] inclines toward it without right reason.[44]

The holiness of God's will is, thus, guaranteed by the intellectualist premise of Arminius' argument, following out the logic of the Thomistic position that the object of the will must be a known good. The good is grasped by the intellect inasmuch as the intellect takes as its proper object the essence and essential goodness of God. The intellect does not itself act but rather directs the will toward its object, the known good.[45]

This argument directly reflects the point made by Arminius in his prolegomena that God, as the highest good, extends himself toward rational creatures as the proper object and goal of their religious knowing.[46] Right religion and true theology reflect from an epistemological perspective the ontological order of the universe. Even so, the doctrine of God—the *principium essendi theologiae*—provides a series of governing concepts that extend back into the prolegomena and forward into the successive *loci* of the system. The character of the divine "extension" toward the finite thus determines both the nature of theology and the form taken by the providential governance of creation and by the plan of salvation.

Granting the rather necessitarian direction of these arguments, Arminius must propose some diversity and distinction in the divine

---

[43] Arminius, *Disp. pub.*, IV.li: "sic voluntas Dei ... vult bonitatem suam et omnia in bonitate sua"; cf. Aquinas, *SCG*, I.77.3: "Ostensum est quod Deus alia vult inquantum vult bonitatem suam." Also, Arminius, *Disp. pub.*, IV.xxiii: "Bonitas essentiae Dei et secundum quam ipsa summum et ipsa bonum est, essentialiter in se ipsa, ex cuius participatione omnia alia sunt, et bona sunt: et ad quam omnia alia tanquam ad summum finem sunt referenda"; cf. Aquinas, *Summa*, Ia, q.5, art.5, ad 3: "quia Deus est bonus, summus, refertur ad causam finalem"; q.6, art.4: "Et quia bonum convertitur cum ente, sicut et unum, ipsum per se bonum dicebat esse Deum, a quo dicuntur bona per modum participationis"; *SCG*, I.41.3: "Deus est bonus per suam essentiam, alia vero per participationem.... Est igitur ipse summum bonum."

[44] *Disp. pub.*, IV.li

[45] Cf. *SCG*, I.45, 72, 74.

[46] *De auctore*, p. 49 (*Works*, I, pp. 361–62).

willing. Such diversity and distinction cannot, of course, arise out of the divine essence in its simplicity. Rather, it must arise out of the character of the possible objects known to God and actualized by him in his act of creation. The will of God, in other words, relates to and accommodates to its objects—first in terms of an order of willing objects in relation to other objects and in relation to God's purpose and, second, in terms of distinctions in willing arising out of the order and relation of the objects willed. Only by means of these two series of distinctions can the contingency and freedom recognized in the world order be explained as existing under, indeed, as resting on the divine will.

"As the simple and eternal act by which the divine understanding knows all its objects does not exclude order from them, so likewise may we be allowed to assign a certain order according to which the simple and single act of the will of God is extended toward its objects."[47] The parallel with Arminius' early presentation of the order of objects in the divine intellect is quite apparent.[48] As in the case of the divine understanding, where God is said first and foremost to know himself, so also in the discussion of the divine will is God said, first and foremost to will himself. Second, and as a result of the plenitude of divine goodness, God wills all things.[49] At this point the identification of an order is crucial, inasmuch as God can hardly be said to will all things, the creatures, acts of creatures, contingent events, and defects in creatures, in their acts and in the contingent order, in precisely the same way. It should be clear from the outset that God does not will the good, sin, and the punishment of sin in the same way.

Arminius presents the order of divine willing according to a pattern extending from the general to the specific: from those things resting solely on God's will to those things that arise in the context of creaturely willing. Thus, after God wills himself, in a secondary and derivative sense,

he wills all those things which, out of infinite things possible to him, he has by the final judgment of his wisdom determined to make.[50]

This general will is further distinguished into five aspects:

First, he wills to make them to be; then second he is affected toward them by his will, according as they possess some likeness to his nature, or some vestige of it. The third object of the will of God, are those

---

[47] Disp. pub., IV.lii.
[48] Cf. Disp. pub., IV.xxxiv and Disp. priv., XVII.iv.
[49] Disp. pub., IV.lii; Disp. priv., XVIII.ii.
[50] Disp. priv., XVIII.iv.

things which he judges fit and equitable to be done by creatures who
are endowed with understanding and with free will; in which is
included a prohibition of what he wills not to be done. The fourth
object of the divine will is his permission, that chiefly by which he
permits a rational creature to do what he has prohibited and to omit
what he has commanded. Fifth, he wills those things which, according
to his own wisdom, he judges ought to be done about the acts of his
rational creatures.[51]

Arminius' central concern is clearly not the theodicy question that
would become a major issue with the rise of rationalism in the
seventeenth century but rather the scholastic question of the operation of the *concursus divinus*—the divine willing of all things that
operates concurrently with and that therefore concurs in and, in
effect, sustains the willing of all rational creatures. There is no particular concern to argue how such unpleasant results of contingencies
in the natural order like fire, famine, flood, or earthquake somehow
belong to the divine will.

These arguments create a paradox: on the one hand God is infinite
and simple in his willing and in no way caused by anything external
to himself to will in one way or another—but on the other hand, God
is responsive to the wills of his free, rational creatures, permitting
them to act against his will and responding positively or negatively to
their acts, as he deems fit. How is this possible? If indeed God wills all
things by one eternal and immutable act, he must, in some sense,
simultaneously will all of the defects, problems, and sins of the temporal order, together with his response to those defects, problems, and
sins. But this explanation verges on a monism that deprives the
created order of its freedom. The opposite explanation, that would
emphasize the freedom of creatures and the responsiveness of God,
militates against the divine eternity, simplicity, and immutability.
Arminius recognizes the paradox and, without resolving it, frames it
with a definition that attempts to do justice to the terms of the
problem:

> There is outside of God no inwardly-moving cause of his will; nor is
> there any goal [i.e., final cause] outside of him. But the creature, its
> action or passion, may be the outwardly-moving cause, without which
> God would supercede or omit that volition.[52]

Thus, the understanding, will, and power of God cause all things,
simply and immutably so, but also in such a way that the divine will
for a creature concurs in and with the will of the creature for itself.
"When he acts either through his creatures, with them or in them,

---

[51] Ibid.
[52] Ibid., XVIII.v.

he does not take away the distinctive mode of acting or experiencing (*modum proprium agendi vel patiendi*) that he has divinely placed in them, but [permits] them to produce their own effects and to receive in themselves the actions of God, according to their same distinctive mode, either necessarily, contingently or freely."[53] Arminius notes the parallel between this point and the point made previously concerning divine foreknowledge: just as God can have certain knowledge of future contingencies without either any diminution of divine knowledge or any reduction of contingency to necessity, so too can the divine will coincide with contingency in the created order, indeed, with the "certain futurition" of contingent events. If a future event is certain, and known with certainty by God, its contingent character is also known.[54]

Whereas the first point—that the divine will sustains all things in their necessity, contingency, and freedom—could have been made by any of Arminius' Reformed contemporaries,[55] the problem underlying the second point—the divine foreknowledge of future contingency—leads Arminius toward a qualification of the language of divine willing that is quite opposed to the Reformed thought of the day. The problem of the way in which a foreknown event of "certain futurition" can become the "outwardly-moving cause" of divine willing[56] presses Arminius beyond the question of an order in the objects of divine willing toward the question of distinctions in the divine will relating to "the manner and order of its extension toward objects."[57] The basic point that the eternal and in some sense necessary will of God in no way interferes with but actually sustains the contingency of secondary causes is, moreover, a common feature of Thomism, whether Catholic or Reformed,[58] whereas the modifications introduced by Arminius represent attempts to modify the Thomistic point in the direction of a less clearly defined relationship between divine and creaturely causality.

In order to resolve the problem of the simple, eternal, and immutable divine will over against the multiple, free, and contingent willing of temporal creatures, Arminius proposes a series of nine distinctions in the divine will.[59] These sets of distinctions, like most

[53] Ibid., XVIII.vi.

[54] Ibid.; cf. *Disp. pub.*, IV.liv.

[55] Cf. *RD*, pp. 82, 144.

[56] Cf. *Disp. priv.*, XVIII.vi with XVIII.v.

[57] Ibid., XIX.i.

[58] Cf. Aquinas, *Summa*, Ia, q.19, art.8; *SCG*, I, 84; with Ursinus, *Explicat.*, cols. 136–37 (*Commentary*, pp. 161–62); Zanchi, *De natura Dei*, III.iv.6; V.i.4; Junius, *Theses theologicae* (Leiden), XVII.7.

[59] Cf. *Disp. pub.*, IV.lvi–lxiii with *Disp. priv.*, XIX.ii–ix; the *Public Disputations* and the *Private Disputations* both contain eight distinctions—however, the second distinction from *Disp. pub.* does not appear in *Disp. priv.*, while the third numbered

of the preceding doctrinal arguments, rest on an acquaintance with late medieval theology and reflect the borrowings of Arminius' Reformed and Lutheran contemporaries. As in the distinctions concerning the *scientia Dei*, the differences between Arminius' definitions and those proposed by the early orthodox Reformed theologians point ineluctably toward the debate over predestination and human free will.

Arminius makes an initial distinction between the operation of the divine will according to "the mode of nature" and its operation according to "the mode of liberty."[60] This distinction returns us, momentarily, to the question of the objects of the divine willing. According to the mode of nature, God naturally wills the primary and direct object of his will—which is to say, himself. According to the mode of liberty, however, God freely wills other things, things *ad extra*. This free mode of willing must be subdivided into a "liberty of exercise" and a "liberty of specification," the former being an extension of will generally toward all things, the latter an extension of will specifically toward good things or toward things insofar as they are good.[61] This distinction and limitation arise because of the existence of things deserving of the divine anger or hate. Such things are willed by God generally insofar as God wills the existence of all things but are clearly not specifically willed by God to be sinful or defective.

The basic distinction between two modes of willing, one natural, the other free, or, as it was more commonly stated, between a *voluntas necessaria sive naturalis*, a necessary or natural will, and a *voluntas libera*, a free will, parallels and echoes the distinction between *scientia necessaria* and *scientia libera*.[62] It was used equally by Lutheran and Reformed contemporaries of Arminius and has little debate or controversy associated with it.[63] The *voluntas naturalis* is the will that God has according to his own nature. God therefore has it by a natural necessity and by it wills his own goodness, justice, and holiness. The *voluntas libera* like the *scientia libera* is directed *ad extra* and is the will that is referred to in the general, nontechnical language concerning the attribution of will to God. It is therefore this "mode of liberty" of the divine will that becomes the subject of further discussion and

---

(actually the fourth stated) distinction from *Disp. priv.* does not appear in *Disp. pub.* There is also the problem in the *Disp. priv.* that only seven distinctions are numbered: XIX.iv ought to be distinction 3 and not a second part of distinction 2 (XIX.iii). In any case, a comparison of *Disp. pub.* and *Disp. priv.* yields nine distinctions.

[60] *Disp. priv.*, XIX.ii.

[61] Ibid.

[62] Cf. *DLGT*, s.v. *"voluntas Dei."*

[63] Cf. Walaeus, *Loci communes*, III.9 (p. 176) with Gerhard, *Loci communes*, II.xv.10; also note *RD*, p. 84, and *DTEL*, p. 26.

distinction. (Arminius' choice of language—"mode of liberty" rather than the more frequent *voluntas libera*—is probably a reflection of a concern to observe the problems of predication of the various divine attributes. Rather than speak improperly of two wills in God, one natural and one free, Arminius identifies two modes of the one divine will.)

Arminius next comes to one of the distinctions typical of late medieval scholastic theology, that between the *voluntas beneplaciti*, "the will of [divine] good pleasure," and the *voluntas signi*, "the will of the sign" or "will of the precept."[64] This distinction, like the distinction noted by Arminius between the liberty of exercise and the liberty of specification, is typically used by medieval, Reformed, and Lutheran scholastics as a distinction within the *voluntas libera*.[65] Arminius does not specifically note a connection at this point, although the implication of a relationship between the first and second distinctions is clear: by moving from the "mode of nature" to the "mode of liberty," Arminius has followed the divine will in its movement or tendency toward objects *ad extra*. All subsequent distinctions refer to the divine will as active *ad extra*.

The will of divine good pleasure Arminius defines as the absolute will of God "to do or to prevent anything." This will is "partly revealed" and "partly hidden (*occulta*)" and is an efficacious will that employs divine power to achieve its ends. Arminius argues that this power is either utterly irresistible or so great that its object cannot withstand it. In other words the power of God is "accommodated to the object and subject in order that the effect might occur even though it could happen otherwise."[66] The *voluntas beneplaciti* is, therefore, the ultimate and irresistible will of God. This will is not to be confused with the absolute and necessary *voluntas naturalis* by which God wills himself; rather it is the ultimate will that God freely wills toward creatures, a category of *voluntas libera*. It is not, however, a category of divine willing that Arminius typically uses to explain events in the world, since his interest lies in the identification of the relationship of God's will to the creature in its freedom and contingency.[67] Reformed orthodox writers not only agree with this basic definition but, assuming the identity of the will of divine good pleasure with the decretive will of God, also view the *voluntas beneplaciti* as crucial to theological explanation: thus Walaeus can define

---

[64] Cf. *DLGT*, s.v. "*voluntas Dei*"; and note the use of the distinction in, e.g., Alexander of Hales, *Summa*, I/1, inqu.1, tract.6, q.3, memb.1–2; Gregory of Rimini, *I sent.*, d.46–47, q.1, art.1; Capreolus, *Defensiones*, I, dist.46–47; Scotus, *Op. oxon.*, I, dist. 46, n.2 and II, dist.37, n.21, in Minges, II, pp. 170–71.

[65] Cf. *RD*, pp. 84–85 with *DTEL*, pp. 126–28.

[66] *Disp. priv.*, XIX.iii; cf. *Disp. pub.*, IV.lvii.

[67] Cf. *Disp. priv.*, XVIII.vi.

the *voluntas beneplaciti* as the will by which God immediately decrees both in and concerning mankind whatever he wills—whether it is an event that will occur or one that will not occur, whether it tends toward salvation or toward condemnation. The *"bene"* in *beneplaciti*, adds Walaeus, refers not to temporal events but to the eternal *consilium Dei* that is always good (*semper bonum*) whether it punishes or confers blessings (*sive punit sive beneficiis afficit*).[68]

The *voluntas signi*, the will of the sign or perhaps, better, signified will, is a completely revealed will of God by which God "wills something to be done, or not done by creatures endowed with understanding."[69] This is an "inefficacious" will insofar as creatures can resist and disobey the revealed will of God. Their resistance or disobedience, however, is limited in a sense by the revealed will itself: for the disobedient still fall under the rule or order of the revealed will and risk the imposition of God's will upon them.[70] Over against the Reformed language of *voluntas signi*, Arminius excludes from consideration here the universal call of the gospel: he will not juxtapose a revealed universality of promise with a hidden particularism of salvation. To the Arminian mind, Reformed theology hypothesizes a contradiction in God: God wills the salvation of all (*voluntas signi*) and, at the same time does not will the salvation of all (*voluntas beneplaciti*).[71] Indeed, Arminius' construction of the distinction between *voluntas beneplaciti* as an absolute and *voluntas signi* as a conditional will of God perfectly echoes the definition of absolute and conditional will proposed by Molina for the specific purpose of declaring how God can, conditionally, will all men to be saved while also willing, absolutely, the existence and freedom of sinful creatures and, in addition, the punishment of those who do not repent.[72] For Arminius, as for Molina, the potential contradiction is resolved in the concept of a divine *scientia media* and in a revised conception of the divine causal concurrence in creaturely acts.[73]

The *voluntas beneplaciti* and *voluntas signi* also, according to Arminius, have their negative corollaries—a "twofold ... remission of the will" paralleling the twofold declaration of God's will. The will of divine good pleasure is reflected in a divine permission for the

---

[68] Cf. Walaeus, *Loci communes*, III.9 (p. 179) with *RD*, pp. 85–88. Heppe is incorrect in his conclusion that Reformed theology has "generally ... disapproved" of the distinction between *voluntas beneplaciti* and *voluntas signi* (p. 88).

[69] *Disp. pub.*, IV.lviii.

[70] Ibid. This expanded definition of *voluntas signi* is absent from *Disp. priv.*, XIX.

[71] Cf. *RD*, p. 87 with Walaeus' attempt to deal with the Arminian objection, *Loci communes*, III.9 (p. 179).

[72] Cf. Vansteenberghe, "Molinisme," *DTC* 10/2, col. 2120.

[73] Cf. above, pp 110–21 and below, pp. 195–99.

creature to transgress the ultimate good pleasure or purpose of God: God withdraws or remits his "efficacious will" and allows the successful action of "the will of the creature by not imposing an effective impediment," or, more simply, "permits something to the power (*potestati*) of a rational creature, by not circumscribing [its] act with a law (*lege*)."[74] The signified or preceptive will of God is reflected in a remission of divine will "which permits something to the power of a rational creature, by not circumscribing its act with a law."[75]

As we have recognized in the various distinctions used by Arminius to explain the concept of theology, the divine nature, the essential attributes, and the divine intellect or understanding, Arminius' theological views are rooted in late medieval scholastic theology. These distinctions in the divine will are no exception to the generalization: every one of them, beginning with the basic distinction between *voluntas beneplaciti* and *voluntas signi*, can easily be identified in virtually any of the great summas and sentence commentaries from Alexander of Hales[76] to Gabriel Biel.[77] Arminius' definitions reflect this tradition, draw on its vocabulary, and in places adjust the definitions to his own purposes. Thus, Arminius does not use the distinction between *voluntas beneplaciti* and *voluntas signi* as the foundation for all the rest—even though certain points of connection between it and subsequent definitions can easily be detected. As a basis for comparison with the scholastics, we note Altenstaig's summary definition:

> the will of God truly and properly defined is in God and is [identical with] his essence. It is, moreover, one and not understood as a multiplicity. Whence it is typically distinguished into the will of divine good pleasure (*voluntas beneplaciti*) and the will of the sign or signified will (*voluntas signi*). The *voluntas beneplaciti* is twofold, namely, the antecedent and consequent will (*voluntas antecedens & consequens*). The *voluntas signi* is fivefold, namely, prohibition (*prohibitio*), precept (*praeceptio*), counsel (*consilium*), fulfillment (*impletio*) and operation (*operatio*).[78]

The reason that Arminius departs from the typical scholastic pattern of using the distinction between *voluntas beneplaciti* and *voluntas signi* as the basic pattern for the whole definition may be found in the *Articuli nonnulli*, or *Certain Articles* where he writes, "the distinction of the will of God into that which is secret or of his good

---

[74] *Disp. pub.*, IV.lviii; *Disp. priv.*, XIX.iii.

[75] *Disp. pub.*, IV.lviii.

[76] Alexander of Hales, *Summa*, I/1, inqu.1, tract.6, q.3.

[77] Gabriel Biel, *Sacri canonis misse expositio resolutissima* (Basel, 1510); cols. 68–69 as cited in Oberman, *Harvest*, pp. 103–4.

[78] Altenstaig, *Lexicon theologicum*, s.v., "*voluntas Dei.*"

pleasure, and that which is revealed or signified, cannot bear a rigid examination."[79] Arminius clearly objects to the idea that God may will one thing in an ultimate and hidden way and will another contradictory or opposite thing in a penultimate and revealed way. His positive definition of the distinction bears this out inasmuch as he views the *voluntas beneplaciti* as an ultimate, irresistible will and limits the *voluntas signi* to the revealed law: the former is the ultimate end of God, the latter is merely the ideal for human conduct and not in any way a departure from or contradiction of the divine purpose.

Arminius next presents his own reading of the distinction between the proper and alien work of God (*opus proprium; opus alienum*). Some work is said to be "proper to God," he argues, when God wills certain objects "from himself, not on account of any other cause placed beyond him."[80] Other divine work is said to be "extraneous and alien" (*extraneum & alienum*) when it is done by God "on account of a preceding cause provided by the creature."[81] Even so, some of the things that God wills—like morally good works—are "pleasing and acceptable to God in themselves," while other things willed by God— like ceremonial acts—"please accidentally and on account of some other thing."[82] This reading of the distinction between *opus proprium* and *opus alienum* is unusual, to say the least.

In the first place, the distinction is not typically presented in the discussion of the *voluntas Dei*, but rather as an element of the doctrines of creation and providence. In the second place, the alien work of God performed "on account of a preceding cause afforded by the creature" is typically defined by the scholastics as a divine working of good ends in and through the evil acts of creatures.[83] The distinction between intrinsically good works and ceremonial acts—as things differently willed by God—has little bearing upon the meaning of proper and alien work. Arminius does, however, have recourse to the concept of an alien work of God in his discussion of the relation of providence to sin: here he observes the traditional definition but does not explicitly draw on the vocabulary.[84] The typical scholastic definition of the *opus alienum* appears in Arminius' *Declaration of Sentiments* as an element in his theology of creation: the proper work of God is the creation itself, whereas "the actions of God that tend

---

[79] *Articuli nonnulli*, II.7.
[80] *Disp. priv.*, XIX.iv.
[81] Ibid.
[82] Ibid.; cf. *Disp. pub.*, IV.lix.
[83] *Disp. priv.*, XIX.iv.
[84] Cf. *Disp. pub.*, X.x, xii.

toward the condemnation of the creature, are alien acts of God (*alienae Dei actiones*), because God consents to them for some other extraneous cause" [i.e., to his ultimate purpose].[85]

Why Arminius varies his definition of this distinction is not clear. It is particularly curious that Arminius' *Private Disputations,* in which he is making an effort to provide normative definition, would stray so far from the typical definition of *opus alienum.* Both definitions of the alien work of God do, however, emphasize a point integral to Arminius' revision of the Reformed doctrine of the will of God: rather than emphasize the way in which the divine *opus alienum* works the will of God and, therefore, serves the divine purpose in and despite the sinful wills of creatures, Arminius emphasizes the way in which the divine *opus alienum* is a response to the willing of contingent beings—over against the *opus proprium* as an absolute will of God.

The fourth distinction noted by Arminius in his *Private Disputations* (omitted from the *Public Disputations*) is between the peremptory and the conditional will of God. The peremptory will of God is a will that "strictly or rigidly obtains." Here Arminius gives as an example the words of the gospel, "the wrath of God abides on him who does not believe" and "he that believes shall be saved" (cf. John 3:36).[86] Both of these texts are direct statements of divine intention. Sometimes, however, the will of God is expressed conditionally—as in Jeremiah 18:8, "If that nation, against whom I have pronounced, turn from their evil, I will repent of the evil that I thought to do unto them."[87] Here the intention of God is to influence the creature; but in both cases, peremptory or conditional, the will of God is described as related and responsive to the free and contingent willing of creatures.

In his fifth distinction, Arminius returns to the issue indicated in his reinterpretation of the distinction between the proper and the alien work of God—the relationship of the divine willing to actions on the part of creatures. Indeed, as indicated in the final sections of the preceding disputations (*On the Will of God*), this is the central concern of Arminius' entire discussion of the divine will. The will of God toward creatures, the *voluntas libera,* is either "absolute" or "respective":

> The absolute [will] is that by which he wills anything simply, without regard to the volition or act of the creature; such as is that about the salvation of believers. The respective is that by which he wills something with respect to the volition or act of the creature.[88]

[85] *Dec. sent.*, p. 108 (*Works*, I, p. 627).
[86] *Disp. priv.*, XIX.v.
[87] Ibid. (referencing but not quoting Jer. 18:7–10).
[88] *Disp. priv.*, XIX.vi.

The definition draws directly on Aquinas who, in defining predestination, distinguished between a simple and a relative willing in God.[89]

The distinction between absolute and respective will can also be presented as a willing of things for what they are in themselves or as a willing of things "in their antecedents."[90] (Arminius presents this point as his eighth distinction in the *Private Disputations*, noting its identity with the fifth distinction.) When God wills a thing in its antecedents, he wills it not directly in and for itself, but relatively, in and through its causes. In other words, he wills the cause primarily or directly but "in such an order that effects may follow." Granting that the effects do follow, they have been willed "in their antecedents." Arminius adds that, nonetheless, these effects can still be willed so that, in themselves, they are also pleasing to God.[91]

The respective will of God, moreover, is either antecedent or consequent:

> The antecedent is that by which he wills something with respect to the subsequent will or act of the creature, as, God wills all men to be saved if they believe. The consequent is that by which he wills something with respect to the antecedent volition or action of the creature.... Both depend on the absolute will, and according to it each of them is regulated.[92]

This distinction, as formulated by Arminius, is not very different from the issue addressed by his definition of the divine *opus alienum* or from the preceding distinction between the peremptory and conditional will of God. Since Arminius' definition directly reflects Aquinas,[93] the significance of the formulation must be identified in terms of the spectrum of Reformed teaching, which included Thomistic formulae in addition to the more nominalistic views opposed by Arminius. Arminius' other writings offer testimony to the importance he set on this distinction properly defined: he calls it correct and useful while at the same time raising questions about the distinction between *voluntas beneplaciti* and *voluntas signi*,[94] and he appears to use it in his language of the four decrees of salvation.[95]

The Thomistic view had been advocated among the Reformed prior to Arminius by Zanchi and contemporaneously with Arminius

---

[89] Aquinas, *Summa*, Ia, q.23, art.4, ad obj.3.

[90] *Disp. priv.*, XIX.ix; cf. *Disp. pub.*, IV.lxii.

[91] Ibid.

[92] *Disp. priv.*, XIX.vi.

[93] Cf. Aquinas, *Summa*, Ia, q.19, art.6, ad obj.1; q.23, art.4, ad obj.3 with Garrigou-Lagrange, *Predestination*, pp. 80–84.

[94] *Articuli nonnulli*, II.6–7.

[95] Cf. ibid., XV.1–4 with *Dec. sent.*, p. 119 (*Works*, I, pp. 653–54).

by Polanus. After Arminius, it would continue to be represented by Walaeus. In all cases, these theologians defined the antecedent will as a general will of God toward human beings, prior to and not predicated upon human faith, human merit, or human actions. The consequent will stands as a divine response to faith, merit, or actions. Like the *voluntas signi*, the *voluntas antecedens* is not always fulfilled, whereas the *voluntas consequens* is absolute and simple and is always fulfilled.[96] A rather different view of antecedent and consequent will appears in Perkins, who seems to have identified the antecedent will with the *voluntas beneplaciti*.[97]

Against Perkins' use of the language of antecedent and consequent will as a distinction between an absolute, irresistible will and a will that is conditional in the sense that it arises in relation to secondary causes, Arminius argues pointedly that the antecedent and consequent wills of God must be defined, not in relation to the divine being as such, but instead in relation to the temporal acts of creatures. The antecedent will logically precedes God's knowing and willing of a creaturely act; the consequent will logically follows the creaturely act and responds to it. The only other meaning that Arminius will allow for the distinction relates to the internal and logical order of the divine will itself: "God wills one volition before another in order, though not in time" with "the former as antecedent, the latter as consequent."[98] Thus, "if we consider the order of the things willed by God before all action or volition of the creature, ... some are antecedent and some are consequent volitions, but all preceding every act of the creature." The will that is normally called consequent arises in response "to creature's act or volition."[99]

Since both the antecedent and the consequent will stand in relation to the creature, Arminius can deny that either is an absolute will— whether absolute is understood as irresistible or unconditioned. God, therefore, does not damn anyone by an absolute will, even if the divine will to damn can be grounded on antecedent conditions, nor, conversely, can the antecedent divine will to save all men be identified as absolute:

> God seriously wills all men to be saved; yet, compelled by the pertinacious and incorrigible wickedness of some, he wills them ... to be condemned. If you say that ... God could have corrected their wickedness ... I answer that God can, indeed, by his absolute omnipotence, but that it is not fitting for him to correct the wickedness of the creature in that

---

[96] Cf. Zanchi, *De natura Dei*, III.iv, q.3; Polanus, *Syntagma*, II.xix; Walaeus, *Loci communes*, III.9 (p. 180).

[97] Perkins, *Treatise of the Manner and Order of Predestination*, pp. 606–7.

[98] *Examen modestum*, p. 740 (*Works*, III, p. 429).

[99] Ibid., p. 741.

mode. God therefore wills their condemnation, because he is unwilling for his own justice to perish.[100]

There is no irresistible will operative here and, indeed, no will that stands outside of the realm of relationship to concrete existents. Arminius denies that God can have any dominion over "creatures indefinitely foreknown, that is, possible creatures" that "are not entities."[101]

The antecedent will, Arminius comments, ought to be called *velleitas* rather than *voluntas*.[102] *Velle est in se volitionem habere*, writes Altenstaig: "to will is to have volition (i.e., the exercise of will) in one's self."[103] If *voluntas* is the faculty that exercises volition, *velleitas* is the inchoate, imperfect because incomplete character of will addressing impossibility or, perhaps, not to be actualized possibility. Thus Aquinas contrasts the *voluntas absoluta et completa seu perfecta* that attains its goals and *voluntas incompleta* or *velleitas* that wills impossibles or possibles that do not exist.[104] By identifying the antecedent will of God as *velleitas*, Arminius, therefore, removes it from consideration as an absolute or effective willing. Gomarus, who, like Perkins, assumed an absolute, omnipotent, and inalterable antecedent will, would clearly have grounds for concern over Arminius' definition and, specifically, over the way in which, in concert with Arminius' other distinctions, it tended to lessen the immediacy and necessity of divine involvement in the life and activity of all things.[105] As Wendelin would later comment, "Strictly considered, *velleitas* does not apply to God, since it denotes imperfection,"[106] that is, an incapacity or inefficacy in willing.

Much of the debate between Arminius and the Reformed, therefore, relates to the character of the divine knowledge of possible creatures and to the character of the divine will toward such known (or foreknown) possibles. Or, to state the problem somewhat differently, the debate is over the implication of the precedence of the antecedent divine willing over creaturely existence and creaturely acts: Is the precedence such that it implies an indefinite divine knowing or does God always will in relation to definite objects, whether to create them or to act toward or upon them? The Reformed object to the Arminian use of the concept of antecedent willing in relation to the divine decree in order to hypothesize a general, indefinite divine willing by

[100] Ibid., p. 742 (*Works*, III, pp. 430–31).
[101] *Examination of the Theses*, in *Works*, III, p. 627.
[102] *Disp. pub.*, IV.lx.
[103] Altenstaig, *Lexicon theologicum*, s.v. *"velle"* (p. 932).
[104] Aquinas, *Summa*, Ia, q.19, art.6, ad.1; III, q.21, art.4, corpus.
[105] Cf. Gomarus' accusation in Dibon, *L'Enseignement philosophique*, p. 66.
[106] *RD*, p. 81.

which God ordains means of salvation without reference to man's
good or evil use of his power of choice or to the work of grace upon
the human will.[107] In other words, the Reformed deny that God can
will salvation, specifically, the means of salvation, apart from a full,
definite knowledge of the results of his willing. Later Reformed dogmaticians, like Voetius, Heidegger, and Mastricht, allow the early
definition of a general antecedent willing of the conditions of salvation but argue, on the ground of the divine eternity and simplicity,
that there is but one will of God that wills all things. To postulate
indefinite and unfulfilled willing in God is, they declare, an error.[108]

As a sixth distinction, Arminius notes that God wills some things
"insofar as they are good when absolutely considered according to
their nature" and other things "insofar as, after an inspection of all
the circumstances, they are understood to be desirable."[109] This distinction, by Arminius' own admission, is virtually identical with the
concept of an antecedent will of God. Similarly (seventh), "God wills
some things *per se* and others *per accidens*."[110] Thus God wills some
things of or in themselves because they are good: even so, "he wills
salvation to the obedient man." God wills those things accidentally
that are not simply or fully good but that are in some way evil. God
thus wills punishment which is in itself an evil—but he wills it for
the sake of his justice: "he wills that the order of justice be served by
punishment rather than the sinful creature go unpunished."[111] In
a related distinction that appears only in the *Public Disputations*,
Arminius argues that God "wills some things as an end, and other
things as the means to that end." The former are willed by a "natural
affection or desire," the latter by a "free choice."[112]

All of Arminius' distinctions concerning the divine will are analyses or modifications of traditional scholastic argumentation. His
modifications are significant not only because they direct the doctrine
away from the typical Reformed definitions but also because they all
tend to display a mutual or reciprocal relation between God and
world rather than a purely sovereign or absolute relation of God to
the world. Whereas the Reformed doctrine of the will of God tends to
resolve all distinctions into a single, simple, eternal will of God to
actualize certain possibilities and not others, the Arminian doctrine
tends to emphasize the distinctions for the sake of arguing interaction
between God and genuinely free or contingent events in the created

---

[107] Cf. Walaeus, *Loci communes*, III.9 (p. 180).
[108] *RD*, pp. 91–92.
[109] *Disp. pub.*, IV.lxi; cf. *Disp. priv.*, XIX.vii.
[110] *Disp. priv.*, XIX.viii; cf. *Disp. pub.*, IV.lxiii.
[111] *Disp. priv.*, XIX.viii.
[112] *Disp. pub.*, IV.lvii.

order. Just as in the Arminian language of the two *momenta* of the divine nature, essence and life, and of the primary and secondary actuality of the divine life, there is, in this language of distinctions in the divine willing, a movement away from the strictest notion of divine simplicity and transcendence toward a view of God as conditioned and, therefore, somehow limited by his relation to the temporal order. Arminius has, on the one hand, identified genuine qualitative and quantitative differences, between divine willing that is absolute, antecedent, and *per se* and divine willing that is respective, consequent, and *per accidens*. On the other hand, he has refused to resolve these tensions in terms of concepts of a hidden, ultimate, and a revealed or signified will in God. Thus, as in the general pattern and movement of his doctrine of the divine attributes, Arminius has here identified an extension or tendency of the divine toward the created order, a movement of God into relationship, indeed, an ordination or ordering of the divine toward the created order that, in its turn, has an effect upon the divine willing. (Viewed in this way, the contrast between antecedent and consequent divine willing looks very much like the traditional distinction between *potentia absoluta* and *potentia ordinata*, with, however, the absolute power defined simply as primacy or ultimacy and the ordained power arising not only out of the consistency of God's will for the created order but also out of the created order itself as it relates to and fixes a limit upon the exercise of divine power and will.[113]) This language had a major impact not only on Episcopius and Limborch, but also on the philosopher Leibniz, who cited Arminius' arguments on antecedent and consequent divine will with strong approbation in his *Essai de Theodicée*.[114]

In the case of Episcopius in particular, the Arminian distinctions in the divine willing bore fruit in the fuller development of a non-deterministic conception of God's relationship to the world. Like many codifiers and followers, Episcopius was capable of drawing together the issues addressed by his teacher's distinctions and stating the underlying point more clearly, in summary form. Thus, Episcopius begins his discussion of distinctions in the divine will not with the traditionally primary distinction between *voluntas beneplaciti* and *voluntas signi* but, before introducing that distinction, with an extended discussion of the dictum, "Nulla est voluntas Dei nisi efficax"—the will of God is nothing if not efficacious. The dictum is, of course, incorrect and, argues Episcopius, must be replaced with the

---

113 See below, chap. 12.
114 G. W. Leibniz, *Essai de théodicée: Abrégé de la controverse*, in *Opera philosophica quae exstant*, ed. J. E. Erdmann (1840; repr. Aalen: Scientia Verlag, 1974), p. 627, col. 1.

contrary statement, "Non omnem Dei voluntatem esse efficacem"—not all of God's willing is efficacious. The latter principle alone accounts for the existence and benefits of religion! If God's will is always efficacious and, moreover, ultimately unitary, voluntary obedience and disobedience become impossible.[115]

Even so, Episcopius follows Arminius in insisting that the hidden will of God's good pleasure cannot be severed from the revealed or signified will in such a way as to nullify in the hidden recesses of divine intentionality the redemptive value of human acts performed in obedience to the revealed will.[116] Following out the principle and the line of Arminius' argument, Episcopius redefines the *voluntas* and *potentia absoluta*, in effect merging the terms with the *voluntas antecedens*: the absolute will and power of God no longer stand as a possibility hovering behind the established order of things but are now defined as a will and power without relation to the creature that are subject to modification when they enter into relation as *voluntas conditionata* and *consequens*.[117]

Once the will of God has been defined in its relation to the created order, the character or affective aspects of that relationship can be defined. Since, moreover, this free willing of God is an *ad extra* willing, toward finite objects, it is more capable of an analogical approach than was the divine essence considered in itself by way either of preeminence or negation. Arminius can therefore address "the attributes of God that are to be considered under his will" primarily as attributes that have "analogy to the affections or passions" typically attributed to the wills of "rational creatures."[118] These affections or passions can, moreover, be distinguished into two genera:

the first contains those affections which are concerned *simpliciter* with good or evil, which may be called primitive (*primitivi*), the second comprehends those which are concerned with good and evil as absent or present and which are derived from the former.[119]

The primitive or primary affections are love and its opposite, hatred, goodness, grace, benignity, and mercy.[120] The derivative or secondary affections arise out of the primary affections in direct relation to good and evil in particular creatures. These secondary affections are understood by analogy with the "concupiscible" and "iras-

---

[115] Episcopius, *Inst. theol.*, IV.ii.21 (p. 308, col. 1).
[116] Ibid. (p. 308, col. 2).
[117] Ibid. (p. 309, col. 1).
[118] *Disp. priv.*, XX. heading and i.
[119] Ibid., XX.ii.
[120] Ibid., XX.iii.

cible" emotions experienced by the human soul.[121] Some preliminary definition is surely appropriate. Concupiscence, a term usually associated with wrongful lust, indicates in its root meaning simply an ardent desire: the concupiscible operations of the will are, therefore, affections of desire together with joy in attainment and grief in loss. The irascible operations of the will or irascible affections are feelings, like anger, that have to do with aversion or repulsion—but also, in Arminius' usage, with expectation, the opposite of aversion or repulsion.[122] This terminology belongs, typically, to the Aristotelian usage of scholastic faculty psychology and is characteristic of Thomist anthropology:[123] the shift of meaning of the term "concupiscence" from the purely negative Augustinian sense of inordinate desire or lust to a neutral and even potentially positive sense of natural inclination toward an object is usually credited to Aquinas. Aquinas took over the term in his development of a Christian Aristotelian psychology and applied it to the affective aspect of human nature. Concupiscence, then, is an appetite for an object, or specifically, in Aquinas' view, one of the powers of the sensible appetite. Its opposite, the other power of the sensible appetite, irascibility, is an aversion or opposition to an object, particularly insofar as that object stands in the way of the attainment of something that is desired.[124] Aquinas himself did not press these categories into the doctrine of God. Their presence in Arminius' doctrine of God appears to be a speculative extension of the principle of analogy somewhat less than typical among medieval writers, but common currency in the seventeenth century.

Thomistic psychology also recognized the close relationship of concupiscence and irascibility and was able to argue not only the subordination of the latter to the former but also its origin in the former. As Pourrat comments, "We only become angry because we wish to possess at any cost that which we desire for ourselves in order to enjoy it." "Love," therefore, "engenders all the passions."[125] This model for understanding the appetitive affections of will has, by extension, a major impact on the concept of God and of God's relation to the world when it is developed in connection with the divine attributes. (It can, in fact, be viewed as a natural extension of Aquinas' stress on the priority of love in the elective willing of God, itself an extension of the identification of God as the *summum bonum* who

---

[121] Ibid., XX.ix.

[122] See ibid., XX.x–xi.

[123] Cf. Garrigou-Lagrange, "Thomisme," *DTC* 15/1, col. 966.

[124] Aquinas, *Summa*, Ia IIae, q.25 and cf. the discussion in Pierre Pourrat, *Christian Spirituality*, trans. W. H. Mitchell, S. P. Jacques, and Donald Attwater, 4 vols. (Westminster, Md.: Newman, 1953–55), II, p. 144.

[125] Pourrat, *Christian Spirituality*, II, pp. 144–45.

takes himself as the primary object of his willing.[126]) Since the irascible is subordinate to and serves the concupiscible appetite, love must be more ultimate than hate—and the *odio Dei* must be an alien work that serves the goal of God's loving. This divine psychology presses Arminius toward the recognition that God's very nature forestalls any act of ultimate aversion to the creature. God cannot, in effect, will a world or an end for the world and its creatures that is contrary to the primary attributes of goodness and love. Against his Reformed colleagues, particularly against the supralapsarian Gomarus, Arminius would argue against a perfect coordination of love for the elect and hate for the reprobate, of mercy for some and justice for others.

Arminius' presentation of the primary or primitive affections of the divine will focuses, therefore, quite understandably, on the attributes of love and goodness. An underlying difficulty encountered by Arminius in this presentation is the dual identity of divine goodness: it is both an essential attribute and an affection of will. In the former instance it is utterly incommunicable,[127] in the latter it is eminently communicable—indeed, Arminius can state that "goodness in God is the affection of communicating his own good."[128] There is no contradiction here: the logic of the statements is identical to the logic of Arminius' comments on the objects of the divine will. There he had argued that the essential goodness of God, the *summum bonum* or highest good, is the primary object of the divine will and that the divine will, therefore, must extend *ad extra*, toward lesser goods, only secondarily and indirectly.[129] In addition, there is no external object that brings about an inward motion in God: all motion in God, specifically the motion or movement toward the actualization of things *ad extra*, must be grounded in the plenitude of the divine essence itself.[130]

Thus, the essential goodness of God, identical with the divine *esse*, can no more be communicated than the divine *esse* itself. In creation, the Being of God enables creatures to be, just as the goodness of God's Being is the ground of the goodness of creaturely being. But the creaturely *esse* is not identical with creaturely *essentia* and the creaturely *bonitas* exists only by derivation and participation. The volitional goodness of God, however, is in a sense communicable inasmuch as God, by the power of his willing, confers goodness together with being upon his creatures. Arminius' teaching simply reflects the scholastic modification of the language of emanation or efflux out of

---

[126] On Aquinas' doctrine of election, see *Summa*, Ia, q.23, art.4, corpus.

[127] *Disp. pub.*, IV.xxii.

[128] Ibid., IV.lxviii.

[129] Cf. *Disp. pub.*, IV.l–li with *Disp. priv.*, XVIII.iii–iv.

[130] *Disp. priv.*, XVIII.v; cf. *Disp. pub.*, IV.l.

the divine: it is not essential being and goodness that emanate but the *potentia* for being and for the good.[131] The distinction between Creator and creature is maintained while, at the same time, the teleological relationship between the creature and its source and goal of being and goodness is established.

In the previous discussion Arminius had, only with difficulty, explained that the will of God, by willing the plenitude of divine goodness, must also by resting upon and acting in concert with the divine understanding, will also, albeit secondarily and indirectly, the existence of the created order as good. Here in the interrelationship of divine affections, Arminius is able to return to the problem and to supply, on a different level, a more cohesive explanation. In the divine Being, love is in one sense prior to goodness: in the affective order of divine willing, in the primary act or actuality of will by which God wills his own goodness, love is the affection that seeks out the good. Thus, "love is prior to goodness with regard to its object, which is God himself."[132] In the movement *ad extra* of the divine will, however, love seeks out those things that are capable of being loved inasmuch as they are created good and ordered toward the highest good. Thus, "goodness is prior to love with regard to an object that is other than God."[133]

This relationship of the divine love to the divine goodness has profound ramifications for the whole of theology, particularly for the doctrines of creation, providence, and predestination. The priority of love over goodness with respect to the divine object and of goodness over love with respect to the created object establishes an ordering of the divine decrees according to which God primarily loves and wills his own goodness, secondarily wills and loves all things in himself as they arise from the communication of his goodness, and, as a result orders all good things toward himself as their goal, the *summum bonum*. This is not only the logic of Arminius' doctrine of the divine goodness in its creative self-communication, it is also the logic of Aquinas' doctrine of predestination:

> For [God's] will, by which in loving he wishes good to someone, is the cause of that good possessed by some in preference to others. Thus it is clear that love precedes election in the order of reason, and election precedes predestination. Whence all the predestinate are objects of election and love.[134]

Of course, God's creative act communicates goodness apart from and

---

[131] Cf. Pinard, "Création," *DTC* 3/2, cols. 2089–91.

[132] *Disp. priv.*, XX.iii.

[133] Ibid.

[134] Aquinas, *Summa,* Ia, q.23, art.4, corpus.

in some sense prior to election—just as providence is a more general act than predestination—whereas election must be with reference to a particular good granted to certain individuals.[135] It is, moreover, the "love of God [that] infuses and creates goodness."[136] There must be, therefore, an antecedent will according to which God wills the salvation of all. This antecedent willing is, moreover, not a simple or absolute but a relative will.[137] As Thomas elsewhere says, "whatever God simply wills takes place; although what he wills antecedently may not take place."[138] The antecedent will, according to Aquinas, is "the principle of sufficient grace" while the consequent will, which is a simple and therefore definitive will, is "the principle of efficacious grace."[139] Arminius clearly goes farther along the line of Thomistic logic than did the Reformed and he does so, significantly, in relation to his equally Thomistic view of the priority of the divine intellect and the self-diffusive character of the divine goodness. On neither of these points were the Reformed willing to follow out the Thomist logic without modification.

On the grounds of this fundamentally Thomistic logic, the divine love may be defined:

> Love is an affection of union in God, whose objects are not only God himself and the good of [his] righteousness (*iustitia*); but also the creature in relation to God whether according to likeness (*imaginem*) or according to vestige (*vestigium*) or its ultimate reward.[140]

Granting again the distinction of object, the love of God itself is subject to distinction into the "love of contentment" (*amor complacentiae*) and the "love of friendship" (*amor amicitiae*).[141] The former corresponds with the Augustinian identification of love as *frui* or *fruitio*, the enjoyment of the good, the love of something in and for itself as the ultimate goal; the latter with the Augustinian identification of love as *uti* or *utilitas*, the love or use of something as a means to an end. The love of contentment is the love by which God loves himself "in the perfection of his own nature" as the highest good, alone capable of being loved for what it is in itself. This love of contentment extends also to the divine love of works *ad extra* insofar

---

[135] Ibid., Ia, q.23, art.4, ad obj.1, cf. ibid., q.6, art.4.

[136] Ibid., Ia, q.20, art.2, corpus.

[137] Ibid., Ia, q.23, art.4, ad obj.3.

[138] Ibid., Ia, q.19, art.6, ad obj.1.

[139] Garrigou-Lagrange, *Predestination*, p. 80; cf. Aquinas, *Summa*, Ia, q.23, art.4, ad obj.3.

[140] *Disp. priv.*, XX.iv.

[141] Ibid.; cf. Altenstaig, *Lexicon theologicum*, s.v. "*amor amicitiae*" and "*amor complacentiae*" (pp. 38–39).

as they are "evidences" of the divine perfection.[142] The "love of friendship" is reserved for things loved by God as means to his own end. Arminius' definitions of these terms are not particularly distinctive; they simply reflect the general scholastic background.

The divine hatred or *odio Dei* is the opposite of love but not its full coordinate. This lesser status of the divine hatred arises from the fact that it has no ultimate object and does not flow directly from or return to the divine goodness. Hatred flows out of divine love because the divine love "cannot extend toward all of the things that become objects of divine understanding."[143] Whereas love "belongs" to God "in the first act or primary actuality … prior to the existence of any thing" hatred must follow the existence of things as a necessary and natural operation of the will and not as something willed freely by God. In other words, God does not choose or elect to have, rather God naturally and necessarily has an aversion to some things simply because he is God.[144]

Arminius defines the *odio Dei* as "an affection of separation from God the primary object of which is unrighteousness (*iniustitia*) and the secondary object the misery of the creatures."[145] The primary object of divine hate arises out of the "love of contentment" inasmuch as God "properly loves himself and the good of [his] justice, and in the same instant (*momento*) hates the iniquity of the creature."[146] The secondary object, however, arises from the secondary divine love, "the love of friendship" according to which God loves the communication of his goodness to creatures in their existence and in their blessedness and in the same *momentum* hates, not the creatures as such, but the misery of the creature. Nonetheless, Arminius adds, if a creature rejects the goodness of God and refuses to be released from the misery of its sin, God then comes to hate "the creature who perseveres in unrighteousness" and to love its misery.[147] This language of the divine love and its less ultimate opposite, the divine hate, reflects the language and the dynamic of medieval scholastic theories of predestination—and does so specifically at the point that they tend away from making reprobation coordinate with election and move to ground predestination as a positive will of God in the general and universal love of God for creatures as created good.

[142] *Disp. priv.*, XX.iv.
[143] Ibid., XX.vi.
[144] Ibid.
[145] Ibid., XX.v.
[146] Ibid.
[147] Ibid.

The divine communication of goodness by or through the affection of love has, according to Arminius, three positive objects and acts:

> Its first object *ad extra* is nothing; and this is so necessarily first, that, when it is removed, no communication can be made externally. Its act is creation. Its second object is the creature as a creature; and its act is called sustenance (*sustentatio*) as if it were a continuance of creation. Its third object is the creature performing its duty according to the command of God; and its act is the elevation to a more worthy and felicitous condition, that is, the communication of a greater good than that which the creature obtained by creation.[148]

Both of these "outward movements" (*progressus*) that reach out toward the creature can be identified as the benignity or kindness of God.[149] Thus, by his affective willing or love God both desires himself to be the ultimate goal of all willing and loving and desires all things to exist as evidences of his goodness and to tend toward his ultimate goodness as the goal of their being.[150]

Very much after the fashion of Aquinas, these comments appear to indicate that the concept of providence as the divine governance of the finite order—which Arminius discussed at length, following his doctrine of creation—also ought to be discussed in relation to the doctrine of God, as one of the powers or operations predicated of the divine essence.[151] The "good order existing in created things" manifests both the origin and participation of all things in the goodness of God and the goal of all things in God as the *summum bonum*. In addition, since "God is the cause of all things by his intellect ... it is necessary that the type of the order of things towards their end should pre-exist in the divine mind: and the type of things ordered towards an end is, properly speaking, providence."[152] Thus, according to Arminius, the *intellectus Dei* knows "the order, connection, and relation of all [created beings] ... by his own essence."[153] The question remains, however, as to the way in which the providence, eternally predicated of God, functions in the temporal order—particularly in view of the distinctions made by Arminius in the divine knowing and willing. For the moment, all that can be said is that Arminius' intellectualism serves to reinforce the practical and resolvative direction of his theological system by identifying the essential goodness of God as both source and goal of all things—and, equally so, to point

---

[148] Ibid., XX.vii.
[149] Ibid.
[150] Cf. *Disp. priv.*, XX.iv, vii with *Disp. pub.*, IV.lxvii and *Disp. priv.*, XXIV.viii.
[151] Cf. Aquinas, *Summa*, Ia, q.22 and q.103 and note *SCG*, I.76–79.
[152] Aquinas, *Summa*, Ia, q.22, art.1, corpus.
[153] *Disp. pub.*, XVIII.ii.

toward a powerful systematic or dogmatic emphasis on creation as the primary goal of all the divine activity that is ordered, *ad extra*, toward the ultimate goal of the divine goodness. The act of creation itself implies not only the sustenance of creation but the requirement of creaturely obedience and the hope of final "communication of a greater good" in eschatological union with God.

The fourth object of the divine communication of goodness "is the creature not performing its duty, or sinful, and on this account liable to misery according to the just judgment of God, and its act is a deliverance from sin through remission and mortification."[154] This last movement of goodness is called mercy. What Arminius has done in this description of the self-communication of the divine goodness is to argue all of the divine affections as manifestations of the two primitive or primary affections, goodness and love—hatred as the negation of love; benignity, kindness, and mercy as modifications of goodness in relation to its objects. This argument is crucial to his whole theological perspective inasmuch as it has the effect of binding the divine affections to the primary impulse of God *ad extra*, the self-communicative character of the divine goodness, and thereby relating the divine affections to the teleological presupposition of Arminius' theology and, more immediately, to the gracious relationship of God to the created order.

> Grace is a certain adjunct of goodness and love, by which is signified that God is affected (*quod Deum affectum esse*) to communicate his own good and to love creatures, not through merit or of debt, not by any extrinsic impelling cause (*causa extrinsecus impellente*), and not as if anything may be added to God himself, but that it may be well with him on whom the good is bestowed and who is beloved, which may also be termed liberality: and according to this, God is said to be rich in goodness, mercy, etc.[155]

The *sola gratia* rings out as loudly here as in any Lutheran or Reformed theology—but with a significant difference. Whereas the Lutheran and the Reformed orthodox understand grace as primarily, indeed, as virtually exclusively soteriological in operation, Arminius ever so subtly prepares the foundation, here, for a subsequent emphasis on the relationship of grace to nature in the creature and providential order. Of course, the Reformed and Lutheran orthodox do associate grace, as a divine attribute, with the goodness of God and they do state that God's goodness toward and love for the creature is not a matter of debt but of grace. The Reformed, however, manifest a certain discomfort with the notion of a generalized or "common" grace and tend to focus on the special grace of God toward the elect, to

---

[154] *Disp. priv.*, XX.vii.
[155] Ibid., XX.viii.

the point of arguing that the love of God for the "world" (John 3:16) is
not a love for "the entire system of heaven and earth with all their
denizens divinely produced out of nothing, but only for the human
race."[156] The Lutherans do not place so great a stress on election, but,
like the Reformed, the emphasis in their doctrine of grace is on the
unmerited character of the free gift of grace in salvation.[157] Arminius,
however, has broadened the issue of grace by binding the concept of
grace more closely to the divine creative self-communication, so that
the goodness of God in creation is understood as a primary, overarching, gracious act. This perspective will have an enormous impact
on Arminius' doctrines of creation and providence inasmuch as
God's unmerited grace may not be arbitrarily or restrictively bestowed. If grace is both unmerited and implicit in the creative act, it
must be both universal and natural.

Arminius next comes—still under the larger category of divine
will—to the attributes of God that "have some analogy to the moral
virtues." These attributes, he argues, either "preside generally over all
the affections, or specially relate to some of them."[158] Thus,

> the general [attribute] is justice or righteousness (*iustitia*), which is
> called universal (or legal): concerning which the ancients said that it
> contains in itself all the virtues: the special are particular justice,
> patience and all those moderations (*moderatrices*) of anger, and of
> castigations and punishments.[159]

These "moderations of anger" include such attributes as long-
suffering, gentleness, clemency, and readiness to pardon. Arminius'
discussion of these attributes is brief, amounting to no more than a
definition of each—with the exception of the *iustitia Dei*, which he
develops at considerable length.

The justice or righteousness of God is considered by Arminius first,
in its universal or general sense as an attribute or virtue of God, and
then in its particular sense, as relating to objects. This second sense is
divided into categories of "justice in deeds" (*iustitia in factis*) and
"justice in words" (*iustitia in dictis*).[160] Universally or generally considered, the *iustitia Dei* is "a virtue of God according to which he
administers all things rightly and properly (*recte et decenter*), according
to what his wisdom indicates as befitting himself."[161] This primary

---

[156] *RD*, pp. 95–96, 372. On the problem of common grace in Reformed theology,
see Louis Berkhof, *Systematic Theology*, 4th ed. (Grand Rapids: Eerdmans, 1941),
pp. 432–46.
[157] *DTEL*, pp. 471–78.
[158] *Disp. priv.*, XXI., heading and i.
[159] Ibid., XXI.i.
[160] Ibid., XXI.ii–v.
[161] Ibid., XXI.ii.

divine righteousness governs, together with the wisdom of God, all "acts, decrees and deeds" (*actionibus, decretis, factis*) of God—so that God truly may be recognized as "just in all his ways."[162] This universal divine righteousness is, therefore, the foundation of the particular acts or operations of God, in and through which God renders justly to himself whatever is his due and also bestows on his creatures whatever rightly belongs to them.

In a highly significant comment on the implication of the concept of the *iustitia Dei* for the rest of his theology, Arminius notes that this particular justice that renders what is due both to God and to creatures and that is clearly enunciated both in deed and in word is no different in mode, manner, or implication than the mode, manner, or implication of the eternal decree: "whatever God does or says, he does or says it according to his own eternal decree."[163] In other words, the justice of God, manifest in deed and word, stands firm in relation to the decree. There can be no injustice in the decree and no deviation of the revelation concerning the decree from the revelation concerning God's justice. Even so, the *iustitia Dei* rests in agreement with God's "love for the creature and toward [creaturely] goodness."[164] By implication, the decree can be no different: it must agree with the love and the goodness of God as defined in relation both to the obedience of the creature and to the goodness of the creature as created.[165]

The divine justice in deeds follows a threefold order. In the first place, it acts in the "communication of the good, either according to the first creation (*creationem primam*) or according to regeneration."[166] Here we encounter the first usage of *iustitia* that indicates what is normally translated into English as "righteousness." It is worth noting that the Latin, *iustitia*, like the Greek, *dikaiosune*, makes no such distinction but identifies the concepts of legal justice and moral righteousness with the same basic term—and, therefore, holds the two in closer relation in theological discussion. Thus, the second aspect of the justice of deeds is "the prescription of duty or in legislation, which consists in the requisition of a deed, and in the promise of reward and threat of punishment, while the third aspect lies in the judgment of actual deeds in retributive acts either of reward or of punishment. Punishment is to be understood, therefore, not only in terms of a divine hatred of disobedience but also in terms of the vindication of divine justice."[167]

---

[162] Ibid.
[163] Ibid., XXI.iii.
[164] Ibid.
[165] Cf. *Disp. priv.*, XX.vii.
[166] *Disp. pub.*, XXI.iv.
[167] Ibid.

"Justice in words" can also be explained in terms of a threefold order. The divine justice, in the first place, declares truth as opposed to falsehood: God always "declares exactly as the thing is." Second, it is both sincere and simple in the sense that God "always declares as he inwardly conceives, according to the meaning and purpose (*propositum*) of his mind, opposed to which are hypocrisy and duplicity of heart." Third, the justice of God is faithful and constant "in respecting promises and maintaining communicated goods, to which are opposed inconstancy and perfidity."[168] If the use of the term *"propositum"* or *"purpose"* can be taken as a technical theological usage—which would seem to be the case given the technical character of Arminius' disputations and their constant recourse to scholastic vocabulary—Arminius here also points toward his formulations concerning the decree of God and argues against any divergence in purpose between the inward design of God and the revealed demands and promises of God. This was also the implication of Arminius' discussion of the *voluntas beneplaciti* and *voluntas signi*, where the Reformed posited just such a divergence, and of the *voluntas antecedens* and *voluntas consequens*, a distinction denied by the Reformed.

As if to drive home the point that a careful consideration of divine justice in relation to the eternal decree and purpose of God will result in a view other than the orthodox Reformed teaching, Arminius appends a set of three corollaries to his disputation:

Whether the justice of God allows that a sinless rational creature be destined to eternal death? N(egative).

Whether the justice of God allows that a creature persevering in sin be saved? N(egative).

Whether justice and mercy may not be considered, in an accommodated sense, as in some respect opposites. Aff(irmative).[169]

Even if these theses represent a caricature of the Reformed perspective or, perhaps, more precisely, an Arminian overstatement of its dangers, they do provide a clear insight into the thrust of Arminius' doctrine of God and a highly instructive point of transition between Arminius' doctrine of the moral attributes of God and his discussion of the power of God, the *potentia Dei*. Even as the essential attributes of God determine all subsequent discussion of the divine nature and of the divine work, so also do the moral attributes. The will and the power of God may not be construed in such a way as to generate conflict or contradiction in the Godhead. Thus, the divine will is

---

[168] Ibid., XXI.v.
[169] *Disp. priv.*, XXI, ad fin.

regulated by the ultimate goodness of God and the divine power will not violate the divine justice—either by damning the sinless or by vindicating the wicked. Arminius will, therefore, argue against a speculative discussion of the absolute power of God. God is restrained, in some sense, by his justice and his justice is balanced by mercy.

Arminius recognizes the need to define the power of God (*poten-tia Dei*) very carefully in terms of the ultimacy, simplicity, and immutability of the divine essence. God is, after all, uncaused and not in "motion" from potency to actuality. The potency or *potentia* of God cannot, therefore, be defined as one would define the potency of a creature. There can be no "passive potency" in God inasmuch as God is *actus purus*, pure actuality. In view of the divine actuality—the "internal acts" of the Godhead that belong necessarily to God according to his nature, such as the relations of the persons of the Trinity, are also not to be considered exercises of power or as movements from potency to actuality. "We exhibit for examination that power alone which consists in the virtue of acting, and by which God not only is capable of acting beyond himself, but actually does operate wherever it is his own good pleasure."[170] The *potentia Dei* is

> a faculty of life (subordinate to the understanding that shows and directs and to the will that commands) by which [God] is capable of bringing about externally whatever things he can freely will, and by which he does bring about whatever he freely wills.[171]

In other words, the scholastic concept of omnipotence refers specifically to "the freedom of God in his works *ad extra*," whether those works belong to the realm of "supernatural theology"—that is, works such as predestination, incarnation, and redemption—or to the realm of "natural theology" where the transcendence of God is maintained over against the divine involvement in the creation.[172]

Arminius recognizes a distinction of the power of God into absolute power (*potentia absoluta*) and ordained or ordinary power (*potentia ordinaria*), but he refers the distinction to the will of God rather than to the *potentia Dei* properly so-called. He notes that the divine will sometimes wills to exert power and sometimes refrains from doing so—and that God, therefore, could exert his absolute power to "do far more things" than he actually does.[173] Here again, we encounter a somewhat curious modification of a traditional scholastic distinction. It is indeed true, according to the scholastics, that "God can indeed do

---

170 Ibid., XXII.i.
171 Ibid., XXII,ii; cf. *Disp. pub.*, IV.lxxviii–lxxix.
172 Chossat, "Dieu. Sa nature selon les scholastiques," col. 1162.
173 *Disp. pub.*, IV.lxxxv.

many things according to absolute power that he does not do according to the ordained power,"[174] but this statement hardly exhausts the issue or even, taken by itself, indicates the purpose of the distinction.

The scholastic distinction between *potentia absoluta* and *potentia ordinata* had its origins as early as the *De sacramentis christianae fidei* of Hugh of St. Victor, and was therefore an integral part of the scholastic doctrine of God from its very beginnings.[175] The distinction appears in the writings of most of the thirteenth-century doctors—thus, Aquinas can distinguish between the divine omnipotence considered in itself, in terms of what God can do, and the divine omnipotence considered in relation to what God has in fact done.[176] The language of *potentia absoluta* and *potentia ordinata* did not become a central issue in the doctrine of God and of God's relation to the created order, however, until the advent of nominalism in the fourteenth century. As Oberman well says of this development,

> the *irrealis* which indicates what could have happened if God had willed otherwise becomes more and more a *realis*. God's *potentia absoluta* becomes the power to reverse the natural order of things as in fact is the case with miracles. God is not obliged to obey moral or natural laws.[177]

The distinction between the absolute and the ordained power of God does not, of course, imply two powers in God. The nominalist teachers who developed the distinction assumed the radical simplicity of the divine essence: divine attributes are merely various concepts or "names" (*nomina*) applied by us to God. Even so, the divine *potentia* is God himself in his utter unity and simplicity.[178] The language of two powers, then, refers to the way in which God relates to the created order—either absolutely in view of what he can do or ordinarily in view of the laws he has established to govern the natural order. God, in other words, transcends not only the temporal order but also the laws that govern it.[179]

Since the *potentia Dei* operates under the divine will as the efficacy or efficiency *ad extra* of the *voluntas Dei*, it is "circumscribed and limited" by the divine will alone. If God is incapable of willing any

[174] Altenstaig, *Lexicon theologicum*, s.v. "*potentia Dei est duplex*" (pp. 715–16).

[175] Hugh of St. Victor, *De sacramentis christianae fidei*, I.22, in *PL*, 176.214.

[176] Aquinas, *Summa*, Ia, q.25, art.5.

[177] Obermann, "Some Notes on the Theology of Nominalism," pp. 56–57.

[178] Vignaux, "Nominalisme," *DTC* 11/1, cols. 757, 764.

[179] See Francis Oakley, *Omnipotence, Covenant, & Order: An Excursion in the History of Ideas from Abélard to Leibniz* (Ithaca and London: Cornell University Press, 1984), esp. pp. 79–84, 87–92.

particular object, he is also incapable of exercising his power to effect that object.[180]

> But the will of God can only will that which is not opposed to the divine essence (which is the foundation both of his understanding and of his will), that is, [it can will] nothing but good and true being (*nihil nisi ens, verum, bonum*). Therefore his power cannot do any other. Moreover, since the phrase "what is not opposed to the divine essence," comprehends whatever is simply and absolutely possible, and since God can will all of this, it follows that God is able to do whatever is possible.[181]

God cannot, therefore, do what is impossible, that is, what "involves a contradiction," such as

> to make another God, to mutate, to sin, to lie, to cause something at once to be and not to be [or] to have been and not to have been.... that a thing and its contrary should be, that an accident should be without a subject, that a [given] substance should be changed into another substance.[182]

Arminius, then, argues two kinds of limitations on God or, to state the point somewhat differently, notes two kinds of contradictory acts of which God must be incapable. God cannot, of course, be involved in any contradiction and contradictions, generally speaking, must be either essential or logical. God cannot, therefore, violate his own nature: God cannot set aside any of the properties belonging to his essence in order to perform an act contrary to a particular property—as, for example, his goodness or his truth. (This point follows, of course, from the definition of divine attributes not as incidental properties but as perfections identical with the divine essence and essentially identical with one another.) Neither can God create contradictory or noncompossible things. Such acts would indicate, Arminius reasons, an absence of *potentia*, indeed, an *impotentia*, and a fundamental lack of truthfulness and consistency in the divine will.[183]

These limitations, however, in no way detract from the omnipotence of God. God has, indeed, infinite power inasmuch as he is capable of doing anything within the realm of possibility and because no created thing can resist the power of God. "All created things depend on him as upon the efficient principle, both in their being and in their preservation: hence omnipotence is justly ascribed to him."[184] Arminius does not, therefore, rest his concept of omnipo-

---

[180] *Disp. priv.*, XXII.iii.
[181] Ibid., XXII.iv.
[182] Ibid., XXII.v.
[183] Ibid.
[184] *Disp. pub.*, XXII.vi.

tence either on a naive assumption that "God can do anything" or on a more subtle assumption of an absolute power that transcends and is capable of abridging the order of things. The former notion actually deprives God of genuine power and is typically founded on speculations about impossibilities; the latter idea, however, could and did function in the thought of Arminius' contemporaries, notably Gomarus and Perkins. As becomes clear in Arminius' doctrine of creation and providence, Arminius found this second view also to be problematic and moved to set aside the notion of a *potentia absoluta* in the received sense of the term.

Arminius rounds out his discussion of the divine attributes with a disputation on the perfection, blessedness, and glory of God.[185] Two structural or organizational issues need to be noted here before we can pass on to the discussion of these attributes. First, if Arminius' doctrine of God had been constructed deductively rather than analytically or "resolvatively," it could easily have discussed these attributes earlier, as essential perfections, and then used the doctrine of the *potentia Dei* as the point of transition to the doctrine of creation. Indeed, in the logic of divine extension toward objects *ad extra*, as presented by Arminius, the power of God is the last operation of divine life to be discussed in the ordering of attributes leading to the production of creatures. This order will need to be observed in the subsequent analysis of creation and providence. Nonetheless, second, the overarching practical, teleological, and analytical-resolvative pattern of Arminius' system demands the completion of the doctrine of God in such a way as to indicate the final goal of theological praxis— the ultimate perfection, blessedness, and glory of God toward which all creation tends as its ultimate hope and final vision.

"The perfection of God has its existence from the simple and infinite combination of all these [attributes] when they are considered according to the mode of pre-eminence."[186] This idea of perfection is not merely a duplication of what was said under the attributes of simplicity and infinity, inasmuch as this perfection is not the means or mode by which God has all of his attributes but rather the way that God "perfectly possesses all the things that denote any perfection."[187] In other words, the divine perfection is more than just a pattern of attributes, it is also a genuine attribute in its own right which, because of the essential identity of all the attributes, can be inferred from the way in which God is in possession of the various "perfections" of the divine essence. By way of definition, Arminius returns to the pattern offered by Boethius' definition of eternity: perfection "is the

---

[185] *Disp. priv.*, XXIII; cf. *Disp. pub.*, IV.lxxxviii–xcii.
[186] *Disp. pub.*, IV.lxxxvii.
[187] Ibid.

interminable, entire, and, at the same time, the perfect possession of essence and life."[188] This perfection, unlike that of creatures, is not derived from anything external; rather it is the archetype of all creaturely perfection.[189] The divine blessedness is an internal or intrinsic act of God resting on this perfection and the glory of God is an extrinsic relation of divine perfection.[190]

Blessedness, therefore, can be defined as

> an act of the life of God by which he enjoys his own perfection, that is fully known by his understanding and supremely loved by his will and by which he contentedly reposes in this perfection with satisfaction.[191]

The definition may point toward the "love of contentment" (*amor complacentiae*) by which God loves himself as the highest good.[192] Such blessedness must be incommunicable—although it is also the ground of any blessedness that is in creatures. Thus, in relation to creatures, God is the "effector of the act which extends toward" the creature and results in its being made blessed.[193] We see here a reflection of the argument concerning the primary and secondary objects of the divine goodness: the creature is a secondary object of the inward movement of divine understanding and will that both knows the divine essence as the highest good, "perpetually" has "an immediate apprehension of the blessed object and reposes in the same."[194]

The *gloria Dei* is "the excellence above all things, which he makes manifest by external acts in various ways."[195] Here, too, we find a reflection of the teleological and resolvative character of Arminius' system and of the medieval scholastic meditation on the meaning of final causality. The divine glory, in accordance with the inward movement of intellect and will toward the being and goodness of God as their primary object and toward the being and goodness of creatures as their secondary object, is achieved through the work of creation. God cannot be glorified without being made known, specifically without making his perfections known by their communication *ad extra*. Participation in the divine perfections through the creative communication of being and goodness is, in turn, the good and, therefore, the goal of all things. The ultimate end of all things in the

---

[188] Ibid.
[189] Ibid., IV.lxxxviii.
[190] Ibid., IV.lxxxix.
[191] Ibid., IV.xc.
[192] Cf. *Disp. priv.*, XX.iv.
[193] *Disp. pub.*, IV.xci.
[194] *Disp. priv.*, XXIII.iv.
[195] Ibid., XXIII.vi.

glory of God, then, consists both in the revelation of the infinite *gloria intrinseca* of the divine Being and the fullness of *gloria extrinseca* in the creaturely reflection of the divine perfections.[196] God's glory arises, then, from the perfection of God *cum respectu ad extra*, with respect or in relation to externals, and is manifest in two ways—one, by an effulgence of light and of unusual splendor, or by its opposite, a dense darkness or obscurity (Matt. 17:2–5; Luke 2:9; Exod. 16:10; 1 Kings 8:11); the other, by the production of works which agree with his perfection and excellence (Ps. 19:1; John 2:11).[197] God has, in his ultimate purpose, "formed us for his glory" and will bring about that purpose in Christ, "the brightness of his glory, and the express image of his person." All of our religion, moreover, directs us toward this end as evidenced by the revelation of the divine attributes: the perfection and blessedness of God indicate the worthiness and usefulness of religious observance, while our knowledge of God arises directly from "the manifestation of the divine glory."[198]

Thus, in placing the *gloria Dei* last in his list of divine attributes, Arminius has both rounded off his doctrine of God in such a way as to illustrate the resolvative pattern of his system as a whole and to provide a suitable point of contact between his doctrine of God and the doctrine of creation and providence that follows. The language of the *gloria Dei* looks directly—as it had in the medieval scholastic theologies—toward the concept of the primary and secondary goals of creation, the glory of God as *summum bonum*, and the good of the creature by participation in the divine goodness.[199] What is more, in the case of Arminius' system, this statement of goals and ends, with its drawing together of the themes of divine intellect, will, and goodness, and the end and good of the creature, provides a basis for the subsequent declaration, in the doctrine of creation and providence, of a divine self-limitation in creation resting upon the structure of God's relationship to his creatures.

[196] Cf. Aquinas, *SCG*, III.17 with Pinard, "Création," *DTC* 3/2, col. 2085.
[197] *Disp. pub.*, IV.xciii.
[198] Ibid., IV.xcii, ad fin.; *Disp. priv.*, XXIII.viii.
[199] Pinard, "Création," col. 2085.

PART 5

Creation and Providence

11

The Doctrine of Creation

Arminius' doctrine of creation is set forth in the *Disputationes privatae* but not in the *Disputationes publicae*.[1] There is also a section on creation in the *Articuli nonnulli*, but it deals only briefly with the creation in general and passes almost immediately to the doctrine of man.[2] Finally, the doctrine of creation appears briefly in the *Declaratio sententiae* as one element in Arminius' refutation of the supra-lapsarian view of predestination.[3] From these several sources it is apparent not only that Arminius' doctrine of creation, like his doctrine of God, is profoundly indebted to the scholastic tradition, particularly to the tradition of Thomism, but also that his doctrine of creation is one of the fundamental pivots of his theological system. On the one hand, Arminius draws on the scholastic view of God as the *summum bonum* and on the scholastic perception of creation as grounded in this self-diffusive divine goodness. In addition, Arminius' doctrine of creation echoes the teaching, typical of the more Augustinian and Platonizing of the medieval doctors from Alexander of Hales onward, that the work of God in creation, incarnation, and consummation must be understood as a unified work tending toward the single ultimate goal of the divine goodness.[4] On the other hand, it is quite clear that Arminius does not simply reproduce the scholastics in order to develop the doctrine of creation more fully along dogmatic lines than had been done by the Reformers. He makes the scholastic categories his own and allows his conclusions regarding the divine goodness and the character of the divine creative act to determine his view of theology in general and of the external will

---

[1] *Disp. priv.*, XXIV.

[2] *Articuli nonnulli*, VI.

[3] *Dec. sent.*, pp. 107–8 (*Works*, I, pp. 626–27).

[4] Cf. Scheffczyk, *Creation and Providence*, pp. 138–39.

of God, especially the will known in election and reprobation, in particular.

It is also probable that Arminius, who died at age forty-nine after barely six years of teaching in the university, did not live to work out all of the issues raised in his doctrine of creation. As will become clear in the following exposition and analysis there are several directions, if not inconsistencies, in Arminius' language about creation that stand in tension with one another. Since, moreover, the *Public Disputations* almost invariably appear to have been a first draft of system and the *Private Disputations* a refinement, the absence of a doctrine of creation from the former document points toward the theses of the *Private Disputations* as a first attempt at doctrinal definition, perhaps lacking the polish of Arminius' final theses on the essence and attributes of God. These tensions and possible inconsistencies, however, are not without significance inasmuch as they appear to draw on a motif, already present in Arminius' early oration *On the Object of Theology* and clearly recognizable in the theses on providence, of the limitation of God implicit in the very act of creation.

With his practical or teleological purpose in view, Arminius begins his doctrine of creation by noting that Christ is the second object of the Christian religion and that discussion of Christ naturally follows discussion of the first object, which is God himself. A transition from the one object to the other and a proper order of discussion must, however, be observed—and certain topics must therefore be presented by way of preparation for the discussion of Christ. It is therefore necessary to preface Christology with a discussion of the reason why God can in fact "require any religion from man," what religion has been required in view of this divine prerogative, and for what reason, after the creation, God not only retains this right but also needs to constitute Christ as Mediator and Savior[5]:

> Since God is the object of the Christian religion, not only as creator but also as re-creator, in which latter respect Christ also, as constituted by God to be the Savior, is the object of the Christian religion, it is necessary for us first to discuss the original creation (*creatione primaeva*) and those things which are joined to it according to nature and, after that, those things that resulted from the conduct of man—this before we begin to discuss the re-creation, where the primary consideration is of Christ as Mediator.[6]

This identification of the divine creative act as the foundation of all religion and the tendency that it imparts to theology toward a more rationalistic perspective and toward a sense of the created order as fundamentally constitutive of the logic of theological system marks

[5] *Disp. priv.*, XXIV.i.
[6] Ibid., XXIV.ii.

not only a central issue in Arminius' theology, but also a major theme that carries over from Arminius' thought into the work of Episcopius.[7] The structural implication of Arminius' definition, that the work of God is twofold, having to do with creation and recreation or redemption, draws on a fairly standard scholastic distinction concerning the *opus Dei*. Arminius may have seen it used structurally or architectonically in the work of his teacher, Lambert Daneau, who once again takes a concept resident in medieval theology and declares it (in Agricolan or Ramist fashion) at a key point in his discussion of the doctrine.[8] Apart from this structural point, however, Arminius' doctrine of creation appears to draw very little directly from Daneau either by way of order of topics or of content of discussion. Daneau, for example, was very interested in the hierarchical order of the Ptolemaic cosmos, while Arminius manifests virtually no interest in this question.[9]

"Creation is an external act of God, by which he produced all things out of nothing, for himself, by his Word and his Spirit."[10] Arminius proceeds, after stating this basic definition, to present the causality of the creative act in the highly developed language of scholastic Aristotelianism. Thus, God the Father, working according to the pattern of all trinitarian activity *ad extra*, which is to say, through the Word and the Spirit, is the "primary efficient cause" of the created order.[11] (All work of the Godhead *ad extra* is the common work of the three persons, but in the order established by their personal relations *ad intra*: thus the Father works by the Son, through the Spirit.[12])

The primary divine causality of creation can also be explained in terms of the divine attributes, shared by the persons of the Trinity, that have already been used by Arminius to indicate the extension or movement of God toward the finite objects of his creative work: goodness, wisdom, will, and power.

The impelling cause, which we have indicated in the definition by the particle "for" [i.e., produced out of nothing, *for* himself], is the goodness of God, according to which he is inclined to communicate his good. The ordaining [cause] is wisdom (*ordinatrix est sapientia*), the executive is power (*executrix potentia*), which the will employs as a result of goodness (*ex effectu bonitas*), according to the most just ordination of wisdom.[13]

---

[7] Cf. Episcopius, *Inst. theol.*, IV.iii.1.

[8] Daneau, *Christianae isagoges*, I.24 (p. 38r).

[9] Cf. ibid., I.27.

[10] *Disp. priv.*, XXIV.iii: "Creatio est actio Dei externa qua Deus verbo & Spiritu suo omnia propter semetipsum ex nihilo produxit."

[11] Ibid., XXIV.iv.

[12] Cf. *Disp. pub.*, VI.ii, xii.

[13] *Disp. priv.*, XXIV.iv.

The formula relating the divine goodness, wisdom, and power carries over into the theology of Johann Poliander and the Leiden *Synopsis*.[14]

The view of creation as arising, causally, in the self-diffusive goodness of God lies at the heart of Arminius' theology and is indicative of its scholastic roots. He can, alternatively, define creation as "the perfect act of God by which he has manifested his wisdom, goodness and omnipotence" and, in a more philosophical mode, "a communication of good according to the intrinsic property of its nature."[15] That intrinsic property is, surely, the self-diffusive nature of goodness. Granting these premises and their underlying assumption that God is to be known, above and beyond all other identifications, as the highest good and final goal of all things, creation must be viewed as belonging to the ultimate divine purpose. Very much like Aquinas in the *Contra gentiles* and *Compendium theologiae*, Arminius so holds the identity of being with goodness that he can assert both that all things have their *esse* by participation in the divine *esse* and that all existent things are good by reason of their participation in the goodness of God.[16] It cannot be, as the supralapsarianism of Gomarus would have it, a subordinate act of God willed for the sake of some purpose other than the communication of the good. It cannot, in other words, be an act of God subordinate to an ultimate goal of the reprobation of some individuals: "in that case, creation would not have been a communication of any good, but a preparation for the greatest evil both according to the very intention of the creator and the actual issue of the matter."[17]

Following the causal logic of creation, Arminius next comes to the problems of material and formal causality or, more simply, matter and form. There are, he begins, three stages and ways of understanding matter in the creative process.

> The primary is that from which all things in general were produced, and into which they may therefore relapse and be reduced: it is nothing itself (*ipsum Nihilum*) which our mind, by the removal of all entity (*per aphairesin omnis entitatis*), considers as the first matter (*ut materiam primam*): for that alone is capable of the first communication of God *ad extra*: since God would neither have the right to introduce his own form into coeval matter (*materiam coevam*), nor would he be capable of

[14] *Synopsis purioris*, X.xx: "Ejusdem creationis causa directrix est Deus sapientia; exsecutrix potentia ejus infinita."

[15] *Dec. sent.*, pp. 107–8 (*Works*, I, pp. 626–27). Note the similarity to Aquinas' formulation of existence and goodness of created being in *De veritate*, q.21, art.4, discussed by Chossat, "Dieu. Sa nature selon les scolastiques," in *DTC* 4/1, col. 1236.

[16] Cf. Aquinas, *SCG*, I.41; III.17 and *Compendium theologiae*, I.109 with Arminius, *Disp. priv.*, IV.viii; *Disp. pub.* IV.xxiii, lii and with Patterson, *Conception of God*, pp. 262–64.

[17] Ibid.

acting, as it would be eternal and, therefore, not susceptible to change.[18]

The usage here is quite unusual inasmuch as Arminius presents the traditional concept of creation *ex nihilo* while at the same time identifying the *nihil*, the nothing, as in some sense belonging to the material causality of the universe.[19] The form of Arminius' second point, the denial of an eternally existent *materia prima*, appears to be taken from Suárez.[20] When Suárez turned to the philosophical problem of creation *ex nihilo* he had followed the Thomistic argument that reason alone could not disprove the eternity of the world.[21] Nonetheless, Suárez only could allow a notion of the eternity of a contingent order, drawn out of nothing not temporally but ontologically by God: there can be no preexistent matter juxtaposed with God, inasmuch as God would be unable to act upon it.[22] The idea of divine interaction with the temporal order itself demands the conclusion that God creates *ex nihilo*.

This Suárezian language of Arminius' disputation has no parallel in Junius' theses on creation, but it is strikingly similar to Poliander in the Leiden *Synopsis*:

> This universe of things was produced out of nothing, [the *nihil*] being taken not privatively but negatively and, therefore to be conceived by the removal or negation of all entities: loosely or by an invalid usage this has been called matter—indeed, where nothing is, matter is improperly said to be.[23]

Poliander takes Arminius' first point and sets it aside: there is no attempt to identify the *nihil* with primary matter. Indeed, Poliander comments on the oddity and impropriety of the usage. The second point, the Suárezian denial of an external material substratum on logical grounds, is accepted by Poliander without elaboration.[24] Once again, Arminius' theology occupies a position in the developing Protestant scholasticism of Leiden—making, in this case, the point of the reception of Suárezian metaphysics.

[18] *Disp. priv.*, XXIV.v.

[19] See below, this chap.

[20] Cf. Suárez, *Disputationes metaphysicae*, XX.i.18, with Scheffczyk, *Creation and Providence*, p. 182.

[21] Suárez, *Disp. metaph.*, XX.ii.11.

[22] Ibid., *Disp. metaph.*, XX.i.18; cf. ibid., XXXI.ii.3–5 and the translation by Wells in Francis Suárez, *On the Essence of Finite Being as Such*, pp. 59–60.

[23] *Synopsis purioris*, X.xxii: "Haec rerum universitas producta est ex nihilo, non privative sed negative sumpto, ideoque per aphairesin et negationem omnis entitatis, a nostro intellectu concipitur; quod a quibusdam katachrestikos ac valde akurologos materia ex qua nominatur, ubi enim nihil est, ibi improprie materia esse dicitur."

[24] Ibid., X.xxiii–xxiv.

Since the *nihil* is understood as "the removal of all entity," as absolutely nothing, it does not represent any actuality—nor even a potency in any common sense of that term. The potency or potential for being is solely the *potentia Dei*, with the result that the *nihil* becomes potentially something only in the exertion of divine power. Were this divine power or potential for being ever withdrawn, all things would necessarily "relapse" into nothing. Such is the typical scholastic view of creation[25] and it appears also to be that of Arminius. Nonetheless, he refers to this nothing as capable of being considered as first or primary matter, *materia prima*—a statement consistent not with the Christian Aristotelianism of Aquinas or even with the essentially Aristotelian language of primary and secondary matter embedded in the Christianized Neo-Platonism of Augustine,[26] but rather following out the argument of Aristotle's own *Metaphysics*, where the *me on* or nonbeing of Platonism is understood as a material substratum a *me po on* of pure potency or unformed matter.[27] By way of contrast, Aquinas could declare quite categorically that the *ex* ("from") in *ex nihilo* "does not signify the material cause, but only order."[28]

Arminius' Reformed contemporaries tend, on this point, to agree with Aquinas. Indeed, they assume with Aquinas that the term *ex nihilo* does not indicate, strictly, a *making* of something out of nothing but only an indication of the ontological and temporal limit and order of the creative process: first there was nothing and, then, after the creative act, there was something. The term *"ex nihilo,"* therefore, indicates the existence of the material order *post nihilum*.[29] What is significant is that Arminius, who surely had seen this argument, did not use it. His interest in an alternative construction of creation-language and, specifically, of the problem of the *nihil* as it relates to the concept of the eternity of the world may even reflect his year of study at Padua where Pomponazzi and Achillini had, in the early sixteenth century, taught Aristotelian philosophy with a marked predilection for the interpretations of Averroes and Alexander of Aphrodisias over the Christianized Aristotelianism of the Middle Ages and had argued the eternity of matter.[30] Or it may have arisen out of Arminius' contact with subsequent developments in the philo-

[25] Cf. Scotus, *Opus ox.*, IV, dist.1, q.1, n.33, as cited in Minges, II, p. 273 with Aquinas, *Summa*, Ia, q.44, arts.1 and 2; q.104, art.3.

[26] Cf. Aquinas, *Summa*, Ia, q.45, art. 1 with Augustine, *Confessions*, XII.8; and idem, *De genesi ad litteram*, I.xv.29–30.

[27] Aristotle, *Metaphysics*, VII.1–10 (1028a–1035a); IX.6, 8 (1048a–b, 1050b).

[28] Aquinas, *Summa*, Ia, art.1, ad obj.3.

[29] Cf. *RD*, pp. 196–97 with Keckermann, *Systema*, I.vi (col. 109); Zanchi, *De operibus Dei*, I.iii, q.3 (*Opera*, III, col. 35), and note *DTEL*, p. 164.

[30] Cf. Constantin, "Rationalisme," *DTC* 13/2, cols. 1697–99.

sophy and metaphysics of the Renaissance, such as the flowering of the Dutch and German Protestant metaphysics in the early seventeenth century.[31] Nor, of course, should these two possible sources be isolated from each other.

In the Christian Aristotelianism of the Middle Ages—just as in Augustine's meditations on the stages of creation—the nothing out of which God creates is absolute nothingness and the first stage of creation, the chaos or void of Genesis 1:1–2, is identified as *materia prima* or *informis*, the material no-thing or substratum drawn out of absolute emptiness by God.[32] Arminius appears to have reverted to a more genuinely Aristotelian usage on this point. Indeed, he identifies the material substratum made by God out of nothing as *materia secunda*, secondary matter (and not, as the medieval scholastics and his scholastic Reformed contemporaries would have argued, as *materia prima*[33]):

> secondary [matter] is that from which all corporeal things are now distinguished according to their separate forms (*formas separatas*); and this is the rude chaos and unshaped mass made at the beginning.[34]

A similar concept, on which Arminius may have drawn, appears in the *Metaphysicae systema methodicum* (1604) of the Steinfurt philosopher and colleague of Conrad Vorstius, Clemens Timpler. Timpler argues a duality of ultimate principle, of being and nothingness, and, thus, accords metaphysical status to the *nihil* over against Being.[35] If Courtine is correct, moreover, Timpler's argument—and, by extension, perhaps Arminius' also—is the result of the radicalization of Suárez' critical project of identifying the proper object of metaphysics. Suárez recognized that a comprehensive ontology must come to terms with all possible objects and even though he followed the traditional view of the proper object of metaphysics as *ens inquantum ens*, being insofar as it is being, or *ens reale*, real being or being having the character of a thing (*res*), a real, extramental existent, he also believed that mental objects not having real, extra-mental existence (*ens rationis*) entered the discussion at the level of the identification of real being over against possible being. If metaphysics is to be constructed—

---

[31] Cf. Wund, *Schulmetaphysik*, pp. 75–76; Dibon, *L'Enseignement philosophique*, pp. 64–71; Lewalter, *Metaphysik*, pp. 46–59.

[32] Cf. Aquinas, *Summa*, Ia, q.44, art.2; q.66, art.1 with Scotus as cited in Minges, II, pp. 268–69; Lombard, *Sent.*, II, d.2, caps.2, 5; d.12, caps.1–2 and Altenstaig, *Lexicon*, s.v. "*materia potest capi dupliciter*" (p. 521).

[33] Cf. Junius, *Theses theologicae*, XV.7 with *Synopsis purioris*, X.xxii–xxiii and with Lombard, *Sent.*, II, dist.xii, cap.2.

[34] *Disp. priv.*, XXIV.v.

[35] Cf. Wundt, *Schulmetaphysik*, p. 76, citing Timpler, *Metaphysicae systema methodicum*, cap.2.

as Suárez intended—as an intellectually independent science of general metaphysics rather than a theological metaphysics, and its object is being understood in a neutral sense, then, Courtine contends, the result of a radical elaboration of this metaphysics will be a concept not primarily of *ens* as God but of *ens* as the most generalized object, *ens* as a name (*nomen*), as a pure *cogitabile*.[36]

Timpler, by pressing the Suárezian argument a step further, moved from a definition of the object of metaphysics as *ens inquantum ens* to its definition as *intelligibile inquantum intelligibile*: "metaphysics," wrote Timpler, "is a contemplative art that deals with all intelligibles."[37] Metaphysics, therefore, extends consideration to all objects, even purely mental ones, and examines being from its highest to its lowest degree, including what Courtine calls "an essential indeterminacy" or a "neutrality" of the object, with the result that both something (*aliquid*) and nothing (*nihil*), being (*ens*), and nonbeing (*non-ens*) are its proper objects. Indeed, the basic question of metaphysics and also of ontology must now become the opposition between being and nonbeing as establishing the range of their proper objects. *Nihil* is now understood as *nihil negativum*, an absolute nothing, incapable of representation—while *non-ens* in its opposition to *ens* is understood as *nihil privativum*, the purely possible or utterly indeterminate possibility that can be determined or actualized.[38]

Arminius appears to have encountered this development and to have registered the issue in his identification of the *non-ens* or merely possible as in some sense an object in the work of creation. Although the brevity of Arminius' formulae and the vagueness of his language prevent a definitive explanation of the importance of this variant definition to his theology, the implication of some limitation, outside of God, on the work of creation resonates with other formulations throughout his system. As Arminius will argue in his doctrine of providence, the communication of being and goodness to the created order is not an absolute communication but one that is relative to the finitude of the creature,[39] and whereas virtually all scholastic writers would agree to the basic idea of a limit upon the communication of

---

[36] Courtine, "Le projet suarézien," pp. 249–50.

[37] Cited in Courtine, "Le projet suarézien," p. 251.

[38] Ibid., pp. 239–41, 251–52. A similar conclusion appears to have been drawn by Eilhardus Lubinus (1565–1621), a professor of theology at Rostock, who argued two eternal principles, Ens and Non-ens: God, as Ens, is the efficient cause of the created order and the author of all good; Non-ens is the material principle and the source of all limitation, including evil. Lubinus' *Phosphorus de prima causa & natura mali tractatus* (1596) caused considerable controversy in the Lutheran Church beginning around 1600: see Pünjer, *History*, p. 174 and Jocher, *Lexikon*, II, cols. 1146–47, 2254–55.

[39] Cf. *Articuli nonnulli*, VII.1 with *De obiecto*, p. 29 (*Works*, I, p. 326).

any divine perfection to finite creatures, virtually none would allow that a positive limitation arises from the *nihil* viewed as an eternal, material substratum or as a realm of possible being existing independently of the realm of actual being. Arminius seems, at least, to have toyed with the idea as one theoretical option for delimiting and restricting the exercise of divine power over the created order. If, moreover, this is the implication of Arminius' language, his theological questionings appear not only as standing in continuity with the scholastic philosophical debates of his own time but also as standing in a line of philosophical development extending from the early seventeenth-century reception of Suárez in the Netherlands and Germany to the rise of a fully developed rationalist metaphysics in the works of Leibniz, Wolff, and Baumgarten at the beginning of the next century.[40] Without claiming to engage in this larger historical discussion, we can at least point to the affinity of Arminius' thought for the rationalist direction of seventeenth-century philosophy and note that this affinity extends beyond the generalized openness to reason that has frequently been recognized in Arminian theology.[41] Reformed theology had far more difficulty negotiating its brief and partial eighteenth-century alliance with continental rationalism.[42]

It is also the case that later Arminian thinkers followed Arminius in recognizing a philosophical problem in the language of creation— rather than simply setting aside the difficulties and the inconclusive formulations found in Arminius' theology and falling back upon a more traditional statement. Thus, Episcopius, after having identified God as the highest good and as the primary object of his own willing, declares that the "primary object" *ad extra* of the divine will is nothing (*nihilum*). The first effect of such willing is the production of *ens ex nihilo*: the divine act prior to all other divine acts is necessarily concerned with "nothing considered as nothing" (*nihilum qua nihilum*).[43] This *nihil* is not preexisting matter; rather it is an objective potency that is not repugnant or contradictory to the establishment of real being so that, "after non-being, it receives being" (*post non esse, accipiat esse*). "In this way," concludes Episcopius, "the *nihil* does not

[40] Cf. Courtine's views on the importance of Suárez to this development in "Le projet suarézien," pp. 235–43, 245–51, 272–73 with Mahieu, *François Suárez*, pp. 517–21.

[41] Cf. Van Holk, "From Arminius to Arminianism in Dutch Theology," in McCulloh (ed.), *Man's Faith and Freedom*, pp. 38–39 with A. C. McGiffert, *Protestant Thought before Kant* (New York: Harper and Row, 1962), pp. 187–89.

[42] Cf. *PRRD*, I, pp. 88–97, 190–93, 242, 305–8 with Ernst Bizer, "Die reformierte Orthodoxie und der Cartesianismus," *Zeitschrift für Theologie und Kirche* 55 (1958): 306–72.

[43] Episcopius, *Inst. theol.*, IV.ii.22 (p. 310, col. 2).

prevent the establishment of objective potency in the *nihil*."[44] As in Arminius' ruminations, but now with far more philosophical clarity, the nothing is not a *nihil absolutum* or *nihil negativum* but rather a *nihil privativum* or latent potency for being. In addition, Episcopius clearly follows out the implications of Timpler's definition of metaphysics as the art that deals with all intelligibles and therefore both with *ens* and *non-ens*. "Nothing" has not become "something," but it has gained, in Episcopius' view, what Courtine has termed "objectity."[45] The point is carried forward by Limborch.[46]

By way of contrast, the typical Protestant scholastic discussion of creation assumes a primary or first creation (*creatio prima*) of matter out of nothing. This created but as yet unformed matter is *materia prima*. This first matter can be called *nihilum secundum quid* or relative nothingness inasmuch as it is incapable, of itself, of generating fully formed things. Upon this first matter God acts in the second creation (*creatio secunda*) to produce the substances of things—which is to say, *materia secunda*.[47] In this two-stage model, *creatio prima* precedes *materia prima* and *creatio secunda* precedes *materia secunda*, in both cases creation being the precondition for the existence of matter. In Arminius' model, *materia prima* precedes the first creation and *materia secunda* precedes the second creation, with the result that, even granting the identification of this "primary matter" as the *nihil* in a more traditional sense, matter in some way is always the precondition for the work of creation and, indeed, a limiting factor in the work of creation.

Two corollaries appended by Arminius to this disputation help to draw out the implications of this concept of the creation of even the material substratum of things. In the first place, the superabundant plenitude of divine wisdom, goodness, and power stands over against an utter void, a "twofold privation or vacuity." Over against God there is an utter privation of "essence and form, which will bear some resemblance to an infinite nothing that is capable of infinite forms"—and there is, second, an utter privation of "place, which will be like an infinite vacuum that is capable of being the receptacle of numerous worlds."[48] This language, like Arminius' variant on the

---

[44] Ibid., IV.iii.1 (p. 346, col. 1): "*Hujusmodi potentiam objectivam in nihilo ponere nihil vetat.*"

[45] Courtine, "Le projet suarézien," pp. 235, 240–42, 251–52.

[46] Limborch, *Theologia christiana*, II.xix.7.

[47] Cf. *RD*, p. 197 with *DLGT*, s.v. "*creatio*," "*ex nihilo*," and "*materia prima*." Note that this view of two creative acts raises an issue of order, not of time: there is no temporal duration of unformed matter prior to the creation of *materia secunda*.

[48] *Disp. priv.*, XXIV, corollarium ii: "Qui creationem accurate mente sua concipit, necesse est ut praeter plenitudinem sapientiae, bonitatis, & potentiae divinae, duplicem concipiat sive privationem sive vacuitatem; unam secundum essentiam & formam, quaerit instar infiniti Nihili, quod infinitarum formarum capax est;

usage of *materia prima* and *materia secunda*, appears to draw on a purer Aristotelianism or even on a modified Platonic concept of a pure potency that, although unformed and, technically, nothing, still has a receptivity for form and therefore a remote resemblance by way of potential to the multiplicity of the created order. We may also hear, in Arminius' words, an echo of the theory of the plurality of worlds.

In the second place, Arminius can argue that the utter emptiness of the *nihil* out of which God creates the world leads to the realization "that time and place are not separate creatures, but are created with things themselves."[49] Time and place are not, of course, things. Rather they exist relative to things, so that "no created thing can be ... conceived" without them. "They exist together at the creation of things."[50] Time exists only in the mutation of finite things and space only in their relationship: God is eternal, without time, and immense, without measure—time and measure are characteristics of the created order. The point, in its original form, comes from Augustine.[51] It was surely known to the Reformers, but it was discussed at length, before the era of the Protestant scholastics, only in the scholastic tradition.

Having identified as "secondary matter" what his contemporaries generally called *materia prima*, Arminius moves on to define the actual substances of things as "third matter":

> The third consists of both of these simple and secret elements and of certain compound bodies, from which all the rest have been produced—as from the waters have proceeded creeping and flying things, and fishes; from the earth all other living things, trees, herbs and shrubs; from the rib of Adam, the woman; and from seed (*ex semine*), the perpetuation of the species.[52]

This concept of "secret elements," or as they are more typically called *rationes seminales*, has its roots in the thought of Augustine,[53] and carries over into the thought of the scholastics and, to a certain extent even into the theology of the Reformers, whose exegesis of

---

alteram secundum locum, quae erit instar infiniti vacui, quod plurimorum mundorum potest esse receptaculum." On the problem of the plurality of worlds, see Funkenstein, *Scientific Imagination*, pp. 140–43.

[49] *Disp. priv.*, XXIV, corollarium iii.

[50] Ibid.: "Unde & hoc sequitur, tempus & locum separatas creaturas non esse, verum rebus ipsis concreari, vel potius ad rerum creationem simul existere, non absoluta sed relativa entitate, sine qua res creata nulla concipi aut cogitari possit."

[51] See Augustine, *Confessions*, XI.30–31; XII.15; and idem, *De genesi ad litteram*, I.xv.29; V.v.12–13.

[52] *Disp. priv.*, XXIV.v.

[53] Cf. Augustine, *De genesi ad litteram*, V.4 with Gilson, *Christian Philosophy of Saint Augustine*, pp. 206–8.

Genesis 1—for all its appeal to the original language—tended to rest on a traditional view of the beginnings of the world.[54]

The form or formal cause of the created order is "the production itself of all things out of nothing."[55] Arminius, thus, will not allow the actual or real existence of any formal cause or forms of created things apart from the divine productive act: just as no materiality exists in eternity alongside of God, even so no forms of things can be said to have an eternal existence outside of God. Thus, the forms of things "pre-existed already framed, according to the archetype in the mind of God, without any being of their own (*sine ulla propria entitate*), lest anyone should claim an ideal world."[56] Here we have returned once more to the Suárezian point against the coeternity of matter or substance with God apart from the creative act—but now by way of the Thomistic assumption that all of the forms to be conjoined with matter in the creation of the substances of things preexist in the mind of God.[57] God, therefore, by knowing himself in his being and goodness—by having an archetypal theology that is identical with his own essence—also knows all of reality, and knows it eternally.

The divine understanding, therefore, not only knows eternally the plenitude of divine goodness, it also knows eternally all of the forms of possible existence that can arise out of the communication of goodness *ad extra*. This self-communication can also be understood, as Aquinas had argued, as the communication of being, inasmuch as the ultimate Good is identified with Being.[58] Arminius has, in other words, accepted the scholastic merging of the artisan model of creation according to which God fashions the world of things by informing the matter that he has created and the view of creation as an emanation of being (or goodness) according to which the existences of things flow forth from God. Indeed, Arminius has adopted the Thomistic synthesis of these two rather opposite views in the assumption that it is the power or potency for being and not being itself that emanates from God, granting that the divine goodness is not so

[54] Cf. Luther, *Lectures on Genesis*, in *Luther's Works*, vol. 1 (St. Louis: Concordia, 1958), pp. 6, 8; and note Zanchi, *De operibus Dei*, I.i.3.3; II.i.2,4–5 in *Opera*, III, cols. 35–36, 224–25, 251–57.

[55] *Disp. priv.*, XXIV.vi.

[56] Ibid.

[57] *SCG*, I.58.

[58] Cf. *Disp. pub.*, IV.xx, xxiii, lii with Aquinas, *Summa*, Ia, q.5, art.1; q.6, art.4; q.19, art. 2. Note especially, *Disp. pub.*, IV.xxiii: "Bonitas essentiae Dei & secundum quam ipas summum & ipsum bonum est, essentialiter in se ipsa, ex cuius participatione omnia alia sunt, & bona sunt: & ad quam omnia alia tanquam ad summum finem sunt referenda"; Aquinas, *Summa*, Ia, q.6, art.4, corpus: "Et quia bonum convertitur cum ente, sicut et unum, ipsum per se bonum dicebat esse Deum, a quo omnia dicuntur bona per modum participationis" and idem, q.19, art.2, ad 2: "cum Deus alia a se non velit nisi propter finem qui est sua bonitas."

much an efficient as a final cause, drawing things out of nothing toward itself. The absence of any sense of conflict among these three assumptions resident in Arminius' thought only serves to show how fully he has accepted the Thomistic synthesis as the correct metaphysical reading of the creation-narrative: exegesis fades into the background.

The obvious corollary to these arguments is the problem of the eternity of the world. Arminius raises the issue in all its paradox:

> The world was neither established from eternity, nor could it be created from eternity: though God was from eternity furnished with the power (*potentia*) by which he could make the world and afterwards did make it; and though no moment of time can be conceived by us in which the world could not have been created.[59]

The notion of the eternity of the world is, thus, deemed to be an error and, beyond that, an impossibility. Nevertheless, the doctrinal arguments presented by Arminius provided no positive ground for such an assertion. Just as he had done in his introductory proofs of the existence of God, Arminius here rested his entire doctrinal exposition on an Aristotelian, causal model. The argument that *materia prima* (or in Arminius' terminology, *materia secunda*) cannot be eternal inasmuch as eternal substance could not be acted upon, merely duplicates a point made in the proofs,[60] and is hardly conclusive—particularly in the context of Aristotelian concepts that imply the opposite. Arminius does not appear to follow through with the logic of Suárez' realization that the eternity of the world (as opposed to an eternity of co-equal matter) can be explained in terms of an atemporal, ontologically construed creation *ex nihilo*, and that such an understanding of the eternity of the world alone makes conceivable a creative relation between God and an eternal *materia prima*.

The wording of Arminius' corollary indicates a further problem—that God is eternal and eternally able to create and that our temporality, as we experience it, cannot be conceived of as beginning, much less as "beginning in time." On the one hand, the juxtaposition of God's eternity with a notion of beginning in time leaves the question of divine activity before the beginning—or of divine inactivity. On the other hand, the eternity of God, understood in terms of the pure actuality and immutability of the divine being in all its attributes, appears to contradict any concept of beginnings in relation to God. The concept of a creation of the world *ex nihilo* can easily enough be understood in terms of the utter contingency of things and the divine power that holds them eternally in being. All that Arminius can do is

---

[59] *Disp. priv.*, XXIV, corollarium 1.
[60] Cf. *Disp. priv.*, XXIV.v with XIV.vii.

assert the orthodox doctrine, while the way he notes its paradoxical character suggests that he may be somewhat hesitant to resolve the problem caused by his Aristotelian language. His doctrine is too scholastic to avoid the problem—but not developed enough to note the way out of it.[61]

Clearly, Arminius had at his disposal in this and other disputations the outlines of a solution—indeed of the Thomistic solution. He had previously argued that God possesses eternally in his intellect the ideas of all finite things and that this knowledge is not in itself, eternally, the impartation of being to things. Simply by knowing his own essence, which is his own *esse* and, moreover, the *esse* of all things, God eternally and changelessly knows the temporal order *in himself*. Outlines of this argument are not only present in Arminius' doctrine of creation but also, at somewhat greater length, in the discussion of the self-communication of divine goodness found in his doctrine of the divine will and affections.[62] Why, then, does Arminius withhold the solution to the problem? There are several possible answers to the question. Arminius may simply have posed an issue for discussion fully expecting the standard scholastic answer to arise in the course of debate. His system does, after all, take the form of disputations. He may, however, have intended to identify a problem resident in the orthodox scholasticism of his day—or, he may have desired to press by implication toward a solution outside of the bounds of contemporary orthodoxy in order to reinforce his arguments concerning the self-limiting character of the divine creative act. The pattern of Arminius' disputations (and, for that matter, those of Junius, Gomarus, and Polyander) was, normally, to state a point for elaboration not for refutation.

His subsequent examination of the problem of matter and form—both of which lack real existence prior to the divine creative act—points Arminius toward two conclusions that echo the orthodox scholastic solution:

> First, that creation is an immediate act of God alone, both because a creature who is of a finite power is incapable of operating on nothing, and because such a creature cannot shape matter in substantial forms. Second, the creation was freely produced, not necessarily, because God was not limited by the *nihil*, nor was he destitute of forms.[63]

Creation, in other words, must be a divine act because, understood as a creation *ex nihilo*, it is beyond the capability of a creature. Only

---

[61] Cf. the medieval debate in Cyril Vollert (ed.), *On the Eternity of the World*.

[62] See above, 4.2; and cf. Patterson, *Conception of God*, pp. 424–37 for a discussion of Aquinas' arguments.

[63] *Disp. priv.*, XXIV.vii.

the infinite power of God can make something where nothing was before—and only the infinite power of God can make unformed matter into something formed, into a substance. This divine action, moreover, must be understood as a free action inasmuch as the hypothetical constraints of preexistent matter or of eternal forms existing outside of the mind of God have been eliminated in the previous arguments. (We are still left with the problem that Arminius has, in several places, stated the seemingly contrary point that the *nihil* imposes a limit on the divine communication of being and goodness.[64])

The first of these conclusions once again appears to be a reflection of the Thomist position, according to which creation must be "the proper act of God alone" inasmuch as God alone is capable of producing being in an absolute sense. Creatures may be able to produce individual beings, but only God can produce being as such, because the essence of God is being itself.[65] Arminius has, we remember, made precisely this point, thereby laying the foundation for his concept of creation, in his initial definition of the divine essence as the first moment of the nature of God: God is to be understood, in the first instance, "purely and simply" as "*esse.*"[66] As Gilson points out, the Scotist alternative lodges the act of creation in the will of God in order to argue its freedom in a voluntaristic context: here the act of creation arises out of the divine essence, out of the pure act of the divine Being.[67] The Thomistic argument was available to Arminius, moreover, not only in its original form, but also as defended against Scotus' critique in Suárez' *Disputationes.*[68]

The second of these conclusions—the freedom of God in his creative act—also represents the result of lengthy scholastic debate. If, as Arminius has previously argued, the being and goodness of God in its superabundant fullness is such that it "is inclined" toward self-communication[69] and the understanding and will of God, in a sense, concur in the suitability of the communication of this plenitude, and if God is indeed immutable in his being, goodness, understanding, and will, creation would appear to be necessary. Arminius can state the opposite, and state it so simply, without elaboration, because of the earlier debate and its outcome. As indicated in the preceding paragraph, part of the reason for disagreement between Thomists and Scotists over the language of creation was the desire, on both sides, to

[64] Cf. *De obiecto*, p. 29 (*Works*, I, p. 326) with *Articuli nonnulli*, VII.1 and *Disp. priv.*, XXIV.iv.

[65] Aquinas, *Summa*, Ia, q.45, arts. 5 and 6; *SCG*, II.21.

[66] *Disp. priv.*, XV.v.

[67] Gilson, *Christian Philosophy of St. Thomas Aquinas*, p. 122 and p. 460, n. 102.

[68] Suárez, *Disp. metaph.*, XX.ii.23–38.

[69] *Disp. priv.*, XXIV.iv.

affirm it as the free act of God. The problem itself arose out of the philosophical discussion of creation inherited by the West from Arabian sources—specifically from the Averroistic discussion of the eternity of the world—and, in addition, out of the desire of Western thinkers like Aquinas to profit from Aristotelian and Arabian philosophy.[70]

Alexander of Hales explicitly linked the concepts of creation out of nothing and the freedom of God in creation on the ground that the temporal beginning of things could only be accounted for as the result of a freely willed decree to create.[71] Aquinas clarified the point considerably by arguing that God necessarily knows from all eternity the idea of the world inasmuch as he knows from all eternity the fullness of his own essence and goodness and the infinitude of his own intellect (which is identical, essentially, with his essence and goodness).[72] We noted precisely this point in Arminius' location of the forms of all things "already framed, according to the archetype in the mind of God."[73] The freedom of God in creation arises for Aquinas and, indeed, for Arminius, in the relation of intellect and will—inasmuch as the creation and ordering of things toward the good is an act of intellect and will in which the intellect directs the will to act: the knowledge of all things is necessary, but the creation of those things rests upon a free decree to actualize the eternally known possibilities.[74] Even if the act of will is understood as being in God eternally, it is nonetheless the will of God that the world be created in time.[75]

The origin of all things from nothing, by an utterly free act of God serves also to emphasize both the radical contingency of the created order and the distance between contingent beings and their Creator, the self-sufficient and necessary Being. Creatures

> are always nearer to nothing than to their creator, from whom they are removed by an infinite distance and they are distinguished from the nothingness, their primeval source (*primaeva matrice sua*), only by finite properties inasmuch as they may fall back into it once more and can never be raised to equality with God.[76]

The point was made by the nominalists of the late Middle Ages that,

---

[70] Cf. Schwane, *Histoire des Dogmes*, IV, p. 283.

[71] Alexander of Hales, *Summa*, II, q.21, memb.3, arts.1–2.

[72] Aquinas, *SCG*, I.45.7; 49.3–4; 50.8.

[73] *Disp. priv.*, XXIV.vi, cf. ibid., XXIV.vii; and note Aquinas, *Summa*, Ia, q.44, art.3, corpus.

[74] Cf. *SCG*, II.23.4; *Disp. pub.*, IV.1; Schwane, *Histoire des Dogmes*, IV, pp. 284–85; and Jourdain, *La philosophie de Saint Thomas d'Aquin*, I, pp. 229–30.

[75] Cf. Arminius, *Disp. priv.*, XXIV, corollaria i and iii. Suárez, *Disp. metaph.*, XX.v and with Patterson, *Conception of God*, p. 425.

[76] *De obiecto*, p. 29 (*Works*, I, p. 327).

granting the infinite distance between Creator and creature, between Being and all that has origin from nonbeing, even the most exalted creature is no closer to God than the lowest form in the great chain of being: the highest spiritual being is removed from the lowest material form by a finite measure, albeit great, whereas both beings are infinitely removed from God.[77] Arminius appears, in these comments, to reflect this late medieval problem with the chain of being: he recognizes that the use of God or Being and nonbeing as standards or measures of the relative being or nonbeing of things in the temporal order is an exercise fraught with difficulty. Indeed, although he has previously argued that finite things exist by participation in the communication of God's goodness he now appears to argue more affinity between finite things and nonbeing than between those things and God.

Once this infinite distance between God and the most exalted of creatures is recognized, the logic of the chain of being begins to crumble: the chain no longer reaches to God. Its high, spiritual ranks no longer mediate between God and man, God and the tangible cosmos. If Blumenberg is correct about the problem posed not just for rational knowledge of God but for comprehension of the world order by this late medieval argumentation, particularly by the logic of the *potentia absoluta*,[78] Arminius has here stated one of the central theological and philosophical problems of his age—and the way in which he deals with the problem is crucial to an understanding of his place in intellectual history and the history of theology. Nominalism, according to Blumenberg, had avoided metaphysical dualism while at the same time creating "its practical equivalent *ad hominem*: the only dependable and trustworthy God is the God of salvation, who has restricted Himself to his *potentia ordinata*, like a partially constitutional monarch, but who, through predestination, still withholds from man's knowledge the range over which He chooses to be dependable."[79] This view ultimately made ordered knowledge of the creation impossible and removed both reason and nature from the realm of certainty. Arminius' conception of divine transcendence echoed the nominalistic view, but his approach to theological epistemology and to the problem of the created order as the emanation of creatures from the divine goodness points in the opposite direction. The great problematic of theology addressed in his doctrine of creation and providence is precisely that difficulty of maintaining the transcendence and creative freedom of God while at the same time affirming the stability of the created order and the theological as well

[77] Mahoney, "Metaphysical Foundations," p. 238.
[78] Blumenberg, *Legitimacy of the Modern Age*, pp. 152–54.
[79] Ibid., p. 154.

as philosophical validity of conclusions drawn from the nature and character of God's creation.

Of course, as Oberman and Vignaux have shown,[80] the point argued by Blumenberg is an oversimplification. Nominalist language of *potentia absoluta* did focus theology on the problem of divine transcendence and it did, in the case of Occam, provide a final point of critique of the Thomistic attempt to reconcile faith and reason. Granting the divine *potentia absoluta*, revelation might not only be beyond reason, it might also be nonrational or irrational. To this extent Blumenberg is correct. But it is also the case that "Occam's thesis of the irrationality of revelation may not ... be equated with the undermining of the established order."[81] What is more, the language of *potentia absoluta* functioned as much to emphasize the divine immediacy as to indicate the divine transcendence. God can, by his *potentia absoluta*, work immediately with individuals, without reference to the ordained pattern of laws and intermediaries, but he cannot undo history or bring about the noncompossible opposite of a temporal truth foreknown with certainty![82]

If, then, Arminius' rejection of the language of *potentia absoluta* cannot be argued to be a generalized repudiation of nominalist usage, it may still be viewed as a repudiation of a particular approach to the concept of a divine *potentia absoluta*, an approach inherited from the nominalism of Augustinians like Gregory of Rimini and represented in his own day by Perkins and Gomarus. These writers had, indeed, stressed the divine transcendence to the point of admitting no clear correlation between moral activity and election,[83] thus severing the link between the exercise of human freedom in the natural order and the ultimate purpose of God for his creation. Over against this view of Perkins and Gomarus, Arminius' rejection of the concept of *potentia absoluta*, when set into the context of his doctrines of the *scientia media* and divine concurrence, will be seen to point in two directions. On the one hand, as we will argue directly below, Arminius labors to diminish considerably the range of positive divine causality in the world for the sake of the freedom of creatures. In effect, by setting aside the *potentia absoluta* he both limits the divine activity and

---

[80] Oberman, "Some Notes on the Theology of Nominalism," pp. 56–62; Vignaux, "Nominalisme," *DTC* 11/1, cols. 762–69. These conclusions are borne out by Marylin McCord Adams, *William Ockham*, 2 vols. (Notre Dame: University of Notre Dame Press, 1987), II, pp. 1186–1207.

[81] Oberman, "Some Notes on the Theology of Nominalism," p. 60.

[82] Ibid., p. 62, and cf. Occam, *Predestination, God's Foreknowledge and Future Contingents*, p. 36.

[83] Cf. Vignaux, "Nominalisme," *DTC* 11/1, cols. 770–71 with Perkins, *Exposition of the Symbole or Creed*, pp. 278–79 and Arminius, *Examination of the Theses of Dr. Francis Gomarus*, in *Works*, III, pp. 527–29, 650–58.

loosens the causal link between God and world. On the other hand, and at the same time, his rejection of the *potentia absoluta* and redefinition of the absoluteness of divine power in terms of the *potentia ordinata* increases vastly the linkage between the divine being and goodness and the physical and moral logic of the created order. Arminius' denial of a transcendent, essentially arbitrary and irrational *potentia absoluta* has the effect of bringing the divine being and goodness, as evidenced in the creation, into a more direct and consistent relationship to human perceptions of the results of God's work in the created order.

As Oakley recognized, the profound alteration of the significance of the concept of the two powers of God that occurred in the late Middle Ages can be traced to a shift from the intellectualism of Thomist thought to the voluntarism of Scotus and Occam. If all that God wills is governed by the divine knowledge of the goodness of God's own nature, then the ultimate will and power of God will be manifest in the very order of things, with the result that "subjection to law could well be seen to extend to God himself."[84] The Scotist and nominalist assertion of the primacy of will—even granting fully the limitations placed on the divine will and power by the nominalist theologians— placed eternal law, as known to divine reason in some sense below the will and affirmed powerfully the divine freedom and omnipotence. The resurgence of Thomist intellectualism and its modification in the hands of Molina, Suárez, and Arminius meant a return to the earlier, more limited conception of *potentia absoluta* and, indeed, in the case of Arminius to precisely the issue of divine self-limitation against which Scotus and the nominalists had reacted and, therefore, to a clear declaration of the stability, lawfulness, rationality, and inherent morality of the world order as created and maintained by God.

These overarching issues of theological formulation are not immediately obvious in Arminius' next topic—the question of final causality—although, as we have seen in the preceding chapter, the concept of the glory of God, intrinsic and extrinsic, as the goal of creation does relate directly to the issue of a divine self-limitation consequent upon the act of creation. Quite surprisingly he does not return in detail at this point either to the goodness of God as the ultimate and proper object of God's willing of all finite lesser goods or to the eschatological union of all things in God, particularly the union of rational creatures with God in final blessedness. Omission of the second of these points is especially curious in view of the practical, teleological orientation of Arminius' system toward ultimate ends. In any case, the final causality of creation indicated by Arminius is immediate and proximate:

[84] Oakley, *Omnipotence*, p. 80.

The end—not that which moved God to create, for God is not moved by anything external—but that which results immediately and without interruption from the very act of creation, and which is in fact contained in the essence of this act, is the demonstration of the divine wisdom, goodness and power. For those divine properties which concur in the act, shine forth and show themselves in their own nature in action.[85]

Here the transcendence of God is still the dominant concern, even though it is somewhat limited by the *analogia entis*—that is, by the analogical presentation or revelation of attributes in the created order. Goodness is revealed in the communication of existence, wisdom in the order and variety of the world, and power in the production of things out of nothing.[86] In addition, the divine goodness is its own primary object—so that the communication of it to creatures cannot represent an increase in God's own goodness or a necessary act on God's part.[87]

The other end of creation that Arminius notes is usually identified as the *finis proximus creationis*—the proximate, not the ultimate end, of creation:

The end which is called "to what purpose," is the good of the creatures themselves, and especially of human beings, to whom are referred the other creatures, as being useful to him, according to the institution of the divine creation.[88]

Now, perhaps, we have some limitation of the power of God and some indication of a relationship between transcendent Creator and the creature: in the first place, creation is now defined as intending the good of creatures and, in the second place, creatures are defined as being "useful" to God—not, however, in such a way as to subvert the good of the creature. Indeed, the balance of these issues and the way in which the ordained good of the creature limits the power of the transcendent Creator, will be a central concern of Arminius' doctrine of providence.[89]

Once he has defined the causality of creation, Arminius passes over into a consideration of creation as an object or effect capable of general description. The effect of the divine creative act is the "universal world, which in the scripture is identified by the terms 'heaven' and 'earth,' sometimes also 'sea,' as being the bounds within which all

---

[85] *Disp. priv.*, XXIV.viii; cf. *Synopsis purioris*, X.19.

[86] *Disp. priv.*, XXIV.viii.

[87] Cf. *Disp. pub.*, IV.lxviii with *Disp. priv.*, XXIV.iv, viii and with Patterson, *Conception of God*, p. 424 on Aquinas, *SCG*, II.23, 31.

[88] *Disp. pub.*, XXIV.ix.

[89] Below, chap. 12.

things are contained."[90] Arminius assumes that he can speak of the universal order itself as a thing—as a unity with an overarching form given to it by God—so perfect and complete that it has no formal defect either in whole or in part. The form of the world is perfectly fulfilled without redundancy. Thus, the world is a unified whole because there is a perfect "connection and coordination" of all the parts in their "mutual relation" while at the same time all of the parts are "distinguished, not only according to place and situation, but likewise according to nature, essence and unique existence."[91] This unity and diversity in perfect order and perfect fullness "was necessary, not only to adumbrate in some measure the perfection of God in variety and multitude, but also to demonstrate that the omnipotent one did not create the world by a natural necessity but by the freedom of will."[92] Here, once again, we may see a brief reflection of what was, in Aquinas' theology, a major issue elaborated at great length—the absence of natural necessity in the creation of the world. Thus, the overarching unity and order of the creation rest on the divine intellect which, in turn, acts through the divine will. Such activity is voluntary, not bound by a necessity of nature. Moreover, both Aquinas and Arminius add, God does not create *all* possible beings—again indicating, as opposed to a Platonic theory of emanation, the freedom of the creative act.[93]

Arminius has done nothing less than enunciate a crucial modification of the principle of plenitude underlying the scholastic view of the "great chain of being." As Lovejoy defined the concept, it indicates "that no genuine potentiality of being can remain unfilled, that the extent and abundance of the creation must be as great as the possibility of existence and commensurate with the productive capacity of a 'perfect' and inexhaustible Source."[94] The ultimate Good is a *plenum formarum*, a plenitude of forms, that of its own nature as good, must be self-diffusive in such a way that the forms eternally belonging to it are realized or actualized in the temporal order. This basically Platonic view of the cosmos was linked, particularly in the medieval mind, with the Aristotelian concept of a continuum of beings in the temporal order: things do not exist in isolation as discrete entities but rather in continuous relation to other things in time and space. From this latter concept the medieval scholastics theorized a continuous

---

[90] *Disp. priv.*, XXIV.x.

[91] Ibid.

[92] Ibid.

[93] Cf. Aquinas, *SCG*, II.23 with Arminius, *Disp. priv.*, XXIV.X; corollary 5; and with Patterson, *Conception of God*, pp. 408–11.

[94] Arthur O. Lovejoy, *The Great Chain of Being: A Study in the History of an Idea* (Cambridge, Mass.: Harvard University Press, 1936), p. 52.

ontological series of beings in the emanation of things from the Good.[95]

Arminius' association of a modified principle of plenitude with the freedom of divine willing creates something of a paradox—inasmuch as it was the principle of plenitude that seemed, in the first place, to argue the necessity of creation.[96] Lovejoy argues that the "expansiveness or fecundity of the Good ... is not the consequence of any free and arbitrary act of choice of the personal Creator in the myth; it is a dialectical necessity."[97] This necessitarianism, of course, did not carry over into the thought of the scholastics—indeed, it could not, in view of their Christian conception of God freely creating the world *ex nihilo*.[98] Dogmatic appropriation of the concept of plenitude was, therefore, at best partial. The Christian modification of the concept is, perhaps, most clearly seen in the redefinition of the emanation of being from God as, not an emanation of substance, but an emanation of the *potentia* for the being of the finite order.[99] Against Lovejoy, the issue is not that the principle of plenitude yields a necessitarianism but rather how the concept of plenitude, in association with the Christian conception of a free Creator, generates modifications of theological language and, as in the case of Aquinas' and even more so in the cases of Suárez' and Arminius' theology, brings about a sense of the self-limitation of God in his creative act.

The modified concept of plenitude carries over into Arminius' view of the distribution of creatures into "three classes" of beings as the "best" distribution possible. There are creatures who are "purely spiritual and invisible"—the angels—and creatures that are "utterly corporeal." And third, almost as if to provide the order of creatures with its requisite symmetry, there are creatures who are part "corporeal and visible," part "spiritual and invisible," namely human beings endowed with body and soul.[100] This also is the order of creation, Arminius argues, with the angels created first, corporeal creatures next in the six days and "not together in a single moment," and finally man was created—first his body and then his soul was "afterwards ... inspired by creating and created by inspiring." Here,

---

[95] Cf. ibid., pp. 55–56 with Mahoney, "Metaphysical Foundations," pp. 212–14. Mahoney here surveys the debate over the "principle of plenitude" and critiques Lovejoy's view of it as an essentially necessitarian concept; and see further Edward P. Mahoney, "Lovejoy and the Hierarchy of Being," *Journal of the History of Ideas* (1987): 211–30.

[96] Cf. Lovejoy, *Great Chain of Being*, pp. 61–62, 65–66, 72–74.

[97] Ibid., p. 54.

[98] Cf. Schwane, *Histoire des Dogmes*, IV, pp. 281–85 on the scholastic discussion of divine freedom in creation with Patterson, *Conception of God*, pp. 408–11.

[99] Aquinas, *Summa*, Ia, q.65, art.3; cf. q.25, art.1.

[100] *Disp. pub.*, XXIV.xi.

too, in the order of creation are the reality and truth of God reflected: "as God commenced the creation in a spirit (i.e. angels), so he might finish it on a spirit (i.e. the soul), being himself the immeasurable and eternal Spirit."[101]

The creation, Arminius concludes, is "the foundation of that right by which God can require religion from man."[102] If God were not the Creator under whose power and command all things exist, God could not be totally believed or be the sole source of our hope—nor would he be the only being ultimately to be feared. But these acts—belief, hope, and fear—all belong to religion. Therefore religion itself rests on the identity of God as Creator. Here again we have strong evidence of the intellectualist assumptions and rationalist tendencies of Arminius' theology: religion is founded upon the relationship of human beings to their Creator. What is more, if we follow out the logic of Arminius' discussion of the primary end of creation, religion can be grounded on the demonstration of divine wisdom, goodness, and power in the natural order.[103] We may say of Arminius, as Sertillanges said of Aquinas, that his view of "the problem of creation is no less complex and refined than the problem of God" because, "at bottom, it is the same" problem, granting that the whole of theology is concerned with the relation of God to creatures and of creatures to God.[104]

Arminius' thought evinces, therefore, a greater trust in nature and in the natural powers of man to discern God in nature than the theology of his Reformed contemporaries. It also evinces, at a somewhat deeper level, a view of creation that has a virtually principial status for theological system. Whereas the theology of Arminius' Reformed contemporaries tended to place the work of grace prior to the work of creation and, therefore, to understand creation increasingly as a means to God's higher salvific end, Arminius' theology tends to conjoin nature and grace, to understand creation as manifesting the ultimate purpose of God, and, therefore, to conceive of the divine act of creation as standing prior to all other divine acts *ad extra* and as establishing both the context and the limitations within which those acts must occur. An enormous shift in emphasis has, therefore, taken place, a shift away from the Reformed stress on the distinction or even, at extreme moments, the separation, of nature from grace. Arminius not only views the self-communicative or self-diffusive character of divine goodness as the basis for identifying creation as a

---

[101] Ibid., XXIV.xii.

[102] *Disp. priv.*, XXIV.xiii.

[103] Cf. ibid., XXIV.viii.

[104] A. D. Sertillanges, *Les grandes thèses de la philosophie thomiste*, p. 81, as cited in Patterson, *Conception of God*, p. 437, n. 2.

revelation of the ultimate purpose of God, he also views it as a self-limiting act by which God makes the whole of creation necessary, by way of consequence, to the final advancement or glorification of creatures. Creation is so placed at the center and foundation of Arminius' theology that the work of salvation can no longer be construed as a restriction of the universal purpose implemented by God in the creative act: there must be a universal will for the whole behind the universal call to salvation rather than an original intention to create for destruction as well as for eternal fellowship. These implications of Arminius' view of creation become still more apparent in his doctrine of divine dominion and providence.

12

The Doctrine of Providence

In approaching the doctrine of divine providence, Arminius had a wealth of material at his disposal—both medieval scholastic and Reformation era Protestant. His views on the subject clearly reflect both sources and, in addition, reflect the beginnings of the early Reformed orthodox doctrine of providence which, like his own teaching, had been constructed out of medieval and Reformation era materials. The differences between his presentation and the views of other early orthodox writers like Ursinus, Zanchi, Daneau, and Junius, however, lies in the pattern of appropriation of the medieval materials and in the blend of materials appropriated. Whereas the work of Ursinus, Zanchi, Daneau, and Junius had as its goal the restatement of a Reformed or Calvinist view of providence in the language and method of scholasticism, Arminius' effort appears to have been directed toward the reformulation of the Protestant doctrine of providence not merely in scholastic terms but also and primarily in view of late medieval theological themes distinctly at variance with the language of providence found in the thought of Reformers like Zwingli and Calvin. Arminius' doctrine of providence represents the working out of the principles developed in his doctrines of God and creation, directed specifically toward a solution to the problem that has been with us since the discussion of the proofs of God's existence—the problem of the relationship of God to the contingent life of the created order. Where Arminius draws directly and positively on Reformed doctrine his model is, as before, Franciscus Junius' *Theses theologicae*.

As one would be led to expect, moreover, from Arminius' discussion of *scientia media*, his doctrine of providence—where the contingencies foreknown by God according to his middle knowledge must be understood as genuine contingencies in relation to the will of God—is one of the points at which he departs not only from the

typical Reformed view but also from his Thomistic models. Unlike
Thomas, who was concerned to argue how God can "govern things in
diverse ways according to their own diversity" in such a way that all
motion ultimately comes from God but also, at the same time,
respects the being of the creatures and does not rob them of their own
operations,[1] Arminius sought to remove the divine efficacy from
those acts foreknown by God as genuine contingents. In other words,
Arminius' departure from Thomas Aquinas on the doctrine of *scientia media* is paralleled by a departure in the doctrine of providence
precisely where the question of contingency and of the divine relation to the contingent order is raised. Nonetheless, the intimate relationship drawn from Thomism between the doctrine of God and
creation carries over into Arminius' doctrine of providence as does
the relationship, made explicit in both the *Summa theologiae* and
Aquinas' *Compendium*, between divine government and divine
providence.[2]

The relationship established by God with his creatures in the act of
creation carries over into the preservation and governance of the
created order as described in the doctrine of providence. Arminius'
views on providence are set forth in four disputations—"On the
Lordship of God," "On the Providence of God,"[3] and the pair of
debates entitled "On the Righteousness and Efficacy of the Providence
of God concerning Evil."[4] In addition, individual sections of the letter
to Hippolytus à Collibus and of the *Declaratio sententiae* are devoted to
the discussion of providence as are two sections of the *Articuli
nonnulli*.[5] All in all, this is one of the more broadly documented topics
in Arminius' theology—and the only topic out of the group discussed
here that was drawn into controversy in Arminius' lifetime. The two
Private Disputations present Arminius' theology in a relatively
noncontroversial setting and probably provide an indication of his
own proposals for the direction to be taken by theological system in
the doctrine of providence. The other documents, particularly the
Declaratio sententiae, although they clearly set forth aspects of
Arminius' doctrine, tend to be guided by Arminius' apologetical and
polemical concerns.

The doctrine of creation provides Arminius with the foundation

---

[1] *Summa*, Ia, q.103, art.5; cf. Jourdain, *La philosophie de Saint Thomas d'Aquin*, I, pp.
243–49.

[2] Cf. Arminius, *Disp. priv.*, XXVII and XXVIII with Aquinas, *Summa theologiae*, Ia,
q.22 (providence), qq.103–4 (divine government), and *Compendium theologiae*, I.123–
25, 130–32 and with Patterson, *Conception of God*, p. 446.

[3] *Disp. priv.*, XXVII and XXVIII.

[4] *Disp. pub.*, IX and X.

[5] *Epistola ad Hippolytum*, pp. 941–43 (Works, II, pp. 696–98); *Declaratio sententiae*, p.
121 (*Works*, I, pp. 657–58); *Articuli nonnulli*, VII–VIII.

on which to construct his conception of the rule and governance of God. God rightly has dominion over all creatures inasmuch as he is the Creator. The nature or character of the divine creative act, moreover, determines and delimits the nature and character of divine dominion.

> The dominion of God over creatures rests on the communication of the good that he has bestowed on them. Since this good is not infinite, neither is the dominion itself infinite. That dominion is infinite only in the sense that it is lawful and proper for God to issue his commands to the creature, to impose on him all his works, to use him in all those things which his omnipotence might be able to command and to impose on him, and to engage his services or attention.[6]

Arminius argues a virtually unlimited rule of God over the creation: his list of "lawful and proper" commands implies no weakening of the doctrine of providence. Nonetheless, Arminius equally adamantly denies that there can be an arbitrary exercise of absolute power on God's part. The rule of God is limited by the character of the creative act, specifically by the mode of God's communication of the goodness of being to creatures.[7]

In the act of communicating his goodness to objects *ad extra*, therefore, God both establishes and limits his rule over the created order. In its establishment, this dominion of God is primary, ultimate, absolute, and perpetual. God's rule is dependent on no prior dominion and must, therefore, be identified as primary. Even so it is, like God himself and the divine goodness on which it rests, ultimate: there is no greater or higher dominion. This dominion is also absolute inasmuch as it is a rule extending to each and every creature in its entirety, whether "according to the whole" or "according to all and each of its parts" or according to "all the relations which subsist between God and the creature."[8] The perpetuity of divine rule follows from this absoluteness: the creature is under the dominion of God as long as it exists.[9]

This primary, ultimate, and absolute rule of God finds its limitation in the very act of creation that establishes it as absolute: "the dominion of God is the right of the creator and his power over creatures, according to which he has them as his own, can command and use them, and do about them whatever the order (*ratio*) of creation

---

[6] *Articuli nonnulli*, VII.1.

[7] Cf. *Dec. sent.*, p. 107 (*Works*, I, p. 626).

[8] *Disp. priv.*, XXVII.i. Arminius distinguishes between dominion deriving from creation (XXVII.i–iv) and from covenant (XXVII.v–ix) with the result that only the first part of this disputation relates directly to providence.

[9] Ibid.

and the equity which rests upon it permit."[10] As if to press home the point that the limitation of divine rule is intrinsic to the creative act itself, Arminius continues: "The right cannot extend further than the cause from which the entirety of that right derives, and on which it is dependent."[11] The cause is, however, God himself and, specifically, the plenitude of being and goodness in God that has been communicated to creatures in a finite way.[12] In the very act of making finite creatures, of actualizing finite forms and capacities, God has set a "limit and a measure" on the communication of his goodness and of his Being and, therefore, on his right over creatures whose goodness and being are less ultimate than his own.[13]

Arminius' argument here reflects the scholastic distinction between the absolute and the ordained power of God. The *potentia absoluta* is the absolute, ultimate power that God has to do as he wills: it reflects the unlimited possibilities known to the *scientia simplicis intelligentiae* and the unlimited power "to do or prevent anything" lodged in the *voluntas beneplaciti*.[14] The *potentia ordinata*, however, is the will of God known through the covenanted order of the universe. Whereas medieval scholastic theology and the theology of early Reformed orthodoxy had both placed the *potentia absoluta*, as it were, behind the *potentia ordinata* and had assumed that, in certain instances or for certain ultimate purposes, God can and indeed has intervened in the temporal order of things in such a way as to manifest his transcendence over his own universal order,[15] Arminius' theology draws together the concepts of absolute and ordained power in such a way as to argue the divine absoluteness in the ordination of dominion and the divine ordination of things as characteristic of absolute dominion itself.

The *potentia absoluta* no longer hovers behind the will of God, representing the range of all possibility, including possibilities at variance with this world order. God is understood as absolute in and for the present world order, as ordered by his goodness. Arminius, in effect, refers to the distinction in order to set it aside by redefinition. He seems to recognize no power in God that is not in some way limited or regulated by attributes that are logically prior to it in order: the *potentia Dei* stands below the *voluntas Dei;* and the will of God, in turn, answers to the *sapientia, scientia,* and *intellectus Dei* and is, in all its movements or extensions, ultimately grounded in the *bonitas Dei* as

---

[10] *Disp. priv.,* XXVII.ii.

[11] Ibid., XXVII.iii.

[12] Cf. *Articuli nonnulli,* VII.1 with *Disp. pub.,* IV.1 and *Disp. priv.,* XXIV.iv.

[13] *De obiecto,* p. 29 (*Works,* I, p. 326).

[14] Cf. *Disp. priv.,* XVII.ix–x and *Disp. pub.,* IV.xliii (*scientia simplicis intelligentiae*) with *Disp. priv.,* XIX.iii and *Disp. pub.,* IV.lviii (*voluntas beneplaciti*).

[15] Cf. Oberman, *Harvest,* pp. 30–38 with Heppe, *RD,* pp. 103–4.

that goodness is known and desired inwardly or intrinsically by God.[16] Once again, the intellectualism of Arminius determines his approach to doctrine. God's freedom to create is not, therefore, paralleled by a freedom with creation: granting the free decision to create and, in so doing, to actualize certain possibilities, we must also grant the self-limitation of God in relation to the created order. The divine nature itself in its essential goodness is one limiting factor.

In his early oration *On the Author and End of Theology*, Arminius makes the argument for a limitation of the relationship between God and his world in a significantly different way: "God is the author of the universe, not by a natural and internal but by a voluntary and external operation and that imparts to the work as much of what is his as he chooses and as much as the *nihil* from which it is produced will permit."[17] This comment returns us to the problem of Arminius' identification of the *nihil* with *materia prima*. God's dominion, usually understood as limited only by divine ordinance, the *potentia ordinata*, is here understood as limited by a factor outside of God, the "nothing" that in some way determines the constitution of finite things by limiting their receptivity to divine being.[18] This assumption would effectively remove a transcendent *potentia absoluta* and, as Arminius' definitions seem to indicate, redefine the absolute power of God as a uniqueness and soleness of ultimate rule within the created order and within the range of possibilities inherent in creative acts rather than as an absolute capability to make or unmake all things.[19]

When Arminius specifies the various limitations intrinsic to the lordship or rule of God, it not only becomes clear that his redefinition of absolute and ordained rule represents an important departure from Reformed doctrine in general but also that his arguments are framed with particular issues in mind—such as the Reformed doctrine of predestination. It is also the case that his opposition to the Reformed teaching arises not as a disagreement over the exegesis of a few passages but as a fundamental divergence resting upon a highly

16 Cf. *Disp. pub.*, IV.1 with *Disp. priv.*, XVIII.iv.

17 *De auctore*, p. 43 (*Works*, I, pp. 350–51).

18 *De obiecto*, p. 29 (*Works*, I, p. 327).

19 *Disp. priv.*, XXVII.i; cf. Funkenstein, *Theology and the Scientific Imagination*, pp. 135–40: Funkenstein argues "a radical change in the perception of the world" between the time of Aquinas and the time of Occam defined by the Occamist assumption that any thing can be annihilated by the *potentia absoluta* over against the Thomist assumption that the universe is an interconnected order of forms none of which can be arbitrarily destroyed without the destruction of the order. Like Blumenberg (cf. above, pp. 174–75), Funkenstein has exaggerated somewhat the implications of nominalist speculation. It is true, nonetheless, that Arminius' arguments stand against any excessive speculation *de potentia absoluta* and point back toward the Thomistic view that Funkenstein contrasts with a radical nominalism.

developed scholastic conception of the essence, attributes, and operations of the Godhead in primary relation to the work of creation and
providence. Arminius appears to have discerned one of the underlying problems confronting theology in the early modern era, the
relationship of God to an ordered universe, and to have moved away
from a radical notion of divine omnipotence such as was cham-
pioned by several of his Reformed contemporaries toward a concept
of divine self-limitation more in accord with theories of the constancy and stability of natural law.

It would not be in accord with the goodness of God or with the
mode of communication of that goodness to the creature (and therefore not a right of the Creator or an aspect of his power over creatures)
for God to deliver his creatures into the hands of some other, arbitrary power that might inflict ill on the creature apart from any sins
or demerits. Even so, it is not within God's dominion to "command
an act to be done by the creature which it has neither sufficient nor
necessary powers to perform."[20] Nor may God "employ the creature
to introduce sin into the world so that, by punishing or forgiving the
creature, he might promote his own glory"—and still less may God
"do with the creature whatever is possible according to his absolute
power (*absolutam suam potentiam*), that is, to punish or afflict him
eternally, apart from sin" or "merits" on the part of the creature.[21]
Quite pointedly, against his colleague Gomarus, Arminius declares,
"It is therefore false that 'though God destined and created for destruction certain creatures (indefinitely considered) without any consideration of sin as the meritorious cause, yet he cannot be accused of
injustice, because he possesses an absolute right over them.'"[22]

Arminius also declares false Luther's statement in *On the Bondage of
the Will* that we will understand by the light of glory the right of God
to condemn whomsoever he wills, just as now we understand by the
light of grace "by what right God saves unworthy and sinful men."[23]
But, Arminius continues, "still more false" is the claim that "man is
bound to acquiesce in this will of God, nay, to give thanks to God, that
he has made him an instrument of the divine glory, to be displayed
through wrath and power in his eternal destruction."[24] All such
statements misunderstand the character of God's lordship over the
creation and, in particular, misunderstand the nature of God's
absolute power in relations *ad extra*:

---

[20] *Disp. priv.*, XXVII.iii.

[21] Ibid.; *Articuli nonnulli*, VII.2.

[22] *Articuli nonnulli*, VII.3, citing Gomarus' *Theses on predestination* (cf. Arminius, *Works*, III, pp. 626–32 and note pp. 599–602).

[23] *Articuli nonnulli*, VII.4.

[24] Ibid., VII.5.

God can make of his own whatsoever he wills, but he does not will, neither can he will, to make of that which is his own whatever it is possible for him to make according to his infinite and absolute power.[25]

Of course, if God truly *cannot* will such things, then placing them hypothetically under the *potentia absoluta* is nonsense. In effect, absolute power, thus defined, cannot exist.

The concluding portion of Arminius' disputation on the rule of God moves from consideration of God's general or providential rule to consideration of the covenanted relationship between God and his rational creatures. The transition occurs smoothly insofar as the dominion that God has as "the right of the creator" (*creatoris ius*) embodies a covenantal principle—the concept of *potentia ordinata*. Thus, Arminius distinguishes between a "despotic" (*despotike*) rule of God by which God rules his universe "without any intention of good which may be useful or saving to the creature" and a "kingly or fatherly" (*basilikea seu patrike*) rule that arises "through the abundance of [God's] goodness and self-sufficiency" and intends directly and specifically "the good of the creature itself."[26] This fatherly rule stands until the creature, intransigent in its unworthiness and "perversity," no longer deserves its blessings—and then the lordly or despotic rule, which achieves God's ends for creation despite the creature, comes into play. Implied here is the usual reading of the distinction between *opus proprium* and *opus alienum*.[27]

The priority of God's paternal rule in his plan for creatures is seen in the inducements to obedience that accompany divine commands: God does "not exact everything that by right (*iure*)" he might exact of the creature but rather "employs persuasions and arguments" that manifest "the utility and necessity" of obedience.[28] Beyond these inducements, the paternal rule of God is manifest in the contract or covenant into which God enters with his creatures. The purpose of the covenant is to bring about "a spontaneous, free and liberal obedience" that arises out of the "stipulations and promises" attached to the agreement.[29] Underlying all such covenants is the basic condition that refusal to meet the terms of the covenant and to profit from its more gentle rule will lead to the "strict" and "rigid" rule of God according to his lordly dominion.[30]

There is, therefore, a "twofold right" (*duplex ius*) that God has "over his rational creatures"—and, in the case of disobedience and sin, a

[25] Ibid., VII.6.
[26] *Disp. priv.*, XXVII.iv.
[27] Ibid., cf. *Disp. priv.*, XIX.iv and above, chap. 10.
[28] *Disp. priv.*, XXVII.v.
[29] Ibid., XXVII.vi.
[30] Ibid., XXVII.vii.

third right. God has the basic right of lordship or dominion that arises from the creative act and the good given to the creature by God as Creator. A second right arises out of the covenant that is imbedded in the natural order and consists in the "greater benefit which the creature will receive from God, the preserver, promoter and glorifier."[31] The third right arises when a creature refuses to accept the lordship of God and falls into disobedience, giving God the right of "treating him as a sinning creature and of inflicting punishment." This right arises not out of an act of God but out of "the wicked act of the creature against God."[32] The previous point, that the absolute power of God does not confer on God the right or ability to punish innocent creatures with justice, is reinforced and placed into the concrete context of the world order: the right to punish is itself not an absolute but a derived right, resting neither on creation nor even on covenant—not directly—but rather resting indirectly on the positive dominion of God and directly on the creature's disobedient relation to that dominion.

This association of a concept of divine self-limitation in creation with a doctrine of covenantal relationship is also a point of contact between the theology of Arminius and late medieval scholasticism. There is, of course, the background of developing Reformed covenant theology against which Arminius' teaching can also be interpreted both for its common elements and its distinctive features,[33] but the theological argumentation here points back to the covenantal logic of the late medieval discussion of the *potentia ordinata*. Specifically, the first of these sources, the medieval theological tradition, provides Arminius with the connection between the language of *potentia ordinata* in its relation to the act of creation and the concept of a divine covenant or pact (*pactum*) with the creatures. God covenants with the world order to observe the limitations of his ordained power and not to unleash the *potentia absoluta*.[34] Arminius has, of course, modified the argument by dissolving the *potentia absoluta* into a concept of sovereignty grounded both in the antecedent will of God and in the nature of God as Creator and self-diffusive good—and he has modified the argument also by drawing out the concept of a covenant of creation to include the moral law of God.

The latter modification most certainly stands in relation to the Reformed theology of covenant. Arminius' concept of covenant has all of the characteristics of a suzerainty treaty into which God enters

---

[31] Ibid., XXVII.viii.

[32] Ibid., XXVII.ix.

[33] See Muller, "Federal Motif," pp. 102–8.

[34] Cf. Oberman, *Harvest*, pp. 100–111, with Steinmetz, *Misericordia Dei*, pp. 51–55 and Oakley, *Omnipotence*, pp. 55–65, 79–85.

unilaterally but which, once unilaterally decreed, has a bilateral function. Human responsibility before and relation with God arises under conditions set forth by God. Much of the development of Reformed covenant theology can in fact be described in terms of the incorporation of themes of divine sovereignty and human responsibility, of unilateral or monopleuric covenant and bilateral or duopleuric covenant into the federal language of theology.[35] Arminius wrote at a time when covenant theology was still fluid both in its structures and in its terminology—and, in what must be conceived as a more rationalistic approach to the relation of God with the world order, appropriated the Reformed language of moral and soteriological covenanting for his discussion of the primal covenant or pact of God imbedded *de potentia ordinata* in the world order itself. Once again, a clear relationship is established between the order of salvation and the moral order known in the rational observation of the world.[36] Both in the act of creation and in the establishment of covenant, God freely commits himself to the creature God is not, in the first instance, in any way constrained to create, but does so only because of his own free inclination to communicate his goodness; nor is God, in the second instance, constrained to offer man anything in return for obedience inasmuch as the act of creation implies a right and a power over the creature. Nonetheless, in both cases, the unconstrained performance of the act results in the establishment of limits to the exercise of divine power: granting the act of creation, God cannot reprobate absolutely and without a cause in the creature; granting the initiation of covenant, God cannot remove or obviate his promises.[37]

The doctrine of divine providence arises from Scripture and experience and it is inferred from our knowledge of "the very nature of God and of things themselves."[38] This providence is not a property disposition or power in God; rather it is an act *ad extra* directed toward

---

[35] The history of federal theology is recounted in Gottlob Schrenk, *Gottesreich und Bund im älteren Protestantismus* (Gütersloh: Bertelsmann, 1923) and the problem of monopleuric and duopleuric formulae is discussed by Leonard J. Trinterud, "The Origins of Puritanism," *Church History* 20 (1951): 37–57. Recent scholarship has modified Trinterud's arguments considerably—most notably, Lyle D. Bierma, "The Covenant Theology of Caspar Olevian," Ph.D. diss., Duke University, 1980 (forthcoming in *Studies in Historical Theology* from Labyrinth, Durham, N.C.) and John Von Rohr, *The Covenant of Grace in Puritan Thought* (Atlanta: Scholars, 1986); also see Muller, *Christ and the Decree*, p. 41.

[36] On the views of Arminius' Reformed contemporaries, see Schrenk, *Gottesreich und Bund*, pp. 57–82; for a discussion of Arminius' relationship to later Remonstrant theology, see Muller, "Federal Motif," pp. 109–22.

[37] Cf. *Disp. priv.*, XXIV.vii, viii, xi; XXVII.i–iii, v–vi; XXIX.i, iv; *Dec. sent.*, pp. 107–8 (*Works*, I, pp. 626–27); *Articuli nonnulli*, VII.1–3; VIII.1–3; with Oberman, *Harvest*, pp. 42–44, 168–70 and Steinmetz, *Misericordia Dei*, pp. 51–55.

[38] *Disp. priv.*, XXVIII.i.

creatures and which has creatures as its primary object. As such, the act of providence is not to be considered as something belonging eternally to the mind of God but as "separate and really existing."[39] Thus, providence is "an act of the practical understanding" of God or, perhaps more precisely, "of the will employing the understanding" in an act that is "not completed in a single movement, but is continued through the moments of the duration of things."[40] Providence may therefore be defined as

> the solicitous, everywhere powerful and continued oversight of God, according to which he exercises a general care over the whole world, and over each of the creatures, their actions and passions, in a manner that is befitting himself and consistent with the welfare of his creatures, especially for the benefit of pious men, and for the declaration of the divine perfection.[41]

This providence is guided or ordered by the divine wisdom (*sapientia*) so that it is always both just and equitable.[42]

The providential care of God, as Arminius takes great pains to spell out in detail, takes as its proper object both the world as a whole "consisting in many parts which have a certain relation among themselves, and a certain order" and each creature as an individual with its own actions and passions. This twofold operation of providence is intended to "preserve the goodness" in creatures "according to their nature, through creation" and "according to grace, through the communication of supernatural gifts and through elevation to dignities (*iuxta gratiam ex donorum supernaturalia communicatione*)." In addition, providence also superintends "the right use of nature and of grace."[43] Arminius concludes this thesis with the pointed remark that "we ascribe the latter two [operations] also to the act of providence"—as if to drive home the point that providence is not merely of nature and that grace, through providence, is administered universally to all creatures. Grace, therefore, belongs to the created order as part of its fundamental relation to God—and is not merely a divine gift later and only to some as a means to the correction of a problem! Arminius had intimated as much in his first lecture as a professor of theology at Leiden in 1603.[44]

This pointed statement concerning the gracious character of universal providence is more than a general disagreement with the

---

[39] Ibid., XXVIII.ii.

[40] Ibid., XXVIII.iii.

[41] Ibid., XXVIII.iv; Arminius cites and then defends this definition in *Dec. sent.*, p. 121 (*Works*, I, p. 657).

[42] *Disp. priv.*, XXVIII.vi.

[43] Ibid., XXVIII.v.

[44] Cf. *De obiecto*, p. 28 (*Works*, I, p. 325).

tendency of Reformed theology: it is, in fact, a direct counter to Junius' distinction between universal and particular providence. Arminius' predecessor had taught that "the work performed by God in the created order (*in rebus creatis*), according to his twofold providence, is also twofold: a work of nature and a work of grace." The former belongs to God's universal providence over all things in the created order; the latter, according to Junius, is a special work that God "performs in his elect according to the good pleasure of his will (*secundum beneplacitum voluntatis suae*)."[45] Arminius refuses to particularize providential grace and to refer it to a will of God that remains partly hidden.

The difference over the relationship of nature and grace in creation and providence is foundational for the issues raised by Arminius in debate with Junius over the problem of the original condition of man and the meaning of the term *in puris naturalibus*. Junius held the view, inherited from Aquinas and advocated by the proponents of a generally Augustinian view of creation and grace, that the divine act of creation imparted to man both natural gifts (i.e., the intellect, will, affections, actions, and passions) and supernatural gifts of grace by which perseverance in the good might be possible.[46] Junius assumes that the supernatural *donum superadditum* was conferred by an act of God logically distinct from but temporally simultaneous with the act of creation in and by which the natural gifts were bestowed. This supernatural gift was, however, specific to Adam and Eve and incapable of transmission with the natural gifts to their progeny "except by the appointment of grace." Man was, thus, created with supernatural gifts but is now bereft of them after the fall.[47]

Arminius agrees with Junius that the natural and supernatural gifts are given simultaneously in the act of creation and that man never existed without the supernatural gifts. But Arminius appears also to want to strengthen the connection between nature and grace: it is not merely a matter of two coincident divine acts, one bestowing natural gifts, the other supernatural. Rather, Arminius contends that "God was unwilling to desist from the act of communicating his own good to that part of the first matter, or nothing, from which he created man until he had conferred supernatural [gifts] also upon him."[48] Not only is man created with both natural and supernatural gifts; what is more, the supernatural gifts belong to the *imago Dei* in which man was created and were, therefore, to be "transmitted to his

[45] Junius, *Theses theologicae* (Leiden), XVII.3.

[46] *Amica collatio*, pp. 513–14 (*Works*, III, p. 96); cf. Aquinas, *Summa*, Ia, q.95, art.1.

[47] Ibid., pp. 513–14 (*Works*, III, pp. 96–97).

[48] Ibid., p. 522 (*Works*, III, p. 109).

posterity without exception," according to the "administratory decree of creation" and providence,[49] to the end that "the principles and seeds of moral virtues ... remain in us after the fall" even though the original "spiritual virtues" of knowledge according to piety, righteousness, and holiness have been lost to sin.[50] This argument allows Arminius to place predestination below or subordinate to providence and to define its objects as individual sinful human beings.

God does not elect or reject on the basis of a consideration of human beings generally, in their "purely natural condition," prior to the fall, because in that condition, they were endowed with grace and did not evidence sin. Sin is the "condition required in the [human] object" for there to be a decree of predestination.[51] Arminius assumes, in other words, the Thomistic view of the *donum superadditum* but even more than Aquinas, and certainly more than Junius, he emphasizes the intimate bond of nature and grace—of grace perfecting nature—in the acts of creation and providence.[52] This union of nature and grace in creation and providence, in turn, provides a framework and a limit within which predestination must be construed. As in the Molinist and Suárezian models, human acts, including the sins for which some are damned, arise as a result of free choice in the context of divine concurrence. Such acts belong to the realm of human moral responsibility and are known to God according to the *scientia media*. Predestination, therefore, occurs within the context of God's providence, even to the point that grace may be bestowed by God in view of his foreknowledge of the use to which it would be put by its recipients.[53]

The profound interrelationship of nature and grace in providence and the limitation of divine power in relation to the created order together point toward Arminius' conception of the "rule" (*regula*) of providence. This rule is the *sapientia Dei* or wisdom of God that guides and produces the acts of providence and thereby manifests in this world "what is worthy of God, according to his goodness, his severity, or his love of justice or of the creature, but always according to equity."[54] The *sapientia Dei* is the rule of providence, presumably, because *sapientia* is typically defined in the scholastic vocabulary as a knowledge of goals or ends and providence directs all things toward

---

[49] Ibid., pp. 523, 528–29 (*Works*, III, pp. 110, 119).

[50] Ibid., p. 525 (*Works*, III, p. 115).

[51] Ibid., pp. 529–30 (*Works*, III, pp. 119–21).

[52] Cf. *Disp. priv.*, XXVIII.v, where the *dona supernaturalia* are defined as part of the work of providence.

[53] Cf. Mahieu, *François Suárez*, pp. 445–47, citing Suárez, *De Deo*, II.iv–v, with Arminius, *Dec. sent.*, p. 119 and *Articuli nonnulli*, XV.1–4.

[54] *Disp. priv.*, XXVIII.vi.

their proper ends. In addition, the ordination of a thing toward its end by the wisdom of the good God can hardly be conceived of apart from equity. This language of equity returns to the issue raised earlier in the discussion of divine dominion: the existence of creation and, now, the goals of that creation, limit the divine power and will and, in effect, remove the *potentia absoluta* from consideration in the working of divine providence.

The divine providence can also be distinguished into acts of preservation and government and into acts that are mediate and immediate, ordinary and extraordinary. The divine preservation, Arminius asserts, refers to "essences, qualities and quantities" while government "presides over actions and passions" in four basic acts—motion, assistance, concurrence and permission (*motus, auxilium, concursus, permissio*)."[55] The more typical pattern of argument among Protestant scholastics observed a threefold division of the act or acts of providence into preservation, concurrence, and government—separating out from government a category that Arminius subsumes under it. The basic definition, however, is much the same: preservation (*conservatio* or *manutenentia*) is the act of God, the ultimate Being, essentially independent of all lesser beings, that maintains the contingent and dependent being of all creation.[56]

This maintenance of dependent being is typically identified by the Reformed and the Lutheran orthodox as "continued creation" (*continuata creatio*). According to this definition, inherited from the medieval scholastics, creation and conservation are but one eternal act of God by which God calls things into being and preserves them in being. The distinction between creation and providence is a purely rational one arising from our finite, temporal way of understanding the eternal and simple acts of God: the human mind understands by means of rational distinctions and divisions that which is essentially simple and indivisible.[57] This was, incidentally, also Suárez' view: he discusses providence among the divine attributes and identifies the distinction between creation and providence as rational or conceptual, resting not on the character of God's work but on the nature of our temporal perception.[58]

Arminius, significantly, differs on this last point. His basic definition of providence as a temporal, not an eternal act of God—as "continued through ... the duration of things" and not "completed in a moment"[59]—allows no room for the Reformed and Lutheran

---

[55] Ibid., XXVIII.vii.

[56] Cf. *RD*, p. 257.

[57] Cf. Scotus cited in Minges, II, p. 276 with Junius, *Theses theologicae* (Leiden), XVII, prologue, and *RD*, pp. 257–58.

[58] Scheffczyk, *Creation and Providence*, pp. 184–85.

[59] *Disp. priv.*, XXVIII.iii.

argument for the essential identity of creation with providence or for the argument, found in a wide variety of medieval, Protestant scholastic, and post-Tridentine Roman Catholic scholastic systems, that providence is the larger category of the decree of God that includes both the general will to maintain the created order and the special will to save the elect. Arminius appears, consciously, to have narrowed the scope of providence specifically to temporal divine activity in and with the things of the created order and to have maintained this narrow definition by modifying the concept of *continuata creatio*. He had, of course, spoken of continuing creation in his discussion of the self-diffusion of divine goodness in the creative process, but even there he makes a firm distinction between the initial, creative act of drawing things out of nothing and the secondary act of conservation or sustenance.[60]

This temporalized view of providence, however much it diverges from the typical scholastic teaching, may be related to a tension in the thought of Aquinas and of later Thomism. As Scheffezyk notes, Aquinas had divided his doctrine of providence, placing its basic definition as the eternal "reason of order" (*ratio ordinis*) into the doctrine of God and placing its larger exposition as the temporal "execution of order" (*executio ordinis*) after the doctrine of creation.[61] This division, which became normative for Thomism, allows a double problem of not deriving providence from creation and of not maintaining a strong relationship between temporal governance and the eternal working of the divine mind: "the *executio ordinis* as a temporal effect of God's thought ceases to be regarded as Creation continued, with the consequence that the link between the world and its Creator is loosened."[62] One of the ways in which the "link" may be "loosened" is, we add, the development of a category of contingent events foreknown but not directly willed by God.

In the wake of Aquinas' formulation of this problem, Henry of Ghent had argued rather pointedly that it is one act by which a thing is produced and acquires its being and another, distinct act by which it is preserved in being. Such is the conclusion that follows from the doctrine of creation in time inasmuch as the act of conferring being must be instantaneous, sudden, indivisible, and therefore without duration or permanence: conservation in being, which accounts for the duration and permanence of contingent things, must be a second, distinct act.[63] This line of argument was taken up by Peter Aureole

---

[60] Ibid., XX.vii.

[61] Cf. Aquinas, *Summa*, Ia, q.22, art.1 and q.103 with Scheffczyk, *Creation and Providence*, pp. 148–49.

[62] Scheffczyk, *Creation and Providence*, p. 149.

[63] Henry of Ghent, *Quodlibeta*, I, q.7; IX, q.1 cited in Suárez, *Disp. metaph.*, XXI.ii.1.

and Gregory of Rimini,[64] and stubbornly combatted by Thomist or Thomistically inclined thinkers like Giles of Rome, Hervaeus Natalis, and Johannes Capreolus.[65] In the case of Peter Aureole, the radical distinction between creation and providence arose out of his denial of the category of present knowledge to the divine eternity: God knows eternally, but the idea of the present applies to God no better than ideas of past and future.[66]

It is significant, therefore, that Arminius nowhere has recourse to the typical view of eternity as a present without past or future and nowhere grounds the divine knowledge of all things on the existence of God in an eternal present. Indeed, he defines eternity as infinitude with respect to time and as an absence of succession,[67] but identifies the presence of all things, eternally to God, in terms of the divine knowledge of all things as resident antecedently in their causes and, ultimately, as possibilities known to the divine essence.[68] It is equally true that later Thomists argued against Henry of Ghent's distinction between acquisition of being and preservation in being as two distinct acts by falling back upon the language of divine eternity: since the creative act, as performed by God, occurs not in a moment but in eternity, it is one with conservation. The distinction is made only by the time-bound human mind.[69]

Arminius seems to have followed out the problematic of Aquinas' doctrine, perhaps through a reading of the subsequent debates, and, then, in a departure from Aquinas' own pattern and vocabulary, to have omitted the discussion of providence from his doctrine of God and to have identified providence totally with the "execution of order" in time. There is some discussion of the sustenance of the world by the divine goodness in Arminius' doctrine of God,[70] but the term "providence" is applied only to the temporal activity of God— precisely the opposite of Aquinas' identification of "providence" in God and discussion of God's *ad extra* activity as "governance." Arminius may even have discovered the problem by reading Suárez but

---

[64] Peter Aureole, *I sent.*, II, dist.1, q.2, art.2; Gregory of Rimini, *I sent.*, II, dist.1, q.6, concl.4.

[65] Giles of Rome, *De ente et essentia*, q.7; Hervaeus Natalis, *Tractatus de aeternitate mundi*, cap.1; Johannes Capreolus, *Defensiones*, II, dist.1, q.2, art.2.

[66] Cf. Peter Aureole, *I Sent.*, dist.38, art.3 with Copleston's discussion in *History of Philosophy*, VI, pp. 38–39.

[67] *Disp. pub.*, IV.xiv.

[68] Ibid., IV.xxxiii.

[69] Cf. Capreolus, *Defensiones*, II, dist.1, q.2, art.3, with Suárez, *Disp. metaph.*, XXI.ii.12.

[70] See above, chap. 10.

have been convinced by the objections to the Thomist view rather than by Suárez' own resolution.[71]

This problem of the relation of the eternal decree (whether of providence or predestination) to its execution in time is, moreover, one of the problems of medieval theology that was profoundly felt by the Reformed theologians of the sixteenth and seventeenth centuries.[72] On the one hand, the logic of Calvin's powerful theology of grace tended to subordinate providence to predestination and to identify the salvation of the elect as the primary and ultimate purpose of God.[73] This tendency is seen even in those infralapsarian theologians who, like Junius, placed predestination above creation in the order of system and thereby severed it from the doctrine of providence.[74] The Thomistic model, granting its identification of predestination as *pars providentiae*, a part of providence,[75] tends in the other direction toward a view of the salvation of believers as part of the larger purpose of the achievement of the final goal of creation. In Arminius' version of the Thomist model, this tendency is reinforced by the placement of providence within and defined by the created order and the placement of predestination below providence both in the order of system and in its reference to creatures as created, fallen, and "as actually in existence (*ut actu talia existentia*)."[76]

For Arminius, the distinction between the eternal decree and its execution in time is a distinction between the way in which God considers all things eternally in his intellect and the way in which God considers things as actually existent.[77] This definition stands in direct opposition to the Reformed view inasmuch as Arminius does not define the divine intellect or knowledge, in Thomist fashion, as causal. His modification of Thomist intellectualism toward Molina's *scientia media* allows him to define the decree as containing a knowledge of particulars not directly willed by God.

Indeed, Arminius specifically argues that providence must be conceived as logically subordinate to an eternal decree. God has, eternally, decreed "either to do or to permit" everything that occurs in time: this decree is an internal act of God that precedes and grounds the external act, the divine providence.[78] Quite unlike his Reformed

---

[71] Cf. Suárez, *Disp. metaph.*, XXI.ii.1–2, citing Capreolus, *Defensiones*, II, dist.1, q.2, art.2; Hervaeus Natalis, *Tractatus de aeternitate mundi*, cap.1; Giles of Rome, *De ente et essentia*, q.7; and against the Thomist view, Henry of Ghent, *Quodlibeta*, I, q.7; IX, q.1 and Gregory of Rimini, *Sent.*, II, dist. 1, q.6, concl.4

[72] See Muller, *Christ and the Decree*, pp. 20–21, 43, 48–50, 81–8, and passim.

[73] Cf. ibid., pp. 23–24.

[74] Junius, *Theses theologicae* (Leiden), X–XI; cf. XVII.

[75] Aquinas, *Summa*, Ia, q.23, art.1, corpus and art.2, corpus.

[76] *Disp. priv.*, XL.viii.

[77] Ibid.

[78] Ibid., XXVIII.xii.

colleagues, Arminius introduces a causal disjunction between this eternal decree and the providential order of the world. The decree, "by which the Lord administers providence and its acts," does not "induce any necessity on future things; for since it is an internal act of God, it lays down nothing in the thing itself."[79] Things and events occur in the temporal order according to the providential "mode of administration" and occur either necessarily or contingently under providence, without direct causal relation to the eternal decree.[80]

Providence is not only subordinate to an eternal decree of God, it is also "subordinate to creation."[81] Here, too, as in his doctrine of divine dominion, Arminius draws heavily on the covenantal implications of the *potentia ordinata*. Since providence is subordinate to creation, it is "necessary" that God's providential governance of creation conform to the order established by God in the act of creation. Providence cannot "impinge against creation" nor can it "inhibit the use of free will in man." Neither can providence "direct man to another end, or to destruction," but rather must guide him toward the end "that is agreeable to the condition and state in which he was created."[82] Not only was Adam, therefore, capable of refraining from sinning, he was also brought to sin by his own will, voluntarily, freely, "without any necessity either internal or external" and "not ... because of some preceding decree of God."[83] Such limitations clearly do not obtain according to Calvin, who places all things strictly under the divine decree and insists on the immediate divine determination of all things, to the exclusion of contingency and permission.[84]

Rather than claim a direct, causal relation between the eternal decree and the providential concurrence of God in finite things, Arminius defines the things eternally permitted by God in terms of a divine foreknowledge or "prescience" (*praescientia*) that belongs to God as a consequence of his knowledge of contingent events in the natural, providential order. The language used by Arminius here is of utmost importance: the divine prescience is identified as "in part natural and necessary, in part free."[85] The terms are a direct reflection of the categories of divine knowing—*scientia naturalis sive necessaria* and *scientia libera*—but they appear, now, in reverse order, and with reference to temporal events. Thus, the divine prescience is, in the first instance, free, because it results from an act of divine will freely to receive an object. Second, this prescience is "natural and necessary

[79] Ibid., XXVIII.xv.
[80] Ibid.
[81] *Articuli nonnulli*, VIII.1.
[82] Ibid.
[83] Ibid., XI.1–2.
[84] Cf. Calvin, *Inst.*, I.xvi.4, 8–9; xviii.1.
[85] *Disp. priv.*, XXVIII.xiii.

insofar as, when this object is laid down by the act of the divine will, it cannot be unknown by the divine understanding."[86] In other words, prescience is necessary and natural granting the divine ability to know with certainty things and events that will occur in time by reason of contingent or secondary causes.

Arminius reinforces this argument by asserting that God sometimes permits his creatures to know, by "prediction," things that are about to happen. Neither the prediction nor the divine prescience on which it rests "introduce necessity" into the future event inasmuch as the divine prescience is "posterior in nature and order to the thing that is future (*re futura*)."[87] "For a thing does not occur because it has been foreknown or foretold, but it is foreknown or foretold because it is about to be (*futura*)."[88] Here again, as in his language of *scientia media* and of the consequent will of God, Arminius introduces an element of contingency or at least of relational consequence into the divine knowing and willing, a point very much at variance even with the teaching of those Reformed writers like Ursinus and Junius, who were concerned to argue for the freedom and contingency of events in the created order and who also, against Calvin's doctrine, maintained a category of permissive willing in God.[89] Ursinus specifically maintained the causal nature of the divine foreknowledge.[90] Arminius, on the contrary, grounds the freedom of creatures on a concept of noncausal foreknowledge—a divine foreknowledge of future contingents not directly ordained by God.

Significantly, there is some precedent for this argument, albeit without any use of the concept of *scientia media*, in the thought of one of Arminius' Reformed and Thomistically inclined teachers. Daneau argues at length in his doctrine of providence that a distinction must be made between *providentia* and *praescientia* or foreknowledge. Providence, Daneau argues, is the divine ordination of the world order and is, in some sense, the cause of the same things that God foreknows. Foreknowledge imposes no necessity on things —and it therefore precedes providence in a "natural" or logical although not in a temporal order.[91] Divine providence can, therefore, govern free and contingent events, ordering them in accordance with God's will, without rendering them causally necessary: "For God ordains nothing that he does not foreknow; he foreknows, however, many

---

[86] Ibid.

[87] Ibid., XXVIII.xiv.

[88] Ibid.

[89] Cf. Ursinus, *Expl. cat.*, cols. 130, 135–36 (*Commentary*, pp. 153, 160–61); Junius, *Theses theologicae* (Leiden), XVII.8–9; XVIII.6–9.

[90] Ursinus, *Expl. cat.*, cols. 133–34 (*Commentary*, p. 157).

[91] Daneau, *Christianae isagoges*, I.30 (p. 46r)

things that he does not ordain."[92] Daneau insists, nonetheless, that there can be no real distinction in God between knowledge and ordination and that there is no "naked and ineffectual knowledge of things in God." Indeed, both providence and foreknowledge fall under the eternal decree—"since God is not a naked and idle examiner of things, but rather their author and ordained."[93] Unlike Arminius, Daneau takes away with the decree what he gains in the initial distinction.

The second act of providence, government (*gubernatio*), indicates an ordering or governance of the world in a narrower sense than the general preservation or maintenance of things. Governance refers specifically to the divine ordering of both physical and spiritual motions. "Motion" (*motus*) refers to the most general divine governance over physical things—the earth, its rivers and seas, the rain, and the wind. These things are incapable of directing themselves toward ends and are, therefore, ordered and directed by God. Creatures endowed with life, intellect, and will, in addition to being given the basic power of movement by God, are treated in a manner suitable to the preservation and governance of their own spiritual movements—actions and passions. Thus God both assists and concurs in the spiritual movements arising from living creatures.[94]

Concurrence, the *concursus divinus*, refers to the movement of the divine first cause in all finite operations in such a way as to sustain the created thing in its operation and to provide it with the capability of doing its own work and gaining its own ends, even as the ultimate purpose of all things is being worked out in particular finite acts. As Aquinas wrote, "God works in things in such a manner that things have their own proper operation."[95] "God not only moves things to operate ... he also gives created agents their forms and preserves them in being."[96] Scotus similarly refers to God as the first or principal agent in all acts of creatures in such a way as to sustain the causality of the individual creatures.[97] Virtually all of the Protestants concur in these definitions.[98] Arminius, however, follows a different pattern:

[God's] concurrence ... is necessary to produce every act, because nothing can have any being except from the first and highest being, who immediately produces it. The concurrence of God is not his immediate influx into a second or inferior cause, but it is an action of

[92] Ibid., p. 46v.
[93] Ibid., pp. 46v–47r.
[94] Cf. *RD*, pp. 262–63.
[95] Aquinas, *Summa*, Ia, q.105, art.95, corpus.
[96] Ibid.
[97] Cf. Minges, II, pp. 277–79.
[98] Cf. *RD*, pp. 258–60; *DTEL*, pp. 193–94.

God immediately flowing into the effect of the creature, so that the same effect in one and the same entire action may be produced simultaneously by God and the creature.[99]

Here again, Arminius moves away from the Thomist position, as represented in his own day by Suárez, and adopts a view that accords more freedom to the creature by once again loosening the link that bound together creature and Creator. As Suárez argues, the divine concurrence is the continuous "influx" or "inflowing" (*influxus*) by which "God in himself and immediately acts in all actions of creatures" and not merely into the effects of creaturely actions.[100] It was the view of Durandus that creaturely causality, the action of secondary causes as such, distinct from their effects, did not require divine concurrence. The divine concurrence flows not into the secondary cause but into its effect. For Durandus, God merely concurs in the existence of the secondary cause and in the continuance of its abilities—and then concurs in the existence of the effect. The action thus belongs immediately or directly to the secondary cause and only mediately and indirectly to God.[101] Durandus' alternative view of concurrence, as opposed to the basically Thomistic model advocated by most of the Protestant scholastic writers, opened up a realm for creaturely activity under the doctrine of providence equivalent and parallel to the realm of creaturely contingency posed by his conception of a divine *scientia media*.

Arminius, then, accepts neither the nuanced Thomism of Suárez nor, precisely, the views of Durandus. As Durandus' critics, including Suárez, had noted, the concurrence of God as first cause is necessary for all of the actions of secondary causes—so that the influx of divine power into the effect alone leaves the secondary cause itself without the ontological support requisite to its action.[102] Arminius takes from Durandus' view an emphasis on the divine concurrence in the effect —but he recognizes that, in some sense, God must concur in the action of the creaturely secondary cause as well as in the effect. Arminius, therefore, argues that influx of divine concurrence is not directly into the cause, thereby safeguarding the freedom of secondary causality. Rather the divine influx is into the action of the cause, so that "the same effect" is "produced simultaneously by God and the creature" in a unified action of the secondary cause and the concurring first cause.[103] The creature remains a cause in its own right and a

---

[99] *Disp. pub.*, X.ix.

[100] Suárez, *Disp. metaph.*, XXII.i.2; ii.3, 6.

[101] Cf. ibid., with Durandus, *Sent.*, II, dist.1, q.5 and dist.37, q.1, and Vansteenberghe, "Molinisme," *DTC* 10/2, col. 2110.

[102] Cf. Suárez, *Disp. metaph.*, XXII.ii.3–6.

[103] *Disp. pub.*, X.ix: "Est autem concursus Dei non influxus illius immediatus in causam secundam, seu inferiorem, sed actio Dei immediate influens in effectum

causal structure has been developed that resonates with Arminius' view of the general doctrine of providence and, more importantly, of the divine *scientia media* and of the various distinctions in the divine will.

Once again, Arminius appears to have been influenced by the argumentation of Molina's *Concordia*. Molina had rejected the conception of concurrence according to which God was understood as acting *in* or *on* the secondary cause—the conception held in common by Aquinas, Scotus, Suárez, and the Reformed orthodox—and had replaced it with a conception of God acting *with* the secondary cause and flowing, with it, into its action and effect.[104] The divine *concursus* is, thus, necessary not only to the existence of the cause and of the effect but also to the existence of the causal activity, but the divine involvement is such that the secondary cause is determinative of its own action and, therefore, free. Even so, Molina could argue of prevenient grace that it, together with the free will of the creature, is the cause of faith and that the will is free to accept or to reject this offer of grace, but not capable of faith apart from grace. As Vansteenberghe states, "prevenient grace and freedom [of will] are two aspects of one single integral cause, and that salvific acts depend on both for their eventuality."[105]

Just as the *scientia media* and the various distinctions in the divine will were defined by Arminius in such a way as to loosen and limit the grip of divine power on the temporal order, so too is his view of concurrence constructed in such a way as to remove the immediacy of divine causality from the causal activity of the creature. Unlike Aquinas, who assumed that all actions of secondary causes must be traced back to the primary cause—and, therefore, unlike his Reformed brethren who almost universally accepted this Thomist assumption—Arminius here balances the activity of the finite will with the divine concurrence. Indeed, this theory of concurrence ought to be regarded as the corollary, in the temporal order, of the doctrine of *scientia media* and the parallel distinctions in the divine will, inasmuch as they presume events or acts known to God but lying outside of his direct or immediate causal activity. In other words, Arminius has adopted a fairly consistent Molinism. Arminius' point, moreover, carries over into later Arminian theol-

---

creaturae, sic ut effectum idem una et eadem totali actione a Deo simul et creatura producatur."

[104] Cf. *Concordia*, II, q.14, art.13, disp.26.5: "Quo fit ut concursus Dei generalis non sit influxus Dei in causam secundam, quasi illa prius eo mota agat et producat suum effectum, sed sit influxus immediate cum causa in illius actionem et effectum" with Vansteenberghe, "Molinisme," *DTC* 10/2, cols. 2111–13 and Pegis, "Molina and Human Liberty," pp. 106–7.

[105] Vansteenberge, "Molinisme," *DTC* 10/2, col. 2113.

ogy. Limborch briefly defines *concursus* as the divine influx into the actions of all creatures, granting that God is the first cause, that maintains the creature in its activity while at the same time establishing the creature's ability to determine a result. Limborch specifically denies that divine concurrence in any way predetermines an act of the creature.[106]

The acts of divine government are executed or enacted, with the exception of divine permission, "universally and at all times" by the power of God and "specially and sometimes ... by the creatures themselves."[107] This generalization leads Arminius to his distinction between "immediate" and "mediate," "extraordinary" and "ordinary" acts of providence. An immediate act of providence is a direct action of God upon the order of the world or upon an individual being, performed without the means or instrumentality of secondary causes. It is, in other words, an unmediated act. Since such acts are "beyond, above," and even "contrary" to the established order of things, they can also be identified as extraordinary (*praeter ordinem* or *extraordinaria*).[108] Even such extraordinary acts, however, are in harmony with the needs of creatures and conformable to the being and the goodness of God.[109] The divine *opera extraordinaria*, therefore, are not violations of the ordained patterns of the universe as implied in the divine act of creation itself. Junius had made the same distinctions between immediate and mediate, extraordinary and ordinary providence, but without such strong insistence on the bounds set even upon the immediate and extraordinary power of God.[110]

The usual or ordinary operation of providence, however, in moving, assisting, and concurring in the existence and acts of creatures, "employs creatures" and "permits them to conduct their movements in agreement with their own nature."[111] Such providential acts are, therefore, "executed by creatures themselves" in accord with the normal pattern or operation of nature and of grace.[112] In all providential acts, whether of nature or of grace, the end or purpose is twofold: "the declaration of the divine perfections, wisdom, goodness, justice, severity and power" and the realization of "the good of the whole, especially of elect men (*praesertim hominum electorum*)."[113] Here again we encounter the probable influence of Aquinas and Junius—indeed, the distinctions in providence and the interpretation

---

[106] Limborch, *Theologia christiana*, II.xxv.16–17.
[107] *Disp. priv.*, XXVIII.viii.
[108] Ibid., XXVIII.viii–ix.
[109] Ibid., XXVIII.ix; cf. XXVIII.iv.
[110] Junius, *Theses theologicae* (Leiden), XVII.4–5.
[111] *Disp. priv.*, XXVIII.viii.
[112] Ibid., XXVIII.viii–ix.
[113] Ibid., XXVIII.xi.

of the ordinary or mediate governance of things appear to rely on Aquinas, while the final point, concerning the end or goal of providence, appears to come from Junius.[114] Where Arminius would differ with both of these predecessors is over the balance between mediate and immediate acts of providence: granting his definition of concurrence, the divine support of most finite actions must be mediate. Perhaps in the wake of Arminius' teaching, the *Synopsis purioris theologiae* argues that God works "immediately in all things" although in such a way as to conserve the proper motion and action of secondary causes.[115]

Whereas the divine motion, assistance, and concurrence refer primarily to finite good, the fourth act of divine governance, permission, refers specifically to the problem of evil.[116] We have already seen Arminius argue a category of the divine knowledge of actual things that refers to contingent events only indirectly or hypothetically willed by God (the *scientia media*)—and a series of categories in the divine will toward objects *ad extra* that refer to acts done by creatures outside of the bounds of God's positive and declared will. Here, under the category of providential permission, Arminius addresses in detail the problem of the existence of sin and evil under the divine causality. He assumes "that nothing in the world happens fortuitously or by chance" and that both the free will and the "actions of the rational creatures" are "in subjection to divine providence" in such a way that "God both wills and performs good acts" but only "freely permits those which are evil."[117]

Arminius was deeply concerned with the problem of the divine permission of sinful acts—particularly with the way in which God can be considered just and genuinely the ruler of his creation while at the same time evil exists. This problem underlines much of his reasoning concerning distinctions in the divine understanding and will and many of his basic definitions of divine providence. In 1605, in response to a set of theses proposed by his colleague Gomarus, and to Gomarus' accusation that Arminius had provided the student disputant, Abraham Vlietius with arguments antagonistic to Gomarus' views, Arminius presented his own disputation "On the Righteousness and Efficacy of the Providence of God Concerning Evil" (*Disp. pub.* IX).[118] This disputation became, in turn, the basis for a series of accusations against Arminius—namely, that God is the cause of sin

[114] Cf. Aquinas, *Summa*, Ia, q.22, art.3 with Junius, *Theses theologicae* (Leiden), XVII.2–6.

[115] *Synopsis purioris*, XI.xv–xvi.

[116] See Junius, *Theses theologicae* (Leiden), XVII.8.

[117] *Dec. sent.*, p. 121 (*Works*, I, pp. 657–58).

[118] Cf. Bangs, *Arminius*, pp. 266–67 with the letter to Uitenbogaert cited by Nichols in *Works*, I, pp. 658–59.

and that he induces hesitant creatures to sin as part of his providential work. Arminius responded to these allegations in the *Apology against Thirty-one Defamatory Articles*, the *Declaration of Sentiments*, and the Letter to *Hippolytus à Collibus*, all written in 1608.[119]

There is some irony in these accusations and debates of 1608. The opponents of Arminius appear to have used his theses of 1605 as the grounds of their accusations although, a year before, in 1607, he had presented a second set of theses on exactly the same theme but considerably clearer in its arguments and quite incapable of being interpreted in the direction of the accusations. These latter theses appear as the tenth *Public Disputation*.[120] In point of fact, the development of Arminius' thought is considerable: in direct response to the argument that God, as in some sense willing sin to occur (even if only by permission) is the true author of sin, Arminius not only clarified his arguments but also added a major discussion of the doctrine of concurrence.[121]

Arminius takes, as his central theme, the problem of "the efficient causality of God concerning sin." He notes immediately that this causality must be considered in three stages, corresponding to the process of sinning in the individual, and that each of these stages is also subject to logical and topical division:

> the efficiency of God concerning the beginning of sin is either hindrance or permission (*impeditio vel permissio*) and, added to permission, the administration both of arguments and occasions inciting to sin, as well as an immediate concurrence to produce this act. With regard to the progress [this efficiency] concerns its direction and delimitation (*determinatio*). With regard to the completion of sin, it is concerned with punishment or remission.[122]

The divine permission, therefore, relates to the conception of sin, the act of sinning, and the result of sinning—and in each of these stages there are, according to Arminius, two distinct relations between the divine will and the sin, all of which are to be understood in terms of the general divine administration of all things and the *concursus divinus*.

Arminius' purpose in developing this language of "the efficiency of divine providence concerning evil" is to "demonstrate from this

---

[119] Cf. *Dec. sent.*, p. 121 (*Works*, I, p. 658), noting the two disputations of the same title, and *Apol.*, XXIII (III), pp. 167–71 (*Works*, II, pp. 35–42).

[120] See Bangs, *Arminius*, pp. 322–23 where he dates the second of the disputations "On the Righteousness and Efficacy of the Providence of God Concerning Evil" (*Disp. pub.*, X) from 1607; and note *Apol.*, XXIII (*Works*, II, p. 36), where the theses of 1605 rather than those of 1607 are the subject of debate.

[121] *Disp. pub.*, X.ix.

[122] Ibid., X.ii; cf. *Epistola ad Hippolytum*, pp. 942–43 (*Works*, II, pp. 697–98). The letter merely summarizes the arguments of the two disputations.

efficiency that God cannot possibly be charged with injustice, and that no stain of sin can attach to him: on the contrary, that this efficiency is highly conducive to the commendation of God's righteousness."[123] Arminius attempts to make clear from the first that the divine relationship to sin is fundamentally negative even as God also, in a most fundamental sense, respects the freedom of the creature. Thus "the first efficiency of God concerning sin is hindrance ... with respect both to the [divine] efficiency and to the [human] object."[124] In order for God to hinder sin or place impediments in the way of evil, God must be somehow involved in the creation of possibilities (and impossibilities) in the order of secondary causality, but in a manner corresponding with the way in which he knows future contingency and the way in which he wills the free and contingent acts of his rational creatures. In other words, Arminius' distinctions in the divine knowing and willing now find their concrete application in his interpretation of human activity and its present or temporal result.

The divine hindrance to sin ought to be understood in terms of six categories of divine activity—three directly relating to the efficiency or efficient causality of God and three relating to the object of divine efficiency, that is, to the human being. An impediment, such as a divine warning or a moral prohibition, is of "sufficient efficacy" to halt sin, but not to intervene directly in preventing the sinful act; or it can be a divine intervention "of such efficacy that it cannot be resisted"; or it may be "of an efficacy administered in such a way by the wisdom of God, as in reality to hinder sin with regard to the event, and with certainty according to the foreknowledge of God, although not necessarily and inevitably."[125] The last of these categories calls for some explanation. Arminius clearly believes that God, whose omniscience is not causal, can construct or guide future contingency in such a way as to exclude certain events from happening without at the same time imposing any external necessity on the finite wills and acts that might otherwise lead to these events.

If such impressively effective noninterference is to be made possible in the concrete, temporal situation, the divine hindrance or placing of impediments must extend somehow to the human object, specifically to human power, capability, and will.[126] All such impediments arise only in terms of the limitations of divine rule set down by the divine goodness in its creative self-communication: "it belongs to a Good to hinder evil as far as the Good knows it to be lawful to do so"—so that impediments can be "placed by God upon a rational

[123] *Disp. pub.*, X.i.
[124] Ibid., X.iii.
[125] Ibid.
[126] Ibid.

creature as far as (*qua*) he has right and power over it."[127] In view of Arminius' views on the dominion of God, this placement of imped-iments in the way of sin must be quite limited.[128] God does not have the right to engage his absolute power in bending the will of the creature to the good if the creature itself has either inclined to evil or remained neutral—nor can God bend the will of a creature to sin if the creature is not so inclined.

Thus God can limit the power of a creature by the declaration of moral law: an "act is taken away from the power of a rational crea-ture, for the performance of which it has an inclination and sufficient powers" when God makes it impossible to "perform that act without sin."[129] The potentially sinful act is, thus, "circumscribed" by God.[130] Furthermore, God can hinder the actual capability of a rational creature by removing the creaturely inclination and ability to act. This may be done "by depriving the creature of essence and life, which are the foundation of capability" or (less drastically!) by diminishing the capability of the creature, by "the opposition of a greater capability or, at least, one that is equal," or by "withdrawing the object toward which the act tends."[131] Finally, the will itself may be impeded by the "unpleasantness, inconvenience, uselessness or injuriousness" or by the "injustice, dishonor or indecency."[132] (Arminius provides biblical references for the sake of illustrating each of these kinds of divine hindrance.) By the sheer weight of argument and example, Arminius places his emphasis not on direct, powerful divine intervention but on indirect divine suasion in and through the order of secondary causality: as indicated in the discussion of divine dominion, we should expect no interventions of absolute power.

If we ask the question posed by the Reformed doctrine of grace— how can a divine intervention that defines or in some way deter-mines the outcome of events in the finite order be accomplished without violating the freedom of the creature?—Arminius provides an answer both different from the Reformed view and profoundly like the teaching of Suárez. Whereas the Reformed insist upon the almost paradoxical point that an eternal and all-powerful God can in fact predetermine that some events will occur as a result of contin-gent or free acts of creatures and can therefore foreknow such events according to his *scientia libera seu visionis*, Arminius follows Suárez in placing the divine foreknowledge or *scientia media* prior to the divine

---

127 Ibid., IX.vii.
128 Cf. *Disp. priv.*, XXVII.iii; *Articuli nonnulli*, VII.1, 2, 6.
129 *Disp. pub.*, X.iii.
130 Ibid., IX.vii.
131 Ibid., X.iii.
132 Ibid.

intervention, with the result that God can and does offer inducements to his creatures on the basis of his knowledge of their disposition toward or against certain acts.[133]

Indeed, so little does God actually abridge the freedom of the creature that the correlate of his hindrance of sin is his permission. God does in fact permit creatures to engage in acts that he has previously forbidden. The legal impediments placed in the way of sin are in no manner either removed or contradicted by the divine permission: permission is not the ratification of a sinful act, not a divine sanction that makes the sin no longer a sin.[134] Divine permission does, however, run contrary to the hindrance of creaturely capability and will, inasmuch as permission is a removal of impediments to this life or abilities of the creature and a clear "presentation of the object" of a potentially sinful act. Similarly, permission implies the removal of impediments to the will—not all impediments, notes Arminius, but only those which would necessarily interfere with the willing of a sinful act.[135] God's permission never involves a removal of the moral law itself.

Recognizing that he has set up a paradox in this contrast of hindrance and permission, Arminius proceeds to argue how it is possible to regard God as just, true, and also in control of his world—granting that God could effectively and absolutely impede the commission of all sinful acts but, by his permission, allows those very sins to occur. How is it that this paradox of hindrance and permission does not lodge a contradiction in the very being and life of God? Permission is, in the first place, grounded in "the liberty of choice, which God has implanted in his rational creature." Such is "the constancy of the giver" that this gift cannot be taken away from the creature.[136] This argument can be made somewhat more convincingly in the context of Arminius' doctrines of God and creation than in the context of his opponents' teaching: whereas Gomarus was content to allow the absolute power of God to obtrude into the world order and to realize goals nominally inconsistent with the revealed natural and moral order of the world, Arminius has argued a limitation on the divine willing brought about by the very act of communication that resulted in the limited goodness of the created order. Thus, the communication of liberty of choice to the creature in the act of creation places a limit on the divine ability to hinder sin and makes necessary the category of divine permission.

[133] Cf. Arminius, *Disp. pub.*, IX.xi; X.vii with Suárez, *De scientia Dei futurorum contingentium*, II, cap.4, nn.4–5 (*Opera*, 11, pp. 354–55) and with Adams' analysis in "Middle Knowledge," pp. 89–90.

[134] Cf. *Disp. priv.*, IX.x with ibid., X.iv.

[135] *Disp. pub.*, X.vi.

[136] Ibid., X.v.

Ultimately, this permission, like the self-limiting divine act of creation, rests on "the infinite wisdom and power of God by which he knows and is able to bring light out of darkness and to produce good out of evil."[137] God therefore in some sense "permits what he does not permit." The divine permission is not an act "in ignorance of the powers and inclinations of rational creatures" inasmuch as God is omniscient. Nor is it an act only reluctantly extracted from God "for he could have refrained from producing a creature that had freedom of choice."[138] In the second of his two disputations, Arminius adds the comment—quite inconsistent with his views of divine dominion—that God might also have "destroyed" such a creature once it had been produced.[139] This latter statement can hardly represent the genuine teaching of Arminius and most certainly arose out of an attempt to reduce controversy: it sounds much more like Gomarus than Arminius.[140]

Even so, the divine permission does not arise out of an incapacity to hinder sin—inasmuch as God does have the power, granting the limits of his rule, to act upon the capability and will of creatures. Nor is it the case that God is "uninvolved (*otiosus*) or negligent (*negligens*) of what is done [by creatures], because before anything is done he has already observed the various actions which concern it and, as we shall subsequently see, he presents arguments and occasions, determines, directs, punishes and remits sin."[141] Clearly, God has a foreknowledge of future contingencies that lie outside of his positive willing—the *scientia media*—and has categories of willing in himself that are consequent upon the foreknown acts of independent creatures. Arminius adds, however, that "whatever God permits, he permits it designedly and willingly, his will being immediately occupied about its permission, and its permission is itself occupied about sin."[142] "This order," Arminius concludes, "cannot be inverted without great peril."[143]

The relationship of divine hindrance to divine permission can be clarified by distinguishing sin as the "act" of sin strictly so-called and sin as the "transgression of the law" connected to the act. There are times when God may, thus, hinder or permit a particular act regardless of it being a transgression of the law—or he may permit a transgression of the law but, at the same time impede the sinful act or its

---

137 Ibid., IX.xi; cf. ibid., X.v.
138 Ibid., IX.xi.
139 Ibid., X.v.
140 Cf. *Articuli nonnulli*, VII.2, 3, 6 and note *Examination of the Theses of Gomarus* in *Works*, III, pp. 596–611.
141 *Disp. pub.*, IX.xi.
142 Ibid.
143 Ibid.

intended result. Even so, God hindered the plan of Joseph's brothers to commit murder, intervening more against the act than against the sinfulness of Joseph's brothers; but God permitted the sale of Joseph, allowing the transgression and then using the act itself for his own ends.[144]

The hindering and permitting of sin may, moreover, be understood in terms of the divine dispensation or administration of "arguments and occasions which incite to an act that cannot be committed by the creature without sin, if not according to the intention of God, at least according to the inclination of the creature."[145] These arguments and occasions can be presented to the mind or to the senses either directly by God or "by means ... of creatures," for the sake of testing the creature "to abstain from sinning" or, if the creature yields to temptation, as part of God's purpose "to effect his own work by the act of the creature." It is not as if, Arminius adds, God needs the creature or its sins to perform his work; rather, in such use of the acts of creatures, God can "demonstrate his manifold wisdom."[146]

At this point, having presented his thoughts on the divine relationship to the beginning of sin under the categories of hindrance and permission, Arminius comes (in his second disputation) to the issue omitted from his first discussion of the subject—the divine "concurrence that is necessary to produce every act."[147] Whatever Arminius' reasons for omitting this issue from the earlier discussion, it is fairly obvious that the simple presentation of categories of hindrance and permission yields an unsatisfactory solution to the original problem of the relation of divine providence to sin. Without the explicit reference to concurrence, hindrance and permission appear to be discrete temporal acts of God—moments of divine involvement that punctuate a history of non-involvement. This, however, is impossible inasmuch as all things come into existence and continue to exist by the will of God, the highest Being and the ground of the existence of all other beings.[148]

It would be a contradiction, Arminius argues, "to permit to the power and will of creature to commit an act" and then "to deny [the divine] concurrence without which the act cannot be done."[149] God concurs in the act, but not in its sin, "and therefore God is at once the effector and the permitter of the same act, but the permitter prior to

---

[144] Ibid., X.vii.
[145] Ibid.
[146] Ibid.
[147] Ibid., X.ix; cf. ibid, IX.vi ad fin, where Arminius specifically notes the omission.
[148] *Disp. pub.*, X.ix; cf. ibid., IV.l.
[149] Ibid., X.ix.

being the effector."[150] Perhaps here we see the importance, stated previously by Arminius but without elaboration, of maintaining the right order of will, permission, and sin:

> if it had not been the will of the creature to perform such an act, the influx of God, by concurrence in the act would not have occurred, and because the creature cannot perform that act without sin, God ought not on that account to deny his concurrence to the creature who is inclined to the performance of the act. For it is right and proper that the obedience of the creature should be tested, that it should abstain from an unlawful act from the desire to be obedient and not because of an absence of the necessary divine concurrence.[151]

The divine concurrence is the foundation of one of Arminius' central arguments against Perkins' view of predestination.[152] Arminius assumes that, in a most fundamental sense, "God is the cause of all actions that are performed by creatures" but that this divine causality cannot be explained in such a way as to undermine "the liberty of the creature" or to attribute sin to God. God can, indeed, be understood as both effecting and permitting the same act of a creature. Perkins overstates his case and must attribute sin to God when he argues that the lawlessness of an act belongs to the creature but the act itself, understood as something "positive," must be referred to God as the first cause.[153] It is true, Arminius contends, that God is "the effector of the act but only the permitter of the sin" but it is also true "that God is at the same time the effector and the permitter of the same act" and, if the *concursus divinus* is rightly understood, in such a way that the creature is truly free and God truly good.[154]

The creature, as a secondary cause, turns freely to its own act and, argues Arminius, determines both "the general influence of God in this particular act" and the "species" of the act itself. This can be so inasmuch as God does "not constitute the will [of the creature] *in actu primo*, but only *in actu secundo*, and therefore presupposes in the will whatever is necessary to the action."[155] The creature has its own inclination and its own potency to act prior to any actual operation—and God allows to the will, as secondary cause, the origin and the disposition of its own acts, even as he also "joins his concurrence to the creature's influence." Without such concurrence "the act cannot at all be performed by the creature."[156] In the case of the sinful act of

---

150 Ibid.
151 Ibid.
152 *Examen modestum*, pp. 730–34 (*Works*, III, pp. 413–19).
153 Ibid., pp. 730, 731 (*Works*, III, pp. 413, 415).
154 Ibid., p. 731 (*Works*, III, p. 415).
155 Ibid., p. 732 (*Works*, III, p. 416).
156 Ibid., p. 733 (*Works*, III, p. 418).

the creature, the divine concurrence and consent take on the aspect of an alien work, inasmuch as God does not will the sin, but for the sake of his own granting of life and liberty to the creature, cannot deny concurrence.[157] Concurrence, thus, is the continuing ontological support of the creature in its willing as well as in its being, necessary to the very existence of the creature and predicated on God's fundamental will to communicate his own goodness—concurrence in sin, in an alien way, subserves this good end.

Arminius' argument not only takes issue with Perkins, it is also opposed to the view of *concursus* found in some of the more radical causal passages of Calvin's *Institutes*. Calvin, for example, disputes a view of providential *concursus* that assumes no divine hindrance of the contingent motions of creatures or of the free choices of human will. The teachers of this view "so apportion things between God and men that God by his power inspires in a man a movement by which he can act in accordance with the nature implanted in him, but [God] regulates his own actions by the plan of his will."[158] Such a teaching, argues Calvin, presents a governance by power or might without divine determination. Arminius, of course, would agree—on the ground that divine determination must be somehow limited or withheld if there is to be any freedom and contingency in the created order, or, as he might well add, if the created order is to be granted the kind of existence intended in the divine act of creation!

God does not, therefore, enter positively into the causality of sin: "since God is the *summum bonum*, he does nothing but that which is good," and is neither the efficient nor the deficient cause of sin. Sin arises neither in the understanding nor in the will of God—and the divine permission is no more than a "cessation" of hindrance.[159] The reason for this permission belongs to the hidden will of God, but it is clear that in the sin of Adam, God "neither perpetrated this crime through man, nor employed against man any action, whether internal or external, which might incite him to sin."[160] Similarly, God "neither denied nor withdrew anything that was necessary for the avoidance of this sin and the fulfillment of the law."[161] How different this is from Calvin's declaration that "God foreknew what end man was to have before he created him, and consequently foreknew because he so ordained by his decree.... God not only foresaw the fall of the first man, and in him the ruin of his descendants, but also

---

[157] Cf. ibid., with *Dec. sent.*, p. 108 (*Works*, I, p. 627).
[158] Calvin, *Inst.*, I.xvi.4.
[159] *Disp. priv.*, XXX.v; cf. Junius, *Theses theologicae* (Leiden), XVIII.1.
[160] *Disp. pub.*, VII.viii.
[161] Ibid.

meted it out in accordance with his own decision."[162] It is also at this very point in his argument that Calvin rules out the distinction between will and permission.[163]

Calvin's view on this point did not, however, become normative for the Reformed tradition. Even the arch-predestinarians Beza and Perkins followed out the Thomistic logic of Vermigli by arguing for a category of permissive willing in God.[164] Ursinus and Zanchi also argued divine permission in the context of their decidedly infralapsarian view of the plan of salvation.[165] Junius could declare that the sin of Adam occurred "without instigation or impulse from God" inasmuch as God did not impede but rather permitted Adam's act.[166] God, of course, does not will iniquity, but God is also, strictly speaking, not unwilling (*non nolente*) that the creature should exercise its free will. Thus God can be said willingly to permit sin.[167] Once again, Arminius appears to develop his position in the wake of Junius, modifying the Reformed or Reformed Thomist position with a distinctly Molinist view of the divine concurrence. Indeed what has been characteristic of Arminius' definition, throughout his refutation of Perkins, has been the Molinist argument for the balance or coordination of primary and secondary causes in all acts of free rational agents—rather than the typical scholastic view, shared by Thomists, Scotists, and Protestant orthodox alike that secondary causes must be consistently subordinated to the primary cause if events are to occur at all in the world order.[168]

From the concept of divine concurrence there does, however, arise the assumption that the "efficiency of divine providence" is also active, somehow, in the "progress of sin." God can be said both to "direct" and to "delimit" sin.[169] The divine direction of sin is in relation both to objects and to ends": when God permits sin, he also allows the act of sin to be directed toward an object, not infrequently an object *not* willed by the sinner. Similarly, God "does not allow the sin that he permits to lead to any end that that creature intends, but he uses it for the end that he himself wills."[170] The point clearly

---

[162] Calvin, *Inst.*, III.xxiii.7.

[163] Ibid., III.xxiii.8.

[164] See Muller, *Christ and the Decree*, p. 86.

[165] Ibid., pp. 66, 690, 106–8, 112, 116.

[166] Junius, *Theses theologicae* (Leiden), XVIII.5, 10.

[167] Ibid., XVIII.12.

[168] Cf. Molina, *Concordia*, p. 152 with Arminius, *Disp. pub.*, X.ix (cited above, p. 196) and with Garrigou-Lagrange, "Thomisme," *DTC* 15/1, col. 888; also note *RD*, pp. 258–61 and *DTEL*, pp. 179–87.

[169] *Disp. pub.*, IX.xvi–xix; ibid., X.x–xi.

[170] Ibid., X.x.

reflects the distinction, made elsewhere by Arminius, between the proper and the alien work of God.[171]

God also delimits sin by circumscribing it temporally and by determining its magnitude. Sin is permitted only within a limited sphere:

> God places a boundary on the duration of the act, when he takes the rod of iniquity from the righteous, lest they commit any act unworthy of themselves (Ps. 125:3) and when he delivers the godly out of temptation (II Pet. 2:9). He places a boundary to the duration of the sin when he hedges up the way of the Israelites with thorns that they may no longer commit idolatry (Hos. 2:6–7) and when he commands all men everywhere to repent (Acts 14:16).[172]

Sin is also restrained so that it cannot "increase to excess and assume greater strength"—as Arminius also attempts to document from a series of scriptural examples.[173] Finally, in the divine efficiency "concerning sin already perpetrated," God both punishes sin according to his justice or righteousness, whether in this life or in the life to come, whether corporally or spiritually, and pardons sin by removing the guilt of the creature and restoring it to fellowship with him, not by disregarding his justice or by absolving all temporal chastisements.[174] (Arminius' discussion of divine hindrance and permission is, again, paralleled by a lengthy discussion in Episcopius' *Institutiones*.[175] Episcopius argues, for example, that divine permission includes not only the removal of hindrances to sinful willing but also the provision of aid (*auxilium*) sufficient to the avoidance of sin. The cause of sin, moreover, is never immanent in God, but is *extra Deum*, in the disobedience of the creature.[176] Like Arminius, Episcopius assumes that a distinction must be made between the direction and determination or delimitation of sin—God both determines the object toward which sin ultimately may be directed and the extent of the consequences of the sin. This point Episcopius cites specifically from Arminius' disputation, praising the beauty of Arminius' "most erudite" argumentation.[177])

By way of conclusion to his disputations on providence in its relation to sin, Arminius returns to his originally stated theme—the vindication of divine justice and the assertion of the existence of providence despite the existence of sin:[178]

[171] See *Disp. priv.*, XIX.iv.

[172] *Disp. pub.*, X.xi.

[173] Ibid.

[174] Ibid., X.xiii–xiv.

[175] Episcopius, *Inst. theol.*, IV.iv.10–16 (pp. 375, cols. 2–399, col. 1).

[176] Ibid., IV.iv.11, 15 (pp. 380, col. 2; 396, cols. 2–397, col. 1).

[177] Ibid., IV.iv.16 (pp. 397–98).

[178] *Disp. pub.*, IX.xxiii; ibid., X.xv.

it is evident that because evils have entered into the world, neither providence itself, nor its government respecting evil, ought to be denied. Neither can God be accused of being guilty of injustice on account of [his governance], not only because he has administered all things to the best ends (that is, to the chastisement, trial and manifestation of the godly, to the punishment and exposure of the wicked, and to the illustration of his own glory); but, since ends alone do not justify an action, much more because he has employed a form of administration that allows intelligent creatures both of their choice and freely to perform and accomplish their own motions and actions.[179]

Even so, the divine permission, rightly understood, is neither the "efficient" nor the "deficient" cause of sin: it is a "suspension of the divine efficiency" that presupposes the ability of the creature, with the aid of a universally available providential grace, to abstain from sin.[180]

By way of evaluation, Arminius' doctrine of creation and providence can be described, in accord with our evaluation of his doctrine of God, as a modified Thomism set forth in the context and in response to the early orthodox Reformed scholasticism of his contemporaries. His method of exposition and the categories of his thought are no more and no less scholastic, no more and no less biblicistic, than the methods and categories of the Reformed writers who opposed him. Although all of the Protestant theologians of his era manifest indebtedness to the scholastics and, typically, to Aquinas, Arminius' use of Thomistic arguments and, even more importantly, his modifications of the Thomistic view of creation and providence appear to be intended as modification not only of the Thomist but also of the Reformed perspective. Specifically, Arminius so defines creation as a self-limiting act of God, so defines providence as bound within the created order, and so binds nature to grace under providence that his doctrine of creation becomes a primary determinant of the course of theological system and, in effect, an indicator of the goal of the divine plan not only temporally but also logically prior to the work of salvation. If the Reformed systems can be called without excessive reductionism and distortion, a theology of grace, the Arminian system may, perhaps, be called a theology of creation.

[179] Ibid., IX.xxiii.
[180] Ibid., X.xv; cf. *Disp. priv.*, XXVIII.v.

Conclusion

God, Creation, Providence, and the Shape of Arminius' Theology

The theology of Jacob Arminius has been neglected both by his admirers and by his detractors. The restrictive conception of Arminius' theology as a counter to the Reformed doctrine of predestination, indeed, as an exegetical theology posed against a predestinarian metaphysic, has led to an interpretation of Arminius as a theologian of one doctrine somehow abstracted from his proper context in intellectual history. Arminius' theology must, in fact, be interpreted in the context of the development of scholastic Protestantism as a scholastic theology in its own right. In addition, Arminius must be understood as a theologian adept in the methods and well versed in the concepts of scholasticism, Protestant and Catholic. As H. E. Weber, Ernst Lewalter, and others have shown for the Lutheran and, by extension, for the Reformed orthodox, Arminius' theology also bears witness to the impact of late medieval and Renaissance Aristotelianism, the logic and method of Zabarella, and the metaphysics of Suárez.

Once it is recognized that Arminius read deeply not only in the works of medieval scholastic theologians like Thomas Aquinas but also in the works of contemporary scholastic philosophers and theologians—Zabrella, Suárez, Molina, Vorstius, and Timpler—and in the works of early Reformed scholastics like his predecessor Junius, it becomes possible to view Arminius not merely as a Protestant scholastic but also as a teacher of theology immersed in the life and thought of his time, aware, as any teacher of theology must be, of issues at the forefront of theology, logic, and metaphysics. Arminius, in other words, cannot be placed into an intellectual vacuum and viewed as a biblicist somehow immune to the main currents of theological and philosophical thought in the late sixteenth and early seventeenth centuries. Quite to the contrary, certain key issues in the development of Protestant scholastic theology, such as the ectypal character of theology and the doctrine of the divine essence and attributes, were not only addressed by Arminius, but were addressed in such a way as to provide a stimulus to later discussion. Arminius took up these themes from his predecessor at Leiden, Junius, and mediated them not only to his Remonstrant successor at Leiden, Episcopius, but also to his Reformed successors, Walaeus and Polyander. Other themes, like the *scientia media*, do not carry over positively into the thought of Walaeus and Polyander—but they are taken up and developed in later Remonstrant theology, notably by Episcopius and Limborch.

The scholastic theology of early Protestant orthodoxy can perhaps be best described as the ecclesial, confessional, and academic institutionalization of Protestantism in its progress toward the full declaration of its doctrinal catholicity. Far more explicitly than the Reformers, the early orthodox writers looked back into the catholic past of the church and made its doctrines, its philosophical insights, and its methods of disputation and discourse their own. The elaboration of doctrine, particularly in such crucial areas as theological prolegomena and the essence and attributes of God, necessarily brought with it a renewed interest in metaphysical problems and a more speculative, philosophically adequate language of theology—if only for the sake of dealing with the fundamental problems inherent in presuppositional statement and in language about God.[1] Arminius' theology is no exception to these generalizations.

Although Aquinas is the only scholastic specifically cited by Arminius as a source of his own teaching, it is clear that Arminius was acquainted with a wide variety of scholastic sources and engaged, as was typical of Protestant writers of his time, in the critical modification and adjustment of Thomistic themes to his own needs. Thus, Arminius' emphasis on the divine goodness and the principle of plenitude, moreover, although akin to elements of Aquinas' thought, particularly when Aquinas is dealing with themes drawn from the Christian Platonism of Pseudo-Dionysius, appear to go beyond the Thomist interest in these themes. Arminius also moves away from the traditional Christian views of the *nihil* and of *materia prima*, shared by Aquinas, toward a more classical Aristotelian view, learned perhaps during his stay at Padua. A Scotist or nominalist critique of theological knowing is evident both in his contrast between archetypal and ectypal theology and in his cautious approach to the proofs of the existence of God. The impact of Zabarella, Suárez, and Molina

---

[1] See Lewalter, *Metaphysik*, pp. 35–38; and Muller, "*Vera Philosophia*," pp. 356–65.

is evident in both the method and the doctrinal content of Arminius' thought.

The accusations leveled against Arminius by Gomarus and by the theology student, Caspar Sibelius, now appear in a new light. On the one hand, it becomes clear that there was a measure of truth in the accusations and that Arminius' biographers and defenders, by simply denying the charge that Arminius read and recommended Jesuit theology, have ignored important sources and antecedents of Arminius' theology. On the other hand, it is also clear that there was a measure of truth in Arminius' denials: he was hardly a Jesuit sympathizer— nor was he a thoroughgoing Suárezian. The truth of the matter appears to be that Arminius, like many of his Protestant contemporaries, dipped heavily into medieval scholastic theology and into the writings of contemporary Roman Catholic writers like Suárez. He borrowed ideas and sometimes even words and phrases from their writings without ever agreeing totally with their theology.

Indeed, many Protestant theologians of the late sixteenth and early seventeenth centuries held what can only be called a modified Thomism.[2] Arminius, again, is no exception. Where Arminius differs from his Reformed and Lutheran contemporaries is in the direction taken by his modifications. He does, certainly, modify some elements of Thomism in the direction of the Leiden theology of his predecessor, Junius: thus, Arminius' theological prolegomena, despite their almost Thomistic sense of the positive relationship between theology and an ancillary philosophy, indicate also an utter transcendence of the divine archetypal theology over human, ectypal theology. This is, most certainly, a Scotistic modification.[3] In addition, Arminius moves still farther down the Scotistic path than Junius by insisting that theology in this life is entirely nonspeculative or noncontemplative—that is, that it is practical.[4]

Similarly, in the doctrine of God, both the proofs of the existence of God and the discussion of the divine nature and attributes have an obvious rootage in Thomist intellectualism. We have seen clear reflections of the argument not only of Aquinas' *Summa theologiae* (a work that was rediscovered for the sixteenth and seventeenth centuries by Cajetan, Vitoria, and by the Jesuit theologians Vásquez and Gregory of Valencia) but also of Aquinas' *Summa contra gentiles*. Nonetheless, Arminius also accepts modification of the Thomist position reflecting both the late medieval debate over problems of predication and of ordering divine attributes and the late sixteenth-

---

[2] Cf. Donnelly, "Calvinist Thomism," pp. 451–53 with Muller, *"Vera Philosophia,"* pp. 356–65, Althaus, *Die Prinzipien*, pp. 230–31, and *PRRD*, I, pp. 310–11.

[3] Cf. *PRRD*, I, pp. 124–36.

[4] Cf. Minges, I, pp. 517–20.

century debate between the Dominicans and the Jesuits over Molina's concept of a divine *scientia media*. On this latter point in particular Molina's and, consequently, Arminius' modification of the Thomist teaching points away from the more strictly Augustinian views of the Reformed orthodox.

The contrast, moreover, between the modified Thomism of the Reformed and the modified Thomism of Arminius takes on a larger significance in the history of thought when it is seen to reflect the Roman Catholic controversies of the day. The Reformed modified Thomist arguments are, typically, in the direction of a more critical epistemology and a somewhat more strictly Augustinian view of human sinfulness and its effects, a modification characterized by Scotist overtones and accents of scholastic teachers like Thomas of Strasburg, Henry of Ghent, Giles of Rome, and Gregory of Rimini— and, in their own time, writers like Dominic Bañez and Michael Baius. Arminius, by way of contrast, modified Thomism in the direction of Molina and Suárez, who themselves had dipped deeply into the well of late medieval scholasticism and its critique of the Thomist synthesis of theology and philosophy. These developments parallel and, in the case of Arminius' theology, draw upon similar developments within Roman Catholicism. The history of scholastic theology in the later Middle Ages is not only the history of the rise of nominalism but also the history of the modification of other trajectories in scholastic thought, particularly the Thomist and the Scotist. In his *Disputationes metaphysicae* Suárez had analyzed and compared the *Thomistae* and the *Scotistae*, drawing from both groups and frequently identifying a median path between the two. His reverence for Aquinas, Capreolus, and Cajetan was profound—enough, as Vollert points out, to lead non-Thomists to view Suárez as a Thomist.[5] Typically, however, Suárez modifies Aquinas and later Thomist arguments in a critical dialogue with Scotist and nominalist teaching without becoming a follower of either school: he is best described as an eclectic philosopher with a profound knowledge of historical antecedents.[6] Molina, too, must be regarded as eclectic—although, like Suárez, he retained a profound respect for Thomism over against which he formulated his concept of a *scientia media*. Aquinas remained the primary point of reference for his formulations.[7] It was, after all, the intention of the Jesuit order, beginning with Loyola himself, to found its theology on the thought of the Angelic Doctor: the

[5] Vollert, "Introduction," Suárez, *On the Various Kinds of Distinction*, p. 11.

[6] See Mahieu, *François Suárez*, pp. 81–95, 115–19, 123–29 and passim; also see idem, "L'eclectisme suarézien," in *Revue Thomiste* VIII (1925): 250–85.

[7] See Pegis, "Molina and Human Liberty," pp. 76–77, 109–15, 129–31 and note, in particular, how Pegis presents Molina in terms of the debates of his day and as viewing Aquinas "across Bañez and especially Duns Scotus" (p. 77).

constitution of the order, written by Loyola, included the statement that theology should rest on a reading of the "Old and New Testament and the scholastic teaching of Thomas" and the general of the order in the time of Molina and Suárez, Aquaviva, reaffirmed and developed the point in a circular letter of 1613.[8]

Similarly, the Reformed orthodox and Arminius appear to have found in Aquinas' theology a primary point of reference in their formulation of a fully developed scholastic system. The Reformed, after all, included in their ranks such Thomist-trained or Thomistically inclined teachers as Vermigli, Zanchi, and Daneau. The theology of the late sixteenth-century Reformed orthodoxy, by drawing on the thought of these teachers together with the systematic and exegetical insights of Reformers like Calvin and Bullinger, can well be described as a modified Thomism—indeed, specifically, as a Thomism modified in an Augustinian and, on epistemological issues, a Scotist, direction.[9] Arminius, by moving away from this Reformed position toward the teachings of Suárez and Molina, turned from the Augustinian tendencies of the Reformed, just as Suárez and Molina rejected the strict Augustinianism of Baius and the Augustinian language of grace resident in Bañez' Thomism. Arminius arrived, therefore, at a position that still, in its intellectualism and in its respect for the *analogia entis*, accepted Aquinas as its primary point of reference but that, nonetheless, was no longer in agreement with the Augustinian and modified Thomist thought of his Reformed teachers and contemporaries. It is worth noting that the parallels between the Roman Catholic and the Protestant debates did not go unnoticed in the sixteenth century: the judicious and extremely well-read Robert Bellarmine argued, in defense of the predestinarian views held by his order, that the views of their Dominican opponents could be excused only on the assumption that the Dominican were ignorant of the heretical writings of the Lutherans and Calvinists.[10] Arminius, on his own side of the debate returned the compliment: he recognized, without accepting Bellarmine's own theology, that the cardinal had well pointed out the dangers of Reformed predestinarianism in its more extreme forms. Specifically, Arminius could note, in a passing reference to the problems of predestination and *concursus*, that Bellarmine had seen that some of the Calvinist formulations pointed logically to a view of God as the author of sin, indeed, as "the only sinner."[11] Like Bellarmine against the Dominicans, Arminius sought a theological alternative: nor is it surprising that Arminius,

---

[8] Jourdain, *La philosophie de Saint Thomas d'Aquin*, II, pp. 254–55.

[9] Cf. *PRRD*, I, pp. 123–36, 310–11.

[10] See La Servière, *Théologie de Bellarmin*, p. 582.

[11] Letter to Vorstius, cited in *Works*, I, p. 644.

when refuting Perkins' doctrine of predestination, would liken his Protestant adversary's views to the teachings of Dominicans like Ferrariensis and Bañez.

The theology of Arminius, like that of his Reformed predecessors and contemporaries, albeit from a somewhat different perspective, points toward a relationship between the Reformation and the medieval scholastic tradition very different from that hypothesized almost a half-century ago by Joseph Lortz. Lortz argued that Luther's theology and, by extension, the Reformation, arose out of a rebellion against the decadent nominalist theology of the later Middle Ages—and that the Reformation might have been avoided had the Thomist model been available as a basis for Luther's formulations.[12] Quite to the contrary, we must not only affirm with Donnelly that the Thomist tradition was alive and well in the thought of several major Protestant writers,[13] but also argue that Protestantism embodied within itself a scholastic development in many ways parallel with the scholastic development of Roman Catholicism in the sixteenth century. The revival of Aristotelianism, the modification and revival of scholasticism particularly in terms of the *locus* method of dogmatics, and the creation of dogmatic and philosophical models based on a comparative evaluation of medieval scholastic debate, were features of both Protestant and Roman Catholic theology.[14] This eclecticism was reflected in the theological searchings of a host of Protestant thinkers from Franciscus Junius, to Amandus Polanus, to Franciscus Gomarus, to Jacob Arminius.

Set against this background of the ongoing history of scholasticism and the continuing modification of its fundamental intellectual trajectories, the debate between Arminius and his Reformed colleagues can be understood, at least in part, as a debate caused by the choice of different directions in the modification of Thomist and, to a lesser extent, Scotist models. Even so, the Protestant debate over predestination parallels the Catholic debate: the Reformed successors of Vermigli, Zanchi, and Daneau followed a line of argument not at all surprisingly like that of a Dominican like Bañez while Arminius also followed out but modified quite differently and, in this case, far more

---

[12] Cf. Joseph Lortz, *The Reformation in Germany* (1941), trans. R. Walls, 2 vols. (New York, 1968), I, pp. 194–201 with idem, "The Basic Elements of Luther's Intellectual Style," in *Catholic Scholars Dialogue with Luther*, ed. Jared Wicks (Chicago, 1970), pp. 3–33.

[13] Donnelly, "Calvinist Thomism," pp. 441–45.

[14] Cf. *PRRD*, I, pp. 28–36, 198–209, 251–57 with Richard A. Muller, "Scholasticism Protestant and Catholic: Francis Turretin on the Object and Principles of Theology," *Church History* 55/2 (1986): 193–205. On the use of the Agricolan locus method in Roman Catholic theology, see A. Gardeil, "Lieux théologiques," *DTC* 9/1, cols. 712–47.

extensively, the Thomistic doctrine, advocating a view virtually identical with that of Molina and other Jesuit thinkers.[15] Vollert's assessment of this Jesuit theology bears also on Arminius' thought and that of other "Protestant Thomists":

> the philosophical bent of the Jesuits veered toward Thomism. However, since the Society had no direct roots in the medieval tradition, and was not bound by fraternal ties to the *Doctor Communis*, it was freer to heed an original urge in philosophical speculation.[16]

As a colleague of mine recently observed, the conflict between the scholastic Arminius and the scholastic Reformed theologians is, like many of the bitter philosophical and theological debates we continue to experience, a battle between brothers. Had Arminius been a biblicistic pietist promulgating a message that was stylistically and doctrinally widely divergent from and foreign to the Reformed mind of his time, he could have been ignored or at least easily dismissed. His scholastic style, however, was precisely the style characteristic of Reformed thought in his day and his modified Thomism was different from the teaching of the Reformed not in its Thomism but in its modification. Nor was the genuineness of Arminius' Protestantism ever really in question.

The undeniably scholastic approach of Arminius to theology provides, therefore, a clue to the problem of the phenomenon of Reformed and Protestant scholasticism in general. The fact that Arminius, who did not follow the Reformed down the path of radical monergism and strict predestinarianism, is as scholastic in his theological method and as apt to draw on scholastic categories in the discussions of divine essence, attributes, and work *ad extra* as his Reformed adversaries demonstrates the incongruity of the thesis found in much earlier scholarship that the rise of a scholastic Protestantism was related in an almost causal way to the development of the Reformed doctrine of predestination.[17] When the whole spectrum of scholastic Protestant teaching is examined—from Arminius and the Reformed to the Lutherans—we encounter not the view of a specialized "scholasticism" drawn to its method by a predestinarian metaphysic but rather a broad, generalized use of scholastic method as the means to a sound, detailed, and well-defined exposition of doctrine. In other words, the scholasticism of the late sixteenth-century

[15] Cf. the debate in Garrigou-Lagrange, *God: His Existence and His Nature*, II, pp. 465–562 over the Jesuit argument that Molinism is a legitimate development of the Thomist position.

[16] Vollert, "Introduction," in Suárez, *On the Various Kinds of Distinctions*, p. 3.

[17] Cf. for the older view, Basil Hall, "Calvin Against the Calvinists," pp. 19–37; Armstrong, *Calvinism and the Amyraut Heresy*, pp. 131–39; Weber, *Reformation, Orthodoxie und Rationalismus*, II, pp. 98–102, 125–26.

Protestant world represents a philosophical and theological pattern almost as diverse as the late medieval and Renaissance scholasticism from which it drew its method and form.

Rather than view Protestant scholasticism as a borrowed theological style—as a style of exposition taken over from Catholic thinkers of the Middle Ages and sixteenth century—we should, perhaps, be ready to recognize the continuity of scholasticism, Protestant and Catholic, in the sixteenth century with earlier forms of scholastic exposition, and to recognize Calvinist Thomists like Vermigli and Zanchi as Protestant participants in the sixteenth-century revival of Thomism and Aristotelian scholasticism that is usually credited, almost exclusively, to their Catholic contemporaries, Cajetan, Bañez, de Sylvestris, and de Victoria. Arminius, together with Reformed writers like Polanus, Keckermann, and Gomarus, represents an extension of this development and an indication of the continuity of scholasticism, Catholic and Protestant, despite the humanism of the Renaissance and the protest of the Reformers, as the normative academic style in the European university well into the early modern era. In particular, Ramus' denial of full logical and methodological status to an analytic or inductive order of argument, for all its popularity among a few English logicians, could hardly withstand the force either of the genuine Aristotle as rediscovered by the Renaissance or of the logic of the Paduans—or, indeed, of the more empirical exponents of early modern science, who knew all too well that the deductive pattern of the syllogism functioned in the logical but not in the natural order.

If Arminius, like many other theologians of his generation, expressed an admiration for the logic of Peter Ramus, he did not follow Ramus either to the point of allowing his thought to be dominated by the elaborate schema of logical bifurcations typical of Ramist thought or to the point of setting aside any of the fundamentally Aristotelian arguments that he learned from the older scholasticism and from the school of Padua. Indeed, Arminius was genuinely in agreement on this point with his Reformed contemporaries and adversaries—even with such writers as Perkins and Polanus who were profoundly influenced by the Ramist technique of logical bifurcation. In particular, Ramus' denial of full logical and methodological status to an analytic or inductive order of argument, for all its popularity among a few English logicians, could hardly withstand the force either of the genuine Aristotle as rediscovered by the Renaissance or of the logic of the Paduans—or, indeed, of the more empirical exponents of early modern science, who knew all too well that the deductive pattern of this syllogism functioned in the logical but not in the natural order.[18]

---

[18] Cf. McKim, *Ramism in William Perkins' Theology*, pp. 27–29, 39–40; Ong, *Ramus*, pp. 252–258; Weisheipl, "Scholastic Method," p. 1146; Gilbert, *Renaissance Concepts of*

As this study has shown, the impact of Ramism on Arminius' thought was minimal, particularly when compared with the influence of medieval scholastic philosophy and theology and specifically of Thomism. The Aristotelian philosophy that Arminius is thought to have shunned looms large in his teaching. He, together with his Reformed colleagues, was a part of the revival of Aristotelianism and scholasticism that scholars have typically traced through the Roman Catholic theology and philosophy of the Renaissance or through the Melanchthonian heritage of German Lutheranism.[19]

Arminius' theological style, as illustrated in the present essay, can hardly be said to draw on the early Reformation. Rather it is a fully scholastic style patterned after the work of his teachers and mentors, although frequently in doctrinal disagreement with them. He shared with them—as is evident from a perusal of Daneau's *Christianae isagoges*—an admiration for the medieval tradition and, in particular for Thomas Aquinas' theology, that influenced both the structure and the content of his thought. Junius' scholastic meditations had a major impact on Arminius' prolegomena and the impact of Daneau's structural use of Thomist distinctions is evident, as we have seen, in several places in Arminius' doctrines of God and creation. In both cases Arminius looks to the thought of the mentor and then, having found access to the scholastic argument, through the thought of the mentor toward its sources. As noted in several places above, Arminius carried forward from Junius several themes that can only be called a "Leiden theology"—but he did so frequently in contrast to the thought of his Reformed contemporaries. From Beza, who wrote virtually no full-scale systematic theology, Arminius appears to have taken still less.

The picture that we have drawn here of the scholastic and Aristotelian development of Protestantism in the sixteenth century is, admittedly, quite different from the traditional, popular view of the Reformation as a radical break with the scholastic tradition and a repudiation of all forms of medieval teaching, whether Thomist or Scotist or nominalist. This traditional Protestant view, with its attendant pejorative use of the terms "scholastic" and "scholasticism" not only has difficulty explaining the positive use of themes from medieval scholastic theology by the early Reformers (despite their vociferous assaults on scholasticism), it also has difficulty explaining why, after a supposedly total rejection of scholasticism by the first and second generations of Reformers, the scholastic method and the arguments of scholastic theology reappeared in the works of third- and

---

Method, pp. 145–63, 168–69; and Randall, "Development of Scientific Method," pp. 185–91.

[19] Cf. Kristeller, *Renaissance Thought*, pp. 33–42.

fourth-generation Protestants. It is, in fact, a gross oversimplification to argue two such radical breaks in the history of Western theology. Not only did the most anti-scholastic of the Reformers, writers like Luther, Zwingli, and Calvin,[20] use concepts drawn from scholastic theology, other Reformers, like Bucer, Musculus, and Vermigli, drew on the older theology with far fewer polemical disclaimers.

A considerable amount of scholarship in the last several decades has been devoted to the analysis of late medieval theology and the elements of continuity as well as the discontinuities between this theology and the thought of the Reformers.[21] Arminius' theology not only manifests the long-term result of these continuities, it also makes clear that the scholasticism of the late sixteenth-century was itself a consciously conceived amalgam of ideas drawn both from the new Aristotelianism of the Renaissance and from the older medieval doctors as well as from the Reformers. Among Protestants in particular the absence of allegiance to particular schools of thought—Dominican, Franciscan, Augustinian, Eremite—permitted an eclectic gathering from and modification of medieval sources, although it is clear that for Arminius as for Vermigli, Zanchi, and to a certain extent Daneau, Aquinas was the primary medieval doctor to be reckoned with.

Beginning with Paul Althaus' important study of the principles of Reformed orthodox theology, scholars have been content, typically, to speak of the Reformed orthodox as Thomistic, in a rather general sense. With the exception of the thinkers studied by Donnelly, Vermigli and Zanchi, none of the founders and formulators of early Reformed orthodoxy were trained as Thomists in Roman Catholic universities—the others all came to medieval scholastic theology, as it were, from the outside. Whereas therefore, Vermigli and Zanchi (more so the latter even than the former) can be called Thomists in Kristeller's primary sense—as thinkers "who tend to support most of [Aquinas'] major and characteristic doctrines"—other of the Protestant teachers, like Daneau and, as we have argued, Arminius, "combine [Aquinas'] ideas with other ideas that are original or from another source,"[22] without, however, losing sight of certain crucial insights of Aquinas, like the priority of intellect in its identity with

---

[20] On Zwingli, see W. P. Stephens, *The Theology of Huldrych Zwingli* (Oxford: Clarendon, 1986), pp. 6–7.

[21] See, e.g., Heiko Oberman, *The Dawn of the Reformation: Essays in Late Medieval and Early Reformation Thought* (Edinburgh: T. and T. Clark, 1986); idem, *Masters of the Reformation: The Emergence of a New Intellectual Climate in Europe*, trans. Dennis Martin (Cambridge: Cambridge University Press, 1981); Denis R. Janz, *Luther and Late Medieval Thomism: A Study in Theological Anthropology* (Waterloo, Ontario: Wilfrid Lauries University Press, 1983).

[22] Kristeller, *Medieval Aspects*, p. 37.

the divine essence. Arminius can, as we indicated in the introduction, perhaps best be classified as an eclectic thinker with a Thomistic focus or center.

This center appears primarily in his discussions of the essence, goodness, intellect, and will of God in their relation one to another and to the created order. Arminius' basic definitions frequently resemble the definitions found in Aquinas' summas—more frequently the *Summa contra gentiles* than the *Summa theologiae*. There is little attempt on Arminius' part, however, to incorporate lengthy arguments either from Aquinas or from any other thinker: his theology is presented in a series of basic theses, without elaboration. (The theses were, of course, presumably, developed in the classroom discussion and debate, but we have no record of these developments.) In several of his departures from Aquinas, moreover, Arminius remains indebted to what may be called a modified Thomism, inasmuch as he draws consistently (particularly in his teaching on the *scientia media* and the divine *concursus*) on thinkers who themselves took Aquinas' theology as a primary point of reference in their own work, modifying it to suit the needs of their own theological context—notably, Suárez and Molina.

The eclectic aspect of Arminius' thought, evidences, perhaps, in his willingness to merge materials taken from Aquinas with arguments found in the work of Suárez and Molina, was most clearly seen in his definitions of theology. There, despite the profoundly intellectualistic cast of his system as a whole, a Scotistic emphasis on theology as praxis and on the diastasis between theology in itself and our theology provides a sense of structure and direction to Arminius' theology that merges well with the Zabarellan language of resolutive order and analytical method. On these points, arguably, Arminius drew inspiration not only from medieval models and from the new Aristotelianism of the day but also from his Reformed teachers and contemporaries in their effort to define the issues of theological prolegomena in a way suitable to Protestant theology. The eclecticism arose, at least in part, out of the perception that no single previous model but rather elements from several were useful to the Protestant cause, as well as out of the varied background of the early Reformers.

As I have argued elsewhere, the Reformers objected to only a small part of the body of doctrine taught by the medieval scholastics: the doctrines of grace, justification, sacraments, and the church were debated but the doctrines of Scripture, God, creation, providence, human nature, sin, Christ's person and work, and the last things were left largely untouched. Protestant theological system developed in the sixteenth century by drawing the insights of the Reformers on disputed points of doctrine into relation with the whole body of

Christian doctrine.[23] During this process, it became increasingly evident that the categories and distinctions of scholastic theology could not be dispensed with—not surprisingly inasmuch as those categories and distinctions had arisen as part of an effort to resolve theological problems left unsolved or, occasionally, created by the work of exegesis.[24] Arminius' theology is a case in point. The resources of scholastic theology, increasingly brought to bear on doctrinal problems by Arminius' predecessors and teachers, were used to their fullest by Arminius in his effort to resolve the problem of the freedom of contingent beings resident in the doctrine of the all-knowing and all-powerful Creator of the temporal order. Lewalter's assessment remains valid: Protestant theology, simply by developing full-scale system, found it necessary to raise and answer metaphysical questions.[25]

As for the doctrine of predestination that made Arminius famous —it was surely fashioned with a whole series of carefully enunciated, formally scholastic, and substantially Thomistic and Molinistic theological principles in mind. Arminius' conception of the order of grace must be viewed in the larger context of his assumptions concerning the nature of God, the relation of the divine intellect and will, the *scientia media* and its corollaries in the distinctions concerning the will of God, and the relation of God to the world in creation and providence. The theological, indeed, the metaphysical premisses of Arminius' system did not lead him toward a view of the divine decrees as an absolute power capable of effecting a seemingly arbitrary solution to the problem of human finitude and sinfulness. Rather, Arminius' assumptions led him toward a view of God as self-limited by his creative act and as active for the salvation of the world within these limitations. The concept of *scientia media* provided Arminius with a way of understanding the temporal grounds of this self-limited divine activity.

The thought of Arminius, thus, can be reduced to a protest against the Reformed doctrine of predestination *only* if considerable violence is done to the intention, shape, and content of the Arminian system. Arminius did, to be sure, protest against the Reformed view of predestination and of the order of salvation, but his protest arose out of a larger theological vision—specifically, out of a different view of the purpose and method of theological system as a whole, a different set of emphases in the exposition of the so-called essential foundation of

23 Preus, *Theology of Post Reformation Lutheranism*, I, pp. 35–44.

24 Cf. Beryl Smalley, "The Bible in the Medieval Schools," in *The Cambridge History of the Bible*, 3 vols. (Cambridge: Cambridge University Press, 1963–69), II, p. 198 with idem, *The Study of the Bible in the Middle Ages* (Notre Dame: University of Notre Dame Press, 1964), pp. 64–75.

25 Lewalter, *Metaphysik*, pp. 35–38.

theology, the doctrine of God, and a very different perception of the place and importance of the created order both in theological system and in the ultimate purpose of God.

In other words, it is this larger theological vision of Arminius, evidenced by his doctrines of God, creation, and providence, and by the various scholastic models present in and behind his exposition, and not merely Arminius' views on predestination, that stand in the way of Bangs' interpretation of Arminius as a Reformed theologian. Arminius certainly shared many sources and attitudes with his Reformed contemporaries—and he was trained primarily by Reformed theologians in Reformed universities. He also bears witness, as Bangs points out, to a diversity of opinion on the doctrine of predestination in the early Dutch Reformation.[26] Arminius' system, however, can only be interpreted as a full-scale alternative to Reformed theology: his doctrine of predestination rests on a view of the relationship of God and world opposed to virtually all of the tendencies and implications of Reformed theology. Arminius argued, in a manner quite foreign to the Reformed, whether infra- or supralapsarian, that the divine rule of the created order is limited and that this limitation provides the only conceivable ground of human freedom.

Arminius' God is the utterly transcendent, simple, immutable, and omnipotent God of the late Middle Ages—but without what Oberman has called "the dialectics" of the two powers.[27] When Arminius addresses the nominalist definition of *potentia absoluta* held by Reformed contemporaries like Perkins and Gomarus, he raises objections and, as far as his own theological system is concerned, sets the definition aside as erroneous. Arminius' own conception of God's absolute power as a sole governance of universal extent measured and therefore limited by the order of creation contrasts profoundly with late medieval and the Reformed tendency to place God above all law and points toward a worldview in which an inviolable temporal order stands as the primary indicator of the nature of God. This is not to say that Arminius' theology ought to be placed in the forefront of the movement toward modernity described by Blumenberg:[28] rather it stands as an indicator of shifting perspectives in the theological world parallel and, indeed, profoundly related to the changes in philosophical and scientific thought beginning to take place in the late sixteenth and early seventeenth centuries. Indeed, as Oakley has shown, the modification of language concerning the absolute and ordained power of God—particularly in terms of a concentration on the *potentia ordinata* and its covenantal character—would have a posi-

---

[26] Bangs, "Arminius as a Reformed Theologian," pp. 216–17, 220–21.
[27] Oberman, *Harvest*, pp. 30–47.
[28] Blumenberg, *Legitimacy of the Modern Age*, pp. 145–203.

tive impact on the scientific work of the Royal Academy, as evidenced in the thought of Robert Boyle.[29]

Arminius was deeply aware, from a theological perspective, of the difficulties faced by the Christian doctrines of salvation and human responsibility in a universe where the divine order and the created order with man at its center could not be rationally understood as standing in a coherent relationship one to the other. Specifically, Arminius resisted a view of God and world in which the ultimate divine plan had no necessary and consistent point of contact with the moral and physical events of the temporal order—and, by extension, a worldview in which human obedience and providential justice do not provide the human reason with a valid representation of the divinely ordained goal of all things. An eclectic theology and philosophy drawing heavily on a modified Thomism appeared, most certainly, to offer a partial solution to the problem: the world and all things in it are an emanation of being as good, grounded in the self-communicative nature of God, the *summum bonum*. To this perspective Arminius needed only add the qualification that God's power over creation is bounded by the limitation of the communication of his goodness to finite things. God is, to be sure, transcendent, absolutely good, the ultimate standard of justice—but he is no longer conceived as operating at the same time within the world order and beyond its laws. The temporal order itself now measures and defines the ways of God, and the practical, morally goal-directed character of theology discerns this truth both for this life and the next.

It is, thus, no accident that Arminian theology proved more open to rationalism than either Lutheran or Reformed thought. The irrationalism of the late medieval nominalist model has been replaced, in Arminius' thought, with a thoroughly dependable, rationally accessible relation of God and world that focuses all attention on the temporal order in which the divine plan is played out according to the (divinely given!) laws of nature, both physical and moral. The physical and moral harmony of the natural order becomes a rationally accessible index to the identity and will of nature's God and, even more importantly, to the meaning of human existence. Arminius' views of God, creation, and providence provide a theological and metaphysical framework for his views of predestination, grace, and salvation, but they also provide a positive point of contact between theology and rational philosophy and, in addition, between theology and the presuppositions of early modern science. The order of the world, as we apprehend it in the course of human existence, has become—over against the inherent fideism of the Reformed and Lutheran positions—an open door to moral and metaphysical truth.

---

[29] Oakley, *Omnipotence*, pp. 84, 88–92.

This sense of the interrelation and, potentially, even the reciprocity of the divine with the temporal order, together with its redefined *analogia entis* and its increased interest in natural law as an evidence of the ultimate ethical goodness of God as the goal or end of creation passed from Arminius into the theology of his successors in the Remonstrant tradition, Episcopius and Limborch. Limborch, for example, argues a close relationship between the law of nature, the revealed moral law, and the moral precepts of Christ—on the assumption that God at first provided human beings with an inward morality sufficient to their needs; that access to this inward law was little diminished by the fall; and that subsequent revelation merely augmented, without altering, this basic law. Indeed, for Limborch, the gospel itself is a clearer, higher law that stands in little contrast to the law of the heart, the law of nature, and the Mosaic code. Sin, in other words, in keeping with the intellectualism of Arminius' theology, distorts the function of the will and affections, but leaves the intellect quite intact.[30] Similarly, Episcopius could discuss at length the grounds of religion and law in the *recta ratio* of the creature prior to sin and maintain that the reason, far less debilitated by sin than the will, could discern the right through an examination of the created order.[31]

This positive relationship between Arminianism and rationalism in turn points toward the need to reevaluate the relationship between theology and rationalism in the seventeenth century. We cannot, simplistically, argue a shift from a world dominated by scholasticism, Aristotelianism, and entrenched dogmatic orthodoxy to a world of new rational philosophies, modern science, and religious indifferentism.[32] The decline of Aristotelianism is not linked absolutely either to the loss of scholastic method or to the end of theological orthodoxy. For if Arminianism stands as a protest against Reformed orthodoxy, it in no way represents—as we have seen in the preceding chapters—either a rejection of Aristotelianism or of the scholastic tradition and its method. Indeed, Arminius' theology manifests, at least, a theoretical openness of a highly scholastic and

---

[30] Limborch, *Theologia christiana*, V.i.4–5.

[31] Episcopius, *Inst. theol.*, I.viii (pp. 17–25); cf. Muller, "Federal Motif," pp. 110–11, 115, 121–22.

[32] Cf. John Dillenberger, *Protestant Thought and Natural Science* (Nashville: Abingdon, 1960), pp. 100–103, 164–78, which is still the best account of the theological transition from orthodoxy to Enlightenment in English, with Dorner, *History*, II, pp. 252–58 and with the astute remarks on the role of Arminianism in J. H. Randall, *The Making of the Modern Mind: A Survey of the Intellectual Background of the Present Age* (Cambridge, Mass.: Houghton Mifflin, 1940), p. 285. Also note the argument in Michael J. Buckley, *At the Origins of Modern Atheism* (New Haven: Yale University Press, 1987), especially the summary point, p. 347.

Aristotelian system to a rationalist worldview. This openness would remain characteristic of later Arminian theology as witnessed by the intellectually positive and mutually fruitful relationship later in the seventeenth century between Philipp van Limborch and John Locke.[33]

Quite contrary to the assumption that scholasticism foundered over the issue of sin, free will, and grace or that its distinctions between antecedent and consequent divine will, absolute and ordained power, and necessary, "middle," and free divine knowledge somehow failed to provide a structure for dealing with those issues,[34] the thought of Arminius and his successors points toward an appropriation of scholastic categories, distinctions, and methods that provided the seventeenth century with a cogent resolution of those issues that was capable of surviving the demise of Aristotelianism and of satisfying the demands of the new rationalism and of the dawning scientific perspective of the early modern era. In England, as well as on the Continent, Arminian or Remonstrant theology and its modified scholasticism made considerable inroads into the domain once claimed by Reformed theology and, specifically, by Calvin. The works of Episcopius appeared (in their original Latin) in a British edition and Limborch's *Theologia christiana* became the basis of a large theological system consisting of a translation augmented with quotations from the works of eminent English divines.[35] There is even some evidence that Episcopius' *Institutiones theologicae* replaced Calvin's *Institutes* as a basic, beginning textbook for theological study.[36]

Conversely, the frequently negative relationship between the Reformed (and Lutheran) orthodox and rationalist philosophy in the seventeenth century points toward the fact that theological content, far more than rational form, provides the primary foundation for an alliance between theological system and rationalism. The claims of historians like Weber and Bizer of a new rationalism in the logical, dialectical, and methodological interests of the Protestant orthodox and in the development of central dogmas needs to be modified not

---

[33] Cf. Muller, "Federal Motif," pp. 120–22 with Van Holk, "From Arminius to Arminianism in Dutch Theology," in McCulloh, ed., *Man's Faith and Freedom*, pp. 38–39.

[34] Cf. A. H. T. Levi, "The Breakdown of Scholasticism," in *The Philosophical Assessment of Theology: Essays in Honor of Frederick C. Copleston*, ed. Gerard Hughes (Washington, D.C.: Georgetown University Press, 1987), pp. 113, 117.

[35] Simon Episcopius, *Opera theologica* (London, 1678); Philip van Limborch, *A Complete System, or Body of Divinity*, trans. William Jones, 2 vols. (London, 1702, 1713).

[36] Cf. Benjamin B. Warfield, "On the Literary History of Calvin's Institutes," in *Institutes of the Christian Religion*, by John Calvin, trans. John Allen, 7th ed. (Philadelphia: Presbyterian Board of Education, 1936), I, p. xxxiii, n. 3.

only by the recognition that orthodoxy had carefully ruled out the principial function of reason and had not in fact deduced systems from central dogmas,[37] but also by the realization that the seventeenth century witnessed the development of a complex relationship between Protestant thought and the philosophical tradition in which logically and methodologically similar theological systems established, on the basis of diverse views of God and world, very different approaches to the use of reason and philosophy. Of the three major systematic models arising out of Protestantism, the Reformed, the Lutheran, and the Arminian, only one, the Arminian, proved genuinely open to the new rationalism, particularly in its more empirical and inductive forms.

[37] Cf. *PRRD*, I, pp. 82–97, 236–49, 295–311 with Muller, "Perkins' *A Golden Chaine*," pp. 69–81.

Abbreviations

Altenstaig	Altenstaig, *Lexicon theologicum*
CO	Calvin, *Opera quae supersunt omnia*
Dec. sent.	Arminius, *Declaratio sententiae*
Disp. priv.	Arminius, *Disputationes privatae*
Disp. pub.	Arminius, *Disputationes publicae*
DLGT	Muller, *Dictionary of Latin and Greek Theological Terms*
DTC	*Dictionnaire de théologie catholique*
DTEL	Schmid, *Doctrinal Theology of the Evangelical Lutheran Church*
Minges	Minges, *Ioannis Duns Scoti doctrina philosophica et theologica*
NCE	*New Catholic Encyclopedia*
PRRD	Muller, *Post-Reformation Reformed Dogmatics*
RD	Heppe, *Reformed Dogmatics*
RE	*Realencyclopädie für protestantische Theologie und Kirche*
SCG	Aquinas, *Summa contra Gentiles*
Arminius, Works	*The Works of James Arminius* (1825–75; repr. 1986)

Bibliography

Primary Sources

Altenstaig, Johannes. *Lexicon theologicum quo tanquam clave theologiae fores aperiuntur, et omnium fere terminorum, et obscuriorum vocum, quae s. theologiae studios facile remorantur* . . . . Köln, 1619.

Alexander of Hales. *Summa theologica.* 4 vols. Quaracchi: Collegium S. Bonaventurae, 1924–58.

Alsted, Johann Heinrich. *Methodus sacrosanctae theologiae octo libris tradita.* Hanoviae, 1614.

―――. *Praecognita theologiae, I–II,* in *Methodus,* as books I and II.

Alting, Jacob. *Operum.* 5 vols. Amsterdam, 1687.

―――. *Methodus theologiae didacticae,* in *Operum,* vol. 5.

Arminius, Jacobus. *Opera theologica.* Leiden, 1629.

―――. *Oratio de Sacerdotio Christi,* in *Opera,* pp. 9–26.

―――. *Orationes tres: I. De obiecto theologiae. II. De auctore & fine theologiae. III. De certitudine ss. theologiae,* in *Opera,* pp. 26–41, 41–55, 56–71.

―――. *Oratio de componendo religionis inter Christianos dissidio,* in *Opera,* pp. 71–91.

―――. *Declaratio sententiae I. Arminii de praedestinatione, providentia Dei, libero arbitrio, gratia Dei, divinitate Filii Dei, & de iustificatione hominis coram Deo,* in *Opera,* pp. 91–133.

―――. *Apologia adversus articulos XXXI, in vulgas sparsos,* in *Opera,* pp. 134–83.

―――. *Disputationes publicae,* in *Opera,* pp. 197–338.

―――. *Disputationes privatae,* in *Opera,* pp. 339–444.

―――. *Amica cum Francisco Iunio de praedestinatione per literas habita collatio: ciusque ad theses Iunii de praedestinatione notae,* in *Opera,* pp. 445–619.

―――. *Examen modestum libelli Perkinsianae,* in *Opera,* pp. 621–777.

―――. *De vero et genuino sensu cap. VII. epistolae ad Romanos dissertatio,* in *Opera,* pp. 809–934.

_____. *Epistola ad Hippolytum à Collibus*, in *Opera*, pp. 935–47.

_____. *Articuli nonnulli diligenti examine perpendendi, de praecipuis doctrinae Christianae capitibus sententiam plenius declarantes*, in *Opera*, pp. 948–66.

_____. *The Works of James Arminius*. London ed. Trans. James Nichols and William Nichols. 3 vols. London, 1825, 1828, 1875; repr. with an intro. by Carl Bangs. Grand Rapids: Baker, 1986.

_____. *Examination of the Theses of Dr. Francis Gomarus respecting Predestination*, in *Works*, III, pp. 521–658.

_____. *The Writings of James Arminius*. Trans. James Nichols and William Bagnall. 3 vols. Buffalo, N.Y., 1853; repr. Grand Rapids: Baker, 1956, 1977.

_____. *The Auction Catalogue of the Library of J. Arminius*. A fascimile edition with an introduction by C. O. Bangs. Utrecht: HES, 1985.

Beza, Theodore. *Quaestionum et responsionum christianarum libellus*. Geneva, 1584.

Bibliotheca fratrum polonorum quos Unitarios vocant. 6 vols. Irenopolis (Amsterdam), 1656.

Bullinger, Heinrich. *Compendium christianae religionis decem libris comprehensum*. Zurich, 1556.

Calvin, John. *Institutes of the Christian Religion*. Trans. F. L. Battles. 2 vols. Philadelphia: Westminster, 1960.

_____. *Opera quae supersunt omnia*. Eds. Baum, Cunitz, and Reuss. Brunswick: Schwetschke, 1863–1900.

Capreolus, Johannes. *Defensiones theologiae Thomae Aquinatis in libros Sententiarum*. 4 vols. in 3. Venice, 1483–84.

Chemnitz, Martin. *Loci theologici*. 3 vols. Frankfurt and Wittenberg, 1653.

_____. *Examination of the Council of Trent*. 4 vols. Trans. Fred Kramer. St. Louis: Concordia, 1971–86.

Cocceius, Johannes. *Opera omnia theologica, exegetica, didactica, polemica, philologica*. 12 vols. Amsterdam, 1701–6.

_____. *Summa theologiae ex Scriptura repetita*, in *Opera*, vol. 7, pp. 131–403.

_____. *Aphorismi per universam theologiam prolixiores*, in *Opera*, vol. 7, pp. 17–38.

Episcopius, Simon. *Opera theologica*. Amsterdam, 1650.

_____. *Institutiones theologicae*, in *Opera*, vol. I.

Gerhard, Johann. *Loci theologici*. 9 vols. Ed. Preuss. Berlin: Schlawitz, 1863–75.

Gomarus, Franciscus. *Disputationes theologicae*, in *Opera theologica omnia*. Amsterdam, 1644.

Heidanus, Abraham. *Corpus theologiae christianae in quindecim locos*. 2 vols. Leiden, 1686.

Junius, Franciscus. *Opuscula theologica selecta*, ed. Abraham Kuyper. Amsterdam: F. Muller, 1882.

Keckermann, Bartholomaeus. *Systema sacrosanctae theologiae, tribus libris adornatum*, in *Operum omnium quae extant*. Geneva, 1614.

Limborch, Phillip Van. *Theologia christiana ad praxin pietatis ac promotionem pacis christiana unice directa*. Amsterdam, 1735. (In its first edition, 1686, the work was entitled *Institutiones theologiae christianae*.)

Maccovius, Johannes. *Loci communes theologici*. Amsterdam, 1658.

Melanchthon, Philip. *Opera quae supersunt omnia*. 28 vols. Ed. C. G. Bretschneider. Brunswick: Schwetschke, 1834–60.

_____. *Loci communes*, in *Opera*, vol. 21.

_____. *Loci praecipui theologici*, in *Opera*, vol. 21.

Molina, Luis de. *Concordia liberi arbitrii cum gratiae donis, divina praescientia, providentia, praedestinatione et reprobatione*. Ed. Johann Rabeneck (1588) Onia and Madrid: Collegium Maximum Societatis Jesu, 1953.

Musculus, Wolfgang. *Commonplaces of Christian Religion*. 2d ed. London, 1578.

_____. *Loci communes sacrae theologiae*. Basel, 1560; 3d ed., 1573.

Peter Lombard. *Sententiae in IV libris distinctae*. Editio tertia. 2 vols. Grottaferrata: Collegium S. Bonaventurae ad Claras Aquas, 1971–1981.

Perkins, William. *The Workes of . . . Mr. William Perkins*. 3 vols. Cambridge, 1612–19.

_____. *A Golden Chaine*, in *Workes*, vol. I.

_____. *A Treatise of the Manner and Order of Predestination*, in *Workes*, vol. II.

_____. *An Exposition of the Symbole*, in *Workes*, vol. I.

Polanus, Amandus. *Syntagma theologiae christianae*. Geneva, 1617.

Ramus, Petrus. *Commentarii de religione christiana*. Frankfurt, 1576.

_____. *Dialecticae, libri duo*. London, 1576.

Scharpius, Johannes. *Cursus theologicus in quo controversia omnes de fide dogmatibus hoc seculo exagitate*. 2 vols. Geneva, 1620.

Scotus, John Duns. *God and Creatures: The Quodlibetal Questions*. Trans. with an intro., notes, and glossary by Felix Alluntis and Allen B. Wolter. Washington, D.C.: Catholic University of America Press, 1981.

Suárez, Franciscus. *Opera omnia*. 26 vols. Paris: Vives, 1856–77.

_____. *De scientia Dei futurorum contingentia*, in *Opera omnia*, vol. 11.

_____. *Disputationes metaphysicae*. Salamanca, 1597. (In *Opera omnia*, vols. 25–26.)

_____. *On the Essence of Finite Being As Such, On the Existence of That Essence and Their Distinction* (*Disputationes metaphysicae*, Disputatio XXXI). Trans. with an intro. by Norman J. Wells. Milwaukee: Marquette University Press, 1983.

_____. *On the Various Kinds of Distinctions* (*Disputationes metaphysicae*, Disputatio VII). Trans. with an Introduction by Cyril Vollert. Milwaukee: Marquette University Press, 1947.

Synopsis purioris theologiae, disputationibus quinquaginta duabus comprehensa ac conscripta per Johannem Polyandrum, Andream Rivetum, Antonium Walaeum, Antonium Thysium, S.S. theologiae doctores et *professores in Academia Leidensi*. Leiden, 1626; editio sexta, curavit et praefatus est Dr. H. Bavinck. Leiden: Donner, 1881.

Thomas Aquinas. *Compendium of Theology*. Trans. Cyril Vollert. St. Louis: B. Herder, 1947.

_____. *In IV libri sententiarum*, in *Opera omnia* (Parma, 1852–73), vols. 6–8.

_____. *On the Truth of the Catholic Faith: Summa Contra Gentiles*. Trans. Anton C. Pegis, et al. 4 vols. Garden City, N.Y.: Doubleday, 1955.

_____. *Summa contra gentiles*. Rome: Leonine Commission/Vatican Library, 1934.

_____. *Summa theologiae, cura fratrum in eiusdem ordinis*. 5 vols. Madrid: Biblioteca de Autores Cristianos, 1962–65.

Trelcatius, Lucas. *Scholastica et methodica locorum communium institutio.* London, 1604.

_____. *A Brief Institution of the Commonplaces of Sacred Divinitie.* London, 1610.

Ursinus, Zacharias. *Opera theologica.* Ed. Quirinius Reuter. 3 vols. Heidelberg, 1612.

_____. *Loci theologici,* in *Opera,* vol. I.

_____. *Explicationes catecheseos,* in *Opera,* vol. I. [Earlier editions are entitled *Doctrinae christianae compendium.*]

_____. *The Commentary of Dr. Zacharias Ursinus on the Heidelberg Catechism.* Trans. G. W. Williard, intro. by John W. Nevin. Columbus, Ohio, 1852; repr. Phillipsburg, N.J.: Presbyterian and Reformed, 1985.

Vollert, Cyril (ed.). *St. Thomas Aquinas, Siger of Brabant, St. Bonaventure: On the Eternity of the World.* Trans. with an intro. by Cyril Vollert, Lottie Kendzierski, and Paul Byrne. Milwaukee: Marquette University Press, 1964.

Vorstius, Conrad. *Tractatus theologicus de Deo, sive, de natura et attributis Dei . . . .* Steinfurt, 1610.

Walaeus, Antonius. *Loci communes s. theologiae,* in *Opera omnia.* Leiden, 1643.

William of Ockham. *Predestination, God's Foreknowledge, and Future Contingents.* 2d ed. Trans. with intro., notes, and appendices by Marylin McCord Adams and Norman Kretzman. Indianapolis: Hackett, 1983.

Wollebius, Johannes. *Compendium theologiae christianae.* New edition. Neukirchen: Moers, 1935.

Zabarella, Jacob. *Opera logica.* Intro. by W. Risse. Hildesheim: Olms, 1966.

Zanchi, Jerome. *Operum theologicorum.* 8 vols. Geneva, 1617.

Secondary Sources

Adams, Marylin McCord. *William Ockham.* 2 vols. Notre Dame: University of Notre Dame Press, 1987.

Adams, Robert Merrihew. "Middle Knowledge and the Problem of Evil," in *The Virtue of Faith and Other Essays in Philosophical Theology*. New York: Oxford University Press, 1987.

Althaus, Paul. *Die Prinzipien der deutschen refomierten Dogmatik im Zeitalter der aristotelischen Scholastik*. Leipzig: Deichert, 1914.

Amann, É. "Occam, Guillaume d,'" in *Dictionnaire de théologie catholique*, vol. II/I, cols. 864–904.

Armstrong, Brian. *Calvinism and the Amyraut Heresy: Protestant Scholasticism and Humanism in Seventeenth Century France*. Madison: University of Wisconsin Press, 1969.

Bakhuizen van den Brink, J. N. "Arminius te Leiden," *Nederlands Theologisch Tijdschrift* 15 (1960–61): 81–89.

Bangs, Carl. *Arminius: A Study in the Dutch Reformation*. Nashville: Abingdon, 1971.

_____. "Arminius as a Reformed Theologian," in *The Heritage of John Calvin*, ed. John H. Bratt (Grand Rapids: Eerdmans, 1973), pp. 209–22.

Berkhof, Louis. *Systematic Theology*. 4th ed. Grand Rapids: Eerdmans, 1941.

Bertius, Petrus. *De vita et obitu reverendi & clarissimi viri D. Iacobi Arminii oratio*, in *Opera*, fol. 001–0004.

_____. *An Oration on the Life and Death of that Reverend and Very Famous Man, James Arminius, D.D.*, in *Works*, vol. I.

Bierma, Lyle D. "The Covenant Theology of Caspar Olevian," Ph.D. diss., Duke University, 1980.

Bizer, Ernst. *Frühorthodoxie und Rationalismus*. Zurich, 1963.

Blumenberg, Hans. *The Legitimacy of the Modern Age*. Trans. Robert M. Wallace. Cambridge, Mass.: MIT, 1983.

Boehner, Philotheus. *Collected Articles on Ockham*. Ed. Eligius M. Buytaert. St. Bonaventure, N.Y.: Franciscan Institute, 1958.

Brady, I. C., J. E. Gurr, and J. A. Weisheipl. "Scholasticism," in *New Catholic Encyclopedia*, vol. 12, pp. 1153–70.

Brandt, Caspar. *Historia vita Jacobi Arminii*. Brunswick, 1725.

_____. *The Life of James Arminius, D.D.* Trans. John Guthrie, with an intro. by T. O. Summers. Nashville, 1857.

Brandt, Geeraert. *The History of the Reformation and Other Ecclesiastical Transactions in and about the Low Countries: From the Beginning of the Eighth Century, down to the Famous Synod of Dort* . . . . 4 vols. London, 1720–23; repr. New York: AMS, 1979.

Buckley, Michael J. *At the Origins of Modern Atheism*. New Haven: Yale University Press, 1987.

Burrell, David B. *Knowing the Unknowable God: Ibu-Sina, Maimonides, Aquinas*. Notre Dame: University of Notre Dame Press, 1986.

Chenu, M.-D. *Toward Understanding St. Thomas*. Trans. A. M. Landry and D. Hughes. Chicago: Henry Regnery, 1964.

_____. "Le Plan de la Somme Théologique de S. Thomas," *Revue Thomiste* 45 (Jan.–Mar. 1939): 93–107.

Chollet, A. "Aristotélisme de la scolastique," in *Dictionnaire de théologie catholique*, vol. 1/2, cols. 1869–87.

Chossat, M. "Dieu. Sa nature selon les scolastiques," in *Dictionnaire de théologie catholique*, vol. 4/1, cols. 1152–1243.

Constantin, C. "Rationalisme," in *Dictionnaire de théologie catholique*, vol. 13/2, cols. 1688–1778.

Copleston, Frederick. *A History of Philosophy*. 9 vols. Westminster, Md.: Newman, 1946–1974; repr. Garden City: Image, 1985.

Courtine, Jean-François. "Le projet suarézien de la métaphysique: pour une étude de la thése suarézienne du néant," *Archives de Philosophie* 42 (1979): 234–74.

Courtnay, William J. "Nominalism in Late Medieval Religion," in Trinkhaus and Oberman, eds., *Pursuit of Holiness*, pp. 26–59.

De Finance, Joseph. *Etre et agir dans la philosophie de saint Thomas*. Paris: Beauchesne, 1945.

DeLubac, Henri. *Augustinianism and Modern Theology*. Trans. Lancelot Sheppard. London: Geoffrey Chapman, 1969.

Dibon, Paul. *L'Enseignement philosophique dans les Universités néerlandaises à l'époque précartesiénne (1575–1650)*. Paris: Elsevier, 1954.

Dictionnaire de théologie catholique. Ed. A. Vacant, et al. 23 vols. Paris: Librairie Letouzey et Ane, 1923–50.

Dillenberger, John. *Protestant Thought and Natural Science*. New York and Nashville: Abingdon, 1960.

Donnelly, John Patrick. *Calvinism and Scholasticism in Vermigli's Doctrine of Man and Grace.* Leiden: Brill, 1975.

_____. "Calvinist Thomism," *Viator* 7 (1976): 441–55.

_____. "Italian Influences on the Development of Calvinist Scholasticism," in *Sixteenth Century Journal* 7/1 (1976): 81–101.

Dorner, Isaac A. *History of Protestant Theology Particularly in Germany.* Trans. Robson and Taylor. 2 vols. Edinburgh: T. & T. Clark, 1871.

Doyle, John P. "The Suárezian Proof for God's Existence," in *History of Philosophy in the Making: A Symposium of Essays to Honor Professor James D. Collins on His 65th Birthday,* ed. Linus J. Thro. Washington, D.C.: University Press of America, 1982, pp. 105–17.

Dumont, Paul. *Liberté humaine et concours divin d'après Suárez.* Paris: Beauchesne, 1936.

Eschweiler, Karl. "Die Philosophie der spanischen Spätscholastik auf den deutschen Universitäten des siebzehnten Jahrhunderts," in *Gesammelte Aufsätze zur Kulturgeschichte Spaniens,* ed. H. Finke. Münster: Aschendorff, 1928.

Fatio, Olivier. *Méthode et théologie: Lambert Daneau et les débuts de la scolastique reformée.* Geneva: Droz, 1976.

_____. *Nihil pulchrius ordine: Contribution à l'étude de l'établissement de la discipline ecclésiastique aux Pays-Bas ou Lambert Daneau aux Pays-Bas (1581–1583).* Leiden: Brill, 1971.

Faulenbach, Heiner. *Die Struktur der Theologie des Amandus Polanus von Polansdorf.* Zurich: EVZ-Verlag, 1967.

Fritz, G., and A. Michel. "Scholastique," in *Dictionnarie de théologie catholique,* vol. 14/2, cols. 1691–1728.

Funkenstein, Amos. *Theology and the Scientific Imagination from the Middle Ages to the Seventeenth Century.* Princeton: Princeton University Press, 1986.

Ganoczy, Alexandre. *The Young Calvin.* Trans. David Foxgrover and Wade Provo. Philadelphia: Westminster, 1987.

Gardeil, A. "Lieux theologiques," in *Dictionnaire de théologie catholique,* vol. 9/1, cols. 712–47.

Garrigou-Lagrange, Reginald. *God: His Existence and His Nature. A Thomistic Solution of Certain Agnostic Antinomies.* Trans. Dom Bede Rose. 2 vols. St. Louis: B. Herder, 1946.

_____. *Predestination.* Trans. Dom Bede Rose. St. Louis: B. Herder, 1939.

_____. "Thomisme," in *Dictionnaire de théologie catholique*, vol. 15/1, cols. 823–1023.

Geiger, L. B. *La participation dans la philosophie de S. Thomas d'Aquin.* Paris: J. Vrin, 1942.

Gilbert, Neal W. *Renaissance Concepts of Method.* New York: Columbia University Press, 1960.

Gilson, Etienne. *The Christian Philosophy of St. Thomas Aquinas.* Trans. L. K. Shook. New York: Random House, 1956.

_____. *The Christian Philosophy of Saint Augustine.* Trans. L. E. M. Lynch. New York: Vintage, 1960.

_____. *The Spirit of Medieval Philosophy.* Trans. A. H. C. Downes. New York: Scribner, 1936.

Graves, F. P. *Peter Ramus and the Educational Reformation of the Sixteenth Century.* New York: Macmillan, 1912.

Hall, Basil. "Calvin Against the Calvinists," in *John Calvin: A Collection of Distinguished Essays.* Ed. Gervase Duffield. Grand Rapids: Eerdmans, 1966.

Harrison, A. W. *Arminianism.* London: Duckworth, 1937.

_____. *The Beginnings of Arminianism to the Synod of Dort.* London: University of London Press, 1926.

Heppe, Heinrich. *Reformed Dogmatics Set Out and Illustrated from the Sources.* Foreword by Karl Barth; rev. and ed. Ernst Bizer; trans. G. T. Thomson. London: George Allen and Unwin, 1950; repr. Grand Rapids: Baker, 1978.

Hoenderdaal, G. J. "Arminius en Episcopius," *Nederlands Archief voor Kerkgeschiedenis*, 60 (1980): 203–35.

_____. "Arminius, Jacobus," s.v. in *Theologisches Realencyclopädie.* Berlin and New York: DeGruyter, 1977– .

_____. "The Life and Struggle of Arminius in the Dutch Republic," in Gerald McCulloh, ed., *Man's Faith and Freedom*, pp. 11–26.

_____. "De theologische Betekenis van Arminius," *Nederlands Theologisch Tijdschrift* 15 (1960–61): 90–98.

_____. "The Debate about Arminius Outside the Netherlands," in *Leiden University in the Seventeenth Century*, pp. 137–59.

Itterzon, G. P. van. *Francis Gomarus*. The Hague: Nijhoff, 1930.

_____. "De 'Synopsis purioris theologiae': Gereformeerd Leerboek der 17de Eeuw," *Nederlands Archief voor Kerkgeschiedenis* 23 (1930): 161–213, 225–59.

Jacobs, Henry E. "Scholasticism in the Lutheran Church," in *The Lutheran Cyclopedia*. New York: Scribner, 1899, pp. 434–35.

Janz, Denis R. *Luther and Late Medieval Thomism: A Study in Theological Anthropology*. Waterloo, Ontario: Wilfrid Laurier University Press, 1983.

Jocher, Chr. G. *Allgemeines Gelehrten Lexikon*. 11 vols. Leipzig, 1750–1897.

Jourdain, Charles. *La philosophie de Saint Thomas d'Aquin*. 2 vols. Paris: Hachette, 1858.

Kendall, R. T. *Calvin and English Calvinism to 1649*. New York and London: Oxford University Press, 1979.

Klauber, Martin. "The Context and Development of the Views of Jean-Alphonse Turrettini (1671–1737) on Religious Authority," Ph.D. diss., University of Wisconsin-Madison, 1987.

Kristeller, Paul Oskar. *Medieval Aspects of Renaissance Learning. Three Essays*. Ed. and trans. Edward P. Mahoney. Durham, N.C.: Duke University Press, 1974.

_____. *Renaissance Thought: The Classic, Scholastic, and Humanist Strains*. New York: Harper and Row, 1961.

_____. *Renaissance Thought and Its Sources*. Ed. Michael Mooney. New York: Columbia University Press, 1979.

_____. "The Validity of the Term Nominalism," in Trinkhaus and Oberman, eds., *Pursuit of Holiness*, pp. 65–66.

La Servière, Joseph de. *La théologie de Bellarmin*. Paris: Beauchesne, 1909.

Le Bachelet, X. "Baius, Michel," in *Dictionnaire de théologie catholique*, vol. 2/1, cols. 37–111.

Leiden University in the Seventeenth Century: An Exchange of Learning. Eds. Th. H. Lunsingh Scheurleer and G. H. M. Posthumus Meyjes. Leiden: Brill, 1975.

Levi, A. H. T. "The Breakdown of Scholasticism and the Significance of Evangelical Humanism," in Gerard Hughes, ed., *The Philosophical*

Assessment of Theology: Essays in Honour of Frederick C. Copleston. Washington, D.C.: Georgetown University Press, 1987.

Lewalter, Ernst. *Spanisch-jesuitisch und deutsch-lutherische Metaphysik des 17. Jahrhunderts.* Hamburg, 1935; repr. Darmstadt: Wissenschafttiche Buchgesellschaft, 1968.

Loemker, Leroy E. *Struggle for Synthesis: The Seventeenth Century Background of Leibniz's Synthesis of Order and Freedom.* Cambridge, Mass.: Harvard University Press, 1972.

Lovejoy, Arthur O. *The Great Chain of Being: A Study in the History of an Idea.* Cambridge, Mass.: Harvard University Press, 1936.

Mahieu, Léon. "L'eclectisme Suarézien," *Revue Thomiste* 8 (1925): 250–85.

_____. *François Suárez: sa philosophie et les rapports qu'elle a avec sa théologie.* Paris: Descleé, de Brouwer, 1921.

Mahoney, Edward P. "Metaphysical Foundations of the Hierarchy of Being According to Some Late-Medieval and Renaissance Philosophers," in *Philosophies of Existence, Ancient and Modern,* ed. Parviz Morewedge (New York: Fordham University Press, 1982), pp. 165–257.

Mandonnet, P. "Bañez, Dominique," in *Dictionnaire de théologie catholique,* vol. 2/1, cols. 140–45.

Maruyama, Tadataka. *The Ecclesiology of Theodore Beza: The Reform of the True Church.* Geneva: Droz, 1978.

Maurer, Armand. *Medieval Philosophy.* New York: Random House, 1962.

McCulloh, Gerald O. (ed.). *Man's Faith and Freedom: The Theological Influence of Jacobus Arminius.* New York and Nashville: Abingdon, 1962.

McGiffert, A. C. *Protestant Thought before Kant.* London, 1911; repr. New York: Harper and Row, 1961.

McKim, Donald K. *Ramism in William Perkins' Theology.* New York and Bern: Peter Lang, 1987.

Minges, P. Parthenius. *Ioannis Duns Scoti doctrina philosophica et theologica quoad res praecipuas proposita et exposita.* 2 vols. Quaracchi: Collegium S. Bonaventurae, 1930.

Müller, Johannes. *Martin Bucers Hermenutik.* Gütersloh: Gerd Mohn, 1965.

Muller, Richard A. "Arminius and the Scholastic Tradition," *Calvin Theological Journal* 24/2 (1989): 263–77.

_____. *Christ and the Decree: Christology and Predestination in Reformed Theology from Calvin to Perkins*. Durham, N.C.: Labyrinth, 1986; second printing, with corrections, Grand Rapids: Baker, 1988.

_____. "The Christological Problem in the Thought of Jacobus Arminius," *Nederlands Archief voor Kerkgeschiedenis* 68 (1968): 145–63.

_____. *Dictionary of Latin and Greek Theological Terms: Drawn Principally from Protestant Scholastic Theology*. Grand Rapids: Baker, 1985.

_____. "'Duplex cognitio dei' in the Theology of Early Reformed Orthodoxy," *Sixteenth Century Journal* 10/2 (1979): 51–61.

_____. "The Federal Motif in Seventeenth Century Arminian Theology," *Nederlands Archief voor Kerkgeschiedenis* 62/1 (1982): 102–22.

_____. "Perkins' A Golden Chaine: Predestinarian System or Schematized Ordo Salutis?" *Sixteenth Century Journal* 9/1 (1978): 69–81.

_____. *Post-Reformation Reformed Dogmatics*. Volume I, *Prolegomena*. Grand Rapids: Baker, 1987.

_____. "Scholasticism Protestant and Catholic: Francis Turretin on the Object and Principles of Theology," *Church History* 55/2 (1986): 193–205.

_____. "*Vera Philosophia cum sacra Theologia nusquam pugnat*: Keckermann on Philosophy, Theology, and the Problem of Double Truth," *Sixteenth Century Journal* 15/3 (1984): 341–65.

The New Catholic Encyclopedia. Ed. William J. McDonald, et al. 15 vols. New York: McGraw-Hill, 1967.

Oakley, Francis. *Omnipotence, Covenant, & Order: An Excusion in the History of Ideas from Abelard to Leibniz*. Ithaca and London: Cornell University Press, 1984.

Oberman, Heiko A. *The Dawn of the Reformation: Essays in Late Medieval and Early Reformation Thought*. Edinburgh: T. & T. Clark, 1986.

_____. *The Harvest of Medieval Theology: Gabriel Biel and Late Medieval Nominalism*. Rev. ed. Grand Rapids: Eerdmans, 1967.

_____. *Masters of the Reformation: The Emergence of a New Intellectual Climate in Europe*. Trans. Dennis Martin. Cambridge: Cambridge University Press, 1981.

_____. "Some Notes on the Theology of Nominalism," *Harvard Theological Review* (1960): 47–76.

Ong, Walter J. *Ramus: Method and the Decay of Dialogue.* Cambridge, Mass.: Harvard University Press, 1958.

Owens, Joseph. *St. Thomas Aquinas on the Existence of God: Collected Papers of Joseph Owens, C.Ss.R.* Ed. John R. Catan. Albany: State University of New York Press, 1980.

Patterson, Robert L. *The Conception of God in the Philosophy of Aquinas.* London: George Allen and Unwin, 1933.

Pegis, Anton C. "Molina and Human Liberty," in Gerald Smith, ed., *Jesuit Thinkers of the Renaissance,* pp. 75–131.

Pinard, H. "Création," in *Dictionnaire de théologie catholique,* vol. 3/2, cols. 2034–2201.

Platt, John. *Reformed Thought and Scholasticism: The Arguments for the Existence of God in Dutch Theology, 1575–1650.* Leiden: Brill, 1982.

Pourrat, Pierre. *Christian Spirituality.* Trans. W. H. Mitchell, S. P. Jacques, and Donald Attwater. 4 vols. Westminster, Md.: Newman, 1953–55.

Preus, Robert. *The Inspiration of Scripture: A Study of the Seventeenth Century Lutheran Dogmaticians.* London: Oliver and Boyd, 1955.

_____. *The Theology of Post-Reformation Lutheranism.* 2 vols. St. Louis: Concordia, 1970–72.

Pünjer, Bernhard. *History of the Christian Philosophy of Religion.* Trans. W. Hastie. Edinburgh: T. & T. Clark, 1887.

Raitt, Jill. *The Eucharistic Theology of Theodore Beza: Development of the Reformed Doctrine.* Chambersburg, Pa., 1972.

Randall, John Herman, Jr. "The Development of Scientific Method in the School of Padua," *Journal of the History of Ideas* 1 (1940): 177–206.

_____. *The Making of the Modern Mind: A Survey of the Intellectual Background of the Present Age.* Rev. ed. Cambridge, Mass.: Houghton Mifflin, 1940.

Raymond, P. "Duns Scot," in *Dictionnaire de théologie catholique,* vol. 4/2, cols. 1865–1947.

Ritschl, Otto. *Dogmengeschichte des Protestantismus: Grundlagen und Grundzüge der theologischen Gedanken- und Lehrbildung in den protestantischen Kirchen.* 4 vols. Leipzig: J. C. Hinrichs, 1908–12; Göttingen: Vandenhoeck and Ruprecht, 1926–27.

Rousselot, Pierre. *The Intellectualism of Saint Thomas.* Trans. with a foreword by James E. O'Mahony. New York: Sheed and Ward, 1935.

Schaff, Philip. *The Creeds of Christendom, with a History and Critical Notes.* 3 vols. 6th ed. New York, 1931; repr. Grand Rapids: Baker, 1983.

Scheffczyk, Leo. *Creation and Providence.* Trans. Richard Strachan. New York: Herder and Herder, 1970.

Schmid, Heinrich. *Doctrinal Theology of the Evangelical Lutheran Church.* Trans. Charles E. Hay and Henry Jacobs. Minneapolis: Augsburg, n.d.

Schrenk, Gottlob. *Gottesreich und Bund im älteren Protestantismus vornehmlich bei Johannes Coccejus: Zugleich ein Beitrag zur Geschichte des Pietismus und der heilsgeschichtlichen Theologie.* Gütersloh: Bertelsmann, 1923.

Schwane, Joseph. *Histoire des Dogmes.* Trans. A. Degert. 6 vols. Paris: Beauschesne, 1903–4.

Scorraille, Raoul de. *François Suarez de la Compagnie de Jésus, d'après ses lettres, ses autres écrits inédits et un grand nombre des documents nouveaux.* 2 vols. Paris: Lethielleux, 1912.

Sepp, Christian. *Het Godgeleerd onderwijs in Nederland gedurende de 16e en 17e eeuw.* 2 vols. Leiden: De Breuk and Smits, 1873–74.

Sinnema, Donald W. "The Issue of Reprobation at the Synod of Dort (1618–19) in the Light of the History of This Doctrine," Ph.D. diss., University of St. Michael's College, 1985.

Slaatte, Howard A. *The Arminian Arm of Theology: The Theologies of John Fletcher, First Methodist Theologian, and His Precursor, James Arminius.* Washington, D.C.: University Press of America, 1978.

Smith, Gerard (ed.). *Jesuit Thinkers of the Renaissance.* Milwaukee: Marquette University Press, 1939.

Sprunger, Keith L. "Ames, Ramus, and the Method of Puritan Theology," *Harvard Theological Review* 59 (1966): 133–51.

Steinmetz, David C. *Misericordia Dei: The Theology of Johannes von Staupitz in Its Late Medieval Setting.* Leiden: Brill, 1968.

Stephens, W. P. *The Theology of Huldrych Zwingli.* Oxford: Clarendon, 1986.

Tachau, Katherine. *Vision and Certitude in the Age of Ockham: Optics, Epistemology and the Foundations of Semantics, 1250–1345.* Leiden: Brill, 1988.

Tjalsma, D. *Leven en Strijd van Jacobus Arminius.* Lochem: Uitgave de Rijstroom, 1960.

Toussaint, C. "Aséité," in *Dictionnaire de théologie catholique,* vol. 1/2, cols. 2077–80.

_____. "Attributs divins," in *Dictionnaire de théologie catholique,* vol. 1/2, cols. 2223–35.

Trinkhaus, Charles E. and Heiko A. Oberman, eds. *The Pursuit of Holiness in Late Medieval and Renaissance Religion.* Leiden: Brill, 1974.

Tukker, C. A. "Theologie en Scholastiek: De Synopsis Purioris Theologiae als Theologisch Document (II)," *Theologia Reformata* 18 (1975): 34–49.

_____. "Vier Leidse Hoogleraren in de Gouden Eeuw: De Synopsis Purioris Theologiae als Theologisch Document (I)," *Theologia Reformata* 17 (1974): 236–50.

Van Holk, Lambertus, "From Arminius to Arminianism in Dutch Theology," in Gerald McCulloh, ed., *Man's Faith and Freedom,* pp. 27–45.

Vansteenberghe, E. "Molina, Louis," in *Dictionnaire de théologie catholique,* vol. 10/2, cols. 2090–92.

_____. "Molinisme," in *Dictionnaire de théologie catholique,* vol. 10/2, cols. 2094–2187.

Von Rohr, John. *The Covenant of Grace in Puritan Thought.* Atlanta: Scholars, 1986.

Vignaux, Paul. "Nominalisme," in *Dictionnaire de théologie catholique,* vol. 11/1, cols. 717–84.

Waddington, Charles. *Ramus, sa vie, ses écrits et ses opinions.* Paris: Ch. Meyrueis, 1855.

Wallace, Dewey. *Puritans and Predestination: Grace in English Protestant Theology, 1525–1695.* Chapel Hill: University of North Carolina Press, 1982.

Wallace, William A. *Causality and Scientific Explanation.* 2 vols. Ann Arbor: University of Michigan Press, 1972–74.

Weber, Hans Emil. *Der Einfluss der protestantischen Schulphilosophie auf die orthodox-lutherische Dogmatik.* Leipzig: Deichert, 1908.

_____. *Die philosophische Scholastik des deutschen Protestantismus im Zeitalter der Orthodoxie.* Leipzig: Quelle und Meyer, 1907.

_____. *Reformation, Orthodoxie und Rationalismus*. 2 vols. Gütersloh, 1937–51; repr. Darmstadt: Wissenschaftliche Buchgesellschaft, 1966.

Weisheipl, J. A. *Friar Thomas D'Aquino: His Life, Thought, and Work*. Garden City: Doubleday, 1974.

_____. "Scholastic Method," in *New Catholic Encyclopedia*, vol. 12, pp. 1145–46.

Wippel, John F. *The Metaphysical Thought of Godfrey of Fontaines: A Study in Late Thirteenth-Century Philosophy*. Washington: Catholic University of America Press, 1981.

Wundt, Max. *Die deutsche Schulmetaphysik des 17. Jahrhunderts*. Tübingen: J. C. B. Mohr, 1939.

Zöckler, Otto. "Socin und der Socinianismus," in *Realencyklopädie für protestantische Theologie und Kirche*, vol. 18, pp. 459–80.

Zuylen, W. H. *Bartholomaus Keckermann: Sein Leben und Wirken*. Leipzig: Noske, 1934.

Index of Names

Index of Subjects

Accommodation, 61, 72
Actuality, 116–17, 125–26, 168
Actus primus. See Actuality
Actus secundus. See Actuality
Analogia entis, 60, 100, 104, 107, 230, 273, 283
Analogy: 104, 109, 114; of man, 114; of nature, 114, 123–24
Aristotelianism, 4, 16: and Arminius, 38; Christian reconstruction of, 27, 28, 35, 94; decline of, 4, 283; and the Prime Mover, 94–95; Renaissance, 4, 16, 21, 64–65; revival of, 35
Arminianism, 9: Aquinas' influence on, 38–39, 279; continuity with Reformed theology, 26–27, 42–43, 66–67, 277; doctrine of God in, 66, 84; historical context of, 15–51; and Ramist dialectics, 16, 58; and rationalism, 282–85; relationship of disputations to, 50; sources of, 37–38, 44–47, 64, 72; as theology of creation, 233–34, 268
Arminius: biographers of, 5–10; condemnation of, 27–30; theological library of, 44–47
Articles of faith, fundamental versus nonfundamental, 69–70
Attributes: communicable, 110, 117, 122, 127; formal distinction of, 130; incommunicable, 110, 117, 122, 127, 131
Augustinianism, 6–7

Being (*Ens*), 59–60: and the *analogia entis*, 60; chain of, 227, 231, 232; classes of, 232–33; dependence of, 59–60; language of, 59; as moment, 114–15; and nonbeing, 218–20
Blessedness: as the goal of theology, 77; of God, 206

Calvinism, 9: and Arminius, 19
Causality, 94, 111, 214–15: in Arminius, 99; efficient, 67, 258; final, 67, 99, 229–30
Christ, as the object of theology, 73–74, 212
Christology: Arminius', 109–10; Lutheran, 109; Reformed, 110
Concupiscence, 192
Concursus divinus, 178, 253–56, 258, 263–66

Confessions, Reformed, 41–42
Congruism, 162
Contingency, 154–55, 157, 158, 179, 226
Covenant: doctrine of, 71; theology of, 68, 242–43
Creation: Arabian sources of, 226; causality of, 213; contingency of, 226; "continued," 247, 248; Creator-creature distinction in, 226–27; definition of, 213, 214; doctrine of, 211–34; end of, 230; eternity of, 92, 94, 95–96, 97, 132, 223; *ex nihilo*, 97, 215–16, 223, 224–25; formal cause of, 222; freedom of God in, 225, 226; goal of, 138; as goal of divine activity, 198; as God's self-limiting act, 234; order of, 231; in relation to the divine will, 171, 191; as revelation, 75; two-stage model of, 220; unity of, 231

Decrees, divine, 162, 163, 250–51
Disputationes, 25, 26, 49, 50, 67, 111, 212: doctrine of God in, 84; provisional character of, 169
Doctrine of God: as final goal, 68; medieval models of, 84–88, 121
Duplex cognitio Dei, 76, 106–7

Eclecticism, theological, 48, 56, 62, 132, 274: in Arminius, 21, 39, 279
Emanation of being, 105, 106, 193–94
Eternity, 133–35, 249: Boethian definition of, 120, 134, 157, 205; comparison with time, 132; derivation of, 132, 133
Existence of God, proofs of, 90–91, 100–101: in Aquinas, 86, 87; in Arminius, 89, 91–93; logic of, 98; in Reformed systems, 87–89, 99
Exposition, pattern of, 108

Faculty psychology, 119, 143, 168, 192
Foreknowledge, 152, 154–55, 159, 160, 179, 251–53: Boethian concept of, 149

Glory, of God, 206–7
God: attributes of, 113–39; as Being, 59–60, 114, 115, 124–25, 133, 134, 225; essence of, 103–12;